# DONNY

## AN UNDERCOVER COP
## WITH A DEATHWISH

## TODD MAGUIRE

Donny: An undercover cop with a deathwish.
Facebook: Todd Maguire - Writer - Story Teller
Website: www.toddmaguire.com.au

Disclaimer: This book is an autobiography written by the author to recount personal experiences, memories and perspectives on various aspects of their life. The content is based on the author's recollection and interpretation of events and is presented to provide insight into their journey and growth.

While every effort has been made to ensure the accuracy and authenticity of the information provided, memory is subjective and individual perceptions of events may differ. Therefore, certain details or accounts may be subject to interpretation or may vary from other sources.

The author may have omitted certain details or altered names and circumstances to protect privacy or for other reasons.

This book is not intended to serve as a comprehensive historical record or objective account of events, but rather as a personal narrative intended to inspire, entertain or provoke thought. The author may have chosen to emphasise certain themes or experiences to convey their intended message or theme.

The author disclaims any responsibility for any misinterpretations or misunderstandings that may arise from reading this autobiography. By reading this autobiography, you acknowledge and accept that personal narratives are inherently subjective, and that the author's experiences and interpretations may not necessarily reflect your own.

**Trigger warning**

This book contains content that addresses traumatic events, including but not limited to suicide, violence, accidents and other distressing experiences. It may include descriptions or discussions of events that could be triggering for individuals who have experienced trauma or are sensitive to such topics.

Published by Todd Maguire with assistance from Ignite & Write Publishing, www.igniteandwritepublishing.com

ISBN: 978-1-7643844-0-7 (paperback)     978-1-7643844-1-4 (eBook)

NATIONAL LIBRARY OF AUSTRALIA

A catalogue record for this book is available from the National Library of Australia

# DEDICATION

This book is dedicated to those who have stood by me through it all—my family.

To my beautiful wife, Peta, and to my son, Fletcher: you've both weathered the storms that came with Donny's chaos and the quiet wreckage that followed. You've stood beside me through every battle, seen the shadows I tried to outrun and held steady when I couldn't. I know it hasn't been easy, far from it, and I haven't always had the words. But please know this: your love has anchored me, your patience has pulled me back from the edge and your presence is the reason I keep putting one foot in front of the other every day. You are my heart, my grounding force and I am endlessly grateful for you both.

To my mum, dad, brother and sister, thank you for loving me unconditionally, even when I was lost in the depths and couldn't find a way out. Your strength, belief in me and unwavering love have meant more than I could ever express.

## DONNY

To Clarke, the innocent four-year-old who was forced to face the unthinkable reality of losing his mum far too soon. Despite it all, you've grown into an impressive young man, wise beyond your years (some might even say more mature than me already). Thankfully, your memories of that devastating time are few, but know this: your mum, Karen, loved and adored you with all her heart. This book ensures that her love, fierce, unwavering and eternal, is forever preserved in ink.

# AUTHOR'S NOTE

It was only after stepping away from the Queensland Police Service in 2023, that I began to confront the full weight of the trauma and loss that had silently shaped my life and eroded my mental health. For twenty-seven years, I served on the frontline not just as an officer, but as a witness to the darkest corners of human experience. The suicide of my de facto partner in 2000 shattered my world in in a way words can't fully capture, and it became the catalyst for stepping into the dangerous and isolating role of undercover policing. What followed was a descent into the shadows of crime and chaos, compounding the emotional toll I was already carrying.

As a police officer, I witnessed the worst of humanity: violent assaults, road fatalities, suicides, child abuse, domestic violence and sexual assault, each leaving invisible scars. Among the most harrowing were the deaths of babies and young children, sudden and senseless losses that left behind an unbearable silence. I stood at the doors of shattered families to deliver the kind of news that stops time. I held the hands of the broken and stood inside the raw aftermath of overwhelming grief, again and again. I brought down armed men barricaded in isolated outback properties, where backup was distant and danger was immediate. The kind of moments that teeter between life and death with no room for error. These weren't just incidents; they were soul-deep imprints. On top of that were the burdens of managing mental health crises, confronting systemic failures and enduring the moral injury of being part of a justice system that too often failed its victims.

Only when the noise stopped, when the shift ended and the radio went quiet, did the impact of it all begin to roar. In breaking my silence, I'm finally shedding light on my lived reality of complex Post Traumatic Stress Disorder (CPTSD), a condition that has insidiously unravelled my relationships, sleep and health. What I've written here is not just a story of survival, but a raw, unflinching account of what is carried long after the badge is returned.

Through sharing my lived experiences, especially those from my time working undercover—a role I took on amid profound personal grief—I hope to connect with others who may feel isolated in their struggles. My reflections offer hard-won insight into the destructive ways trauma is often suppressed, masked or denied. But more importantly, I want this book to show that healing is possible, even when it feels out of reach. Recovery is deeply personal, often messy, and never linear.

My willingness to be vulnerable speaks to the power of healing, a process that begins with unearthing what's long been buried, unpacking the closet of demons carried in silence. In choosing to share my story on paper, I've found strength in the telling. And I've come to believe that true resilience lives in the raw act of being seen. There is power in being honest about pain. There is life in giving voice to what was once unspeakable. And there is hope in knowing that connection, compassion and being heard can begin to stitch together even the most fractured parts of ourselves.

I was never much of a reader, and I'm sure my old English teacher would laugh knowing I somehow managed to put a sentence together to write this book. The only things I ever read were *Rugby League Week*, the sports pages of the *Gold Coast Bulletin* and, of course, my favourite books, the *Les Norton* series, by the legendary Australian author Robert G. Barrett.

What I loved about Barrett's writing was that it never pretended to be anything it wasn't; it was crude, unapologetic, hilarious and uniquely Australian. He captured the grit and madness of everyday life in a way that made you laugh out loud one minute and shake your head the next. His characters were flawed and real, people you could almost smell from across the page, and his stories never strayed too far from the truth, no matter how outrageous they got.

This book is for anyone who has gone through tough times, and trust me, we all will, in one way or another. Living with PTSD isn't a straight line out of the darkness. You will fall and get back up, only to fall again. Some days will break you and others will surprise you. But just when you think you've outrun it, the weight of it returns in ways you didn't expect. That's the truth of trauma, it doesn't vanish. It becomes part of you.

This story was never meant to see the light of day. For years I refused to acknowledge it. 'This' was never meant to become a defining part of my life. And yet I found myself sitting in the offices of numerous mental health professionals. I had no idea how I had ended up there. I guess I was playing the ignorant card. You see, unlike many people, I don't carry the weight of childhood trauma. My childhood was almost idyllic, with a family bond that still holds strong to this very day. So, I knew that wasn't the reason I needed to seek help.

Each professional had their theories, their tools—some of them urged me to pick up a pen and pour out the moments that had shaped me. Again and again, they pointed to one particular moment: the morning I woke to find my de facto girlfriend's lifeless body. She had taken her own life right before my eyes. That single, harrowing moment shattered my world.

For a long time, I resisted. Writing about it felt like lifting the lid on a Pandora's Box of pain I wasn't ready to face. I've never believed in the old saying, 'time heals all wounds'. To me, time's more like a cheeky trickster; it doesn't erase the pain, it just changes the angle from which you see it. Still, something eventually shifted. A flicker of courage sparked inside me, nudging me towards the page.

And so, I wrote it. The whole gut-wrenching story of that day. I poured my soul into it, reliving every detail. Then I folded the piece of paper up and tucked it away in my bedside drawer. There it sat for years, gathering dust. Locking it away felt safer than letting it breathe. But life, with its twisted sense of humour, has a way of dragging you back to the truth. Over time, I realised that this story, my story, needed a voice. I needed to find some kind of meaning in all the madness. Maybe, if I faced the shadows, I could find a speck of light. Maybe, one day, my grandkids or their kids would read this and see a story worth telling. A life worth remembering.

So here it begins. This is my first step towards healing and understanding. It's not just about the pain. It's about the resilience that grows in the middle of it.

# AUTHOR'S NOTE

I also found myself drawn to books and podcasts written by former Queensland Police undercover operatives like Keith Banks, Mick Cacciola and Dan Crowley. Their stories hit hard. These weren't just gritty war stories; it felt like someone had written down the feelings I never dared say out loud. Some of the authors I knew personally, others I didn't, but reading their words felt like sharing beers with old mates at the pub.

They brought the 70's, '80s and '90s roaring back to life, a time when the badge stood for something different. Policing then was wild and unfiltered. The lines between right and wrong smudged like spilled beer across a pool table. That world is long gone, but the stories are still electric; real lives lived on the edge. But the more I read, the more I noticed something missing. No one was talking about what came after this era.

And that's when it dawned on me, maybe *I'm* supposed to tell that part. The madness of the early 2000s, the turn of the century. Maybe a young copper a hundred years from now will read this and laugh at my screw-ups and small wins. Maybe they'll see themselves in the mess, and if I can offer a laugh and a little perspective, then maybe that's enough.

I've done my best to keep this account honest and real. But memory's a funny bugger. What I remember might not match up with someone else's version of events. That's just the nature of it. Some names have been changed, some events reshaped, not to deceive, but to protect the people who walked these roads with me. This isn't a historical account; it's a patchwork of my lived experience. A mosaic of moments, some light, some dark, and every chapter was chosen with purpose. These are the parts of my life that have stuck with me. The moments that shaped me, and the ones I still carry.

I'm not some polished author, just a bloke telling his story. A storyteller writing about what's helped him, what's broken him and what's made him laugh. You'll find footy, music, mateship, heartbreak and plenty of stupid decisions along the way. It starts in childhood, when life felt like a lazy cruise down Easy Street, family barbies, schoolyard laughs and weekends spent kicking the footy like I was destined for the big league, like every young kid. By the time I hit my twenty's, life felt like a playground, full of promise, freedom and a solid career. Then, in a split second, my world changed. Everything I once knew to be 'normal' and 'safe' disappeared before my eyes, and there was not one thing I could do about it. The suicide of my girlfriend Karen shattered my world. At 25 years of age, everything I believed in, everything I thought I knew, was obliterated. The joy and innocence of those early years vanished overnight, replaced by silence, guilt, grief and an intense hatred for the world.

Searching for something, anything to make sense of it, I turned to the world of undercover policing. That's when Donny Wilson was born. Donny wasn't just an alias; he was a new skin, a shield, a way to survive. He was me, in a trench coat, with a dodgy haircut and a badge, living life on the edge. This story is about how quickly life can turn. How one moment you're cruising, and the next, you're spinning out. What follows is a rollercoaster through the highs and lows, the heartbreaks, the laughs, the near misses, and the tiny wins that kept me going.

Through it all, I've learned one thing: even in the darkest of places, there's room for resilience and for reflection and, most importantly, even for a laugh. So here it is: my journey. If you find something in these pages that resonates with your own story, then maybe this was all worth it.

That fatal day drew a line through my life; there was everything before 2000 and everything after. In the before, I was young, wide-eyed and charging through life like nothing could touch me. Full of fire, full of hope, like most blokes in their twenties. Life felt like one big open road. But after, well, the light went out and I became cold, bitterly angry and shamelessly hardened. The world felt heavier and darker, and I had an unstoppable inner rage. I was angry at everything, at nothing, at the world, but mostly at myself. But underneath it all, I was just… alone.

I invite you to walk alongside me through this mess and see what can come from broken places.

Things *can* get better. You learn to ride the emotional highs and lows, and, over time, you reach a kind of acceptance. That acceptance doesn't mean you're done with the pain. It doesn't mean the dark days won't come. It just means you've stopped pretending they're not real and started learning how to live *with* your experience, not despite it. For me, accepting my trauma and the events that led to it will be a lifelong process. I know that now. The memories, the scars, the internal noise, they're part of who I now am. But they don't define me. And they don't get the final word.

So, feel it all. Own your story. Carry your scars. And then push forward again and again and become the fuckin' legend you're meant to be.

# PROLOGUE

'Just pull the trigger,' Donny silently pleaded to himself. 'Make it quick.'

His stomach twisted as the shotgun barrel pointed straight at his noggin—what a bloody nightmare this had turned into. But fate, that cruel bastard, wasn't having a bar of it. They never found his hidden wire, and instead of the heroic death he desperately sought, more accolades were heaped upon him. The recognition turned his insides like a dodgy curry, because deep down, Donny knew he had failed in his one true mission.

His desire for a noble exit was continually disrupted by his own skill and tenacity, or maybe just dumb luck. It was like flipping the script on the classic 'suicide by cop' scenario. Here was Donny, a cop, trying to provoke a criminal into finishing the job he couldn't bring himself to do. What a plot twist!

Still, he persisted, sinking deeper into the criminal world, openly courting death with reckless abandon, hoping it would finally take him, even as it slipped through his fingers. The never-ending search for his shattered sanity drove him to places darker than he'd ever imagined. One night, he found himself in an outlaw bikie club, surrounded by ten enormous bikies, all glaring at him like he'd just insulted their mothers. They accused him of being a cop or a 'narc,' and for the first time, Donny snapped.

'You're right, I'm a cop!' he spat at them, channelling his inner tough guy. 'Now do your end and kill me already, you cowards!' But to his utter horror and frustration, they simply laughed. 'Yeah, good one, idiot. You're not even worth the bullets.' They slapped each other's backs, howling like they had told the joke of the year. Then let him walk away untouched. Talk about a bad punchline! It seemed Donny was doomed never to get the release he craved, no matter how far he strayed from the light. The cycle kept spinning, his soul sinking deeper into a mire of violence and depravity, still chasing the elusive end that refused to claim him. Try as he might to let go, oblivion always slipped its leash.

He was a dead man walking. The only question was: when would the reaper come?

# PART 1

*'Back before everything went to shit,*
*life was pretty bloody good.'*

– Todd Maguire

I was just another knockabout kid from Brisbane—footy under one wing, and not a single bloody clue what was waiting around the corner. Thought I had it all figured out. Had a solid crew of mates I'd bleed for, a family name worth something, and enough crazy neighbourhood brawls to reckon I was ten feet tall and made of bloody titanium.

Life back then was backyard cricket, Mum's Sunday roasts that could feed a small army, and this unspoken rule: if you just rocked up, had a dig, and didn't carry on like a dickhead, everything would be sweet. And for a while, it was.

Footy. Pub work. Mateship. Long nights, sore ribs and enough half-cooked plans to fill a pub jukebox. I lived loud, loved hard and thought that was all I'd ever need.

What I didn't see coming was how quickly the whole bloody lot can flip.

One moment. That's all it takes.

You wake up one day and the world you knew is gone. The good times vanish in a heartbeat—and all you're left with is the silence.

Back then, I was just Todd. Big dreams, a bigger heart and no bloody idea the world I'd built was about to burn to the bloody ground.

# 1

# BLOODLINES OF GRIT AND GRACE

Our family was steeped in Irish Catholic tradition, never missing Sunday Mass and carrying the kind of unspoken pride that only comes from deep roots and shared struggle. The Maguire name traces back to 10th century Fermanagh, Enniskillen, a county in Northern Ireland, and arrived in Australia in the 1800s with my great-grandparents bringing with it a legacy of resilience, faith and quiet strength.

That legacy was never more evident than in my grandfather, Vincent Aloysius Maguire, a man forged in war, defined by sacrifice and remembered for his unwavering devotion to family and country. Vincent lived a hard but honourable life. Though I was only three when he passed at just 55 years old, his story has never left me. He enlisted in the Citizen Military Forces (CMF) in 1939 at the age of 19, alongside his older brother, Eugene Ignatius Maguire, before joining the Australian Imperial Force (AIF), where he was promoted to Corporal.

He fought in the brutal New Guinea campaign during World War II, enduring the horrors of jungle warfare, recurring malaria and enemy fire. In 1943, during an assault on Sattelberg, he was both bayoneted and shot in the hand and still, he pressed on. Though he could have pursued further military accolades, he chose instead to come home. He put his family before fame, a decision that tells you everything you need to know about the man. His courage and humility laid the moral foundation for what it means to be a Maguire.

At the centre of that legacy was my grandmother, Patricia Mary Maguire, the true matriarch. After Vincent's death, she never remarried. Instead, she poured her life into raising five children and serving her community through Saint Vincent de Paul in the Queensland suburb of Sandgate. She was awarded the Medal of the Order of Australia for her tireless charity work, an honour she rarely spoke of, preferring instead to lead by example through quiet service.

Patricia kept a handwritten diary of every single family member's birthday and never missed one. That simple gesture told us how much we mattered. Her legacy now spans twenty-two grandchildren and twenty-six great-grandchildren, a living testament to her strength, grace and steadfast love.

Mum's side of the family wasn't as prominent as Dad's, but there was something special there too. I remember watching my Uncle Barry on the *Today* show in the '80s reporting as the Los Angeles correspondent for US Channel 9. He later became a senior producer for *The Great Outdoors* and a respected travel writer. What many don't know is that he also graced the airwaves more than 40 years ago as the original host of the groundbreaking Sunday morning news show *Night Watch*. He was a pioneer, and I watched him with wide eyes, thinking: *That's my family.*

Today, the Maguire connections remain strong. We still gather, still laugh, still lean on each other in the same way our grandparents taught us. There's pride in our name, not just for what's been but for how we've grown. I'm proud to be a Maguire, proud of our history, proud of our traditions and proud of how our family has evolved. The name carries weight for me, and it reminds me where I come from. It keeps me grounded when the world around me starts to spin.

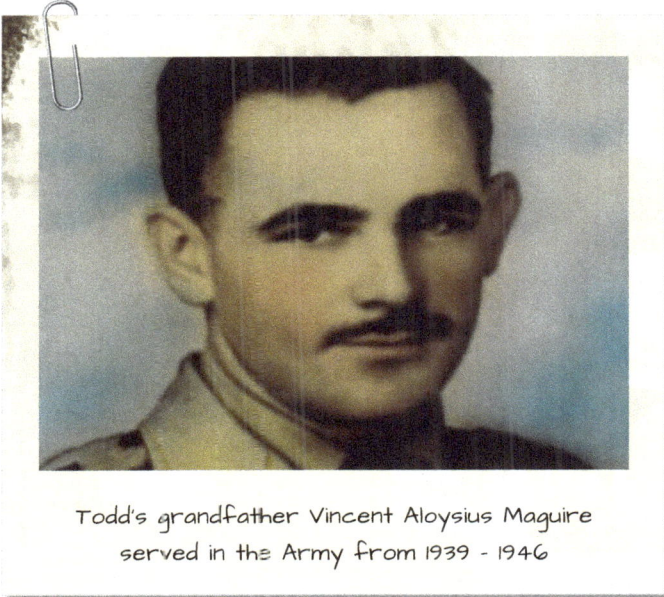

Todd's grandfather Vincent Aloysius Maguire
served in the Army from 1939 - 1946

# 2

# WHERE LEGENDS
# WERE MADE

'Two bucks worth of chips and a couple of potato scallops, please,' I said, slapping my coins onto the counter. The woman behind the register gave a knowing smile, scooping up the change with a well-worn hand. The shop was filled with the scent of deep-fried everything. Salt, vinegar and hot oil clinging to the air like a second skin. The dull hum of the bain-marie, the rattle of the fridge door and the crackle of the fryer were the background music of our weekends.

It was a typical Saturday arvo in Brisbane's northern suburbs— arcades game at the corner store, a packet of Redskins in one pocket and grease-stained paper in the other. My life was simple and carefree, filled with adventure on my trusty silver Mongoose bike, complete with red tuffs. I'd cruise the streets of suburbia from sunup to sundown. It was the 1970s and '80s after all, the best of all eras to be a youngster. Well, in my humble opinion.

Every day brought a new kind of mischief. My mates and I were a ragtag bunch of suburban warriors, taking on the world one reckless stunt at a time. Whether it was launching off homemade ramps, re-enacting footy games under the glow of streetlights, or sneaking into places we definitely shouldn't have been, we were inseparable. We had our own roles, too: the daredevil, the brains, the peacemaker and together, we ruled the neighbourhood with nothing but our bikes, scraped knees and an endless supply of imagination.

Sporting roots ran deep in our family and weekends revolved around competition. My brother Scott and I threw ourselves into everything: cricket, athletics, swimming, soccer. We went on to make a few of the representative teams. Backyard cricket battles were a daily ritual, our rivalry as fierce as any test match. We'd imitate our favourite bowlers from the '80s, each delivery feeling like the defining moment of a World Cup final.

But if anyone in our family had true sporting credentials, it was Dad, Patrick Maguire. A record-breaking swimmer at St Pat's Shorncliffe and a Queensland U19 rugby union rep, Dad was the kind of natural athlete people talk about years later in pubs. He switched to rugby league thanks to a nudge from his boss and joined the Brothers' club, where he trained under none other than Brian 'Bull' Davies. Dad ran with legends like Johnny Gleeson and Barry Dowling and made his name known. In the 1967–68 A-grade grand final at Lang Park, Dad scored a 60-metre try, the kind of effort that still gets retold at reunions over beers. His reward was a crisp twenty bucks. Not bad coin back then. Not quite immortality—but not far off.

My Mum, Cheryl Maguire, was always Dad's biggest fan. There's a famous photo of her in the newspaper, proudly wearing Dad's Brothers jersey before the '67 grand final, a moment frozen in time; all pride and love. Dad's career later took him to the national level with a three-year stint at South Sydney Rabbitohs, where he played alongside legends like John Sattler and Bob McCarthy. By the '90s, Dad had well and truly hung up his boots and was back at Brisbane Brothers, this time as club president, pouring his heart into the club and its community. Dad's legacy wasn't just in stats or stories; it was in the way people lit up when they talked about him. He was respected, admired and loved.

I remember one afternoon sitting with him in the backyard, my head full of questions, wondering how someone like him hadn't worn the green and gold. My godfather, Noel Cavanagh, had played for Australia, and it seemed only natural that my dad should have too. So, with all the innocence of youth, I asked, 'Hey Dad, why didn't you ever play for Australia?'

I expected some grand, inspiring story, maybe a heroic near miss or a sacrifice for the greater good. Instead, Dad leaned back in the chair, a familiar twinkle in his eye, stretching the moment out like it was a punchline worth waiting for.

'Well, Todd, there were three reasons,' he said, dragging it out like he was about to reveal the secrets of the universe.

I leaned in, hanging on every word. 'What were they?' I asked, practically bouncing with anticipation.

He let the silence hang for a moment, then, with a cheeky grin, answered with a single word.

'Selectors.'

That was it. No drama. No excuses. No tragic twist. Just classic Dad, dry as the outback and twice as funny. I laughed, but even then, I understood what he meant. He didn't chase glory; he just showed up, did the work and let others talk about it later. It's a trait that stuck with me. That quiet pride. That sense of knowing where you come from and carrying it with you, even when life gets messy. Especially when it gets messy. Because through all the twists and turns my life would take, from sunburnt childhood afternoons to the darkest corners of the criminal underworld, one thing never changed: I was a Maguire. And I was goddamn proud of it.

# 3

# THE FIGHTING IRISH

In 1982, I kicked off Year 5 at Padua, a renowned Franciscan Catholic boys' college located in the northern suburbs of Brisbane. Here, rugby league was treated with more reverence than the Bible. You could flunk religion, but God help you if you missed training.

By the time I hit high school, I was playing grand finals at Lang Park which, back then, felt like the bloody Colosseum. In Year 12, I landed in the Firsts XIII Rugby League, following the footsteps of some serious talent who went on to wear NRL jerseys. We were lucky enough to have Dad coaching the Firsts, and that made it all the more special, or awkward, depending on how badly you played.

My older brother, Scott, was already a name. A Queensland Confraternity Carnival legend, he made the Queensland Residents side and even had a crack at Parramatta before becoming a local hero at Brisbane Brothers in the Queensland Cup.

And let's not forget my little sister, Sally, who was crowned Ms Brisbane Rugby League in 1995. That's right, the Maguires weren't just producing footballers; we were turning out pageant winners too. Full credit to Mum and Dad. Talk about a well-rounded gene pool.

Scott and I were like chalk and cheese on the field. He was a silky five-eighth with a golden boot who could kick a goal from bloody Mars. But when it came to defence, well, let's just say the opposition loved running at him. He earned the nickname 'Turnstile'. Always open for business. But I'll say this: he was the Queensland Cup's highest point scorer for years. That's how we Aussie blokes do it; we hand out nicknames instead of compliments. But behind all that, I was proud as hell of him.

As for me, well, I was built differently. I loved a big hit. I wasn't there to finesse the game; I was there to flatten anything that moved. Passing wasn't my strong suit. In fact, I'd rather tackle a grandstand than throw a cutout ball. One coach reckoned if he could have combined Scott's finesse and my fire, he would have had the perfect rugby league player. Instead, Mum and Dad got two half-decent ones, one who ran around people and one who ran through them.

Rugby league wasn't just a sport; it was religion, therapy and identity all rolled into one. Weekends were footy chaos: multiple games, half a dozen meat pies and Mum driving like a madwoman to get us across town. Dad was everywhere—coaching, mentoring, yelling from the sideline. You couldn't escape it, and honestly, I didn't want to.

I started out with Brothers Juniors with the legendary Joe Borg as coach and fell in love with the club culture instantly. The smell of Dencorub, the clack of sprigs on concrete and that feeling of putting on the jersey? Bloody magic. Then came 1990. I was 17 and barely shaving when the call came—an invitation to trial with the North Sydney Bears. Big time stuff. I packed my footy bag, a bit of misplaced confidence and a whole heap of nerves. I landed in Chatswood, Sydney and walked into a share house to discover that my housemates were none other than A-graders Kelly Egan, Gary Larson and Barry Mulquin. Absolute units and bloody legends. My stomach did a triple somersault and nearly landed on the floor.

But the real shock was our glamorous accommodation: two tents in someone's backyard. That's right. Tents. Like Boy Scouts but with more grog and less supervision. Welcome to the big time, 1990s style. The night before my trial, my tent mate and I decided we needed to 'settle the nerves'. And by settle, I mean hit up Kings Cross—Sydney's hedonistic nightlife hub—like we were rock stars. One pub turned into five, maybe ten. Next thing you know, it's five in the morning and we're stumbling back into our tents like a couple of busted shopping trolleys.

We had a 10am trial. Spoiler: it did not go well.

If I had a soundtrack for that morning, it'd be Paul Kelly's *I've Done All the Dumb Things*—played on repeat, full volume.

Looking back now, I wonder if that one night, that one stupid decision, cost me a shot at the big league. Maybe. Maybe not. But what I do know is I played like a busted arsehole that day. And even more than the hangover, it was that gut punch of regret that stuck with me. I was at a crossroads. One path led to chasing the party scene, and believe me, the party scene was calling. The other, buckling down and committing to a career in rugby league and seeing how far I could take it.

What path did I choose? Keep reading, mate. The story's just warming up.

# 4

# FROM PUB CRAWLS TO PAINKILLERS

Faced with uncertainty after Year 12 in 1989, I resolved to embrace the possibilities ahead.

So, I did what any carefree 17-year-old Aussie bloke would do. I leaned into what I knew best: having a laugh, sinking a few cold ones and chasing whatever good times came my way.

What followed was a glorious stuff-around phase, lived one schooner at a time, all while U2 belted out *I Still Haven't Found What I'm Looking For* like it was written just for me. Except instead of pondering life's great questions, I was more focused on which pub served the best steak sandwich and chips.

Hospitality was the obvious choice. Believe it or not, I enrolled in and completed a Diploma in Hotel Management with the aim of becoming a successful hotel manager or publican. I loved a party, never said no to a cold one and could yarn the leg off a barstool. Whether it was spinning stories across the counter or hyping up a quiet crowd, I thrived on the chaos. People fascinated me; the heartbreak kings, the pub philosophers, the wide-eyed first timers and the old boys who'd been welded to the same stool since the '70s.

Brisbane's nightlife in the early '90s was where I really cut my teeth. Before long, I was working the scene in joints like The Underground and Mary Street Nightclub, home of the legendary one-dollar drinks on Thursday nights. If you know, you know. When local band Solar Baby belted out *Smells Like Teen Spirit*, you knew the night was about to go sideways.

I started out as a humble glassy, dodging flying Powers stubbies and chasing towers of empties. But it wasn't long before I landed behind the bar, channelling the *Cocktail* era of Tom Cruise only with less charm, more stumbles and a serious spill rate. I even practised bottle flips at home with water bottles. That's right, commitment.

Hospitality wasn't just a job; it was a lifestyle. Long hours, late nights, bad decisions and better stories. And yeah, there were a few mornings I woke up feeling like I'd been hit by a truck full of rum and no regret. But I wouldn't trade those years for anything. They gave me people skills, resilience and a sense of self that I was just starting to figure out. But while I was pouring pints and dodging hangovers, rugby league was still tugging at my sleeve.

In 1992, I cracked the senior squad with the U19 Brothers Colts. Out of one hundred hopefuls, I made the final cut, a feeling like finding a twenty-dollar note in your old footy shorts. Brothers had strong ties to the Brisbane Broncos NRL club, so the selection process was no picnic. The squad was stacked with junior rep players and hungry locals all chasing the dream. Our coaches were the real deal; Trevor Bailey, a former Brothers and St. George star, backed by Internationals David Wright and Graham Quinn in the higher grades. Between the three of them, they had more knowledge than every pub trivia team I'd ever joined combined. The squad was a melting pot of talent from across Queensland, many of them already schoolboy reps, and the rivalry was intense. It felt like Sunday nights at City Rowers: tense, electric and full of promise. And then, just when life felt like it was building towards something, footy decided to give me a slap across the face.

We were mid-season, playing the Wests Panthers at Purtell Park in Brissy's west. I lined up what I thought was going to be a textbook try-saving tackle. But instead of a big hit and a round of applause, I found myself colliding headfirst with one of their forwards, a human brick wall. My cheekbone shattered. My eye socket caved in like a dodgy beer can. I looked like a Picasso painting mid-explosion. To add insult to injury, a stray fingernail lacerated my eyeball. Yep, I was nearly Brothers' first one-eyed warrior. After a few nights in hospital, staring at the ceiling and wondering if I'd ever see straight again, literally or metaphorically, the doctors hit me with the kicker: I'd be in an eye patch for three months while they 'monitored the situation'. Just what every young athlete dreams of, a pirate phase.

When I returned to training, Trevor 'Bails' Bailey took one look at my battered mug, burst out laughing, and dubbed me 'Cyclops'. And you know what? I wore that name like a badge of honour. It wasn't just a nickname; it was proof that I could take a hit and come back swinging. Despite the injury, the Brothers' culture kept me going. The bond with the boys, the dirt under the nails, the shoulder slaps after a brutal session; it was the kind of mateship you couldn't buy. That injury taught me more than any win ever could: resilience, humility and how to laugh even when your face looked like it'd gone ten rounds with Mike Tyson.

Footy was never just about footy. It was about loyalty, brotherhood, showing up and digging deep. Taking the knocks and getting up again. The game shaped me, scarred me and set the stage for what came next. Because, as it turned out, life still had a few bigger hits waiting for me.

# 5

# FIGHTS, FUMBLES AND A WHOLE LOTTA NOODLES

In the early years after school, I was your classic young Aussie bloke, all piss and vinegar, living by the motto: 'You either get a fuck or a fight.' I didn't always get the former, but I sure had a knack for the latter. I found myself in more street scraps around Brisbane city than I care to remember, usually outside places like the Victory Hotel, where the drinks were cheap, the nights were messy and the punches flew quicker than the bar staff could pour.

It wasn't just about being a hothead; it was the era. There was an invisible, reckless confidence that wrapped around us like armour. We were untouchable. Ten feet tall and bulletproof. Fuelled by youth, bravado and a few too many schooners, I thought I was the king of the city. One night, I was out with my mate Kenny. We were at some pub, half lit and full of confidence, cutting shapes on the dancefloor. I was mid-conversation with a girl I thought I was charming the absolute pants off, when out of nowhere, bam! Some surfer-looking bloke spun me around and king hit me. Dog shot. My front tooth hit the dancefloor faster than a dropped meat pie at a B&S ball, and my mouth started bleeding like a stuck pig. The bouncers, bless 'em, barrelled in like drop bears on a mission, dragging everyone outside in a chaotic blur of arms, accusations and spilled bourbon.

Outside, this bloke, looking like an extra from a Red Hot Chilli Peppers music video, started throwing spinning kicks like he was auditioning for *Mortal Kombat: Queensland Edition*. Then his mates showed up; four against two. Kenny and I were clearly outnumbered. Ah, Kenny, he's a great bloke, but not exactly Bruce Lee. Me? Well, I panicked, threw the first punch and dropped Chilly Pepper cold. Kenny clocked the second. The third came at me, swinging like he was in a windmill, and I stayed in tight and got lucky again; down he went. The fourth took one look and bolted. We thought it was over, but it turns out Chilly Pepper was some sort of Muay Thai state champion. No joke. You'd never have known it the way he hit the pavement.

As he stumbled off, bloodied and bruised, he pointed and yelled, 'I know where you live. You're dead!'

I just smirked. 'Mate, good luck—I don't even know where I live half the time.'

The next morning, I woke up with a head like a dropped watermelon. My lip was split, my jaw ached and when I looked in the mirror, I saw a version of myself that had definitely seen better days. My head looked like a lollipop with bruises. Mum was not impressed. Telling her I'd lost a tooth was like confessing I'd joined a nudist cult. I copped the classic Irish Catholic mum look of death and a guilt trip for good measure. But did I slow down? Not a chance.

The very next night, we were back on the town at our go-to venue. City Rowers. An iconic spot. The floors were so sticky you could lose a thong mid-step and never see it again. The drinks were suspiciously cheap, and the DJ… well, he worshipped MC Hammer like he was the messiah in parachute pants. I swear, if you even *whispered* 'Can't touch this,' he'd dive across the decks like it was a defibrillator.

Anyway, after a long night of power drinking, I stumbled back to my mate Oliver's place in Taringa around three in the morning. His real name is Oliver Clozeoff but everyone called him TJ for some reason. You know that magical hour when you're just sober enough to use a key but too drunk to care about volume control? Yeah, that was me.

I crept inside, trying to be quiet but sounding like a drunken possum in a bin. All the lights were on. As I shuffled through the hallway, I spotted a trail of clothing leading towards my mate's bedroom. It started with a pair of jeans, then a lacy bra, a tweed jacket, then a single sock just… floating there, like a lost dream. I thought, *Well done, champ. Someone's punching above their weight tonight.*

I moved to close the bedroom door—you know, be a respectful bloke. But then, as always, curiosity showed up wearing a trench coat and whispering, 'Just a little peek won't hurt…'

Big. Mistake.

What I saw… cannot be unseen. My mate was mid-performance, putting in a real Olympic effort. The chick? Folded like human origami. He had her legs up around his ears like he was trying to use her kneecaps as headphones. It looked less like sex and more like interpretive dance with adult themes.

I backed out of that room like it was a live crime scene, eyes wide, soul slightly damaged. *Nope. Nope. That never happened.*

I retreated to the kitchen for some emotional damage control—and maybe a snack.

Now, if you've ever been in a true bachelor pad, you'll know: food is optional. Alcohol? Abundant. Snacks? Mythical.

But I dug deep—and there it was. A single packet of two-minute noodles. It was slightly dusty and bent at the corners, like it had been through war, but it was mine. I was *winning*.

Now, back then, getting your kit off after a night out was pretty standard. It wasn't weird. It was tradition. Like taking your shoes off at the door, only way more inappropriate. So off came the clothes. Fully nude, 3:30am, mid-winter. I looked like a frozen chicken trying to make ramen.

But then the cold hit. And I don't mean 'Brrr, it's a bit chilly'. I mean Arctic tundra, penguin-slapping-you-in-the-face cold for Brisbane.

There I was *completely starkers*, cooking noodles at 3:30 a.m. in the middle of winter, freezing my arse off. I spotted the tweed jacket draped over a chair, probably the headphone girls, so I slipped it on. However, it didn't fit. I ended up tearing the shoulder trying to jam my arm in. I looked like a half-drunk scarecrow with a hunger problem. And because I only had two hands, one was holding a beer and the other a cigarette, I needed a third hand for stirring the pot. So, in a moment of deranged problem solving, I tucked the cigarette into the one place I had left, at the end of me old fella.

Yes. That happened.

Then, as if on cue, Right Said Fred came on the radio singing I'm Too Sexy. I was swaying to the beat, in nothing but an undersized tweed jacket, cradling a pot of noodles, a ciggy sticking out of my prawn, a tin in me other hand, thinking *this is living*. Then all hell broke loose, the bedroom door slammed open against the hallway wall. Headphone girl stormed out screaming at my mate. She finally reached the kitchen, saw me standing there in all my glory. She looked into my eyes then down to the lit cigarette, then back to my eyes again. She gave a double, no, triple blink and looked again at the cigarette in utter disbelief. It was like she was some sort of stunned mullet, totally bamboozled by my multi-tasking. She finally pulled herself together and then found her rage again and screamed, 'Give me my jacket, I'm going home!'

I nearly dropped the noodles and my beer as she ripped the jacket off me in a violent motion. She grabbed her gear and stormed out, and I swear she left a trail of judgment behind her that still haunts the kitchen tiles. My mate wandered in just as Ace of Base started playing. *All That She Wants* blared from the stereo as we sat there, still half pissed, singing along like idiots. 'All that she wants… is her ripped tweed jacket.'

Only in Australia can a weekend end with a fight, a cook up, a scarecrow strip show and a cigarette in your old fella. That was life back then for twenty-something young blokes, probably not much different to today. It was loud, reckless and unfiltered. I wasn't just partying; I was untouchable. Or so I thought.

# 6

# MATES, MAYHEM
# AND MEMORIES

As life would have it, my next move wasn't exactly part of some well-thought-out career plan. One minute I was tearing up Brisbane's pub scene, high on banter and Bundaberg 'Bundy' rum, and the next, I was boarding a plane to Cairns, hopping a sweaty bus to Mission Beach and catching a water taxi to Dunk Island. No roadmap. No grand plan. Just a hazy idea that working on an island sounded like a bloody good idea at the time.

Back in the mid-90s, Dunk Island wasn't home to just a resort; it was *the* resort. White sand, rainforest walks, reef views and sunset bars full of honeymooners, celebrities and pissed backpackers. I figured I'd work a few months mixing cocktails and living like a king. Fourteen months later, I was still there.

I took to bartending like a hungover duck to water. Think Tom Cruise in *Cocktail*, minus the cheekbones and with a lot more dropped schooners. I'd sling drinks to anyone. Celebrities, dive instructors, international bikini models who didn't speak a word of English (we managed) and tourists whose life stories poured out faster than the rum. I was in my element. Life was sun, salt, sweat and late-night chaos. My uniform: a bar apron, a deep tan and a cocky grin. Like any young fella I would have rooted a barber shop floor – anything with hair on it.

It wasn't all about the drinks either. This is where I discovered the Aussie writer Robert G. Barrett, and let me tell you, it was like finding gospel in a paperback. Les Norton's world wasn't just relatable, it was *mine*. Dodgy bookies, pub blokes and no-nonsense yarns written in a voice that sounded like half the people I'd grown up with. It planted a seed I wouldn't fully understand until years later.

But paradise, as always, comes with strings attached.

Two nights before it all blew up, I got caught up in a 'situation' with a fellow staff member, nothing unusual there. The catch? Well, she had only just got engaged and her fiancé was the lead singer of the island's main entertainment band. When she vanished that one night, he and his bandmates conducted a full-blown manhunt across the resort. When they found us, well, let's just say it was more awkward than explosive. The next morning, they packed up their gear and left the island. This left Dunk without a band. No tambourines. No triangle. No nothing. Most of the blokes on the island thought I was a legend, but the women weren't exactly VIP members of my fan club. In fact, they had to line up to hate me.

Two days later, I was sitting at the bar, beer in hand, enjoying happy hour, when the general manager strolled over. This bloke was about as cheerful as a tax audit, so when he smiled, I knew I was stuffed.

'Hey Todd, what are you drinking? My shout.'

Warning bells. I had never seen him shout anyone the whole time I was on the island. He took a sip, leaned in and said, 'So… enjoyed working here?'

'Yeah, mate, love it.'

'Good. Because today's your last shift. Your water taxi leaves at 10am tomorrow.'

I blinked. 'Oh... right.'

Then he slammed his beer down and exploded: 'Do you know I now don't have a fucking band or any entertainment? I'm fucked!'

The next morning, I packed my one busted suitcase, a few rum-stained memories, a sun-faded staff shirt and then caught the 10am water taxi. As the island shrank in the rear view and the boat bounced across the waves, I felt like a bloke being deported from his own fantasy.

Dunk Island would later be devastated by Cyclone Yasi in 2011, reduced to ruins and left abandoned; now just a memory for those of us who lived there. But back then, it was paradise. And I, for a fleeting moment, was the king of it until I cocked it up in true Maguire fashion. No job. No plan. Just a cracking story, a slightly bruised ego and a tan that wouldn't last the winter.

Back in Brisbane, four weeks into the grind, I felt like a caged bird. I missed the chaos. I missed the adventure. So, I did what any twenty-something with a restless soul would do: I borrowed a couple of hundred bucks off my brother Scott, bought a one-way ticket back to Cairns and took off chasing whatever came next.

I landed on the floor at a mate's place; one of the Dunk Island crew. The welcome was peak Aussie: a crate of beer, filthy jokes and more noise than a footy team on Mad Monday. It felt like home. That very Saturday, I made a critical financial decision: spend my last cash wisely or blow it all at a sports bar on the punt.

Spoiler alert: I backed the horses. And the horses, well, they mugged me blind. I dumped my last rock lobster on a ten-to-one shot, which was also a tip from the local bookie. The horse ran so slow I'm pretty sure it stopped for a snack on the way. By the time it crossed the finish line, the race was long over. I left the bar with lighter pockets and a belly full of laughs. My mates nearly choked on their beers.

But a loss is only temporary—unless you're broke. Which I was. So, I scabbed eleven dollars for a Coral Coach -transfer to Port Douglas and headed north, broke but undefeated. I crashed at my mate GG's place. GG was a solid friend from school, the kind of bloke who was the school captain and First XV vice-captain. Some might say he was the 'golden boy'. And here I was, broke, homeless and sleeping head-to-toe in his double bed. It was ridiculous. And hilarious.

We spent our days exploring the area, hitting the beach and hustling for odd jobs to keep us in beer and instant noodles. Most days were spent half sunburnt, half hungover and fully committed to the noble pursuit of doing as little as possible while pretending we were just 'taking in the serenity'.

Those early days in Port Douglas were electric, raw, ridiculous and completely crazy. I had no money and no plan. The future? I had no idea. The fridge? Well, it was mostly beer. And the feeling? Freedom in its purest form. I was seriously flat broke and living out of a duffel bag, and yet, I felt more alive than I had in months. That had a lot to do with GG.

GG was the kind of mate who didn't just open his door, he opened his life. I rolled into Port Douglas with nothing but a hangover and a backpack, and he didn't hesitate for a second. Cleared some space, tossed me a spare pillow, and that was it, I was in. Sleeping head to toe in his double bed for weeks. That's how tight things were. But GG, he didn't complain once. No weirdness. No ego. Just a shrug and a 'She'll be right, mate.' It was like the world's least romantic honeymoon; two blokes sharing a bed in the sweaty tropics, dodging each other's feet like it was a contact sport. Every night, we'd collapse into that bed after a day of snorkel fails, job hunts or long stints at the pub talking absolute nonsense. And every morning we'd wake up slightly dehydrated, slightly more sunburnt and laughing before we'd even had our first coffee.

That time together forged a bond that no distance or time can undo. It was more than just sharing a room; it was sharing a moment in life where nothing made sense, but everything felt possible. GG had my back before I even knew I needed it, and we forged a mateship that to this very day still brings belly laughs whenever we catch up. Even now, years later, if someone mentions Port Douglas, I don't think of the reef or the palm trees. I think of GG and his generosity.

I think of two idiots living on two-minute noodles, laughing till we cried, not caring what tomorrow looked like. That was living. And back then, that was more than enough.

After a few weeks of couch surfing, noodle scabbing and near-drownings during my snorkelling attempts, GG managed to get me a job on the bell desk at the Sheraton Mirage. Fancy, right? There I was, a busted-up footy bloke with limited vision—my eye had still not recovered from that footy incident all those months ago—and no sense of direction, parking Porsches, greeting high-end guests and zipping around the resort in a golf buggy like a Queenslander James Bond.

'Welcome to the Sheraton! Can I park your car? No worries, if it's in reverse, I'll work it out eventually.' Around the same time, GG and I scored a cracking two-bedroom apartment just off the main drag in Port Douglas. Walking distance to every pub, club and pie shop that ever regretted staying open past midnight. It wasn't just a place to live—it was the ultimate bachelor pad. Mismatched furniture, empty beer cartons as decor and a distinct aroma of Deep Heat and Old Spice. But it was ours. For the next 18 months, that joint would become a shrine to unfiltered youth.

And then came Chubby.

Now, every town has a local legend, and in Port Douglas, it was Chubby, a truckie from nearby Mossman, with a handshake like a vice and a heart the size of Far North Queensland. Chubby knew everyone. He could walk into any pub, nod once and there'd be a schooner waiting for him by the time he reached the bar. For some reason, he took a shine to the two out-of-towners who had more confidence than credentials. He ushered us into the local scene like we were his long-lost sons.

By this time, my vision had sort of... settled. I still saw double on the edges, but straight ahead was mostly clear, give or take the odd blur. Naturally, the next step was obvious: play rugby league. GG and I signed up for the Mossman Port Douglas Sharks A-grade side in the Cairns and District Rugby League comp. It felt a bit like joining the Avengers, what with one working eye and a deep fear of passing drills. But once I stepped on that field, I felt unstoppable. Sure, I had no depth perception, and yes, I sometimes tackled shadows instead of players, but I had the heart of a lion and a cheekbone that took hits like a champion.

We weren't exactly premiership contenders, more like enthusiastic cannon fodder. We got flogged most weekends, but the post-match beers made it worth every bruise. And when we weren't playing, we were out stirring up mischief, becoming infamous for our 3am bakery missions. We'd roll into the local bakery, usually shirtless, shoeless and shameless, like three heat-stroked pirates—me, GG and Chubby—hunting sausage rolls. We'd devour whatever was hot, laugh until our guts hurt and stumble home before sunrise, covered in flour and dignity in tatters. When we were in Cairns, the ritual was the same, only it usually involved a 'nude kebab' from the Esplanade. Don't ask how it started. Don't ask how it ended. Just know that the food was always good and the stories, even better. But Port Douglas wasn't just laughs and liver damage. We were outsiders, and at first, that mattered.

The community in Mossman was predominantly Aboriginal and Torres Strait Islander, and GG and I were two of the only white fellas in the team. At first, we copped some sideways looks, and fair enough. But rugby league, that great leveller, does what it does best: it brings blokes together. Once we started showing up, putting in the hard yards and showing respect, the walls came down fast.

The bonds we built with the fellas, especially the older players and the local legends, ran deep. We weren't just teammates; we were brothers in arms, on and off the field. They taught me more about respect, resilience and cultural pride in a few months than I'd picked up in a lifetime. I learned to listen. I learned to show up. And I learned that real community is something you earn, not something you're handed. One night at the Exchange Hotel, Louie, our fullback and a bloke with the sharpest wit in town, jokingly tried to marry me off to his sister. I laughed, nodded respectfully and promptly changed the subject. But it wasn't about the joke. It was about acceptance. That moment, and many like it, were small but powerful signs that we'd made it in, not as tourists, but as part of the tribe.

The footy, the nude bakery runs, the absurdity of two blokes with no clue, living like kings with nothing but laughs, a bit of luck and a shared mattress when times were tight. We weren't winning much on the field, but we were absolutely killing it in the game of life. That year and a half in Port Douglas taught me more than any textbook ever could about mateship, culture and backing yourself even when you're half-blind and half-broke. Those were the days of barefoot ambition and beer-fuelled wisdom. And they'll stay with me forever.

# 7

# HYATT BY DAY, HIT-UPS BY NIGHT

As careers often do, mine took another one of those sharp left-handers with no indicators. One minute, I was deep in nudie kebabs and bakery runs up in Port Douglas, and the next, I found myself donning a collared shirt (barely ironed) and calling myself head concierge at the Hyatt Sanctuary Cove on the Gold Coast.

At 22 years of age, a greenhorn in management, I'd gone from one working eye and dodgy biceps to answering phones and parking BMWs like I was born to do it. How did I land it? Easy, GG got the job first, and I rode his coattails harder than a hungover apprentice in fluoro clinging to a pie and a Powerade.

We found ourselves a proper battler of a three-bedroom apartment in the suburb of Labrador, not exactly beachfront bliss, but it had a telly, a couch and plumbing that mostly worked. Perfect. We even convinced another schoolmate, known to all as 'The Spazman,' to take the third room. That house became a shrine to the holy trinity: footy, frothies and filthy feeds. Every Friday night was either a trip to the Parkwood Tavern (Mum's place we called it) or some dodgy Chinese joint where you were guaranteed heartburn but never boredom. Then one day, flicking through the *Gold Coast Bulletin* (mostly the sports and crime pages), I spotted a lifeline in print: Robert Grogan and Keith 'Cow' Neller were coaching the Nerang Roosters in the Gold Coast/Group 18 comp. For a footy tragic like me, it was like winning lotto. Well, almost. With Groges, a Brothers' legend from their 1987 BRL Grand Final win, that 'fighting Irish' spirit would be alive and well at the Roosters.

I charged into the Roosters' training like a meat pie sliding off a paper plate—fast, hot and with no brakes. Within two weeks, I'd gone from Reserves to A-grade and signed on the dotted line with NSW Country Rugby League contract; $300 for a win, $100 for a loss. I remember thinking that if I couldn't make it as a professional footy player, at least it'd pay for me piss.

We had a blockbuster coming up against Runaway Bay, the top dogs. Their backline looked like something out of a rugby league who's who. I was named to start in the centres. One bloke I was marking had Brisbane A-grade rep credentials. The other was set to debut with the Gold Coast Chargers in the ARL. No pressure. Just a casual baptism by fire. But footy gods were smiling that day.

Midway through the first half, Ali Davys, ex-Seagulls halfback and magician with a mullet, threw me a peach of a ball off our own half. It was like time slowed down. The line opened up like Moses parting the sea, and I hit the gap with legs pumping and zero regard for my hamstrings.

I could've sworn I heard a gospel choir singing in the background. I palmed one bloke, skinned another, rounded the fullback and, just as I started dreaming about the newspaper headline, *Unknown Centre Stuns the Bay,* their hooker blindsided me. Bang. I bounced, then bounced again. Then somehow bounced myself *over* the line and planted the ball, like a madman, under the black dot. Try time. Felt like the footy version of pulling a full Esky out of thin air at a dry party.

Not a bad way to announce yourself.

# 8

# FROM FROTHIES
# TO THE BADGE

One afternoon in late 1995, I found myself at the Parkwood Tavern with my mate Benno, who was deep into his career with the Queensland Police Service. We were enjoying a few frothy schooners, shooting the breeze about life. I was venting about the relentless demands of the hotel industry, how the long hours were constantly clashing with my footy games and how it was starting to grind me down. Benno, always the enthusiast, saw an opportunity and began to push me to join the police force.

I was hesitant, of course. Who in their right mind would trade a life of resort jobs, cold beers and footy games for a badge and a cap? Ha! Not me. But Benno wouldn't back down. He started spinning stories about playing footy in the police rugby league, name-dropping legends and former cops like Wayne Bennett and Mal Meninga as if they were our best mates.

'Imagine running around with those big names, mate!' he said, his eyes gleaming with excitement.

After a few more beers and a lot of eye-rolling on my part, I gave in. At that point in my life, playing footy was everything, and the hospitality industry was getting in the way. I'd throw in an application, just this once, I agreed. I figured if I got in, great! If not, no harm done; I'd go back to my footy and frothies without thinking twice about it. A few weeks later, I got the call up from the Queensland Police Service for physical testing.

Now, keep in mind that my eyesight was still a little average. So, I studied the eye chart with my good eye like I was sitting for a uni exam. When the doctor asked me to close the good one and read with the dodgy eye, it was blur city. But somehow, I scraped through. Either the doc had a good heart, or they needed numbers. Next thing I knew, I had a letter in my hand congratulating me on being accepted into the Queensland Police Service. I was set to start in nine months. Nine months?! That was almost an entire season of *Home and Away*; ages away, mate.

So I moved back to Brisbane and signed with the Brisbane Brothers for the 1996 season. Dad as president, Scott as club captain, Sally still basking in her glory as Ms Brothers and me. It felt like slipping into an old pair of footy shorts: familiar, slightly stained, but bloody comforting. We had legends like John McGraw, Donny Gailer and Graham 'Shovels' Olling (ex-Eels and Kangaroos front rower) on the coaching staff, and the crew felt solid. I was in form, fired up and ready to smash the season. The camaraderie, the shared history and the sense of belonging were all there, waiting for me. Standing in the change room, surrounded by familiar faces and the smell of liniment, I couldn't help but feel like this was where I was always meant to be.

But as fate would have it, the universe had other plans. During a home game against the Ipswich Jets, I was selected to play in the second row for the A-grade team. I was buzzing, ready to take on the world. As soon as the second half kicked off, I charged forward to make the first tackle, adrenaline pumping. And then, disaster. I collided with an opponent, taking the full force of his elbow directly to my left cheekbone. The impact knocked me out cold, and as I came to, I realised my season was over. Fortunately, my eyesight was unaffected this time, but I had a fractured cheekbone. Yes, the same cheekbone I did in U19s. It was a setback I wasn't prepared for, and it left me frustrated and disappointed. My teammates and coaches rallied around me, supporting me through the recovery process. Once again, I was on the sidelines, but the experience reminded me of the unpredictability of both sports and life.

During my recovery, I took a job pouring beers at the local rissole while I waited to enter the police academy. They took me on right away, and I was told to show up the next day at noon for an eight-hour shift. When I arrived, the supervisor showed me around, introducing me to the other staff. There was Michelle, the poker machine lady, Carol at reception and Jose in the kitchen. Then, I was introduced to one of the chefs, who was busy cutting carrots with a large knife.

As soon as we locked eyes, it clicked. It was Chilly Pepper, the Muay Thai bloke I'd knocked out a few years earlier. He immediately recognised me, gave me a double blink and, without missing a beat, he raised the knife in a menacing gesture. I gave him a smile and a wink and could only laugh internally. After finishing my shift, I never went back. That nine-month wait felt like purgatory; not quite past, not quite future. But it gave me time to breathe, time to recover and time to realise that maybe trading frothies for a badge wasn't selling out. Maybe it was levelling up. And I was ready.

Becoming a copper was never in the grand plan. In fact, there was no grand plan. I'd never dreamed of being a 'Thursday night shopper'. I'd never watched *Blue Heelers* with stars in my eyes, and I didn't have a single copper in the family tree. Up until this point, my interactions with the boys in blue mostly involved breathalysers, suspicious glances or the odd awkward 'Yes officer, I'm fine,' with a pie in one hand and a Bundy rum in the other. But somehow, there I was—enrolment confirmed, buzz cut half-grown back and set to begin a career that would reshape every inch of me.

I kicked off my six-month journey at the QPS Oxley Academy in October 1996. It was a campus that looked like it hadn't had a lick of paint since *Matlock Police* went off air. The buildings were spread out like a bad game of SimCity, the air smelled of lino and government-grade sausages, and the vibe was pure public service: forty per cent hope, sixty per cent paperwork. The training? It was a real mixed bag. Some instructors were legends, passionate, sharp and still gave a shit. Others looked like they'd mentally retired sometime around Expo '88 and were just counting down the days till they could throw the uniform in the bin and piss off to Noosa.

But in my class of twenty-five, I spotted a couple of Padua old boys. Blokes I hadn't seen since the days of dodgeball and tuckshop meat pies. It was like a surprise reunion for the lads who couldn't land a tackle and had nicknames that never died. That made things easier;

the shared banter, the knowing looks during drills, the unspoken understanding that none of us had any idea what we were doing. Academy life was… rigid. March here, stand there, salute this and sign that. It was more of an endurance test than an enlightenment. Half the time, I felt like I was being trained to be a filing clerk with a baton. That year, Regurgitator dropped the iconic track *I Sucked a Lot of Cock To Get Where I Am*. I remember hearing it and thinking, *yeah, sounds about right*. It became the unofficial anthem of our time at Oxley. A loud, ironic middle finger to the bureaucracy we were just starting to swim in.

The glutton for punishment that I was, I figured footy would balance it out. I turned up to Brothers' 1997 pre-season. My vision was still dodgy, but what's a little double vision when you're used to seeing two balls anyway? Bob Lindner, ex-Maroon and Kangaroo great, had taken over as head coach. No way I was missing that chance. I scraped through the first four rounds of A-grade, juggling training by night and academy drills by day. It was madness, but it kept me sane.

Graduation came in April 1997, and just like that, I was no longer just a mug with a mouth. I was a first-year constable. My first posting was to the Gold Coast. Twenty fresh-faced recruits, all eager as a butcher's dog, got sent to one of the busiest policing districts in the state. Real trial by fire stuff. I eventually managed to get into the Kirra Barracks, which was less 'coastal resort' and more 'state-sanctioned share house' for sweaty rookies. The walls were thin, the plumbing suspect and the fridge always empty, but what it lacked in comfort, it made up for in character. The Kirra Hotel became my second home. If those walls could talk, they'd ask us to shut up.

Everyone knew my name, my drink orders and which shift I was meant to be on (but wasn't). It was like a real-life version of *Cheers*, only with more fights and fewer warm fuzzies.

My first shift as a Thursday night shopper was a Friday midnight start at Surfers Paradise on foot patrol. What could go wrong? Answer: Everything, and I loved it. Within hours, we were in the thick of four all-in brawls. Swinging arms, beer breath, someone yelling 'He started it,' the works. I charged in like a drongo with a badge and something to prove, grinning like it was Origin night. It was bloody exhilarating. Adrenaline surging, fists flying, radios crackling, people spewing vodka Cruisers on their shoes. Policing didn't feel like work; it felt like a team sport with legal consequences. I was hooked. Sure, we were rookies—half the time, we had no idea what was legal and what just 'looked assertive'— but we had each other's backs. We stuffed up, sure, but we gave it a red-hot crack, and the old hands guided us (mostly while laughing at us behind our backs).

Those early days on the beat were like footy camp, only instead of orange slices at halftime, you got blood on your boots and a court brief to write. But I knew one thing early on: I might've stumbled into the job by accident, but I was going to run headfirst into it like everything else in life. Settling into life on the Gold Coast or 'Fabulous French Toast' as I liked to call it (don't ask why, it just stuck), wasn't just about strapping on the duty belt and chasing blokes out of Surfers. It was about finding my rhythm. Finding that balance between being a copper and still being... well, *me*. And for me, that always came back to rugby league.

Just as I was settling in on the Gold Coast, still riding the high from being part of the blue shirt brigade, I got the news: Nerang Roosters had folded. So, there would be no going back there. Financial dramas, apparently. The club went belly up faster than a schooner on a summer arvo. It felt like losing your favourite pub—a short moment of grief, followed by the hunt for the next best watering hole. That's when I found the Tugun Seahawks. They were battlers. Gritty, loud and proud of it. My kind of people.

Sunday arvo footy on the Goldie wasn't just a game; it was a full-blown carnival. The scent of sunscreen, sweat and barbecued meat filled the air. Utes lined the oval, cans cracked at kick-off, and if you squinted through the barbecue smoke, you could see half of Tugun hanging off the balcony of the clubhouse. The crowd was a sea of blue and white, as much a part of the game as the players. You could *feel* the atmosphere and the anticipation bubbling, like storm clouds ready to burst. It wasn't just the players who came alive; it was the whole town.

I turned up to my first game and was chucked into reserve grade with about fourteen minutes left on the clock. I figured I'd get a decent cardio session out of it and maybe avoid a concussion. But something must've clicked, whether it was dazzling footwork, blind desperation or just sheer availability; I caught the coach's eye. Ben Gonzalez, a former Penrith and Seagulls player with a footy brain and a face that looked like it had tackled too many knees, tapped me on the shoulder after the match.

'You'll be sitting on the A-grade bench next week, Maguire.'

Boom. Promotion. Just like that. *Straight from the sausage sizzle to the big time.*

Our next game was a local derby against the Tweed Seagulls. Tugun hadn't beaten Tweed in ten bloody years. The *Gold Coast Bulletin* had hyped the game all week. And by kick-off, there were close to 3000 people packing the ground yelling, betting, belching and ready for blood.

With eleven minutes left, we were down sixteen to ten, and I could feel my guts twisting. Gonzalez, the old warhorse, stepped up, dodging two defenders and slamming the ball down just wide of the posts. The conversion sailed through. Sixteen all. Game on. And then came my moment. I'll never forget it. The next set, Tweed went to spread it wide. Their centre threw a lazy cut-out pass, and before I even had time to think, I dragged in an intercept and took off like I'd been shot out of a potato cannon. The crowd roared. The line was in sight. And then *bang*, caught from behind just short of the stripe. Apparently, I still had the speed of a busted wheelie bin, but hey, I got us damn close. From the play of the ball, our lock, Wayne Spence, threw a beautiful long ball out to halfback Luke Swain, who slid over untouched for the winning try. The siren went. The crowd exploded. And suddenly, we were giant killers.

The *Gold Coast Bulletin* headline the next day read: Tugun No Names Upset Seagulls. But in the clubhouse that night? I wasn't a no-name. I was a bloody hero. I didn't buy a single drink that night. Not one. People were patting me on the back, asking where I came from, shouting rounds and thanking me like I'd just delivered a baby on the sideline. It was surreal, wild and, honestly, one of the proudest footy moments of my life.

That game stitched me into the Tugun fabric. The Goldie had officially become home. Copper by day, footy battler by weekend. Between the barracks, the beat and the backline, I'd carved out my little patch of purpose. And the best bit? The journey was only just getting started.

# 9

# SLIDING DOORS AND SEAHAWK SUNDAYS

After a year of dodging cheeky tourists and keeping an eye on the local troublemakers, the twenty first-year constables were summoned into the training office, a sterile room filled with the scent of old coffee and unspoken tension. The Inspector stood before us, a no-nonsense figure with a clipboard and an air of authority that could silence a room. 'Ten of you will stay,' he declared, 'and the other ten are headed to Logan.'

They were taking volunteers first, and the rest would be selected by a random draw, like a twisted game of musical chairs. My heart raced at the thought of returning to Brisbane, the chance to don the Brothers' jersey once more igniting a flicker of excitement in my chest. I loved the Gold Coast, but the pull of the city and the camaraderie of my old mates were too strong to ignore. I raised my hand without hesitation, ready to go.

The following week, we gathered again, the air thick with anticipation. I sat calmly, convinced my name would be read out. But as the list unfolded, a cold wave of disbelief washed over me; my name wasn't called. Silence gripped the room. Eyes turned towards me, a mix of pity and surprise etched across the faces of my colleagues. 'But I volunteered,' I blurted out, still processing the snub. The women whose names had been called panicked, turning to me with desperation spread all across their faces, 'Swap with us'.

If they had approached me with kindness or tact, maybe I would've considered it. But the desperation in their tone sparked a stubborn streak. I smirked and replied, 'Nah, you can't change fate, girls.' In that moment, equal parts absurd and monumental, I sealed my destiny. It was a sliding door moment, one of those forks in the road you only recognise later. That choice would ripple through my life, shaping friendships and rivalries and destroying me in ways I could not yet fathom.

Later that day, I found myself back at the Kirra Hotel with my mates, Pat and Stevo, sinking into a barstool like it was my throne. 'Three schooners of Tooheys, thanks,' I told the barman. We'd wandered up Haig Street and right into our sanctuary. It was my first day off out of four, and nothing kicked it off better than a steak and a cold beer. It was 1998, and there I was, a twenty-four-year-old, second-year copper stationed at Broadbeach, fully embracing the Gold Coast lifestyle. Surfing, footy and pub sessions ruled my days. The speakers at Kirra were belting out TISM, letting everyone know they were on the drug that killed River Phoenix. As Les Norton says, 'You wouldn't be dead for quids.'

Yes, life was good, and the universe would deliver little reminders that I was on the right track. It was like good memories kept sneaking up and whacking me on the head. When I had joined the Seahawks, it was right in the chaos of the Super League war. With the Seagulls and the Chargers folding, a wave of ex-pros flooded our comp. It was wild. One of them was Barry Mulquin, ex-North Sydney Bear and backyard tent lender from back in the day. Talk about a blast from the past.

'Hey Barry! Remember me?' I called out like a hopeful kid. 'The two seventeen-year-old clowns camping in your backyard in 1990?'

Barry laughed so hard he nearly dropped his drink.

'Ha! You two rolled in just as the sun came up, the whole street heard you!'

I grinned. 'The neighbours wanted us strung up, right?'

'Mate, I was just glad you didn't burn the joint down. But yeah, they were ready to riot. Still got earplugs just in case you pop by again!'

We both laughed till our sides ached. It was one of those moments where the past and present collided in the best way.

But the real magic was in the brotherhood of the sport. It reminded me of days gone by and reassured me that I always had family, no matter where I was. As teammates, we backed each other on the field and in life. If we didn't win the game, you could bet we'd win the fight and celebrate together. Someone always had a dodgy speaker blasting The Celibate Rifles' *A Wonderful Life*, and win or lose, we would sing, laugh and dance (badly), knowing full well we'd all be regretting it in the morning.

It wasn't just about what happened on the field; it was everything around it. The rituals, the banter, the community. That was footy. That was family. And on the Gold Coast, that was home.

Looking back, missing out on that Brisbane post felt like a blow. But the truth is, if I'd gone back, I would've missed all of that. The Sundays. The Seahawks. The mates. That one raised hand and a stubborn 'nah' sent me down a different track, and for all its chaos, I wouldn't trade it for anything.

A few weeks after that placement meeting, I found myself stationed at Broadbeach under Sergeant Swift, affectionately known as Swifty. A Brisbane Brothers stalwart from the '80s, he took me under his wing. One day, during a casual chat, he told me about a police rugby league game that was happening at Carrara Stadium, a curtain raiser for the Gold Coast Chargers versus Adelaide Rams ARL game. 'There's a police team coming up from Sydney and they might be short. Do you reckon you could sit on the bench just in case? You probably won't get on, but it'll be good to have you there.'

He downplayed it like it was no big deal, but my curiosity was piqued. Then, I saw a newspaper article promoting the game as Queensland Police versus New South Wales Police. I panicked. *I'm a Queenslander. I can't wear that sky blue jersey!* But I'd already committed. When I arrived, I saw familiar faces from the force cheering me on and, thankfully, the jersey wasn't sky blue; it was a Sydney City Firsts jersey, which was yellow with blue Vs. I breathed a sigh of relief.

The match was fiercely contested, and when injuries struck, I was called onto the field. The pace wasn't as intense as I expected, and I quickly found my groove. With Queensland leading twenty to eighteen, I made a breakthrough the middle, drawing in the fullback before tossing an over-the-head pass to my winger, who scored the match-winning try. The crowd erupted, and my teammates swarmed me. It was a moment I'd never forget.

That night at the postgame function, I received the unexpected news—I'd been selected for the Australian police team for a one-month tour of the UK. My policing career had only just begun, and already, it was taking me around the world.

# 10

# OUT OF MY LEAGUE

It was a Friday night, and I was strutting around The Fabulous French Toast like I owned the joint, when I met up with a mate for a drink.

'Oi Jase, who the hell is the hottie with the dark hair?' I said, giving him a jab to the ribs and gesturing towards the woman nearby.

'Mate, that's Karen,' he replied. 'I knew her from Christchurch. She separated from her husband about six months ago.'

She was stunning, petite, maybe a bit over five feet tall, with dark hair that framed her face just right. But it wasn't just her looks. There was something in her presence, a calm confidence that pulled you in. Vulnerable, sure, but there was quiet strength there too. She looked like someone who knew herself.

'And she's single, hey?' I was trying to sound casual despite already mentally planning our first date.

'Yep.'

Game on. That's blood in the water for any bloke.

Her friendly, kind nature hit me like a rip tide, and I was hooked. I was 25—still figuring out whether I was a grown man or just a kid playing dress-ups. She seemed miles out of my league. I was no Brad Pitt but definitely no arm pit either… I thought I'd give it a crack. We chatted briefly before I somehow convinced her to dance. I accidentally stepped on her toes three times before we said our goodbyes. I was sure she was hoping she'd never see me again.

But I wasn't done.

The next week, I showed up at her workplace, Bond University, in full police uniform. I figured if women liked a man in uniform, I might as well go all in. I strutted in like I was Wally Lewis himself— heart thumping, chest puffed and absolutely no plan for what to do if she actually said 'hi'.

As I made my grand approach, I knocked over a stack of papers. Of course. She laughed. I laughed. And somehow, that clumsy moment became our beginning. I kept finding reasons to visit Bond Uni after that, spinning more yarns than a playwright. Eventually, I asked her out, and to my absolute shock, she said yes. I was happier than a dog with two dicks.

Our relationship started off nice and relaxed, which suited both of us. She was still navigating the aftermath of her separation, and I needed to give her space. Karen lived on a hill in Mudgeeraba in a gorgeous house on acreage, tucked away in the hinterland. She had a three-year-old son, Clarke, who stayed with her part-time. I

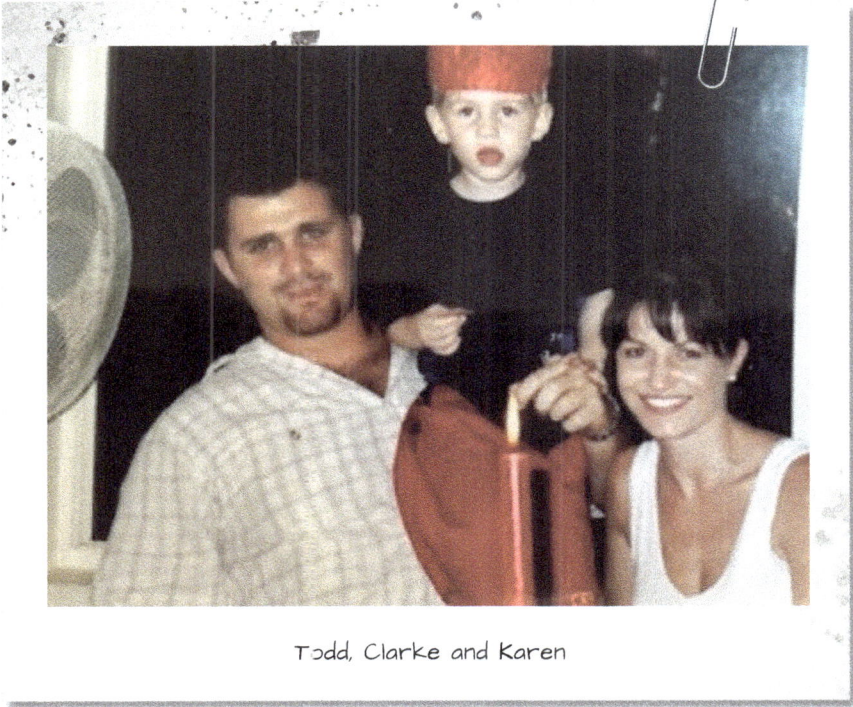

Todd, Clarke and Karen

was still in the barracks at Kirra, but that wasn't going to last much longer. I need to find a new place to live.

Karen and I became joined at the hip, and I never did end up finding my own place to live. Less than a year after meeting, I had somehow become a permanent fixture at Karen's place. One day, I was a single copper. Next, I was stepping over Lego bricks and watching cartoons with popcorn in hand. I never officially moved in. I just stopped leaving. Before I knew it, I was helping with bath time, making Clarke's brekkie and sneaking kisses with Karen in the hallway. For the first time, home wasn't just a place. It was a feeling. It was chaotic, but it was also bloody hilarious. Every day felt like an episode of a sitcom, and I was just stoked to be part of the cast.

Karen was, without a doubt, one of the most stunning women I'd ever seen. A solid ten out of ten. Heads turned wherever we went—bars, pubs, restaurants. People approached her constantly. Sometimes they even asked me for permission to flirt with her. But I never felt jealous. Not once. Karen handled it all with confidence and grace. She'd smile, brush them off and come right back to me, making me feel like the king of the Coast.

One night at the pub, some bloke tried a classic pickup line. 'What's a woman like you doing with a drongo like him?' Without missing a beat, Karen shot back, 'This black belt's gotta keep the drunks in line.' I nearly wet myself laughing. She had this magic for turning any situation into comedy gold. I used to joke that if we charged

Karen

admission for every bloke who tried to chat her up, we could've bought beachfront apartments.

But no matter how many eyes were on her, her heart never wandered. We had something real, our own little bubble, where the outside world just faded away. And somehow, I, the copper from Kirra with two left feet and a pile of Lego underfoot, had landed the girl from Christchurch.

# 11

# WEARING THE GREEN AND GOLD ABROAD

The Australian police footy tour of the UK kicked off in September 1998. It was a surreal moment, knowing I would be representing not just my team but my country. We kicked things off with Korean Airlines, making our way through Brisbane and Seoul before touching down in London. It felt like we were globetrotting in style, even though, at heart, we were just a bunch of blokes on a mission. Originally, we had lined up games against the UK force, but at the last minute, they pulled the rug out from under us. Fortunately, the New Zealand Police stepped up to fill the gap, though we had to foot the bill for the bus to get us to the game. But that was all part of the adventure, and before we knew it, we were deep into an eight-match odyssey against some seriously tough competition.

The standout moment for me was meeting Sir Richard Branson at a London Broncos match. The bloke was every bit as charismatic as you'd expect. With so many memories swirling around, it's hard to recall them all, but that moment sticks out as something special.

As for the footy, we came out swinging. Here's a taste of our triumphs:

- Combined Navy: 44 to 4 (London)
- Midlands Police: 62 to 6 (Birmingham)
- British Civil Services: 30 to 2 (Manchester)
- NZ Police: 36 to 6 (Dewsbury–West Yorkshire)
- BARLA (British Amateur RL) East: 32 to 30 (A nailbiter at St Helens)
- BARLA West: 31 to 10 (Waterhead RFC, Oldham)
- Cumbria Police: 34 to 14 (Cumbria)
- Combined Defence Forces: 18 to 12 (London).

Our squad was packed with talent. We had Harro, our captain and former Rabbitoh; Shakers, Sharpey and Tapey, just to name a few. Queensland players like Bakes, Chalky and Wrighty added to our ranks, creating a formidable team both on and off the field. But this tour was about more than just the scoreboard. It was about pride, camaraderie and the kind of friendships forged in the heat of competition. Representing our country was an honour, and I couldn't have been prouder to stand alongside my teammates on this incredible journey.

In the end, it wasn't just a footy tour; it was a once-in-a-lifetime experience filled with unforgettable moments, hard-fought battles and lifelong mates. The memories we created will be cherished for years to come.

# 12

# CROSSROADS AND COMMITMENTS

**K**aren and Clarke had become my biggest supporters at Tugun Seahawks Rugby League Club. Life felt like it had finally found a rhythm—footy, family and the kind of quiet joy that comes from knowing you're right where you're meant to be. That year, Karen and I took a trip to Bali together, and I swear, it still sits in my top holidays of all time.

The sun in Bali felt different—warmer, slower, golden. We wandered through bustling markets and bartered for souvenirs. We soaked in the sights and smells of incense, sizzling street food and salt in the air. Days were filled with laughter, lazy swims and Bintang-fuelled nights under the stars. It was one of those trips where time didn't matter, where every moment felt light and full. We weren't just travelling, we were making memories, ones that still make me grin to this very day.

Back home, things were just as good. I was selected to play in the Queensland Police versus New South Wales Police match as a curtain raiser to a Broncos versus Knights NRL game, a surreal experience. Pulling on that maroon jersey with the crowd already buzzing in the stands was something I will never forget. From there, things escalated quickly. I was selected in the Australian Police Rugby League side again, and in November 1999, we were scheduled to visit the US for an international test match against the USA Tomahawks in Philadelphia. It was a huge honour, a dream opportunity and something I'd worked hard for.

Todd: 1999 Queensland Police vs New South Wales Police

But just before I left, Karen sat me down.

She was pregnant.

I still remember the moment. The air went still, and everything else faded into the background. My brain tried to catch up, but the words just hung there, echoing. I was stunned. Happy? Yes. Terrified? Absolutely. But mostly, I was unsure. What was I supposed to do? I was about to leave for the other side of the world. Should I stay? Was it selfish to even be considering going on the trip? Was I ready for this next chapter of my life? I didn't know. I tossed and turned over it for days, caught between excitement and panic.

Part of me wanted to call the tour manager and pull out. The thought of Karen going through early pregnancy without me made me feel sick. But we agreed this was an opportunity of a lifetime and that I should go. So off I went. Torn between two worlds. One foot chasing dreams on foreign soil, the other planted firmly back home with the woman I loved and the life we were building.

My second tour with the Aussie police team was a ripper—one of those unforgettable rides that has stamped itself into my memory forever. We kicked things off with a couple of training sessions at Belmore Oval in Sydney before flying out to New York, landing smack bang in the middle of Halloween. Jet lag didn't stand a chance. We shook it off with a jog through Central Park and breakfast at the top of the World Trade Centre—a memory that would take on an entirely new weight just a few years later. From there, it was full throttle: an NYPD harbour cruise, a behind-the-scenes tour of HQ and a whirlwind night through Times Square and the theatre district.

Game day against the USA Tomahawks rolled around and we headed to Philadelphia. We rolled into the stadium like royalty, escorted by police who stopped traffic at ever set of lights. They had marching bands, cheerleaders, the full USA show. After the national anthems they called out each opposed number from each side to run out onto the field a greet each other. My number was called, thirteen for Australia, Todd Maguire, I ran onto the field and faced off against their starting lock, Jeff Preston—a bloke built like an NFL linebacker. He nearly crushed my hand in the pregame handshake. We managed a win for our first game of the tour, coming out on top 24-0. The Americans were big and tough and were still trying to understand the nuances of rugby league. The game was a brutal affair, but we pulled through.

Game two was a showdown, another solid hit out that we won 34-16. Back to Glen Mills for training before the main event against the Glen Mills Bulls, the champion team, in front of 3000 screaming students. The atmosphere was electric, easily one of the best footy crowds I'd ever played in front of outside Australia.

Originally, we were meant to head to Russia for the final leg, but due to some political unrest, that leg of the tour got axed. No vodka for us! Instead, we wrapped it all up in Las Vegas with its bright lights, chaos and roulette tables. I probably dropped more cash than I should've, but the late-night shenanigans, the laughs and the endless yarns made it worth every cent. What began as a footy tour quickly turned into the adventure of a lifetime, packed with mateship, madness and lifetime memories, from Philadelphia to Vegas.

To this very day, I still stir my old coach with the same line every time I see him: 'Who was the best player on that tour—and why was I?' He just shakes his head and laughs.

Austraiia Police v USA Tomahawks

When I was in the US, Karen and I kept in touch the old-fashioned way—pay phones and the occasional fax. I still have those faxes. Words scribbled across a fading page, telling me how much she loved me, how much she missed me and how much she loved our life together. I missed her birthday while I was away, so I had a mate deliver flowers on my behalf. She was doing it tough emotionally, exhausted from the pregnancy, and feeling every kilometre between us.

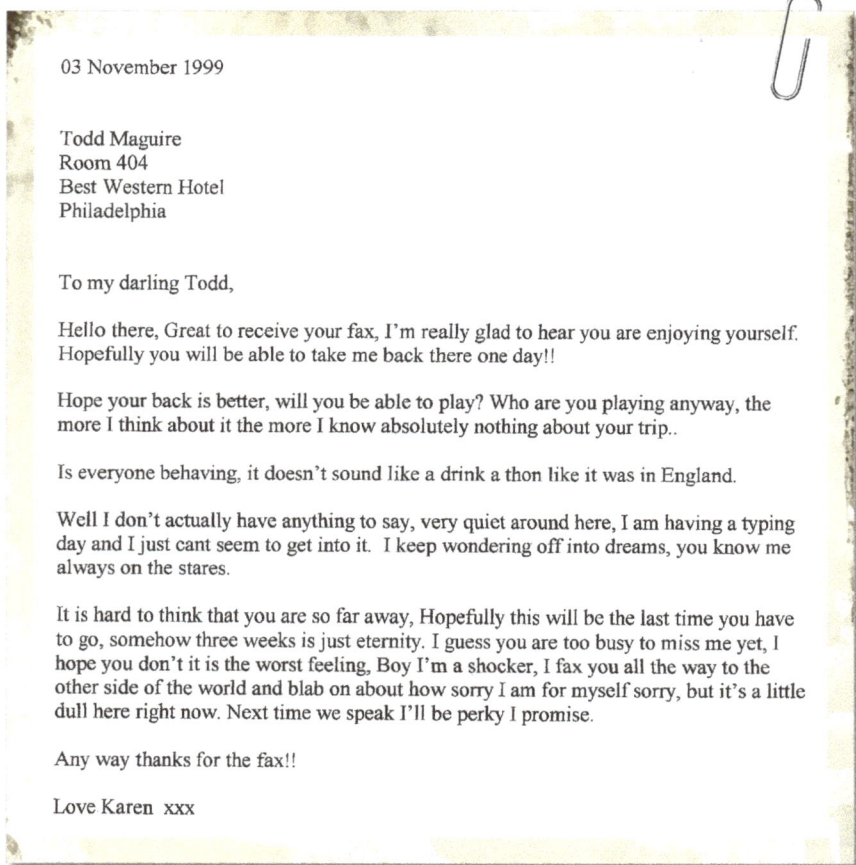

03 November 1999

Todd Maguire
Room 404
Best Western Hotel
Philadelphia

To my darling Todd,

Hello there, Great to receive your fax, I'm really glad to hear you are enjoying yourself. Hopefully you will be able to take me back there one day!!

Hope your back is better, will you be able to play? Who are you playing anyway, the more I think about it the more I know absolutely nothing about your trip..

Is everyone behaving, it doesn't sound like a drink a thon like it was in England.

Well I don't actually have anything to say, very quiet around here, I am having a typing day and I just cant seem to get into it. I keep wondering off into dreams, you know me always on the stares.

It is hard to think that you are so far away, Hopefully this will be the last time you have to go, somehow three weeks is just eternity. I guess you are too busy to miss me yet, I hope you don't it is the worst feeling, Boy I'm a shocker, I fax you all the way to the other side of the world and blab on about how sorry I am for myself sorry, but it's a little dull here right now. Next time we speak I'll be perky I promise.

Any way thanks for the fax!!

Love Karen xxx

When I landed back in Australia, jetlagged and running on fumes, I didn't care. I couldn't wait to see her. She met me at the airport, and I hugged her like I hadn't seen her in years. In a way, I hadn't. I left as one version of myself and came back another. I knew in my mind life wasn't just about the footy anymore. It was about stepping up. And even though I didn't have all the answers, I knew one thing for sure: I loved Karen.

I'd barely unpacked my bags from the US tour when Karen and I decided to take a break—just the two of us. We escaped to Marcus Beach near Noosa for a few days. It wasn't about adventure or sightseeing. It was about space. Space to reconnect, to breathe, to sit in the quiet and figure out where we were heading. In the weeks that followed, the silence began to shift into hard conversations. Conversations about the baby. About whether we were ready. I loved Karen deeply, but I was struggling. She had already walked through two marriages and was raising a beautiful little boy. And me? I was 25, barely figuring out who I was, let alone who I was supposed to become.

Thoughts continually raced through my mind. *What will my Catholic family think? Am I ready to be a father? Is this the life I want? Am I enough?* My mum, always calm in the storm, said only one thing whenever I reached out: 'Follow your heart, Todd.' Things were moving too fast for me. Looking back now, I realise I was young, naïve and unprepared for the weight of the situation.

In December 1999, we made the heart-wrenching decision to terminate the pregnancy. Even now, as I write those words, it feels surreal. It's a moment I still carry quietly and heavily. I remember the ache in Karen's eyes, the way her voice softened and how her laughter started to fade around the edges. She became more distant, like part of her had stepped into another room and left the door half shut. And I didn't know how to knock, let alone walk through. There were moments I would catch her staring into space, her mind seemingly miles away from the present. I felt helpless, unable to reach her.

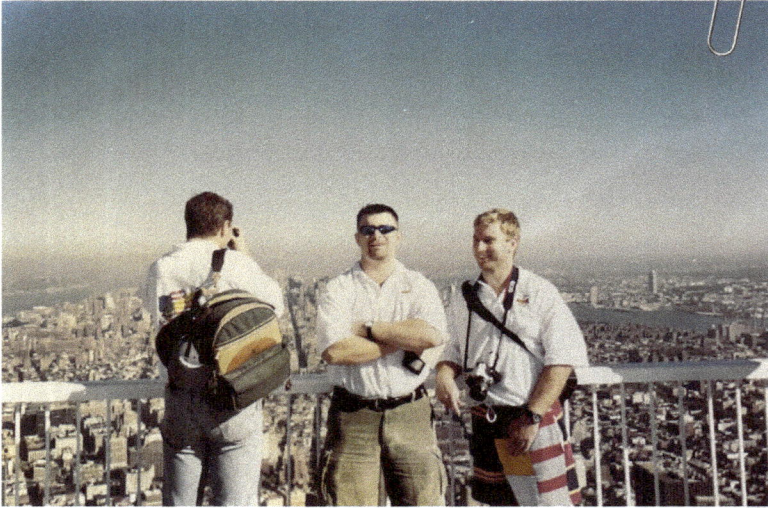

Todd: 1999 Top of the World Trade Centre [Twin Towers]

I started noticing the small things, troubling things. After every meal, she'd disappear into the bathroom. I didn't think much of it at first. But then it became a routine. The sound of the tap running. The lingering scent of toothpaste. The silence that followed. She was making herself sick. Quietly. Painfully. And I hadn't seen the signs until they screamed at me. That Christmas was wrapped in contradiction—joy on the surface, ache just beneath. We smiled for family photos, watched Clarke tear into presents and laughed when we could. But under it all, something fragile was splintering.

At this time, I was still working rotating shifts at Broadbeach Police Station, still relatively new to policing and doing my best to keep all the plates spinning—my job, my relationship, my own mental state. I was trying to hold it together while quietly wondering if

I was already falling apart. From the outside, it all looked fine. Good, even. But inside, I was in the thick of it, wading through guilt, confusion and this stubborn belief that if I just loved hard enough, we'd make it through. That love could be the glue. That things would snap back into place.

And maybe, for a while, they did. But in the quiet moments, the ones without noise or distraction, the truth was always there. Waiting.

# 13

# THE END OF
# EVERYTHING

New Year's Eve, 1999. The big fear was Y2K: The Millennial Bug, a looming computer glitch that had captured the world's paranoia. I was gearing up for a night shift walking the beat at the Gold Coast's Broadbeach Mall. It was the kind of shift no one wanted, but someone always had to wear it. This time, being less than three years in the job, that someone was me.

There was a strange electricity in the air, like the world was collectively holding its breath. Some were bracing for chaos; others anticipated something quieter, an ending, a beginning, or maybe both. Outside, the streets shimmered with anticipation. Glittering lights danced on the waves, but beneath the surface, a current of anxiety thrummed.

## DONNY

In theory, at the stroke of midnight, systems across the globe might fail. The bug, buried in old code, was expected to send digital clocks flipping back to the year 1900 instead of 2000. Banks, power grids, airports, and even nuclear facilities were said to be at risk. Anything run by a computer would be affected. People joked about it, but you could feel the underlying unease. Somewhere between doomsday preppers and nervous IT techs, the idea had taken hold: the world might crash tonight.

Karen had plans to celebrate the new year. She was heading out with her friends Josie and Janelle to Melbas, a buzzing Surfers Paradise hotspot frequented by everyone from cops and crims to dealers. Before the chaos kicked off we all shared dinner. During dinner, I checked my old Nokia 3110 phone. Despite being tucked away in my pocket, three number keys had been pressed, the ole pocket dial. When I looked at the screen, the number '666' stared back at me. I laughed it off. 'Holy fuck,' I said, half joking, 'maybe Y2K really is the end of the world.'

The girls were dolled up, ready for a big night. The boys, all coppers, ate quickly and peeled off to the pickle factory for the night shift. Then the girls disappeared into the glitter and pulse of Surfers Paradise.

As I pulled on my uniform, the weight of the badge felt heavier than usual. I stepped into the humid night, the scent of salt and excitement mingling in the air. Crowds thronged the mall, laughter and music spilling into the streets like a vibrant tide, yet a chill crept beneath my skin. It was as if the universe was holding its breath, waiting for the clock to strike twelve. A distant countdown echoed through the night, a rhythmic reminder that time was slipping away. I scanned the crowd, faces illuminated by the glow of neon signs, each one a story waiting to unfold. Some were lost in celebration, while others clutched their loved ones a little tighter, eyes darting toward the night sky as if expecting fireworks—or something worse.

Tonight, I wasn't just a cop; I was a sentinel on the brink of an unknown era, caught between the familiar and the unimaginable. And as the final seconds of the century ticked down, I couldn't shake the feeling that everything was about to change.

By midnight, the Gold Coast was heaving. New Year's Eve here wasn't just a celebration, it was a riot of noise, neon and wild abandon. I was flat out, run off my feet, dodging drunks and breaking up fights. Karen took half an ecstasy pill that night. Taking pills wasn't an uncommon occurrence on the Coast's nightlife scene, but it was new to her. She messaged and called me throughout the night, full of joy, telling me how good she felt and how much she couldn't wait to see me. Despite the chaos of my shift, I kept checking in, reassured by her happiness and buoyed by her affection.

I knocked off early, at around five-thirty in the morning, and went to pick up Karen and Josie. We dropped Josie at Janelle's place; she had to work a few hours later. It was typical Gold Coast life—party all night, back to reality by dawn and head to work. I drove us home to Mudgeeraba. She was glowing, still riding the wave from the night before. We stumbled into bed sometime around eight or nine, exhausted, happy, and just wanting to hold each other for a little while before sleep took over. I had another shift coming up that afternoon and desperately needed rest. Unbeknownst to me at the time, it wasn't just the start of a new century. It was the edge of something else entirely.

I dozed off, but not long after, Karen's ex-husband, Winnie, dropped Clarke off. I got up to say hello to Clarke, and Karen, who had been downstairs doing laundry, was crying. She told me she felt terrible for forgetting to pick Clarke up that morning. Through sobs, she called herself a bad mother. I sat down beside her, held her close and told her what I knew to be true. She was exhausted, and she was an incredible person—a devoted mother. She nodded slowly and I kissed her forehead. We went back upstairs, tucked Clarke in with a movie, locked the doors and climbed into bed.

I will never forget what came next. It is forever etched in my body and soul. It was exactly one thirty-five in the afternoon. I woke to Clarke's voice.

'Where are you, Mummy? Mummy, where are you?'

I rolled over, stretching my arm across the bed to feel her. Empty. Her side was cold. I wasn't alarmed at first. Clarke walked around to my side of the bed, and I reassured him we'd find her. Still groggy, I wandered the house with Clarke, checking the rooms, the kitchen and the bathrooms. Karen wasn't there. I figured she must have gone downstairs to finish the laundry. Carrying Clarke in my arms, I stepped outside and down the stairs to the lower level, my exhaustion-addled mind trying in vain to steady my racing thoughts.

'Let's find Mummy, mate,' I said, forcing cheer into my voice. 'I bet she's sorting another pile of clothes. Your mum never stops working, does she?'

Clarke just looked at me with his big, curious eyes. Eyes that belonged to Karen, too. I pushed open the sliding door. And my world shattered. There, in the centre of the room, was Karen. My beautiful Karen. Hanging. Lifeless.

Her beautiful, attractive face was ghastly blue, her eyes and tongue grotesquely protruding. Her body swayed ever so gently in the still air. A white electrical cord was wrapped brutally around her pale neck. Her knees were just off the floor, feet tucked back behind her. She was wearing a blue dress that I loved, the one that made her eyes sparkle like the sea. The shock hit me like a freight train. I collapsed against the doorway, unable to breathe, to move, to speak. My mind reeled, slashed open by grief like a blade to the chest.

This couldn't be real. It just couldn't. But it was. As I looked at her body I knew then a part of my heart died with hers. Something shattered inside me at that moment. It was my soul, breaking into a million pieces.

I don't remember what happened next, but I must've thrown Clarke outside somehow, some way, shielding him as best I could. Hoping that image was not burnt into his young mind. I still don't know how much he saw or how much his memory protected him. But I'll never forget the way he clung to me that day, silent and shaking.

I went to Karen and put my arms around her waist, holding her limp body, I screamed her name over and over like an animal. 'What have you done, Karen, why?' There was no response. Her face was vacant, her head slumped unnaturally. I tried to lift her to take the terrible burden from her neck. Her body felt heavier than anything I'd ever held. Her neck was all wrong, twisted at an impossible angle. I knew deep down that her neck was broken beyond repair.

I held her for what seemed like an eternity, weeping violently as I tried desperately to untie the electrical cord that had stolen her from me. But it wouldn't budge. Finally, with a scream of fury and grief, I ran upstairs, grabbed the first knife I could find, and raced back. I slashed through the cord and it gave way at last, releasing her ruined body into my arms like a ragdoll.

My Karen was gone. And I was utterly, irrevocably alone.

I laid her on the ground, I began CPR, desperately breathing into her mouth, forcing life into her lungs. Pleading with her to breathe. Her chest and stomach rose with each breath I gave, but it wasn't her breathing. It was me. She was cold when I touched her, and deep down, I knew she was gone. However, I refused to believe it. I kept going, I couldn't stop. I don't remember how long I tried. I don't know where Clarke was. I was completely gone, drowning in a tidal wave of panic, loss and disbelief.

I lay there with Karen in my arms as I cried uncontrollably, not wanting to leave her. But I knew Clarke needed me. And I knew I was not going to let him see his mum in this way. I did not want his last memory of her to be this. He didn't deserve this, nor did she. Eventually, I reached for my phone. My hands were trembling so badly I couldn't dial. I finally managed to call 000, which went straight to the communications room at the Broadbeach police station. Telling my friends, my colleagues, brought a fresh wave of agony. I remember standing outside with Clarke in my arms, hearing the sirens in the distance, but it felt like they were miles away.

I called my parents. I can still hear Mum's devastated voice on the other end of the phone. I had to repeat myself, again and again, because she just could not fathom what I was telling her. They raced down from Brisbane, arriving within an hour. When the police arrived, the same people I was meant to work with that day, I walked them back downstairs. I knew how this process worked. I wanted Karen to be treated with dignity. I didn't want her to be treated like just another body. The house filled. Sirens. Police officers. Paramedics. Friends. It felt like a TV drama except I was in it, and I couldn't switch it off. Then the Detective Inspector arrived.

'And what did you need the knife for?' he barked at me.

'I'm sorry, what?' I replied in utter disbelief. He repeated it. Again.

A uniformed police officer put the knife into an exhibit bag. My head spun. *What the fuck is happening?* Even in the depths of trauma, I knew what that question meant. They were treating me like a suspect. *How bloody dare they accuse me of that!* To this day, I still carry a deep resentment that the question was even asked of me.

Josie and Janelle, who had been with Karen the night before, came over. We stood in disbelief, grieving together. Through my tears, I said, 'Remember when I joked about 666 being the end of the world? Well, it is. It's the end of my world now.'

That number, once just a joke, now felt ominous. Biblical. 666, the number of the beast. The symbol of chaos. Did it have a meaning here? Did evil visit us that day?

Everything after that moment turned into a haze. It was like I was there, but not really. Like I'd stepped out of my own body and was watching it all happen from somewhere far away. People were talking, sirens were blaring, but it was all muffled, like I had cotton wool jammed in my ears. I couldn't think, couldn't breathe. I just moved through the motions like a ghost.

The next thing I remember is sitting in the back of Mum and Dad's car, head against the window, tears rolling down my face as we drove back to Brisbane. The world was spinning, people walking dogs, cars on the road, cafés open like it was just another day. But for me, time had stopped. Everything had changed. Everything hurt. I had a deep, sickening ache in my gut. It felt as though someone had violently ripped my body in half and stuffed my chest full of bricks.

My world, my future, was gone, and all that was left was this heavy, crushing silence. *Why, Karen? Why the hell did you do it?*

I've turned it over in my head more times than I can count. Maybe it was something from her past, some dark shit she never told me about. One of her mates made a cryptic comment at the funeral, like there was more to the story, but clammed up when I asked. Maybe it was the baby. Maybe it all got too real, too fast. Maybe it was the half an ecstasy tablet she took the night before, something she barely ever touched, and it messed with her head more than we realised. Or maybe it was the guilt. Forgetting to pick Clarke up that morning broke her. She was shattered about it, saying she was a bad mum. Maybe that was the final straw.

Maybe... maybe it was all of it. Maybe none of it.

I've tortured myself with it ever since. Trying to figure out what it was that made it all too much for her Looking back, searching for signs, for something I missed. But the worst part is that I'll never bloody know. And not knowing—that's what eats me alive.

# 14

# THE BLACK DOG

**K**aren didn't leave a note. Not a word. No hint that she was planning to leave this world. One day, she was there, laughing and dancing. The next, she was gone. It wasn't until I started packing up the house that I found a stash of Zoloft tablets hidden away. Anti-depressants. She never told me. Not once. And that hit me like a punch to the gut. I was a copper for Christ's sake, trained to spot signs in strangers. But I couldn't even see it in the woman I loved. That guilt has never left me.

For years, I kept asking myself the same question on repeat—was this her way out? Not just from life, but from me? Did she no longer want to be with me? Was her choice the most final, brutal breakup? One that I never saw coming and would never have the chance to respond to. Either way, I will never know. And that's what wrecks me. The not knowing. The silence that never answers back.

The one thing I'll never forgive myself for is going back to sleep that day. I keep thinking if I'd stayed up with her, if I'd held her a little longer, maybe she'd still be here. Maybe she just needed one more moment. One more reason to pause. I've dealt with a lot of suicide attempts as a police officer. Do you know how many people actually try it again after surviving? In my experience, it's bugger all. Most of them never do. They get a second chance, and they take it. Maybe Karen would've too. Maybe she just needed someone to stop her, just that once.

What I could never wrap my head around is how she left Clarke. She adored him. He was her world. So how could she do that to him? With both of us in the house? She had to know one of us would find her. Could've been me. Could've been him.

Years passed. I carried the silence like a stone in my chest, unspoken, unmoving. Then one day, when Clarke was about ten, he asked me about that fateful day. He didn't remember much. But what he did remember chilled me to the bone. He said he recalled standing outside the downstairs room, pressed against the wall, pinned there by a big black dog. It wouldn't let him move.

I froze. We never owned a dog. I never saw one roaming the street, not then, not ever.

That question has never left me. I've turned it over in my mind more times than I can count. I still don't know what he saw. I don't know what it meant. But sometimes, I wonder. *Did Karen's black dog, the one she couldn't outrun, come for her that day?*

Winston Churchill used the phrase *'the black dog'* to describe his depression, and over time, it's become a symbol for that relentless, invisible weight. Did Karen battle with hers for longer than I ever knew? Maybe that day, it finally caught her. And when it left her body… did it enter mine? Did I inherit her pain? Did I take on her burden so she didn't have to carry it anymore?

I don't have the answer. Maybe I never will. But I've carried that black dog ever since, and some days, I swear I can hear it growling at my heels.

# 15

# THE FRONT ROW

I had never played in the front row before this day. There is nothing more gut-wrenching than sitting in the front seat of a funeral, especially when you are only twenty-six years of age. That front row—that's when you know it's personal. You're not just there to pay respects, you're there because you've lost part of your heart. I never want to sit in the front row EVER again. It was the loneliest day of my life.

I could not talk that day. I wish I had now. But back then, my throat was closed, my mind was numb. I remember just staring out the window behind the coffin, locking my gaze on a single bird perched in the trees, far away. I don't remember what was said in the service. It all blurred. I do remember the music. I'd asked them to play *You're Forgiven, Not Forgotten* by The Corrs as we carried Karen out. Beautiful and brutal all at once.

Fellow coppers (my work family) from Broadbeach station and the rest of the Gold Coast District turned up in force. They'd arranged a guard of honour—hundreds of uniforms lining the chapel path. It was incredible. It was heartbreaking. And then, after it all faded, I turned to the only thing that dulled the pain: alcohol. It got me through the next few days, hour by hour.

In the case of death, many families struggle to understand, to find any sense in what has happened. They try to explain the unexplainable. Especially parents burying their child. Karen's folks came over from Christchurch. They were shattered. Her dad, gentle and softly spoken, was the kind of bloke who looked like he'd never hurt a fly. It tore me apart to see him like that. But grief has sharp edges and sometimes, it needs somewhere to land. For them, that place was with me. How didn't I see it? How didn't I stop it? I was a cop, for God's sake.

I wore the blame like armour. If it took it off Karen's shoulders, I'd carry it. I really wanted to be close to her family. But I can only assume it was too painful for them. I don't hold it against them. Sometimes, you've got to aim your anger somewhere. I just happened to be standing there when they needed to let it out.

Going back to the house to clean and collect my belongings was next-level hard. Not only was it the first time back in the house since Karen left me, but it was going to be the last time. The final time I'd ever set foot in the place we called home. I walked through it slowly, room by room, every corner heavy with memories.

Then I found the box. It was tucked away, containing papers and cassette tapes. Karen had mentioned she'd been seeing a psychic, and we'd had casual chats about it. But as I read through the handwritten notes and listened to the tapes, I realised something I wasn't ready for. It was dark. Really dark. It wasn't the soft, comforting kind of guidance you hope someone's seeking when they're hurting. It felt twisted—like this psychic wasn't guiding her towards the light but dragging her deeper into the dark. Feeding her fear. Validating her worst thoughts. And I never knew how far it had gone until it was too bloody late.

I walked out of that house for the last time with bugger all to my name—just a head full of questions and a silence I reckon I'll carry for the rest of my life.

That was the day I learned that grief doesn't always come in swinging, smashing things up. Sometimes, it just hangs back. Lurks in the corners. Waits for you when things go quiet. It doesn't need to shout to break you.

# 16

# GONE COLD

After Karen's death, everything I knew just fell away. Time warped. Days bled into nights. I was there, but not really. I had no money, no home and no will to live. The grief was so thick it clung to my skin like sweat. I couldn't breathe in it. Couldn't move through it. So, I did the only thing that felt easy—I drank. And I drank a lot. Around the clock, like it was medicine. Alcohol became my only friend.

In the days after the funeral, the support rolled in. People called, hugged me, told me they were there. But soon enough, they all had to get back to their own lives. I couldn't blame them, but it left me feeling even more alone. I still had Karen's phone, and when it rang, I answered. Some people hadn't heard the news. Others had but didn't believe it. And I had to keep saying it, over and over again, like some sick punchline to the worst joke ever told. I told strangers. Mates. Acquaintances. Anyone who rang. Each time, it drained a bit more out of me.

Eventually, I ended up living in my younger sister Sally's garage at The Gap in Brisbane. I had nothing but a bed, a TV and a pile of clothes. I remember sitting on the edge of the bed one night when it collapsed, the legs giving way. I just sat there on the floor, staring at the mess, crying for hours and wondering how the bloody hell my life had got to that point. I had it all once. A life on the Gold Coast. A partner I adored. A future. Then nothing.

I couldn't see a path forward. Not then. Not for a long time. I know I hurt my parents a lot during that period. The pain I put them through haunts me, especially now, being a dad myself, I can imagine what they went through. But back then, I couldn't see anyone else's pain. Just my own. My grief swallowed everything. I was at my lowest, and rock bottom was three floors up.

As my friends and family reached out, desperately trying to pull me back from my own self-destruction, I pushed them away. All of them. Anger coursed through my veins, a raw, seething fury directed at the world for having the audacity to keep turning while I felt frozen still. I would spiral into two or three days of drinking binges, drowning my sorrow in Bundy rum, completely blind to everything around me. The pain was unbearable, a constant ache that gnawed at my insides. All I wanted was Karen. I just wanted to see her again. Hear her voice. Feel her beside me. She was the light of my life, the laughter in my soul, and without her, everything felt hollow. I knew I lacked the courage to end my own life, yet the desire to continue living had evaporated. *If I die, so be it.*

Thoughts of drinking myself to death floated through my mind like a dark cloud, whispering sweet promises of oblivion. I engaged in reckless shit, seeking that thrill that might lead to a permanent exit from my pain. Alcohol stopped working, so I turned to sleeping pills, temazepam, from the doctor, just to get some rest. Even that wasn't enough.

During this chaotic time, something significant shifted within me. I began to challenge every belief I had ever held. The world I once understood had crumbled and nothing made sense anymore. All that was left was a hollow feeling, a dark pit in my chest that ached with hatred. Not just for my own pain but for the world, for people and for anyone who dared to cross my path.

*Why did this happen? Why the fuck did it happen to me?* I was less than three years into my career. I'd worked hard, built something. And then, it was gone. It felt like someone had yanked the ground out from under my feet and left me in free fall. I replayed everything in my head. Every conversation, every glance and every moment I might've missed. Things I said. Things I didn't say. I obsessed over them as if picking apart the past could somehow bring Karen back.

As the days turned into weeks, I began to internalise my suffering, convincing myself that, somehow, I had deserved it all. *Maybe this is my punishment. Karma for being a dickhead once. Or twice. Or a hundred times. Maybe this is what I get for the times I didn't show up, for being selfish, for every wrong I'd ever done.* The painful reality of Karen's death added another layer of torment. It was no longer just about grappling with loss but also about facing the belief that I was now destined to endure a life filled with pain and heartache. I felt trapped in a cycle of self-punishment, as if I were being forced to atone for my past mistakes.

The weight of this conviction was suffocating. I was caught in a storm of guilt and grief, where every thought reinforced my belief that I was unworthy of happiness or peace. It felt as though I was walking through a dark tunnel with no light at the end, resigned to the notion that I had brought this suffering upon myself.

My heart had gone cold, encased in a layer of ice that felt impenetrable. I began to walk through life like a ghost, hating the places I used to love, feeling the echoes of laughter and joy turn to whispers of grief. Each day was a battle, and I was losing ground, retreating further into the shadows. The weight of my sorrow was truly suffocating, a heavy blanket that wrapped around me, keeping me from reaching out for help. I was trapped in my own mind, a prisoner of my own emotions, longing for a release that seemed forever out of reach.

I say my life is broken into two parts, before 2000 and after 2000, because each timeframe represents two significantly different people. The person I was before was an innocent, naïve boy full of optimism and joy in life. The person after was an angry man, consumed by hate who could not see any good in the world.

# 17

# GRIEF, GUILT AND THE GHOST OF TODD

The harshest truth I have learnt: The world will not treat you better just because you're a good person.

When the clock ticked over to the year 2000, the world didn't stop. Everyone was alive and everything continued just as it was. Well, everyone except Karen, or so it seemed. The light had well and truly gone out of my life.

'You were only with her for a couple of years. There are plenty more fish in the sea, mate.'

'Lucky it happened now. Imagine if it was years down the track.'

'She is in a better place now.'

'Let me know if you need anything.'

That was the kind of advice I was getting. Well-meaning? Yes. Useless? Also, yes.

My friends and family were worried, urging me to make a change. They wanted me to move on, to get out, and to start again. Yet I felt lost, trapped in a cycle of destruction I couldn't escape. It felt like being on a rollercoaster that had no stop button. I stood at a crossroads, faced with a daunting choice. I could continue down the destructive path that had consumed me or muster the courage to seek a new direction. The thought of change was terrifying, but staying the same felt even more suffocating in the face of grief.

Grief doesn't play fair. People treat it like it's a bad mood, like a case of man flu you can shake off with a sleep and a schooner. 'Come on, mate, let's get you out for a beer.' As if a cold one could patch the hole in my chest.

It doesn't work.

Here's what I've learned. Acknowledgement is key. It's way more helpful to sit there and share the pain than to toss out those well-meaning but utterly clueless platitudes. You know the ones. 'Time heals all wounds' or 'You'll be stronger for it'. Seriously, grief doesn't come with a deadline. There's no due date for its end. And don't even get me started on people saying, 'I know how you feel, I just lost my great uncle to cancer.' Great Uncle? Really, that's a bit of a stretch, mate!

I get it. Most people mean well—they're coming from a good place. But here's what I wish they had said:

'I can't imagine your heartbreak.'

'This is really fucked. It's not fair.'

'I'll be here, even when you're not okay.'

'My favourite memory of Karen is…'

This is the kind of support that matters—the kind that acknowledges the struggle without sugar coating it. Because grief doesn't follow a tidy arc. It is said that there are seven stages of grief, but those stages aren't on some sort of time-dependent checklist. They can come and go and come back again. Grief is a shapeshifter, quiet one day, crushing the next. It's a rogue wave, a punch in the throat, a whisper from someone who isn't there anymore. It sneaks up when you least expect it, crashing over you in the middle of the grocery store or when you hear a song or see a dress in the back of a wardrobe.

There are a few things I've learned about grief, and let me tell you, it's no fleeting feeling. It's a companion that sticks around for life, ebbing and flowing. Some days, it's a gentle rain, a reminder of loss that you can almost bear. At other times, it's a storm raging, relentless and impossible to navigate. It is a flood of pain that reminds you of the unbearable wait you will endure until you once again see your lost love.

And healing? It doesn't have a clock. So, please, stop with the 'you will heal with time' comments. And, while I'm on it, for the love of all that's good, let's ditch the phrase, 'everything happens for a reason'. Sometimes, shit just happens. It's senseless. Instead, let's just say, 'This must feel so terribly senseless right now.' Because guess what? It does, and acknowledging the chaos can be a comfort.

When words fail, when you are left grasping for something to say, remember this: you don't need to try to find the perfect phrase. Remember that love speaks in silences, too. A simple touch. A shared look. Sitting beside someone in their mess without saying a damn thing.

Let's be the kind of friends who sit with each other in the messiness, who offer understanding instead of empty reassurances. In those moments amidst the pain, we can find a deeper connection, reminding each other that we are not alone in this wild, unpredictable ride called life.

During that foggy stretch of weeks and months that I experienced, an ex-girlfriend, someone who knew me well, stepped up. She showed up for me when most people didn't know how. We were friends, nothing more. But grief does strange things. After a few drinks and too much sadness between us, we crossed a line. We slept together.

The moment it happened, I was hit with a wave of sickening anger and disappointment in myself. Not because of her, she was kind and supportive, but because I felt like I'd betrayed Karen. It was like defacing a memorial with my own hands. We talked about it the next day and agreed it was a mistake, promising it wouldn't happen again. That should have been the end of it. But life had other ideas.

A month or so later, she told me she was pregnant. It hit like a gut punch. Six months after Karen's death, I was facing the possibility of becoming a dad under circumstances that felt impossible to explain, let alone accept. The confusion, the guilt, the disorientation, it all came rushing back. This body of mine?

It was a walking contradiction. Capable of creating life but still drowning in loss. And then, without discussion, she made her decision. She terminated the pregnancy. I understood why. I did. I knew she was dealing with her own version of hell. But it tore something else open inside me. Another grief layered onto the one already eating me alive.

This chapter of my life wasn't just heavy—it was fucking absurd. Like I was the butt of some cosmic joke that wouldn't stop playing. What was I meant to learn from all this? Karma became a concept I couldn't shake. Had I done something so wrong in this life or the one before? Is that why I was being handed loss after loss? The Catholic guilt from childhood collided with the raw chaos of adulthood and I started to believe I was being punished. For being reckless. For not being good enough. For not saving her.

It is said that the depth of the wound is the depth of the healing. It's a poetic way of saying that the more profound the pain, the greater the potential for healing and growth. I understood that concept, I really did. But knowing it didn't make my situation easier to swallow. It didn't stop the ache. And yeah, I'd heard stories of others who'd suffered more. People who'd lost kids, partners, entire families. I had empathy for them, truly. But pain doesn't work like a leaderboard. There's no prize for the deepest scar.

Every time I heard someone else's story, I'd remind myself that pain is relative. It didn't minimise my suffering—it just highlighted the fact that we're all trudging through our own muck, trying to find a way to wash it off. I was buried under my own rubble, trying to find a way out. Some days, I thought I could climb. On other days, I just lay still, listening to the sound of my breath to prove I was still alive.

Grief, not just the event but the aftermath, had broken me. The guilt. The decisions. The silence. Grief does something to your brain. You don't just have a broken heart. The search for sanity was not a straight line. It was a maze. And at that point, I was still very, very lost. I was truly a broken man.

# 18

# RECKLESS RESURRECTION

After taking three months off work on sick leave to grieve, but in reality, trying to drink myself to death, I officially transferred from Broadbeach station to Indooroopilly in Brisbane. My new work partner must've had the patience of a saint because I barely spoke a word. I sat in the passenger seat like a ghost, staring blankly out the window, completely unaware of my surroundings. The crooks probably had a field day. I wouldn't have noticed a robbery happening right in front of me. I was physically back at work, but mentally, I was miles away. I didn't care about paperwork, procedures or even people. I was just showing up because that's what you do when you don't know what else to do—when your brain's too fried to quit but too damaged to function. I knew it had to be done, and I just had to keep turning up.

The uniform felt heavier now, almost like a shroud. I wore it as a badge of duty, but inside, I was unravelling. Grief wrapped around me like a vice, squeezing the air from my lungs. I didn't want to talk about it, didn't want to share the weight of my pain. I just wanted to keep moving, to keep pretending that I was still part of the world outside my own head.

But as the days turned into weeks, I began to realise that showing up wasn't enough. I was a phantom in my own life, haunting the corridors of a job that used to ignite passion in me. I felt the walls closing in, the darkness whispering that I needed to confront it all—my loss, my demons, and the ghosts that lingered just beyond my grasp.

After a couple of months, I transitioned into detective work with the Criminal Investigations Branch in Indooroopilly. That's where I was partnered with an ex-undercover agent who hadn't quite let go of the rush. Every shift felt like a scene from a movie—dangerous, unpredictable, and thrilling. He had a knack for drawing me out, pulling me back into the realm of the living, bit by bit.

He was a punish, but was also a whirlwind of energy, always leaning into the next adrenaline-fueled adventure. He shared wild stories from his undercover days, each one more outrageous than the last. I suspected he only relayed the glamorous bits—like the time he infiltrated a drug ring disguised as a dealer—but it was enough to spark something within me. The thrill of his tales ignited a flicker of interest I thought had long been extinguished.

'C'mon, mate,' he'd say, his eyes gleaming with mischief. 'You've got to see this.' He'd drag me along to investigations that felt more like covert operations than routine police work. We'd stake out seedy bars, follow leads into the shadows, and navigate the underbelly of the city. The adrenaline coursed through me, and for moments at a time, I forgot the weight of my grief.

We did stuff I won't write about here, but let's just say it was anything but standard issue. Every moment was laced with danger, every decision a tightrope walk between right and wrong. I found myself laughing again, sharing jokes in the car during long drives, and feeling the warmth of camaraderie begin to thaw the ice around my heart.

Yet, as exhilarating as it was, I was still acutely aware of the darkness lurking just below the surface. The thrill of the chase was intoxicating, but the ghosts of my past weren't easily dismissed. They lingered, just out of sight, waiting for a moment of weakness to creep back in.

After work, I would often find myself indulging in a few too many beers, seeking solace in the amber liquid as the weight of the day washed away. Once the sun dipped below the horizon and the bar buzz faded, it was time for the grand finale of my reckless daily routine. I would slip behind the wheel of my trusty Landcruiser ute and head for home. Gap Creek Road awaited me.

Now, Gap Creek Road wasn't a road; it was a goat track pretending to be one. Narrow, winding dirt road, and thick with trees that crowded close like waiting arms, it was perfect for a bloke who didn't care if he got swallowed whole. In the pitch of darkness, I'd kill the headlights. Then my foot would hit the pedal, and I would count down from ten as I sped wildly. 10…9….8….7….6….5….4….3….2….1 then

I'd turn the lights back on. The world disappeared in the darkness counting down. No road. No sky. Just the feel of the tires chewing gravel, the cold flex of the steering wheel under my palms, the sound of my own breathing—ragged and shallow.

Some nights, ten seconds wasn't enough. I'd stretch it to fifteen. Twenty if I was drunk enough to think I deserved it. The trick wasn't surviving; the trick was steering blind and daring yourself to hope you didn't crash.

In that blackness, I wasn't thinking about Karen. I wasn't thinking about guilt, grief or the wreckage I'd made of my life. I was thinking about nothing. Just a heartbeat. A countdown. A breath between disappearing and surviving. Sometimes, I wondered if Karen would find me there. If I closed my eyes long enough, would I hear her voice? Would I crash into her memory at full speed and finally stop spinning? I never did. The headlights would flicker back on. The trees would snap back into view, cruel and close. And somehow, just somehow, I'd still be there.

I don't know how I managed to survive it. In those reckless moments, I felt invincible, a king of my own chaotic domain, unaware of the consequences lurking just around the corner.

Rugby league was the last thing on my mind and, looking back, it's clear I wasn't exactly firing on all cylinders. Then GG reappeared, fresh from the Gold Coast and back in Brisbane. He twisted my arm to join him at Norths Rugby in Wavell Heights. I showed up hungover, a bit heavier than I should have been and definitely not in any shape to be running around. My knowledge of rugby union was limited. I'd barely touched a rugby ball since I made some rep side back in high school. But I rocked up anyway.

# RECKLESS RESURRECTION

The air was thick with excitement as I stepped onto the field, where former Wallaby Julian Gardner was shaping the A-grade forwards, and the legendary ex-Kangaroo and Queensland start Tony Currie was shipping the back into shape. GG was on fire, playing A-grade rugby down on the Gold Coast and now in Brisbane. He kicked off in reserve grade, while I found myself at inside centre for third grade.

What followed was the most unexpected rise of my sporting career. Third grade to reserves, then straight into premier grade in a matter of weeks. I played my first top-grade game under the lights at our home base on Shaw Road, lining up against GPS. The adrenaline was pumping. My opposition was number twelve, a Queensland Reds player who was about fifteen kilos lighter than me. *Righto*, I thought, *I'll smash this bloke on a crash ball.* But what no one tells you when you switch codes is that in rugby union, a crash ball from the scrum doesn't just mean one bloke coming at you, it means half the bloody pack peeling off at full tilt. I got folded like a camping chair. The same skinny number twelve danced through the line shortly after, stepped me about twenty-three times, gave me a cheeky pat on the head and jogged off laughing. That was my welcome to union. I stuck around for a few more games, but the spark faded. I was sick of asking the fly half what each penalty was for, only to get a 'No idea, mate'.

The late nights and pub sessions called louder than any footy whistle, and just like that, I was out. Boots off. Back to chasing that high through drinks, danger and the only consistency I had left was chaos. In hindsight, those months weren't about sport or work.

The nights all started to blur—one bar to the next, one beer into another, like a cassette on endless rewind. One night, I strolled into

# DONNY

Dooley's Pub in the Valley, the familiar scent of stale beer and fried food filling the air. It was the kind of place that promised a cold beer and a good game of pool, and I was ready for both. As I scanned the room, my gaze landed on a table in the corner, where a group of blokes looked like they had just stepped off stage as the backup band for Mötley Crüe. They were the roughest characters I'd seen in ages, sporting leather jackets, tattoos, long hair, earrings and an aura of reckless abandon. They weren't just drinking—they were holding court. And something about them pulled me in.

As I stood at the bar, the bloke next to me leaned in and barked an order: 'Two double rum and cokes and a schooner of rusty nail.' That voice. I knew it. Clear as day. I turned, squinting through the dim light, and there he was. Benno. I hadn't seen him in a couple of years, and a wave of confusion washed over me. Is he not a cop anymore? What had I missed?

He grinned, a flash of white teeth through the scruff.

'Hello, brother! What's going down?' He looked different, heavier, sharper. Like life had sanded him down to the bone and he'd learned to like it. 'Come over and meet the boys,' he motioned me over casually. 'Did I tell ya that I'm undercover now?'

Undercover?

It hit me like a cattle prod to the ribs. He wasn't just playing dress-up, he was living it. I joined the table, still in a daze. The rest of the crew, all undercover cops, looked like they'd seen and survived every brand of madness. Over the next few hours, they poured out stories like cheap beer. Stories of adrenaline-pumping chases, close calls and camaraderie that burned bright in the chaos of their lives.

Each tale was like a shot of whiskey warming me from the inside out, awakening something deep in me.

As the night wore on, it hit me—a pivotal decision that felt like a lightning strike. I wanted in. I'd become an undercover police officer. Sure, I understood the risks; it was a treacherous path, one with potential pitfalls that would lead to a one-way ticket to nowhere. But the allure of escaping my own dull existence was intoxicating. I didn't want to be the broken shell sitting in the passenger seat anymore or the bloke playing chicken with trees on Gap Creek Road. I needed something that gave me a reason to feel alive again, even if it meant dancing with danger. And this, well, this felt like a lifeline wrapped in leather and adrenaline.

Later that week, I was visiting one of my oldest mates, Kenny, a detective with a bullshit radar so sharp he could call out a lie from across a paddock. We were under his house, in what he called his bar. Really, it was just a fridge full of XXXX Gold and some bar mats from the '80s. I cracked a beer and hit him with it.

'Thinking I might go undercover.'

Kenny almost spat his mouthful across the floor. He laughed so hard he had to grip the bench to stay upright. 'Ah yeah, mate, great idea,' he wheezed.

'What's so funny?' I shot back.

'Mate, after everything you've been through, there is no way the QPS will let you do that,' he said, slapping his knee like a drum.

'You reckon?'

'Bloody oath, mate! And to be honest, that's the last thing you need,' he replied, still laughing. 'Jesus, Todd. You're serious.'

'Dead serious,' I said, and, for the first time in months, that seriousness felt like a relief.

But if I was completely serious with myself, I was the perfect candidate for undercover.

That night, I realised something about myself. I wasn't chasing danger because I wanted to be a hero. I wasn't even doing it for justice. I was chasing danger because I didn't know how to feel safe anymore. And the only time I felt anything close to alive was when I was one wrong move away from the end.

I was going to be a Covert Police Operative (C.P.O.).

# PART 2

'When the world forgets you, sometimes
the only way back is through the fire.'

– Donny Wilson

This is where the real damage began.

Grief tore me apart. The man that I was—Todd— was gone. There was no putting the pieces back together. Going forward, it was only about building something harder, something stronger, someone who could survive.

You think hitting rock bottom means you stop falling.

You don't.

You just get better at pretending you're standing still.

And so, I stepped into the skin of Donny Wilson, a ghost stitched into Queensland's criminal underworld. It was a life where survival meant lying better, running faster, trusting no one—not even myself.

Every deal, every drink, every stitched-up smile peeled away another piece of who I used to be. This wasn't about justice anymore. It was about staying alive long enough to see if there was anything left worth saving.

Goodbye, Todd. Hello, Donny.

# 19

# BECOMING DONNY

**D**espite the negative nancies, I couldn't wait to get back to work and throw my hat into the ring. The application process for covert operations felt a bit like trying to sneak into a nightclub with a fake ID—sweaty palms, questionable answers, and a whole lot of hope. Each question felt like a hurdle, testing my resolve and my sanity. But I pushed through, driven by a longing for something more, something that could pull me from the depths of my own making.

First up was a psychometric test that left me wondering how the hell I passed. It felt like one of those 'Which shape doesn't belong?' challenges from preschool. Take this question, for example: *'Do you prefer a beautifully crafted handgun or a well-written poem?'* I ticked the poem box because if I was going to be sneaky, I figured I might as well do it with flair.

As luck would have it, the next course was scheduled for November 2000. The undercover courses only ran once every two years, and the timing felt almost surreal, like the universe had cracked open just wide enough to let me slip through. I was officially in, booked for the four-week course that would turn my world upside down. The anticipation was intoxicating. I could almost taste the freedom that came with stepping into a new identity, a new purpose. It was a chance to reinvent myself, to embrace the chaos and thrill of a life lived on the edge. I could feel the weight of my past beginning to lift, the shadows receding just enough to allow a sliver of light through.

In those weeks leading up to the course, I threw myself into preparations. I studied everything I could about undercover work, reading articles, watching documentaries, and even reaching out to others who had walked this path before me. I felt alive again, fuelled by the promise of what lay ahead.

But beneath the excitement, a lingering doubt gnawed at the edges of my mind. Could I really pull this off? Would I be able to step into the role and leave my old self behind? The fear of failure lurked in the back of my thoughts, but it was overshadowed by the thrill of the unknown. I was ready to dive headfirst into a world that promised danger, excitement, and the chance to reclaim my life.

The course itself was based at the Oxley Academy in Brisbane. We sat in classrooms and ate in the mess, surrounded by uniformed recruits who knew exactly why we were there. It wasn't exactly discreet. We started rocking up with scruffy beards, tattoo's, piercings, earrings and clothes that screamed midlife crisis. I remember thinking that we should have been undergoing training away from the other cops. But that was part of the test. To see who could blend in and who could handle the whispers, the sideways glances, the judgement.

The training covered all the usual aspects of law, policy and field tests, and was designed to sort the wheat from the chaff. A couple of fake buys in role plays, and that was it. I found the real tests, though, came at night. The instructors didn't just watch you learn. They watched you drink, too. Late-night sessions turned into surveillance exercises of a different kind. Who could hold their piss and stay sharp? Who'd crumble into their chicken salt chips by midnight? Luckily, I'd been training for that part all year. Years of pub sessions meant I wasn't just keeping up, I was usually the last one standing. Not proud, just… prepared. I passed with flying colours and officially joined the unit in January 2001. And just like that, Todd was gone.

I didn't have a clue how the undercover world worked at first, but slowly, I began to figure it out. For the next two years, I'd vanish from the real world, take on a new identity and embed myself inside criminal syndicates. I'd earn their trust, buy their drugs and then betray them. There would be the odd window to step back into normal life between jobs, but nothing was ever guaranteed. The entire situation suited me just fine. Anything to avoid being Todd.

One of the first things I did was hand in my firearm. I locked it in a police-issue safe in some office in police headquarters. Out of sight, out of reach and out of mind. I wouldn't see it again for two years. It wasn't just policy—it was symbolic. A shedding. The uniform, the badge, the authority, all gone. Ditching the gun meant stepping into a world where rules didn't matter, where power came from presence, not protocol. From instinct, not procedure. I was walking off the map towards a version of myself I hadn't yet met.

I was ready to disappear into another life for the next two years. A new name. A new face. A new story. I would no longer be Todd. And so, I became Donny Wilson, a ghost stitched into the criminal underground, slipping through the cracks, earning trust to only betray it. The transformation was physical, too. Long hair. Thick, messy goatee. Tats and piercings. I fully embraced Donny's persona. Donny was rough, reckless and morally untethered. He didn't care about right or wrong. He lived in the shadows, feeding off adrenaline and lies.

It's no secret that the personality traits of an undercover cop can closely mirror those of a psychopath. Here's the thing: psychopaths tend to tick a very specific set of boxes. Firstly, there's a lack of empathy. They struggle to understand or care about how others feel. Then, there's the charm. They can turn it on like a light switch—charismatic, engaging, magnetic—but it's often as sincere as a politician's promise. Manipulation? Absolutely. Lying and deceit come as naturally to them as breathing, all in the name of serving their own selfish goals. Impulsivity is another hallmark. Psychopaths act without a shred of thought for consequences, blowing off responsibility like a kid ditching chores for a shiny new toy. And let's not forget the narcissism—that inflated sense of self-importance big enough to fill a hot air balloon.

After Karen's death, I felt myself morphing into some kind of Aussie psychopath. My heart, well, it had taken a permanent holiday. Empathy was a distant memory and my care factor was as low as the bar at a dry wedding. I was diving headfirst into this treacherous new world, one in which I felt like a shark in murky waters, ready to bite anything that crossed my path. And yet, every now and then, I'd catch my reflection in the mirror. I could still see the old Todd in there, trying to claw his way back out. He just didn't know how. Strangely enough, I was ready to become someone else. To ditch the world that I knew. To forget my past and all the damage it carried.

I now realise why I was drawn to that world so fiercely. It wasn't just the thrill or the danger, it was the chance to disappear. To become someone else. To bury the grief and guilt deep beneath a new identity, allowing myself to feel nothing at all. When you've lived through the kind of trauma that rewires your brain, sometimes pretending to be someone else feels safer than facing the wreckage of who you really are.

Donny didn't carry pain. He didn't love, or grieve, or feel like he was broken beyond repair. He just existed—unapologetic, untouchable, untethered. And for a while, that was easier than being Todd.

CRIME OPERATIONS BRANCH.          Todd.          08/01/2001

Record Number          138

| | |
|---|---|
| NAME: | WILSON, Donald John |
| ADDRESS: | 65 haig street kedron 4031 |

| DATE OF BIRTH: | 29/12/73 | AGE: | 25 | PLACE OF BIRTH: | Bendigo VIC |
|---|---|---|---|---|---|

| GENDER: | Male | HEIGHT: | 180 cm | EYES: | Brown |
|---|---|---|---|---|---|
| HAIR: | Brown | COMPLEXION: | Fair | BUILD: | Medium |

DRIVERS LICENCE DETAILS:

| LICENCE No: | 34773434 | TYPE: | O | CLASS: | A C |
|---|---|---|---|---|---|

| DATE OF ISSUE: | 24/11/98 | EXPIRES: | 29/12/2003 |
|---|---|---|---|

PLACE ISSUED: ft.valley

| | |
|---|---|
| LICENCE ADDRESS: | 65 haig street kedron 4031 |
| CURRENT ADDRESS: | as above |

| SECURITY NUMBER: | 4009848 | MANUAL NUMBER: | E2575089 |
|---|---|---|---|

MOTOR VEHICLE DETAILS:

| Reg No. | Year | Make | Model | Colour Major | Colour Minor | EngineNo | VIN | DueDate |
|---|---|---|---|---|---|---|---|---|
| | | | | | | | | |

FIREARMS LICENCE No.

BOAT LICENCE No:

LICENCE TYPE:

LICENCE ADDRESS:

FURTHER DETAILS:

L/Permit obtained at Bundaberg on Friday 04-01-91. Class A. Expired on 03-01-92. Address shown as 15 Thabeban Street, Bundaberg 4670.

"P" Licence at Bundaberg on Monday 05-08-91. Expired 04-08-94. Class A. Same address.

L/Permit Class C at Charleville on Thursday 09-04-92. Expired on 08-04-93. Obtained Class C at Charleville on Monday 05-10-92. Address shown as Cobb & Co Caravan Park, Ridgeway Street, Charleville. 4470.

Open licence at TOTEWA (Tewantin) on Monday 01-08-94. Effect from 05-08-94. Expires on 29-12-98. Class A & C. Current address.

License issued ft.valley 24/11/98 effective 30/12/98 expires 29/12/2003. address shown as 64 Haig street kedron 4031. PCDL.

# 20

# AN UNEXPECTED MEETING

I didn't go looking for her. In fact, if you'd asked me then, I would've told you I wasn't looking for anything or anyone. I was about to vanish into the role of Donny Wilson, bury what was left of Todd and become a ghost with a job to do. There wasn't room for connection. No space for love. Hell, most days, there wasn't even room for me.

But then I met this beautiful woman named Peta, who was, funnily enough, a flatmate of my previous workmate. We met just before the undercover operative course started. It was one of those almost accidental introductions that didn't feel like much in the moment. No fireworks. No slow-motion scene from a rom-com. Just a beautiful woman with a kind smile and sharp eyes who saw straight through the fog I was living in. I don't even remember what she said at first. Probably something pretty standard and casual. But I remember how she looked at me, not with pity, not with concern, but like she was trying to understand the weight I was carrying without asking me to hand it over.

I'd built up a fortress of silence. People would knock, and I'd just ignore it. But she didn't knock. She just sat nearby. Unbothered by the space, unafraid of the distance. And something about that made me lean in. I wasn't ready for anything. I knew that. My grief hadn't softened, it had just gone quiet, like an old dog that still bites if you step too close. I was still waking up with Karen's name half-formed in my throat, still hearing songs that made my lungs tighten, still catching glimpses of her in strangers and shadows. Sometimes I would wake up in the morning, not remembering how I got to bed, thinking that her death was nothing but a bad dream. Yet once I fully woke, the realisation would hit me again. Hard.

So, when Peta showed up, I didn't think, *Here's someone I could love.* I thought, *Here's someone who sees me, even when I don't want to be seen.*

We had dinner dates. Good conversation. Laughed more than I expected. There were even moments, brief ones, where it felt like I could breathe again. But the truth was, I didn't know what I was feeling. I was still numb most days, still dragging a weight around that I couldn't name out loud. Peta knew about Karen through a mutual friend, so in my mind, I figured she knew what she was in for. That this version of me wasn't whole. That she was stepping into something already broken. And maybe that's why I let it happen.

We had nights that should have felt good. Nights that looked perfect from the outside—quiet, calm, ordinary. I remember one particular night, sitting on her couch. Television on. Movie selected. Dinner done. The kind of night you're supposed to enjoy—no pressure, no complications. Just two people who liked being around each other. She had her feet tucked under her, a glass of red in hand, telling me about some argument she'd had with a colleague at work. She was animated, laughing halfway through her own story. And I was smiling, nodding, even throwing in the right lines to keep it rolling.

But inside, I felt nothing. It wasn't that I didn't care. It's that I couldn't feel it. The warmth. The connection. The comfort. It was like my brain had switched to grayscale while the rest of the room stayed in colour. She leaned into me, her head on my shoulder. It felt familiar, soft and safe. And that's when the guilt kicked in. Because in that exact moment, when the world had finally gone quiet and someone decent was choosing to be near me, I felt absolutely fucking nothing. Not peace. Not love. Not even discomfort. Just static.

I wanted to reach for her, and I wanted to mean it. But I was split down the middle, half of me watching the scene from above, the other half buried in something I couldn't name. All I could think was how she deserved more than what I was giving her. But I didn't say it. I just sat there, letting her rest against me while I tried to remember what it used to feel like to be alive in moments like this.

She looked up at one point and asked if I was okay.

I nodded. Said I was tired. Gave her the smallest smile I could manage. And she didn't push. She just nodded back and said, 'Yeah. Me too.' I think part of her knew. And maybe that's what hurt the most, that she saw the hollowness in me and stayed anyway.

We watched the rest of the movie like that, me frozen in my own skin. Her, holding space for someone who wasn't all there. And when I drove home that night, I didn't feel better. I felt worse. Because the noise in my head should have stopped. But it didn't.

Somewhere along the way, I told her what was coming. That once the undercover course wrapped up, I'd be assigned jobs anywhere across the state. That I'd disappear for long stretches, sometimes with no warning. No schedule. No certainty. No contact. To me, that was just how the job worked. She just nodded, like she already knew the kind of life I was about to step into. Maybe she understood there were no promises here. Maybe she knew there would be no fairytale ending. I had a mission, a mask to wear, a life I was walking into with my real name already fading in the rearview mirror.

I think it's fair to say she didn't fall for Donny. She met Todd just before he disappeared. And maybe that's what kept her close. Maybe she caught a glimpse of the real me before the mask fully locked on. I didn't know it then, but Peta would become one of the few constants in my life as I spiralled deeper into the shadows. A flicker of light in the periphery. A tether to the person I used to be. And in a job where forgetting yourself is half the challenge, she reminded me I was still in there somewhere, even if I couldn't feel it.

But no matter how much light Peta brought in, the dark was still winning. I could feel it like gravity, like an undertow. Grief still owned me. And even with her in the picture, I wasn't climbing out of the wreckage. I was just learning how to function inside it.

# 21

# THE CHAMELEON WITH A CAUSE

It had been twelve months since Karen's death, and in that time, I'd felt myself morph into someone unrecognisable, a strange blend of outlaw and shadow, like I was stuck somewhere between Ned Kelly and a roadie from Bon Jovi.

Oddly enough, that's what made undercover work so appealing. It wasn't just about catching crooks or chasing adrenaline. It was about disappearing. Becoming someone else. Forgetting the grief that haunted me in every quiet moment. As I plunged into the criminal underworld, I discovered a strange duality. One part of me leaned into the darkness—cold, calculating and detached. The other part was still clinging to something real, some echo of who I used to be. That internal conflict was my real battleground. I wasn't just infiltrating syndicates; I was trying to reclaim pieces of myself scattered across the wreckage of my life.

Some mornings, I woke up fired up with purpose. This wasn't just about the next buy or the next bust. It was personal. I was chasing something more than arrests. I was hunting down the very thing I believed took Karen away from me—drugs. Her death left a hole nothing could fill, but it lit a fire that refused to go out. The haunting image of Karen's death was like a bloody storm hanging over my head. It was burnt into my brain.

I couldn't shake the belief that drugs played a role in her death. Whether it was that ecstasy pill or something deeper, darker—it didn't matter. I blamed them. And in some twisted way, that blame gave me a mission.

I wanted to take down the dealers, the traffickers, the soulless parasites preying on the broken. I wanted to stop others from ending up like Karen. Before all this, the strongest thing I'd touched was a left-handed cigarette. But now, drugs were my world: fake names, fake deals, fake friendships. I was walking a tightrope between justice and destruction. It was dangerous. It was lonely. But it was the only thing that made sense.

Because if I couldn't bring Karen back, I'd burn through the shadows trying to make sure no one else had to experience what I did.

Becoming Donny meant diving headfirst into the deep end of a whole new trade. I had to learn the ins and outs of the drug world— terminology, weights, prices, you name it. It was like a crash course in dodgy maths without the benefit of a calculator. Everyone in this game had it all memorised, like some twisted version of a pub quiz.

Kilos, pounds, ounces, halves, quarters, eightballs, grams, each had its own price tag, and you could bet your last stubby that everyone could whip up the math faster than you could say, 'Where's my wallet?' It was a whole new language, and the character of Donny was determined to become fluent in it. He pictured himself standing in a dodgy back alley, confidently spouting off prices like some sort of drug dealing Shakespeare. I could not fuck this up. The job depended on it. My life depended on it.

Donny had visions of being the next Johnny Utah in *Point Break*, but in reality, he was probably more like Jonah Hill in *21 Jump Street*. In all seriousness, he knew this wasn't just a game. These were real lives, broken people tangled in addiction, and if getting his hands dirty meant making a difference, so be it. But being Donny wasn't just about learning the lingo or pulling off a dodgy moustache. It was about disappearing, slipping into shadows, playing the long game. Small talk became a weapon. Bullshit became an armour. Smiles, nods, casual questions, fishing for a thread to pull.

Donny had lines ready for every situation. 'Nail salesman,' he'd say when asked what he did. 'Roofing nails, spiral shank, cyclone proof—take your pick.' It was dull enough to be believable. The more boring the cover, the less likely people are to ask questions. Donny also made people laugh. That was the trick. When people laughed, they let their guard down. They saw a mate, not a threat. And Donny made sure to leave a mark, just enough to be remembered, never enough to be traced.

But beneath the banter was something more serious. Being Donny wasn't just about telling lies. It was about studying people, watching what they said versus what they did. Learning to read micro expressions. How eyes shifted when a lie was told, how shoulders dropped in a relaxed moment. Body language became Donny's gospel. And trust me, that had to be earned, layer by layer.

Donny also had to retrain his instincts. If someone called out his name across a pub, he had to react without hesitation. If someone slipped and used his real name, he couldn't so much as blink. That kind of discipline wasn't just a habit; it was survival. He quickly learned that truly dangerous people were not the loudmouths or the ones throwing punches. No, the truly dangerous ones were quiet. The ones who smiled a second too long. The firm handshakes. The dead eyes. It was a psychological minefield, one wrong word, one sideways glance and it would all be undone.

There was Donny the undercover operative, the nail salesman, the mate at the bar who always knew where to score. He could switch accents, swap backstories and melt into any room. Donny didn't flinch, didn't feel and didn't hesitate. He wore a smirk like body armour and spun bullshit like it was gospel. He was a chameleon with a cause, threading his way through the underworld, gathering trust from criminals who'd kill first and ask questions later.

What no one tells you about undercover work is that it's not just dangerous, it's lonely. It chips away at who you are until you start forgetting which parts were real to begin with. You come home from a job to an empty, lonely room, take off your boots and stare at the man in the mirror, wondering if he's still you. There were times I'd catch glimpses of the old me. A call from Peta. Her voice, steady and warm, felt like the only thing tethering me to who I used to be. She'd ask, 'Are you okay?' Not pushing, just gentle. And I'd lie. Because I didn't know how to tell her that I no longer knew who I was.

Undercover work is said to be like being an actor on set. The only difference is that you don't get a second chance. You don't get a director saying, 'Cut, let's do this again.' If you need to do it again, the consequences are dire.

Donny was always there, waiting in the wings—coiled, restless, ready to take over the moment Todd let his guard slip. And what was most disturbing was how easy it became to let him. The truth was, Donny gave Todd something he couldn't seem to find on his own anymore: control, power, a sense of purpose. Todd, on the other hand, was the one who had to carry the grief. The guilt. The crushing memory of not seeing the signs, of falling asleep, of failing to stop Karen from doing what she did.

The longer he wore Donny's face, the more blurred the edges became. He stopped responding to the name Todd. It sounded foreign, like it belonged to someone else. Every lie came easier. Every truth felt heavier. This stretch of the story isn't just about the actual police work. It's about the emotional whiplash. The fractures that form when you live too long behind someone else's eyes.

Living undercover felt as though Todd was slowly erasing himself— one lie, one beer, one job at a time. And, truthfully, that didn't seem like such a bad thing.

The transformation of Todd from QPS graduation
1997 to undercover police officer in 2002

# 22

# WELCOME TO CABOOLTURE

Donny's first proper undercover job dumped him straight into the cracked teeth of Caboolture, a twitchy, speed-soaked town fifty clicks north of Brisbane where crime was currency and violence came standard. It was early 2001, just four weeks after he'd graduated the covert operative course, and already he was neck deep, and set to spend nine months in the town's drug-ravaged underworld as part of Operation Icepick.

Caboolture wasn't just rough, it was feral. High unemployment, heavy drug use and a meth scene spinning out of control. Everyone was wired, paranoid and volatile. The kind of place where neighbours knew who cooked speed, but nobody said a word. Even the local cops kept their distance.

The target was Eddie 'Mad-Madden' Madden, Queensland's best speed cook and supplier of methamphetamines—speed, goey, wizz, whatever you wanted to call it. Donny's task was to break into that world. To live it, breathe it and gather evidence to get the cook off the streets.

This wasn't textbook undercover work. It was madness wrapped in blood, noise and cow-print car seats. Because, yeah, Donny's ride—a banana-yellow Holden Commodore Vacationer—had black and white cow-patterned car seat covers. And somehow, in Caboolture, that made him fit right in. But fitting in here meant something darker: learning to laugh with psychos, party with dealers and keep your pulse steady while people bled beside you.

Speed, a powerful stimulant that keeps users wired and alert, usually comes as an off-white or coloured powder. It is often stashed in fridges or freezers to preserve its potency. The cooking process is dangerous, ephedrine mixed with hypo phosphorous acid, iodine and methylated spirits. Volatile chemistry for a volatile scene. Most users would inject the speed with a syringe and needle.

What we now know as 'ice' is just a purer crystalline form of methamphetamine, far more potent, addictive and destructive.

Amphetamines and methamphetamines trace their origins back to 1919 when they were first developed by Japanese chemists. During the Second World War, both substances were widely used to combat fatigue and increase alertness among soldiers. However, it wasn't until the 1980s that methamphetamine production began to surge in Australia—thanks in part to a Gympie man who revolutionised illicit drug manufacturing with the invention of the 'box lab,' a portable meth lab compact enough to fit in the boot of a car.

By the time Donny entered the scene, Mad-Madden was already a ghost story among cops. Queensland's most elusive and feared supplier. He operated out of a fortified rural compound tucked away in the bush behind the town. Cameras, lookout points, fences. You couldn't sneeze near the place without someone knowing. Mad-Madden wasn't just a job. He was *Donny's* job.

The Queensland Police Service Organised Crime Squad and State Drug Squad had tried before to catch him many times but had failed. Mad-Madden was careful, kept his hands clean and surrounded himself with loyal enforcers. His name carried weight and fear. One of his enforcers was named Chuck, a six-foot five cage fighter with a short fuse and a steady supply of free product. Chuck was his insurance policy. Chuck was that tough, they reckon he ate left-handed hammers and shit barbed wire.

From internal briefings, Donny heard stories about Mad-Madden that most people wouldn't believe. Victims kidnapped over drug debts. Dragged into the national forest and mutilated, ears cut off as a message. No one ever reported a thing. Even local bikies wouldn't cross Mad-Madden's crew. He was flooding the region with high-purity speed—sixty-five per cent or more—which was considered as pure as it could be. At close to $3,500 grand an ounce, it was lethal and lucrative.

Donny had been in Caboolture for three months, working his way into the scene and steadily making connections. He started off buying stolen property like quad bikes, cars, motor bikes and general household goods. His main contact was a registered informant named 'Eggplant,' a twenty-year-old career pest who'd been on police radar since he was fourteen. He wore board shorts and thongs year-round, and he was never seen in a shirt. He was infamous through Caboolture and Morayfield. Not loved. But known. Where Eggplant went, Donny went. The Morayfield Tavern, the shopping centre and party houses. They needed to be seen. Be regulars. The Tavern was a magnet for sketchy types: users, dealers and people who could sniff out a cop from across the bar.

Donny found hanging with Eggplant brought 'extra' attention. First week in, Eggplant led them through the cemetery as a shortcut—a shortcut to who knows where. It felt like an initiation. Grim, surreal and crawling with the kind of energy that made your skin itch. Dusk settled over the headstones. Eggplant and Donny wandered the narrow paths, Donny's hands deep in his pockets, whistling some half-remembered pub tune. The last of the sunlight cast eerie shadows across the graves. It felt peaceful in a weird way. Quiet. Just them and the dead. That didn't last long.

Four shadows jumped from behind a tombstone. Junkies, strung out and skeletal. Shoulders like coat hangers, eyes hollow, twitchy movements. They'd clearly skipped every gym day imaginable— leg day, chest day and shoulders. The tallest one seemed to be the lead junkie. He was built like a shallot, with shoulders like a brown snake and legs as thin as tent poles, stepped in front of Eggplant and Donny, trying to appear menacing.

'Well,' Donny said, raising an eyebrow, 'this got morbid real quick. I thought I was the only one here with a dead sense of humour, Eggplant.'

The tall one didn't laugh.

'You're in the wrong part of town, mate. Hand over your wallet.'

Donny couldn't help but chuckle as he replied, 'I'd offer you a cold one, but I reckon the barman at the afterlife would ask for ID. Bit of a light crowd tonight, eh?'

The junkie didn't get the joke. Junkies never did—no imagination for banter.

'Look,' Donny said, feigning concern, 'I'm just here to pay respects to the dead. You start disturbing them and they might get cranky. Long naps do that to a soul.'

Then Donny spotted a shovel leaning against a nearby grave. He picked it up without thinking. It was lightweight and balanced with a bit of rust on the edge. Perfect. Donny gave it a little spin, like a conductor warming up before a violent symphony.

'You sure you boys want to dig your own graves? I'm feeling generous. Might even toss in some daisies.'

The lead junkie, Brown Snake, made a move, but Donny was faster. The shovel caught him clean, dropping him like a sack of potatoes. The other three scattered instantly, zigzagging through the cemetery like spooked rats. One of them shouted over his shoulder, 'You'll have to be quicker than that!'

Donny let them go. He only needed one message delivered.

He looked down at Brown Snake, who had blood oozing from his mouth, eyes wide with panic. Donny could smell the piss before he saw it. He dropped the shovel and offered a hand.

'Relax, brother. I'm just fuckin' with ya. But... yeah, you might've pissed your pants.'

Donny laughed again. 'You looked like you've hyperextended your vagina, mate. And when you sit down to pee tonight, try not to get splashback on your arse, yeah?'

In a split second, his smile was gone. Donny closed the distance in a slow, crooked sway, his sour breath—alcohol, cigarettes and pure menace—pouring over Brown Snake like a dare he was too smart to take. His next words came in a whisper.

'If I ever see you again, cunt, you better have your tombstone picked out. I swear on the dead around us, you'll be brown bread.'

And just for punctuation, Donny gave him a quick, sharp right yabby pump to the bridge of his nose. It cracked like dry timber. Blood spilled fast.

In the world Donny was now living in, this was how you dealt with problems. Not with paperwork. Not with warnings. But with fear and violence.

# 23

# BLACK AND WHITE CAR SEATS

After the cemetery incident, Eggplant doubled down on connecting Donny to every dealer and user in the postcode. He was doing his best to fast-track his credibility with the cops, and to his credit, he was doing a decent job of it. The only issue was that every person he introduced Donny to was a street dealer. Soon, word came down from Donny's controller that it was time to level up. His next target was a serious player. Another dealer, higher up the food chain.

'Donny,' his controller began, 'We want Eggplant to introduce you to The Doc.' Donny glanced over at Eggplant, who was busy rolling a smoke with a level of concentration usually reserved for bomb disposal.

'Oi Eggplant, they want you to introduce me to The Doc.'

Eggplant barely looked up. 'Yeah, that's no dramas… if we run into him somewhere.'

'Nah,' Donny replied. 'They want us to go around to his house.'

Well, The Doc was one of the local heavies in Caboolture and high up in a prominent bikie club. His name carried one warning: don't fuck with him. The QPS hierarchy thought he might also lead us to Mad-Madden.

Eggplant froze mid-roll, eyes wide. 'No fuckin' way. You don't just go to The Doc's place. He's got guns, mate. *Many* guns. He's like a brown snake and a condom. You just don't fuck with them.'

Donny relayed the information to his controller and listened through the phone as the controller passed the message on to the Detective Inspector who was with him in the office.

'The undercover reckons it's too dangerous to go around to his place?' the Controller said. 'Jesus! What'd he think undercover work was, a bloody tea party?' the Detective Inspector spat. Classic desk-jockey wisdom.

Donny? He didn't feel fear. But Eggplant? He was shitting himself. After some convincing (and a promise that if he died, I'd make sure he was buried in his board shorts), Donny talked him into it.

The Doc's place looked like a suburban fortress, with seven-foot fences, cameras guarding every angle and two black dogs in the yard that looked like they'd eat your soul for breakfast. As they stepped through the gate, the front door burst open. The Doc barrelled out, shotgun in hand, prepared for some sort of home invasion. Eggplant stepped up fast, hands raised. 'Oi Doc! It's me,

Eggplant! Just came by to say g'day!' The Doc hesitated. The tension hung in the air like static before a storm. Then, slowly, he lowered the shotgun and launched into a profanity-laced rant about the importance of calling ahead. He finished by telling them to piss off. Honestly, it was the best-case scenario.

Back in the car, Donny called his controller to report on the situation. In the background, the same Detective Inspector chimed in.

'See? Nothing happened. Told ya, young fella. But just remember, you're nothing more than an investigative tool on my belt. We don't care what happens to you. You are easily replaced.'

Huh, comforting.

As they were cruising back to town, a skinny blonde junkie teetering along the footpath caught Eggplant's eye. Leaning halfway out the window like a seagull dive-bombing a packet of chips, he shouted, 'Hey Shelley, ya cunt! How ya going?'

The blonde turned mid-wobble and gave a wave. She looked about forty and sported a hairstyle that could only be described as meth-meets-lawnmower. Eggplant turned to Donny, grinning like a kid on Christmas morning. 'Donny, stop the car! I'll introduce you to Shelley—she's one of the biggest dealers in town.' Donny swung the car into a busted old shopping centre car park and the two men headed over.

Donny reached out to shake Shelley's hand. Big mistake. She looked at it like he'd pulled out a live snake. The kind of look that said, *This bloke is either a cop or a Jehovah's Witness.* Donny made a mental note: no handshakes in Shelley's world.

'Hey, Donny's looking to get on,' Eggplant said, switching into business mode like someone haggling over a dodgy used car.

Shelley squinted, then grinned like she'd just remembered where she hid her last rock. 'Fuck yeah. How much ya want?'

Donny wiped his palms on his jeans. 'I got about five hundred bucks. What's that get me?'

'A bloody good time,' she cackled. 'You got the cash on ya? Me mate's just in those shops. I can grab it for ya now if you want.'

Donny nodded, pretending this was all normal. Just another day in paradise. Given his background, Donny knew how to make this deal happen—what to say, what not to do, and especially, not to let the money run. But in that moment, he was feeling adventurous. Or maybe just plain stupid.

'Shit yeah,' he blurted out, handing over five crisp one-hundred-dollar notes.

Shelley's eyes lit up like a pokie machine hitting the jackpot. 'Sweet! I'll be back in five. Wait here!' And, off she went. Donny and Eggplant stood there, watching her vanish into the shop's fluorescent gloom. A few minutes passed. Then a few more.

'She's been longer than five minutes,' Donny muttered, side-eyeing Eggplant, who was watching the street like he had front-row seats at a movie.

'Nah, she'll be right,' he replied, shrugging.

After another five minutes, the unease in Donny's gut turned into a sharp jab in his ribs. 'Fuck this,' he said, storming into the shop.

Inside was a teenage shopkeeper, maybe 15, glued to his phone and completely indifferent to the outside world.

'Hey, you seen a blonde woman come through here?' Donny asked, trying to sound casual. 'She's my sister.'

The kid didn't even blink. Just pointed to the back door and mumbled, 'Yeah, she went through there.'

Donny stepped out into an empty back car park. No sign of Shelley. Not even a tyre mark.

'Fuck me,' he muttered, realising the sting had hit. 'I've been ripped.'

It was like being pickpocketed by a magician—clean, fast and somehow his fault. He stood there for a moment, a hundred thoughts racing through his head, none of them helpful. The golden rule was echoing in his brain like a bad song: *never let the money run.* And louder still, a new voice joined the chorus, *You fucked up young fella.*

Donny was fuming, but he wasn't ready to call it in to his controller just yet. That would be admitting defeat, and if there was one thing he couldn't stand, it was the thought of someone having a good laugh at his expense. Too stubborn to admit defeat, he turned to Eggplant.

'Where's this mole live?'

Eggplant, as calm as ever, shrugged. 'Just down the road, not far.'

'Take me there,' Donny snapped, gripping the door handle like he was about to tear it off.

They cruised through a few backstreets with men's names until Eggplant pointed to a rundown weatherboard government house that looked like it had been weathering storms since the Federation.

Donny jumped out and stormed up the steps like a man on a mission—half debt collector, half fed-up older brother. The front door was wide open. Inside was a lounge room bursting at the seams with about fifteen teenagers—twelve to fourteen, smoking cones, injecting gear, drinking cheap spirits and carrying on like it was Schoolies meets *Trainspotting*. And it was only 11am. Music blared and Donny could see burnt and bended spoons everywhere. Laughter echoed. Chaos reigned. Then, a girl, maybe thirteen at best, came strutting around the corner from the kitchen like she paid the mortgage. She locked eyes with Donny and raised an eyebrow.

'You lookin' for Mum?' she asked, like she'd been through this routine a hundred times.

'Nah, I'm looking for Shelley,' Donny replied, trying to stay composed as the cop inside him screamed for backup.

'She *is* me mum, ya dumb cunt,' she fired back, unimpressed.

'Oh... right. Yeah. I am,' Donny said, swallowing a fistful of pride and pretending like he wasn't having an existential crisis.

'She's not here. You chasing? What do you need? Eight ball? I can do ya an eight ball for a grand.'

Donny blinked, then gave a double blink. He couldn't believe it. A kid who should've been worried about maths homework was casually slinging meth in her mum's living room. Every fibre in his being wanted to stop the whole show, arrest someone, call child protection, *do something*. But he couldn't. Not here. Not now. This wasn't a rescue mission. This was undercover work. And he was still just a rookie trying to learn the game without becoming its next casualty.

'Nah, I'm good. Thanks anyway,' he muttered, backing out the door like he was retreating from a wild animal's den. Walking back to the car, he felt a sick, heavy pit in his stomach. *What the fuck is this place?*

Back in the car, still fuming from the Shelley fiasco, Donny couldn't help but feel like Caboolture was chewing him up, spitting him out and daring him to come back for more. But that was the job— getting stitched up, dusting off and diving right back into the deep end. And there was always another dealer to meet.

As Donny kept working the streets, he started piecing together just how deep Mad-Madden's roots ran. Turned out, the bloke hadn't just flooded the town with gear, he'd fathered a few kids there too. All with a handful of younger women who were, to put it kindly, rough around the edges. One night at the Morayfield Tavern, Donny crossed paths with one of them. Krystal was the mother of one of Mad-Madden's kids, and in her own way, she was a local legend. Late twenties, ginger hair, a face mapped by pockmarks and old acne scars, and a speed addiction that kept her buzzing like a faulty power line. She was flighty, unpredictable and wore chaos like a badge of honour. She'd ridden more geldings than Damien Oliver and couldn't hold a straight thought for more than a few seconds. The only way to handle her, Donny figured, was like a racehorse—blinkers on, keep her in a straight line, and crack the whip when needed.

But unpredictable or not, Krystal was a link to Mad-Madden and Donny needed to get close. Eggplant worked his magic again, this time lining up an intro to Krystal's boyfriend, a local speed dealer with a setup of his own. Before long, Donny was buying off him regularly. The bloke lived in a rundown house buried in the backstreets of Caboolture and Donny practically moved in. He nicknamed him Marshall because of his bleach-blond hair and penchant for the most putrid rap-style clothing known to man. Marshall was an easily dislikeable character, the typical bloke who would have been bullied at school but would have been a bully himself, targeting much younger kids.

Marshall's house was what you would expect. A couple of stained couches sagging under their own weight, a crusty mattress on the floor, a TV that only worked half the time and, pride of place in the living room, a massive DJ setup with speakers that could level a brick wall. The music hit before Donny even stepped inside. By the time he crossed the threshold, his chest was thumping from the bass, and his ears were already begging for mercy. The place had a distinct smell of neglect.

It was 2001, and Marshall had a one-track mind when it came to music. Donny found himself singing along without meaning to—every word from *The Marshall Mathers LP* etched into his brain like muscle memory. At first, Donny thought Marshall might be the one to lead him to Mad-Madden. He was close enough. It felt like he was right on the edge of something big.

Then one day when Donny turned up to buy, Marshall was fresh out of gear. Donny saw an opportunity and casually mentioned that he was keen to try Mad-Madden's gear. Marshall turned the volume down, looked over at Donny and Krystal with a half grin and said, 'Let's go for a drive.'

Donny thought he'd cracked it. This is what he'd be working towards and much quicker than he expected.

As Donny fired up the canary yellow Commodore, Marshall jumped in the front and Krystal in the back seat.

'Where to?' Donny asked, slipping a tape into the stereo as the Commodore growled to life.

Marshall didn't answer. Eventually, he mumbled something about scoring at Deception Bay from his dealer, Davo. The twist? Davo was the brother of an outlaw bikie. Just the kind of connection Donny was looking for.

They cruised down the coastal road, the sun bouncing off the Commodore's fading paint, windows down, Metallica's *Creeping Death* blaring from the stereo. Donny reached for his shoebox of cassette tapes, each one a time capsule, each song a memory. The Commodore wasn't just transport—it was a soundtrack on wheels.

Before hitting the highway, Marshall insisted on stopping off at the bank to withdraw some cash. The plan was that both Donny and Marshall were going to purchase some speed from Davo. All three strolled inside and Marshall filled out a withdrawal form like he was solving a Rubik's Cube with his feet. Common sense did not come easily. Marshall walked to the teller and handed her the slip. After a while the teller said something to Marshall. Then came the arguing.

Marshall, simmering towards boiling point, turned on Krystal and roared, 'Did you take money out of my account?'

Krystal blinked, caught off guard. 'Yeah. We needed it for groceries…'

What followed was a right hook that dropped her cold. She hit the bank floor like a sack of potatoes. It happened so fast that Donny froze. Every cop instinct screamed to step in. But he wasn't Donny the cop. Not here. Not now.

Donny went to walk over to help Krystal but instead he leant over her and yelled, 'You fuckin' heard him, you rotten cunt!'

It was a line he hated saying, but it was the line that kept his cover intact. And out the two men walked from the bank as though nothing had happened.

Donny was rattled. The violence. The speed of it. The total indifference. Minutes later, Krystal stumbled back into the car, nose gushing blood, mumbling apologies like she was the one who'd done something wrong. Marshall exploded again. 'Fuck this! I don't have enough! You fuckin' cunt, Krystal! What the fuck are we gonna do? Let's just go home!'

The scene in the car was pure chaos. Donny swore he was in the car with Mickey and Malory from the movie *Natural Born Killers*. Krystal screeching from the back with blood coming down over her mouth and chin, and Marshall losing his mind in the front. Donny had reached his limit. He wasn't walking away empty-handed. Not after the day he'd had. Not with ten thousand dollars of Monopoly money or 'imprest' as it was called, tucked in his wallet.

'Fuck ya,' Donny growled. 'I'll spot ya, but it's on tick. No freebies here.'

Marshall grinned. 'Thanks, Donny. Let's just call it even, yeah? Seeing as I helped ya get on.'

'Like fuck,' Donny snapped. 'And it doubles every week too, cunt.'

A twisted kind of understanding passed between them. Business was business, even in the gutters of Caboolture.

They pulled into the Red Rooster car park at Deception Bay and kept an eye out for Davo's white sedan. When he rolled in, Marshall sprinted over. He disappeared into the vehicle before appearing again just moments later. He sprinted back to the Commodore with two bags of gear. Mission accomplished. Donny sped off down some streets before stopping the car. Both Krystal and Marshall were frothing at the mouth to use. Bended spoons, lighters, needles in veins, eyes glazing over, they were ready for liftoff. Squeeze, and in went the liquid from the syringe.

'This is good shit!' Marshall yelled, jabbing his Adam's apple with a finger. 'I love the feel of steel. It gets ya right here!'

Krystal started gagging and dry retching like she was going to vomit. Donny panicked. 'Get the fuck out! Don't you dare spew on me cow printed car seats, I'll fuckin' belt ya!'

Jumping out and dashing around to her side of the car, he yanked her out of the back just in time. She spewed like a fire hydrant onto the pavement. And of course, we were parked right across from a bloody primary school. Thirty wide-eyed kids watching like it was school excursion day at the zoo.

Donny shoved her back into the car just as Marshall, cooked to the eyeballs, jumped into the driver's seat. 'Let's go, cunts!' he roared. Donny sprinted around to the driver's side, trying to drag Marshall out, but Krystal had already vaulted from the back seat into the front.

Marshall fought like a madman, and Donny knew he was losing. He hurled himself into the back seat just as the Commodore screeched away, tyres screaming in protest. Marshall floored it, tearing through suburban streets one-twenty clicks an hour, clipping bins, mailboxes and anything dumb enough to be in his path.

'Ace of Spades' by Motörhead blasted from the speakers like a war anthem for maniacs. Krystal screamed, 'Slow down! Watch out!' Then again. 'Go faster, you mad cunt!' Donny, on the other hand, clutched the cow print seat as the Commodore tore through the streets, dodging a used needle and fumbling for the seatbelt like it was a lifeline. The car wasn't just chaos—it was a full-blown psychotic episode on wheels. Absolute frothing madness.

Then Marshall pulled out a hunting knife. Donny clocked it instantly. Where the hell had he been hiding that? 'Shut the fuck up, Krystal,' Marshall screamed, knife in hand, eyes darting like he was watching invisible bats fly past his head. Krystal, never one to back down, started mouthing off. They were hurling insults at each other, like some junkie version of a Shakespearean tragedy.

'Fuck watch out for that car...' Krystal screamed. Marshall swerved to miss a car head on coming the other way.

'Shut the fuck up Krystal', yelled Marshall.

'Don't yell at me you fucken cunt,' Krystal wailed.

'I said shut the fuck up.' Marshall spat back.

'Fuck you...' Krystal was having a full blown episode and the Donny was trying to work out how the fuck is he gonna stop this shit.

And then—he did it. With no warning, Marshall drove the knife straight into Krystal's right thigh with his left hand. She screamed. Blood poured down her leg. He slammed the brakes. 'What have I done? I'm sorry, babe! I'm so sorry!'

Silence.

Then the stereo kicked back in, Slayer's *Raining Blood*. Of course it did. Donny just sat there. Numb. Brain stalled. This wasn't training. This wasn't theory. This was real.

Donny snapped. 'What the fuck was that for?' But Marshall just stared, hollow and shaking. Donny ripped Marhsall from the driver's seat by the hair and threw him into the gutter. He then helped Krystal, dragging her out of the car and laid her on the curb. He then jumped in the Commodore, heart pounding and put the footdown. He rang his controller, voice steady despite the insanity, told him the whole story and asked to send ambos and some cops. It felt like a dream, a B-grade movie you'd turn off halfway through because it was too unrealistic. But it was real. It was recorded. It was Caboolture.

*You gotta start at the bottom*, Donny thought. *That's how you find the big fish.*

*And Marshall, you weak cunt, better get yourself a lawyer, son.*

*Because you're fucked.*

# 24

# DRESS SHIRTS
# AND HANGOVERS

There was a small window in the Caboolture job, which meant a break for Todd back home in Brisbane. A breather and a reset. At least, that's what it was supposed to be. These were the moments I'd have to muster up whatever scraps of Todd I could find. Switch masks. Wash off Donny. Show up. Pretend I still knew how to speak in complete sentences that didn't involve drug slang or dodgy pub lies. Sometimes I wasn't sure if I actually wanted the break, to go back to being Todd. Donny, for all his recklessness, made sense. He had purpose. He knew how to manage a room and how to manage people, even if it was all bullshit.

I found myself at Peta's work fundraising ball, playing the supportive boyfriend, trying not to look like I'd crawled out of the boot of a panel van. Peta was well aware of my 'special' line of work, but her colleagues? Not a clue. So, there I was, at her elbow, surrounded by wine, polite small talk and very confused-looking professionals. I felt like a stray dog at a purebred show. As she introduced me, I could practically hear the collective brain static ripple through the group. *'Wait... that's your partner?'*

'Hi all, this is Todd,' Peta said, somewhere between proud and praying. 'G'day, ladies, how ya going?' I offered. Truth be told, I was a few months into undercover work and well and truly looking the part. Hanging out on the edge of chronic public nuisance—yes, that would be a good way to describe it.

The looks I got were magic. Up and down scans that indicated their surprise and shock. You could almost see Peta's colleagues trying to solve the puzzle, like maybe I was a community service case or part of a work-study rehab program. Then one of them bit.

'So, Todd... what do you do for a living?'

And there it was. A golden opportunity. Showtime. I leaned in and grinned.

'Ah, sort of in between jobs at the moment. Was delivering furniture till I got done for drink driving. They weren't thrilled. Sacked me.'

I felt Peta's elbow in my ribs like a cattle prod.

'Then I got a gig digging graves but got sacked from that too. Apparently, they didn't appreciate me wearing a shirt that read, 'My day starts when yours finishes.' Bit too on the nose, I reckon.'

Silence. I smiled wider.

'So yeah, if you hear of anything going, let Peta know.'

They didn't laugh. But Peta did. She lost it, head down, shoulders shaking, a full-body laugh she couldn't hold back. And just like that, I knew I had my audience. The rest of the night turned into a one-man comedy hour, with me doubling down and Peta trying (and failing) to keep a straight face.

Undercover life came with chaos, danger and lies layered in even more lies. But every now and then, it also came with these strange little windows. These glimpses of something close to normal. Close to connection. Even if I wasn't sure who I was supposed to be in them. Despite the laughs and the charm I managed to pull out for Peta's work crowd, I wasn't in a good place. Not even close. The function was a brief performance. A break in character. But underneath, the engine was overheating. To close out the weekend, I went straight into a five-day bender.

It was my birthday week and only five weeks after the first anniversary of Karen's death. Not that anyone mentioned it. Not a word. Not her name. Nothing. And that silence? That did something to me. It wasn't just that they forgot, it's that they moved on. Or pretended to. Like it was all behind us. Like she belonged to another time. Another life. It made me feel like I was the only one still bleeding. Still waking up next to a ghost. Still carrying the wreckage while everyone else played 'normal'. And that hurt more than I let on.

So I drank. Hard and fast. I tried my damn hardest to drown the ache in noise and booze and bullshit. Tried to be the fun guy, the wild card, the walking train wreck everyone could laugh at because, at least, that version didn't care.

By the time my birthday rolled around, I was four days into my bender and neck deep in denial. I'd told myself this week back home was a breather. A chance to re-group. Step out of Donny's skin and remember who Todd was. Truthfully, all I really wanted was oblivion, and I was doing a bloody good job of finding it.

While I was busy numbing everything that still hurt, my family was trying to do the right thing. They'd booked a birthday dinner at a nice restaurant, hoping to lure me back to the land of the living. It was a gesture of love, no doubt. But also a bit naive. Because at the moment I should have been celebrating with them, I was eighteen schooners deep at a pub, belting out *Khe Sanh* like I was auditioning for *The Voice: Rehab Edition*.

I had been drinking since sunrise, caught up in the euphoria of my binge. I had joined some of my undercover mates at Hotel LA in the city, where we indulged in a game of pool, laughter echoing through the bar. As the sun dipped lower in the sky, my family began to call me… repeatedly. I was unreachable, lost in the haze of my oblivion. Eventually, my sister Sally decided that enough was enough. She hopped in the car and drove to Hotel LA, determined to drag me to the birthday celebration kicking off without me.

She found me in a heated debate with a bloke named Flea over the merits of pineapple on pizza, clearly the most pressing issue of the day. She pleaded. Calm at first. Then desperate. I waved her off, shaking my head like it was an inconvenience. I wasn't going anywhere. But just as she turned to leave, I changed my mind. Maybe I felt guilty. Maybe I wanted an audience. Or maybe I just wanted to cause a bit of damage.

As we drove off, I was told we needed to collect Sally's mother-in-law, Mrs D, who would also be joining the dinner. Coincidentally, it was her birthday too. Mrs D was a picture of polite perfection. Prim.

Proper. Porcelain smile. The kind of woman who used cloth napkins at home. Sally shot me a look that could curdle milk. *Behave,* her eyes said. 'Don't worry,' I smirked. 'She won't even notice I've been drinking. I'm practically an actor now.'

Mrs D climbed into the car with a warm smile. 'Happy birthday,' she chirped. I grinned. 'How the fuck are ya, Mrs D? Happy birthday.'

Sally's heart sank faster than a lead balloon. She caught my eye in the rear-view mirror, horror etched into every muscle of her face. Mrs D blinked. Tilted her head. That plastered-on politeness trembled. Sally jumped in like a lifeguard at Bondi.

'Oh, he's just being silly, Mrs D! He's in a festive mood,' my sister said, her voice brittle and overbright.

I leaned back in my seat with a smirk plastered across my face, enjoying the chaos I'd stirred. The silence that followed was thick enough to choke on.

When we arrived at the restaurant, the family was already gathered—Mum, Dad, Scott, his wife and Peta. It was warm and inviting. The kind of place where people say things like, 'Cheers to another year,' and mean it. But I didn't come for cake. The second I sat down, the air changed. I was loud and boisterous. Buzzing with the energy of a man who'd been drinking for days and didn't care who noticed. I turned the place into my personal stage. Wait staff copped it. Diners got roasted. I mocked haircuts, clothes, portion sizes. I was relentless and reckless. Every sentence was decorated with profanity like tinsel on a Christmas tree. People around us whispered and eyed our table like we were contagious. Dad told me to tone it down, and so did Scott, not once but many times. But the more they tried to keep me quiet, the louder I got, the drunker I acted and the more outrageous I became. Finally, Dad snapped. 'Alright, that's it. Every time you swear, it's a hundred bucks.'

Without missing a beat, I pulled out my wallet that contained the five grand of drug money I had been given for an upcoming job. I flung it onto the table. Notes scattered like confetti. 'Well,' I said, 'that should cover the fucking night.' And then, with a grin, I stood. Pushed the table aside—plates clattering, glasses tipping—and walked out like I'd just finished an encore. The family sat in stunned silence, caught between fury and heartbreak. It was a classic Todd moment, equal parts comedy and tragedy and a masterclass in how to make an exit.

But the truth was much darker. These moments weren't rare anymore. They were becoming the norm. Outbursts. Self-sabotage. Explosions wrapped in punchlines. And my family? They weren't just worried now. They were grieving too. Not for Karen. For me. Because they could see what I refused to admit. That I was on a death wish and they couldn't stop it. They were losing someone they loved. All while he was still sitting right in front of them.

But what gutted me, what I couldn't shake, was this: nobody focused on my mental health. It came down to my anger—that was the concern. Nobody really cares about your mental health...Not until it turns into anger. Not until it disrupts dinner. Until it caused embarrassment. Then suddenly, in their eyes, you're not hurting. You're just an arsehole. A bad person. A problem to fix or avoid. Sadly, people didn't see a man falling apart. They saw a man ruining a birthday dinner. And maybe that's the part that hurt the most.

That week back home had scraped something raw, my family pretending everything was fine, Peta trying to reach the version of me that barely existed anymore, and not one person saying Karen's name. Not once.

It had been a year, actually one year and five weeks to be exact. And still, I felt like I was the only one bleeding. I didn't see the bender as self-destruction. I saw it as survival. No apologies. No regrets. It kept me upright. But underneath all of that I was hurting real bad. Not that I'd ever admit it, not to them and not to myself.

By the time I hit the highway north of Brisbane, the grief had settled in deep, thick and immovable. It wasn't loud or chaotic. It was the kind that wraps around your lungs and makes the air feel heavy. I wasn't hungover. I wasn't crashing. I was just hollowed out. The bender had lasted the week, loud, messy and necessary. It did what it was supposed to do: drown the noise, blur the edges and keep the ghosts at bay. But now it was over. And it was time to go back. Back to Caboolture. Back to Donny.

# 25

# WALK ON
# HOME, BOY

**B**ack in Caboolture, the fallout had already begun. Marshall, barely holding his shit together at the best of times, finally snapped in full view. After stabbing Krystal in the leg in broad daylight, he was arrested and thrown in the lockup. One minute he was barking orders and frothing on speed, the next he was in lockup wondering how the hell it all spiralled.

With Marshall gone, it meant one less ticking time bomb on the board. But taking him out didn't bring us any closer to Mad-Madden. If anything, it just cleared the path for someone worse. That's when the covert ops team decided to play a little dirty. They pitched a new plan, something out of a bad soap opera: two undercover agents moving in together, playing mates, playing dealers, playing normal.

Enter me old mate Benno—the kind of bloke who could start a pub fight and talk his way out of it before the first punch landed. Benno was assigned to crack Chuck, Mad-Madden's right-hand lunatic. A volatile, gun-wielding psychopath with a cage fighter's stare and a reputation that left bruises. He was the next link in the chain and QPS's best shot at reaching the top. While Benno circled Chuck, Donny stayed on Krystal, pushing in from another angle. Different routes. Same destination. And just like that, Donny had a new flatmate. And the real game began.

Chuck was the kind of bloke who didn't just run deals—he terrorised them. One of his favourite moves was to hop into a punter's car, take the cash, pull a pistol, take the car and then boot them out and drive off like it was his birthday. Think Chuck 'The Iceman' Liddell mixed with Chuck Norris high on drugs. You couldn't script someone like Chuck. Every meeting with him was a roll of the dice, and most of them were loaded. Benno lined up a buy. Five ounces. Chuck agreed to meet at the Brisbane Hamilton Hotel car park, a classy place for a dodgy drug deal. As the day crept closer, Benno was twitchy. Pacing. Practising his one-liners with fake confidence like he was about to walk on stage at an amateur comedy night. Donny, ever the support act, slid Pantera's *Walk* into the stereo and turned it up till the windows shook.

*'You can't be something you're not… be yourself, by yourself… walk on home, boy…'*

Benno laughed nervously. 'This'll be sweet. But if he pulls that 'jumps in and robs me' shit, I'll be calling you for a lift.'

Donny grinned. 'Hope you wore sneakers, mate. She's a long jog home with no kneecaps. But in all seriousness, I'll do you a solid and wait inside the pub.'

Benno rolled into the Hammo car park to find Chuck leaning on a post like he was born to menace. Chuck stalked towards the car, slow and deliberate. Every step screamed bad news. They drove around to the back of the car park. Quiet. No foot traffic. Just tension. Benno kept his voice level.

'Let's keep this simple. You got the gear?'

Chuck smirked. 'Yeah, mate. Show me the cash.'

Benno held it out, casually, like he was handing over a bar tab. Chuck's eyes locked on. His grin dropped. The shift in his face was instant, friendly to feral in half a second.

'Everything sweet?' Benno asked, testing the water.

Chuck leaned in, face inches away, voice low and dead-eyed. 'It's sweet, unless you try to be funny. Then it's fuckin' done.'

Benno could feel the breath on his cheek. Could smell the meth, sweat and street-level madness radiating off the bloke.

One wrong blink and that would be it.

Meanwhile, Donny posted up at the bar, had the perfect vantage point. He could keep tabs on Benno while tucking into a feed and knocking back a few cold ones. Occupational multitasking. The chicken parmy hit the table like a wheel off a road train. Golden, melted cheese bubbled deliciously. A schooner of

XXXX Gold sweated beside the plate, dripping condensation like it was trying to escape the midday heat. *What more could a man want?* Donny leaned back, soaking in the atmosphere. It was your typical Friday lunchtime chaos—tradies blowing off steam, locals sinking schooners, petty criminals running side hustles between bets and bullshit. This was Donny's terrain. Loud. Blurry. Nobody watching anyone for too long. He kept one eye on the door. Still no Benno.

'Ah, fuck it,' he muttered to himself, before turning to the barmaid. 'Bundy and Coke, cheers.' By the time he'd hit his third drink, Benno had strolled in, looking pleased as punch.

'Your shout, Donny?' he called out.

Donny raised an eyebrow. 'Where the fuck've you been? Thought Chuck might've used your head to open his glovebox.'

Benno laughed. 'Just chatting about the latest *New Idea* magazine; its full of some great reads. Nothing to worry about.'

Donny shook his head and Benno ordered a pint big enough to drown a dog—no sign that he had just locked in a deal that almost cost him a kidney. The pair clicked glasses and settled into the noise. Just two blokes, sinking piss, lying to the world.

Benno leaned back, a glint of mischief in his eyes. 'So, what's next? A quick game of darts or should we plan an escape route?'

Donny chuckled, swirling his drink. 'I'd say both. This is our job now.'

What no one in that bar knew was that one of them had just bought five ounces of speed off a lunatic, and the other was already planning the next move. But that was the life. Underneath the laughter and the bullshit, this was war. And they were just getting started.

# 26

# GOD HATES US ALL

onny woke just after ten in the morning, the sunlight slicing through the blinds like a scalpel. His skull throbbed with a violence that felt like a jackhammer was tunnelling straight through his forehead. It wasn't just his head. Every muscle, every joint, every cell in his body ached as if he'd been churned through a cement mixer and left out to dry.

He lay still for a moment, eyes half-closed, trying to piece together the night before. The memories came in jagged flashes: the clink of bottles, the bitter burn of rum, the syrupy haze of temazepam, the slosh of beer and red wine. It had been a drinker's mixed grill, and he and Benno had devoured it like starving dogs.

After the pub closed, they both headed back home, sprawled on the back deck under a flickering bug zapper, talking nonsense with the confidence of men who thought they were wise. They weren't. They were drunk, loud, loose and utterly convinced they were solving the world's problems with every slurred sentence. *Philosophers with brain injuries*, Donny thought, wincing at the memory.

At some point, the music had gotten louder. So had they. Benno had tried to explain quantum physics using a beer bottle and a half-eaten sausage roll. Donny had countered with a theory about time being a flat circle, stolen from a TV show he couldn't remember the name of. They'd laughed until they cried, then cried until they passed out. Donny was so drunk that he could have slept under an elephant pissing and he wouldn't have woken up.

In the harsh light of morning, the wisdom of the night before had evaporated, leaving only the wreckage behind. Donny sat up slowly, the room spinning like a carousel. His mouth tasted like regret and ashtrays. He reached for the glass of water on the bedside table, knocking it over instead.

'Brilliant,' he muttered, rubbing his temples.

Somewhere in the distance, a dog barked. A magpie warbled. The world, indifferent to his suffering, carried on.

Donny groaned and swung his legs over the side of the bed. He didn't remember leaving the deck and getting to bed. He didn't remember much at all. But one thing was certain: whatever they'd been trying to solve last night, it hadn't worked.

And he was never drinking with Benno again.

At least, not until next weekend.

His phone buzzed angrily beside him, like a wasp trapped in a plastic cup. Text after text flashed across the screen:

'Turn on the TV!'

'New York!'

'Planes—World Trade Centre-Twin Towers—holy fuck.'

Donny rolled over, grabbed the remote and smacked the power button. Channel Nine flickered to life, revealing smoke, screams and absolute chaos. One tower had already collapsed; the second was barely holding on. 'Fuck me sideways,' he muttered, rubbing his eyes like that would somehow erase the image. Just a couple of years ago, he'd been walking those streets with a grin, stuffing his face with hot dogs and pretending he was some big shot. Now it looked like the world was ending on live television.

'Crikey. What's wrong with the world?' he whispered to no one. Thousands of people just going to work, buying coffee, kissing their kids goodbye—all wiped from the Earth in an instant. The randomness of it twisted something inside him. His mind snapped back to Karen. Her smile, her voice, the way she'd tilt her head when she was curious. Gone. Just like that. No warning. No chance to say goodbye.

He stared blankly at the screen. 'That didn't really happen, did it? Surely it's a fuckin' nightmare and I'll wake up soon.' But he wouldn't. And even in his hazy, booze-fogged state, he knew that. No bravado or gallows humour could fix this. The world was broken. So was he. And through the numbness, a single question clawed its way up from the depths: 'Why do the good people die?'

There were no answers. Just the towers burning. Just a room full of ghosts. On the very same day, US metal band Slayer released their album *God Hates Us All*. September 11, 2001—a day etched forever in memory. The album wasn't some lazy anti-Christian dig. It was a scream. A sentiment that, deep down, a lot of people understood. That feeling of being steamrolled by life. That cosmic unfairness that doesn't care how good a person is—life always has a way of knocking them down. It's that storm cloud that won't piss off. The breakup, the job loss, the gut-punch grief. Drawing the short straw.

But in that shared darkness, there's something cathartic, something real when the world burns. Sometimes the only thing to do is crank the volume, let the guitars wail and scream along. It's a release valve for the misfits, the betrayed and the broken. That album didn't just speak to Donny; it was Donny. Slayer's album was a brutal anthem for those drowning in pain.

Just as Donny was starting to feel like a human again, his phone buzzed. Krystal. 'Hey Donny, what you up to today? You wanna get on?' He smirked. She wasn't calling for a chat. Donny was her payday. She was skimming off the top and getting her gear for free. 'Fuck yeah, I'm hangin'. Did ya see the news about the World Trade Centre in New York?' 'The fuckin' what...' she mumbled.

'Don't worry,' Donny said with a laugh. She lived in a drug-fuelled bubble. World events didn't penetrate her orbit.

He was playing the long game with Krystal. If he could build trust with her, it might be the ticket to Mad-Madden, the dealer he was madly chasing. But it didn't take long for him to figure out that Krystal came from a world where men didn't treat her with even the faintest whiff of respect. Donny was different. He was polite. He didn't hit her. Didn't stab her. Showed up on time. Paid for gear. In her world, that made him look like royalty. To Donny's friends and family, he was off the rails. But to Krystal, he was some clean-cut, too good to be true mystery. And that made her suspicious. Was he real? Or was he a cop? Donny picked up on her hesitations: offhand remarks, subtle glances, the occasional hand on his lap while he was driving. It was a dance. And he knew he had to be careful. If she fancied him too much, things could get messy. If she didn't trust him, the whole thing would unravel.

Eventually, Donny convinced her to do a straight buy from Mad-Madden. 'He won't meet ya. You'll have to wait outside,' she told him. 'Yeah, whatever. I've heard his gear is the best, and that's all I want.' Donny was ready to roll the dice. She agreed, reluctantly.

As they cruised along towards Mad-Madden's property, Krystal glanced over with a casual ease that suggested something was on her mind. 'Hey, Donny, do you know Viper?'

Donny paused, his brain churning like an old washing machine.

'Yeah, I bought a stolen car from him,' he replied, keeping his voice as nonchalant as possible.

Krystal's eyes flickered with recognition. 'Well, I ran into him the other night at Morayfield Tavern and he said he knew we were seeing each other.'

Donny nearly choked on his own spit. 'What?'

Krystal continued, unfazed. 'He told me to tell you that you owe him five grand, and he wants it by Friday. Or else.'

# DONNY

A cold sweat broke out across Donny's brow. Viper (that was his bikie club name) was a cocktail of half-baked bikie, car thief, debt collector, drug dealer and possible hitman. A bloke who could make you vanish faster than a snag at Bunnings on a Saturday.

'I fucking paid him ten grand for that BMW!' Donny said, his voice thick with disbelief.

'Yeah, well, he said he priced it wrong. He reckons it's worth more than that. It's fifteen now, apparently.'

Donny leaned back in his seat, the weight of the world crashing down on him. He was supposed to be en route to a dodgy drug deal, not knee-deep in a financial cluster fuck with a psychopath.

'Well, that's just bloody brilliant,' he muttered, staring out at the passing bushland. 'What's next? Viper's gonna ask for my firstborn?'

'At this rate, you might have to throw in your left kidney too,' Krystal chuckled.

Donny sighed, her laughter quickly fading. 'Looks like it's a "find a way to pay Viper" kind of week,' he grumbled. He should've stayed home and watched infomercials.

Eventually, they arrived at a rural property. There were no neighbours in sight, and the house was hidden down a long driveway that dipped and snaked through the trees. As the Commodore rolled to a stop, Donny clocked the sign bolted to the gate: LOT 666.

'You've got to be kidding,' he muttered.

Krystal leaned forward, scanning the dirt road through the dense scrub. 'Alright, you wait here. Give me the cash, I'll get the gear and come back.'

'No dramas,' Donny said, handing it over. 'But don't fuck with me. Come back. Fast.'

She scoffed. 'Yeah, as if I wouldn't.'

Donny wasn't convinced. As she got out and rounded to the driver's side, she threw a casual, 'You getting out? I'm not walking all that way.'

He narrowed his eyes. 'Fuck no, you're not taking my car.'

'Well, I'm not walking that far.'

A pause. The air thickened. A standoff. Silent. Heavy.

Krystal folded her arms, dug in. Donny didn't blame her, but she wasn't getting the car. What he couldn't tell her was that it had been tricked up by the QPS tech boys with a secret start-up sequence and a hidden recording device. If it stalled, only he could bring it back to life. Not that she'd believe that anyway.

Twenty minutes passed. The sun scorched the bonnet. Flies buzzed like tiny, annoying reapers. Krystal hadn't moved. Donny could see the opportunity slipping away, inch by inch, down that long, dusty drive.

He sighed. 'Alright, how about I drive you down and wait in the car?'

She shook her head emphatically. 'You wouldn't survive. They'd shoot you on sight.'

# DONNY

Donny glanced up again. The gate had a fake padlock, the kind you could pop with a spoon. Above it, a hand-painted sign screamed in red:

PRIVATE PROPERTY. DO NOT ENTER. YOU WILL BE SHOT.

Bush cams were nailed to trees like evil eyes. His gut twisted, but he forced a grin. 'Fuck it. Open the gate. I'm running the gauntlet.'

Krystal's face dropped. 'No fuckin' way. Let's go home. I'm done. These are dangerous cunts, Donny.'

'Fine,' he snapped. 'I'll go down myself. Call Mad-Madden. Tell him I'm coming.'

'There's no phone signal out here,' she shot back, her voice rising.

Donny checked his phone. She was right—there was no service, of course. He might as well have brought a brick with him. He exhaled slowly, trying not to let the dread show.

'Alright. Take the car. But it's been playing up, so don't turn it off. Leave the ignition on, get the gear and come straight back.'

'I'll be ten minutes, tops.'

She popped the gate, slipped through, and the yellow Commodore rumbled away, disappearing into the scrub like it was being swallowed whole.

Donny sat on the roadside, lit a smoke and waited. Ten minutes. Then twenty. Then sixty. The sun dropped lower. Shadows stretched long and menacing. He lit a fifth smoke. Then a sixth. 'Where the fuck is surveillance?' he muttered to himself, scanning the trees. Nothing. No birds. No breeze. No backup. Two hours passed. His nerves frayed. His gut churned. 'Fuck it,' he growled, flicking his butt on the ground. He climbed the gate.

The moment his boots hit the ground on the other side, the bush roared to life. A ute tore up the driveway, engine howling, tyres skidding. Two blokes in the tray, rifles slung. Two in the cab, eyes wild. The ute slid to a stop in a cloud of dust. Donny barely had time to blink before they were on him. Rough hands shoved him against a tree. A rifle jammed into his ribs.

It was Chuck. Donny recognised the mugshot Benno had shown him. The guy looked even worse in person.

'What the fuck are you doing, cunt?' Chuck barked, eyes bulging with rage. Donny tried to stay composed.

'Krystal's got me car. I need to get home.'

Another bloke raised his rifle, safety off. 'Didn't you see the fuckin' sign?' Donny raised his hands. 'I'm not here to start trouble.'

Chuck clicked the walkie, mumbled something, then turned back.

'Get in the ute, cunt.'

Donny climbed in, heart thudding like a war drum. As they crested the hill, the house came into view, a crumbling Queenslander surrounded by rusted car bodies and coiled-up hoses. And there, at the top of the steps, was Mad-Madden. He held a thick chain. On its end was a monstrous black dog foaming at the mouth, thrashing like it wanted to tear Donny's throat out. Krystal was sitting in the Commodore, bawling, banging the steering wheel, trying to get it to start. It coughed. Died. She turned the key again. Nothing.

'I couldn't get it to start, Donny. I'm so sorry!'

'I told you not to turn it off,' he snapped. 'It needs my special touch.'

Donny forced himself to move. Every step felt like walking across a minefield. Had they found the listening device wired into the dash, it was game over. His cover would be blown. His body dumped in the dam behind the shed. He slid into the driver's seat. Hands steady. Heart hammering. The dog lunged; Mad-Madden held it back with a dead stare. Not a word was spoken. Just cold judgment, like he was weighing up the easiest way to kill him. Donny worked the ignition, tapped the sequence and the engine kicked. Relief rushed through his veins like morphine. 'See ya, fellas. It's been real!' he shouted, then jammed the throttle. The Commodore screamed, gravel spitting in every direction as he fishtailed down the drive. He nearly clipped a tree on the bend but didn't care. The night air rushed in through the open windows like freedom.

Donny didn't breathe properly until he hit the bitumen. When he dropped Krystal off, she asked him in for 'coffee'—her code for wanting drugs or perhaps something more. And so, he handed her some gear, gave her a nod and drove off without another word. He wasn't about to complicate things. He headed straight to his controller's place to hand over the drugs and give a full debrief.

'Tell surveillance they did a bloody good job, I didn't see them once out there,' he finished with a smirk.

The controller raised an eyebrow. 'Ah... about that. There was a mix-up. They had a send-off function in the city. That took priority. Sorry Donny, getting pissed with mates was more important.'

Donny stared at him, then let out a dry laugh.

'Well, that explains it. So much for having my back.'

The next morning, Donny woke to fifteen missed calls from Krystal. Still half asleep, he returned one.

'Donny! Viper's coming to your joint today. He wants his money now. And he's off his head. He's gonna give you a touch-up!'

His blood ran cold. That was no idle threat. Viper wasn't some drama queen bikie—he was the real deal. He was known for tuning blokes up and disappearing others for less.

Donny called his controller.

'Viper's coming. He wants money I don't owe him. What now?'

'Sit tight,' the controller replied. 'I'll sort something.'

'Sit tight? Really?' Donny muttered. 'You reckon I can sit tight while my teeth are being introduced to the back of my throat?'

Then came the miracle. His phone rang about 30 minutes later. The controller again, this time laughing. 'You're not gonna believe this. Viper ran a red light on his Harley. Semi cleaned him up. Two streets from your place.'

Donny just shook his head, speechless. That is the kind of luck you don't question. 'Well, seeing I'm still alive, I'd better get a drink.'

He hit the bottle shop, grabbed a carton of beer and a bottle of rum and settled in for a one-man victory lap. With music blaring from his stereo, he danced like a madman, laughing at the absurdity of what had happened. And then, as the beat of the Super Jesus hit *Gravity* hit his ears, he laughed even harder. *Well, Viper, my boy, gravity wasn't your friend today.*

As Donny continued to dance around the living room, fuelled by six stubbies and three double rums, he was hit with a genius idea. It was time to step up and get things happening on the Mad-Madden front. He picked up his phone and started dialling. It was a make-or-break move, but it had to be done. A few rings in and Mad-Madden picked up.

'Hey mate, I was the bloke with Krystal. Sorry for the way that went down, didn't mean any disrespect,' Donny began.

'Listen, cunt,' the crim cut in, 'don't you ever rock up to my joint uninvited again. Got it?'

Donny did a little grovelling and managed to smooth things over. So much so that he ordered two ounces of speed. Mad-Madden even invited him back to the property the next day to collect.

That was the breakthrough.

Four more buys and the job was done. In the end, it was easy, clean and simple. Time to shut down Operation Icepick. The Special Emergency Response Team (SERT) moved in. The boys walked twenty-five kilometres into the bush and camped out there on the property. They stayed there, hidden by the trees for two days, undertaking surveillance. They had to contend with lethal brown snakes and all the bugs and annoyances that come with hiding out in the scrub. They even dodged bullets that whizzed over their heads as Mad-Madden and his crew, unaware they were being watched by cops, randomly fired rifles into the bush for fun.

And then it happened. At four in the morning, they hit the place. Mad-Madden was snoring in an armchair with the TV blaring, a pistol on his lap. His crew were rounded up in minutes. The haul? Five stolen cars. Four bikes. Two jet skis. And the jackpot—two forty-litre drums buried in the yard, packed with half a million dollars and a kilo of speed.

During this operation, Donny bought four separate ounces (28.4 grams each), a 38-gram bag, and a quarter (7 grams) of methamphetamines from Mad-Madden.

Benno grabbed four ounces, two quarters, plus five grams, 13 grams and 8.5 grams from Chuck. And to top it off, Chuck had the bad luck of being arrested on an outstanding armed robbery matter.

Donny got awards, handshakes, back pats and empty praise. 'I didn't save the world,' he told his controller. 'If I wanted a pat on the back, I'd go find a dog.' While the bosses were popping champagne, Donny was dreaming of a pub feed and a pint, anywhere far from the bullshit. For most blokes, a job like that would leave them wired for days, buzzing from the rush, replaying every close call, riding the high of the bust. But not Donny. He didn't celebrate, didn't decompress. He didn't feel much at all. Just a hollow hum where adrenaline once lived. Every handshake, every cheer from the bosses, felt like it belonged to someone else. Because deep down, Donny knew he hadn't really won anything. He was still standing, sure, but only just. Still here, still breathing, but detached. Disconnected. The stakes were high, the danger real, but inside? Nothing. It was like his system never quite hit the brakes after a spike, just redlined and coasted into silence. In the end, it was just another day. He was still alive.

His life had become a slow, deliberate erasure. One lie, one beer, one job at a time. The armour was now well and truly in place. Donny was now the whole damn man. And Todd had become a shadow—the exhausted, fractured soul buried beneath, reduced to a silent passenger, still chasing the fading echo of what *home* used to feel like. The raid was over. The job was done. But the cost? That stuck like smoke in the lungs. Donny walked away from Lot 666 like it was nothing, just another tick on the board. But the truth? The silent man within was breaking down piece by piece. He wasn't living anymore. Just surviving and too far gone to count the damage.

A couple of months after the Caboolture job, Donny was already on his next job in West End when he was called to give evidence against Eddie Madden in a Committal Hearing. He arrived with his controller, Detective Senior Constable Ronnie 'The Rat' Hatchling.

Mad-Madden's barrister was Harry 'Hearsay' McPray, the archetypal slick lawyer from the early 2000s, often retained by bikie clubs and wealthy criminals. He was known to have built his career on things people *might* have said. In the courtroom, Harry had a reputation for objecting to everything, even his own arguments. But worst of all Harry was profiting from the spoils of organised crime and his name often came up throughout the operation.

Finally, Donny stepped into the witness box and met Mad-Madden's gaze, unwavering and intense. The dodgy barrister launched into his usual spiel about legal privilege and the importance of confidentiality regarding informants. Under the Drugs Misuse Act, it was a serious offence for police officers to disclose informants' identities, punishable by imprisonment.

Harry asked, 'So, Mr. Wilson, who introduced you to my client? Oh, wait—I'm sorry, I know you're not allowed to reveal your registered informant. It's in some legislation, correct?'

Donny replied, 'You are very correct, Mr. Barrister. It's under Section 33 of the Drugs Misuse Act. I am fully aware of the legislation.'

'Jolly good, Mr. Wilson,' Harry smirked and winked at the Magistrate.

Donny continued, 'The person who introduced me to your client was ultimately Marshall and Krystal.' He locked eyes with Mad-Madden and gave a slight nod. Mad-Madden's head dipped, and he stared at his feet. Donny knew he had just signed Marshall's death warrant. *Couldn't happen to a nicer bloke.* Donny knew he wasn't committing an offence because technically Eggplant was the Registered Informant not Marshall and Krystal.

After giving his evidence, Donny left the courthouse, and his controller was driving him back to his safe house.

'I've got a mate at a pub not far from here. Want to stop in for a few?' The Rat asked.

'Thought you'd never ask,' Donny replied.

'Now, my mate is a big drinker and loves to gamble. He's hopeless with money, so I guarantee he'll hit you up for a loan. Whatever you do, don't give him money.'

'Got it.'

When they arrived, The Rat introduced Donny to Eric Pouch-House, a Detective Senior Sergeant from the State Drug Squad. Pouch-house was in his forties, towering at about six-foot six and probably 130 kilos. It was clear he had started drinking early; he wasn't just tipsy, he was as full as a doctor's wallet.

Pouch-House rambled on about his numerous drug jobs, boasting more than Donny had probably experienced. Typical of old-school detectives, he exuded self-importance and had an ego larger than Mount Cootha. Donny shot The Rat a look that said, 'Let's get out of here.'

'After the next one, Donny,' was always his reply.

Before long, Pouch-House confronted Donny directly. 'Hey, young fella, I know you've got a stash of imprest money. Hand it over, and I'll get it back to The Rat tomorrow.'

Donny was holding around $5000 in cash but recalled The Rat's warning. He noticed The Rat shaking his head vigorously behind Pouch-House's fat head.

'I don't have any on me, mate. The Rat has everything. He won't give me anything. Doesn't trust me, I reckon.'

Pouch-House turned his attention to The Rat, starting on him instead. Seizing the moment, Donny slipped away to the TAB to place a bet. He chose a horse and approached the teller. 'Ten dollars, thanks,' she said. As he opened his wallet, he was unaware that Pouch-House was looming behind him, able to see inside.

'You little liar. Hand over your wallet!' Pouch-House roared, shoving Donny.

Donny spun around, resisting. 'Get lost! You can't have it.'

'This is your last chance, young fella. Your career depends on it!'

'Get stuffed!' Donny pushed him back, sending Pouch-House stumbling.

The Rat rushed in, 'Okay, fellas, let's go. Eric, I'll drop you home.'

Donny took the front passenger seat while a drunken Pouch-House clumsily settled into the back, right behind him. In the short drive, Pouch-House managed to jab the back of Donny's headrest repeatedly, taunting, 'Your career is over, young fella. Say goodbye to your badge!'

Donny turned to The Rat. 'I don't care who he is or that he's your friend. I'm gonna knock him out!'

Luckily, The Rat slammed the brakes and shouted, 'Get out, Eric. See you tomorrow.' As Pouch-House exited, he continued his tirade.

As they drove away, The Rat reassured Donny, 'Don't worry. He won't even remember this tomorrow.'

Eddie Madden got twelve years gaol and was paroled after eight or so years. Oh, and Krystal? She got done for supply and vanished into the system. Last we heard she vanished interstate. And Marshall. He pleaded guilty to Unlawful Wounding and was doing 2-3 years in the slammer.

# 27

# GREED, HEROIN AND A WOMBAT

West End, Brisbane's bohemian heart in the early 2000s, was alive with colour and contradiction. Cultures clashed and coexisted. Hippies bumped elbows with hustlers. Vintage stores shared street space with Vietnamese grocers and record shops. It was a place where no one asked questions, and no one gave a fuck what you were hiding. The sweet smell of cannabis wafted in the air as Donny walked down Boundary Street.

*This is my kind of place. No rules. No responsibilities. No care factor.*

Beneath the patchouli and reggae beats of West End, a darker current pulsed. It was 2001, and Operation Nifty had embedded Donny deep inside Brisbane's underworld. Boundary Street had become one of his haunts—shared by the homeless, the artists, the good and the bad. Heroin. Money. Power. Trust was as fleeting as a hit. Donny, now deep undercover, was here for one thing: to infiltrate a scene built on paranoia and violence. But what he got was something else entirely.

Enter 'Wombat'—an erratic, manipulative registered police informant with one foot in the grave and the other on a syringe.

A walking tribute to the criminal underworld of the '80s, Wombat looked like he'd stepped out of a Rose Tattoo film clip. Fifteen years in the slammer for armed robbery had done little to mellow him. This was an era when good crooks were tough, loyal and violent. His mullet had defied all laws of nature and fashion. His whole body was covered in gaol tatts, each one of them told tales of mayhem, each ink marked a badge of honour from his days in the can. His tattoos read like a rap sheet. And his blue singlet hadn't come in contact with detergent since Don Bradman retired. He was jacked. Not one day of missing the gym had him looking like someone not to fuck with.

Wombat's claim to fame was that he would tell everyone that wanted to listen that he was part of the Angry Gang, a notorious gang in Sir David Longlands Correctional Centre (now the Brisbane Correctional Centre). He spun tales of blood and betrayal like bar stories, including the one about Bart Hans Vosmaer, Queensland's most notorious prison enforcer. Bart copped his ticket to the next world inside the gym at Sir David Longlands Correctional Centre in 1993, courtesy of the Angry Gang. Lee James Garrett and Jason 'Waxy' John Nixon, foot soldiers in that outfit, took the fall. They were already legends for their 1991 garbage truck escape from Boggo Road Gaol. And in '97, Wombat helped Nixon and Brenden

James Abbott—the infamous 'Postcard Bandit'—break out of Boggo Road Gaol.

Wombat reckoned he was part of it all. Bullshit or not, the man could tell a yarn. And now, he was spinning one to the drug squad, claiming that he could open doors to Brisbane's Vietnamese heroin trade. He just needed a buyer. 'Someone legit.'

Enter Donny.

Before they could sell the lie, Donny and Wombat needed to live it. A backstory. Something airtight. Something that would stand up under scrutiny from criminals who'd slit your throat for a misplaced glance. Donny suggested they head to the Boundary Hotel and start laying the groundwork. When they walked through the doors, the mood shifted. Heads turned. Conversations stopped midsentence. Some even left the bar. Even by West End standards, the duo looked fearsome as they crashed open the front doors of the public bar and walked in with their servo-bought black wraparound sunnies still on. It was almost slow motion as they walked through the public bar and Donny swore he could hear Rose Tattoo playing *We Can't Be Beaten* over the speakers and even thought Angry Anderson could have been the barman.

Donny, of course, had a chip on his shoulder the size of a bloody boulder. Wombat looked like a pub brawl waiting for a reason. They slid onto stools at the public bar and the air turned to wire. Donny and Wombat had to whip up a tale about how they met, and mate, this was gonna be as tricky as getting a straight answer from a politician. See, Wombat had been doing a long stretch in the clink for the last fifteen years. Not the best idea to say Donny met him in the slammer—that's a surefire way to get your story checked by anyone sniffing around for dirt on Wombat's 'mate.'

After five or six schooners, Donny was feeling pretty good—at least until he overheard two tradies nearby, sunburnt and glistening like a couple of roast chooks. They started mouthing off, and it was like listening to a bad stand-up routine gone wrong.

'Oi, mate! Where'd you get that mullet? The two-dollar shop? I thought it was Halloween, not a bloody dress-up party!'

The banter dragged on like a never-ending footy match, ten minutes of cheap jokes and even dumber jabs. It was like listening to a pair of parrots squawking the same old lines but then came the brutal silence that felt heavier than a fully loaded hilux.

Donny, nursing a hangover that felt like a mule had kicked him in the skull—mixed with a cocktail of prescription meds and simmering anger—decided he'd had enough. Without a word, he rose like a man possessed.

The first bloke's face met the bar with a crack that echoed louder than a failed footy kick. Bone and blood splattered like a bad paint job. Out cold. His mate? Well, he got the same treatment, head locked and then bam! Straight into the bar. The poor sod dropped like a sack of potatoes, blood everywhere, turning the place into a scene from a horror flick.

'Disrespectful little cunts,' Donny muttered, plopping back down on his stool like nothing had happened. Wombat, his mate, didn't even blink. He just kept sipping his beer, staring straight ahead like he was watching the footy on a massive screen.

'Right, where were we?' Donny chuckled, raising his schooner in salute. Wombat nodded, as if to say, 'Good work buddy.'

And that's when Donny knew. This world, the one where fists solved problems and chaos was currency, was where he belonged. He wasn't pretending anymore.

Donny started to revel in the simplicity of sorting things out with his fists. There was something liberating about it. Why waste your breath when a quick jab could deliver the message louder than any words ever could? The thrill of it was intoxicating. He'd swagger into a pub or some dodgy back alley, and the opportunity would be right there. Some people just didn't listen, no matter how many times you tried to reason with them. Cunning conversations go nowhere. Out here, it wasn't about charm or clever lines. It was about the power of the punch.

As Donny and Wombat downed a round of beers, he ordered another two. The publican and Angry Anderson picked up each tradie and dragged them out the front and pushed them into a cab. Donny smiled and said, 'No probs we'll wait for the garbage to be taken out.'

Donny and Wombat were supposed to be building a legend. A backstory tight enough to survive the weight of scrutiny. Donny wanted to go over it a few times but Wombat wasn't in it. He was only half there scrolling his phone, eyes glazed, twitchy fingers chasing the idea of a hit more than any deal. Donny sat beside him, wired and tense, trying to hold the narrative together as his sidekick unravelled. Wombat was mumbling things about B-rad this and B-rad that. Then his phone buzzed. Wombat got up from his seat and walked away as he was talking on the phone. He hung up and came straight back.

'Let's go, that was B-rad, he's gonna get us on,' he barked.

'What?' Donny blinked, but Wombat was already out the door.

With Donny driving, they cruised the winding streets of West End, Wombat rambling and erratic. B-rad, triad, standover crews, ghosts in alleyways. His words tumbled over each other, sharp edges dulled by desperation. Donny kept his eyes on the road, unease spreading like a stain.

As they cruised to a quieter street corner, Wombat said, 'pull up here, B-rad will meet me around the corner'.

'Okay,' said Donny. 'But I want to meet him. I have to meet him.'

'Nah mate. Just give me the cash. I'll get it for ya.' pleaded Wombat.

Donny handed Wombat a wad of cash. 'Don't do anything stupid,' he said, trying to sound calm even though his insides were doing backflips. 'Just give me a call when you're ready.' Wombat nodded, took the money and then vanished like smoke.

As he disappeared, Donny felt an unsettling weight settle on his shoulders. The unspoken rule in Donny's line of work was gospel: never let the money run. But Wombat had insisted. 'Too dangerous,' he had said.

Donny knew better. He'd seen this before. Memories of Shelley. And he felt the pressure of it building. Still, he let it go. Sometimes, the rules just had to be broken. Otherwise, the job just would not get off the ground. And as we know Donny and rules really didn't go together.

About thirty minutes later, a frantic figure burst back into the ute. Wombat looked like death with a pulse. Chalk-white skin. Hollow eyes. Pupils like pinholes.

'They're coming for us, mate! Get the fuck out of here!'

'Who is?' Donny yelled back.

'Just go… now,' Wombat screeched.

Donny slammed his foot to the floor. Vulture Street became a blur. On he drove, past the hospital, past The Gabba— the whole time looking in the rear-vision mirror to see if they were being followed. Adrenaline surged like a tidal wave.

'I can't see anyone. What the fuck did you just score?'

Wombat didn't answer.

Donny persisted. 'What fuckin' happened back there?'

With frustration, he turned towards the passenger seat to discover that Wombat was 'on the nod' with blood trickling from the fresh hole in his arm. Donny's chest tightened.

'Fuck me.' He scrambled through the ute—under the seats, around foot wells—searching for the gear, the syringe. The bag. Anything to give him a clue as to how much of the goods Wombat had injected.

'Come on, come on...' he muttered under his breath, desperation creeping into his voice. The world outside faded into a blur. Then Wombat started convulsing and foaming at the mouth. His limbs spasmed violently. Donny snatched the phone and dialled his controller.

'This dumb cunt is OD'ing on smack, I think. What the fuck do I do?'

'What happened?' his controller barked through the phone.

'The prick tricked us. Slammed the full two grams we scored straight into his arm.'

'Jesus. Where are you?'

'Near The Gabba.'

'Get him to the Mater Hospital. Now.'

Donny didn't have to be told twice. That smack had been bought with police money. There was no way in hell that his boss's wanted a death on their hands. As the hospital neared, panic clutched him in its tight grip. The doctors and nurses would ask questions. Names. Details. Why this bloke was barely breathing. Why Donny, a man with dead eyes and no ID, was the one dropping him off. There'd be forms. Cops. Explanations he didn't have time or patience for. Donny had to think fast. Before he knew it, he had swerved into the emergency bay, slammed on the brakes, jumped out, yanked Wombat from the passenger seat and dumped him onto the pavement. 'Get help,' Donny roared, the words raw in his throat. Back in the driver's seat, he leaned on the horn, blasting it long and loud to draw attention to Wombat's plight. He didn't stick around. He peeled out before the questions caught up. As the hospital disappeared from view, Donny's mind raced with thoughts and plenty of regret, but there was no turning back.

Back at the safe house, he made the dreaded call to his controller.

'I left him at the front entrance to the hospital.'

There was a pause before his controller sighed. 'How the hell am I supposed to sell this to the boss's?'

Donny let out a cold, humourless chuckle. 'Not my circus, mate. Not my monkeys. That's why you get paid the big bucks.'

And then, he tossed the phone like it was radioactive, hand already reaching for the bottle. He knocked back a triple rum and Coke in one go and then chased it with two temazepam. No hesitation. No worries.

'Well, old Wombat, me ole mate... that's what you get for nicking shit. If you'd just asked, I might've chucked you a bit,' he muttered with a grin. 'Next time, don't be such a greedy cunt, eh?'

Jane's Addiction exploded through the speakers. *Been Caught Stealing*. Donny barked along, voice cracked and raw. Laughter spilled out of him, manic, jagged, too close to a scream. 'Greedy fuck... should've just asked.'

He wiped his mouth with the back of his hand and slumped into the couch like a man lowering himself into a grave. *I wonder if a heroin overdose is painless?* The thought didn't come like a question.

It landed like a plan. He filed it away. Not for Wombat. For himself. And as the music thundered and the room began to tilt, Donny let the dark swallow him whole. Whatever came next? He was ready. Or didn't give a fuck. Same difference.

# 28

# A BURGER, CHIPS AND A SIDE OF HAMMER

When Donny checked in on Wombat at the hospital, thinking he was going to be in there for a few days, he was surprised to learn that the slippery bastard had already checked himself out. No note. No call. Nothing. He was fine. Everything was fine. 'Fuck me, these cunts are good,' he muttered to himself, shaking his head. 'They'd be the only ones left after a fuckin' nuclear war.'

Back at the safe house, Donny slumped into his chair, scratching his chin like a bloke pondering life's mysteries. The empty rum bottle on the table seemed to be judging him. 'Right, mate, time to cut the dead wood,' he said out loud, more to the silence than himself. Wombat was a liability now, a proper loose unit. Erratic behaviour, reckless decisions and, worst of all, the useless cunt had stolen from

Donny. All trust was gone. The decision was made, Wombat had to go.

Donny picked up the phone and dialled. 'Listen up,' he told Wombat firmly. 'I need you to introduce me to B-rad.' Apparently, B-rad could get his hands on 'hammer' any time. Just the type of scumbag Donny needed to dig deeper.

'B-rad? You serious, mate? That bloke's just a fucked-up junkie!' Wombat slurred down the phone.

'Exactly,' Donny barked. 'How's that any different to you, cunt?'

Wombat wasn't keen to burn his free supply of smack, but Donny applied pressure. He could get pinched for taking the smack and would be back inside before he knew it. Eventually, Wombat caved.

As he stepped further into this tangled web, Donny couldn't help but chuckle to himself. He recalled the old Detective Inspector warning him about the dangers of going undercover. But for Donny, danger was part of the package. For Donny, every misadventure was just another one closer to being with Karen. With that, he took a deep breath, ready to embrace whatever wild ride lay ahead. Donny knew the stakes were high, and navigating this treacherous landscape would require a shitload of finesse.

B-rad was a classic smackie stereotype—scrawny with pockmarked skin and a wardrobe that looked like it had been stolen from the dump. He was swamped in threadbare clothes that tried and failed to hide the frailty underneath. Even in the middle of a Queensland summer, he wore a long-sleeved jumper, clearly trying to cover the railway of track marks lacing his arms. Donny's first impression was a mix of disgust and pity. B-rad's hollow eyes and sunken cheeks told the whole story. But behind that haunted look was sharpness, something calculating and dangerous. Donny could smell it. As they spent more time together, Donny realised B-rad had his finger on the pulse. This was one junkie who knew the drug game inside out, navigating its layers with surprising skill. Underestimating him would be a mistake. Donny understood now this wasn't just a desperate junkie. B-rad was a player.

B-rad had a long wrap sheet spanning back to 1994 with offences including, three armed robberies, numerous drug and break and enter offences. B-rad was no saint.

One afternoon, the pair met near the Boundary Hotel before heading off along Vulture Street. B-rad was dragging along a mangy black pit bull tied to a frayed rope. Classic B-rad. He led Donny to an unassuming burger shop. Inside, he introduced Donny to the owners—Mr and Mrs Tran. They were the quiet couple who ran heroin through the dingy little joint. The place looked innocent enough. Order a burger, some dim sims, maybe a can of Coke. But if you knew the right words, you could tack a bag of smack onto your combo meal.

The atmosphere was thick with paranoia. The Tran's operated behind a mask of calm authority, but it was clear they weren't to be trifled with. In the back room, Donny clocked half a dozen young Vietnamese blokes, tense and watchful, barely out of their teens. B-rad leaned in. 'Here's how it works. Order a full meal, then ask for the good stuff. They don't like customers comin' and goin' without buyin' food. Keeps the cops off their backs.' Donny took it all in.

Every gesture, every rule. One misstep here could cost him more than just the operation. It could cost him his life.

As the days turned into weeks, Donny became comfortable. He started going to the shop solo, slipping into the rhythm. But each visit was more than just a pickup. He was building a case, chipping away at the Tran's defences. He struck up conversations and asked questions with just enough curiosity to be convincing. The more they talked, the more he learned. They lived in a flat above the shop and rarely left. This close-knit living arrangement posed a significant challenge for the QPS, as it complicated their plans to install covert surveillance cameras.

For weeks the QPS tech team worked around the clock, searching for a window of opportunity to install covert cameras so the investigators could see from the inside. Finally, they found a gap. Two cameras went in, one above the shopfront door, another tucked into the living room out back. It felt like a major win. At least, it did until Donny watched the footage. Mrs Tran was sprawled on the couch, half watching TV, digging deep into her crutch for a scratch that lasted way too long. Then she sniffed her hand. Her face winced and scrunched up like she had just eaten a lemon wedge. She then got up and strolled out to make a burger. No hand wash. Nothing. After that, Donny made a new house rule: no more food. Just the heroin, thanks.

Donny kept at it—scoring eight more bags of heroin in two months. But he could feel the tension building. Were they onto him? Was it the fact that he wasn't ordering food anymore? He could feel the shift in the air, the sideways looks. Was it rubbing them the wrong way? With Christmas only days away, he pushed his luck and bought an eightball (three-and-a-half grams) off Mr Tran. Normally, the QPS would rush the gear to the John Tonge Centre, Queensland's leading forensic joint for a purity test, but the lab was shut for the holidays. Leaving him without the means to get it analysed. Every buy so far had been solid. Consistent and reliable. And that gave him a misplaced sense of confidence. By the time New Year's crept up, the boss's wanted one more score before the break. Donny just shrugged. 'Why not, who gives a fuck anyway.'

For Donny, the New Year wasn't a celebration—it was a countdown. Two years since Karen's death. The date sat heavy on his chest. He lowered his voice, 'See you soon, K.'

Donny knew the order from the boss's to make one more buy was reckless, as the last batch hadn't even been tested. That was always the rule: test everything. Know the purity. Know what you're dealing with. If a dealer was ripping you off or, worse, cutting with something dangerous, you needed to know before stepping back into the fire. But this time, he was flying blind. Going in without lab results was a gamble that could cost him everything. But Donny didn't care. Not anymore. Not about the risks. Not about the rules. He was already drowning—the mission just handed him the anchor.

Donny pulled up about 100m from the shop and as he turned the car off he continued singing Beasts of Burbon's *I Don't Care About Nothin Anymore.*

'I used to give my money to the motherfuckin' poor
But I don't care about nothin' anymore
I used to let you in but you can leave it at the door
'Cause I don't care about nothin' anymore…'

Donny casually sauntered into the shop, smiling up at the camera above the shopfront door like he was waving at his mum. He figured it would give the detectives who were monitoring the camera back in HQ a good old laugh. However, he didn't notice Mrs Tran crouched by the fridge, out of sight under the front counter. When he turned, she was staring at him, and then she looked to the corner where the camera was hidden. Donny stepped up to the counter, still trying to play it cool.

'Hey, that last stuff was really good. Can I get the same?'

She didn't even blink. 'Get out. Don't come back.'

She spat more words in rapid Vietnamese, none of which Donny understood. He tried reasoning with her. He was desperate. She wasn't having it.

*Fuck this cunt*, he thought. And then the switch flipped. 'Get fucked. You're dead. I'm gonna fuckin' kill you.'

He shaped his fingers like a gun, mimicking shots in her direction. Then he trashed the shop. Flipped a table. Threw a chair. That's when Mrs Tran snapped. She grabbed a large Asian kitchen knife from behind the counter and came at him swinging like a woman possessed. Donny backed away, hands raised. *Fuck, I don't want to be the cop who gets killed by a Vietnamese grandma with a fuckin' butter knife.* He kicked in a window on the way out and bolted up the street back to his car.

The moment Donny was alone, a sick feeling sank into his gut. Had Mrs Tran seen him look at the camera. Or maybe she thought he was just completely unhinged. Either way, he'd blown it. He got back to the safe house where his controller was waiting.

'Well, wouldn't you know it,' The Controller said, holding a printout. 'Test results came back from the Christmas buy. That heroin? It was fuckin' Plaster of Paris.'

Donny double blinked.

'You inject it,' The Controller added. 'Could be fatal.'

So that was it. The Tran's had set him up. The gear was fake. And he'd walked right into it like a mug. And just like that, Operation Nifty was dead.

Two days later, Donny was front and centre in the Organised Crime Squad briefing room at five a.m. Fifty detectives packed in, gearing up to hit the shop and the houses, to finally shut the whole operation down. Months of footage had given them twenty punters, a maybe-runner, nothing more—just street junkies, scraps. The kind of haul that should've felt like a win. Instead, the room was flat, airless, like everyone knew it wasn't enough. Deflated. Donny barely listened. Faces blurred past. Conversations washed over him. He'd gotten close. Then he'd fucked it. And now, it was slipping away. One of the boss's stood up and rattled off the same old lines about 'confidentiality' and 'officer safety'. Donny didn't buy it. Then came the final twist: he was going back in. One last time. Donny was to buy an ounce of heroin. Eight thousand dollars' worth. The stakes had never been higher.

An ounce represented a significant jump from what Donny was accustomed to purchasing. In his previous dealings, he had always dealt in smaller quantities, just enough to maintain his cover without drawing too much attention. But an ounce was a much larger commitment, a move that would undoubtedly raise alarms and scream 'narc' or 'undercover cop' to anyone who was paying attention. It had become common knowledge that undercover agents were disposable, and the feeling between undercover agents was that their welfare was not a priority.

Donny didn't fear for his safety. He feared screwing the whole thing again. And so, with nerves tight and instincts screaming, Donny prepped for his return. The plan was absurd. Order a full meal—burger, chips, dim sims a Coke and then do the deal. Ten detectives would be waiting nearby for Donny's command.

Just after eight a.m., Donny parked at the same place about 100m from the shop and started walking. That's when he saw him: a well-known crime reporter cruising the street. It was quite obvious he was looking for a scoop. Donny knew him well, and knew he had been taking detectives out for extravagant lunches and, in return, he would get the first tip about any criminal investigations.

'Fuck this,' Donny muttered, grabbing his phone and ringing his controller.

'Tell them all to get fucked. I'm going home. Who the fuck tipped the media?'

His controller rang back a short time later. 'It wasn't the detectives. It was someone higher up. Leak came from the top.'

Of course it did—so bloody typical, more interested in getting a good story than an undercover cop's safety.

Donny pushed the thought away and decided to get it over and done with. He walked into the shop, face calm, hands steady. This time, Mr Tran served him. Donny didn't say much. He just nodded, placed the order, and walked out with a fat bag of what felt like the real deal. High grade heroin 'Hanoi Haze', 'Saigon Silk' or 'Vietnamese Gold'. It worked. Twenty minutes later, the shop was raided. The Tran's were arrested. But as Donny would soon learn, they weren't the big fish. They were bait. And now, the whole game had changed.

Over the next couple of weeks, whispers began to circulate in the shadows of the local underworld. Detectives started hearing rumours of a contract—one hundred thousand dollars, to be exact— on Donny's head. Firstly, for being an undercover cop. Secondly, for trashing Mrs Tran shop. Donny was just plain pissed off. 'Fuck those cunts! I'm worth more than that. That's bloody offensive!' He figured if they were going to put a price on his life, at least make it a reasonable one. In typical Donny fashion, he started joking about it. Plotting ways to meet with the head of the Vietnamese community to negotiate a better deal. 'I'll just have a chat with them, maybe ask for a million,' he chuckled to himself. Of course, making contact was forbidden. Some bureaucratic rule in some bureaucratic handbook said it wasn't a good idea.

So, there he was. Stuck in limbo—with a bounty on his head that he found more insulting than threatening. He even brainstormed ways to boost his market value: 'What if I throw in a couple of footy tickets? Or a backyard barbecue? Everyone loves a snag and a beer.' He considered making flyers: 'Have a hit on your head? Let's negotiate'. As the tension built, Donny found himself becoming more and more paranoid. 'What if they send someone to get me with a rubber chicken or a Peking duck?' he joked. Humour was his only defence. In the days that followed, Donny found solace at the bottom of a bottle. His drinking escalated dramatically—maybe it was even Guinness book-worthy.

# 29

# SUPREME SHITSHOW

**M**onths flew by, and the day finally arrived for Donny to testify against the Tran's in the Brisbane Supreme Court. In his mind, this was the moment he'd been waiting for, the grand finale of his personal soap opera. Rumours from the Vietnamese crime gang were still circling like seagulls at a chip shop, but it seemed the QPS couldn't give a rat's arse. Donny was onto his next job by this time, and his current bosses had no knowledge of the West End job so he didn't give a shit. Donny was on his own. *Great job, boys. That's right, I'm just an investigative tool. There's more of us anyway*, he thought sarcastically. *Keep up the good work!*

Standing outside the courthouse, Donny gazed up at the sky, watching the clouds drift lazily overhead. He felt the familiar pang of longing for Karen. 'I'll see you soon,' he murmured softly, almost as if she could hear him. The words hung in the air, a bittersweet vow echoing back at him from the vastness above. In the recent months, a dark thought had begun to take hold of Donny's brain.

He had been secretly wishing a heroic assassin would leap from the shadows and end his misery. He pictured it like a scene out of a dodgy action flick, where the protagonist meets a swift and intense fate just as they ascend the front steps of their home. 'How cinematic would that be?' he chuckled grimly to himself. It was a fantasy that was both terrifying and oddly appealing, a reckless way out of the constant pain swirling in his gut.

In those moments, he felt a strange mix of fear and yearning. He wanted the pain to stop, the endless cycle of grief and regret that had consumed him since Karen's passing. Yet, deep down, he clung to the hope that maybe, just maybe, there was still a chance for redemption, a way to reclaim his life before it spiralled completely out of control. 'I could start a new career as a motivational speaker!' he joked to himself. 'Step right up and hear how to turn your life from tragic to mildly entertaining, where everyone around you kills themselves.'

But as he stood there, wrestling with his thoughts, he couldn't shake the feeling of being trapped in a life that felt increasingly meaningless. The promise to Karen lingered in his mind, a bittersweet reminder of the love he had lost and the darkness that now surrounded him. Would he ever find a way out, or was he just waiting for the right moment to disappear completely?

He took a deep breath. 'Alright, mate, let's do this,' he said out loud, perhaps to bolster his motivation. Who knows, maybe testifying would be the kick in the pants he needed to get his life back on track. Or, at the very least, it would make for a hell of a story down the pub later. Donny walked into the courthouse alone and simmering with anger. He was a bit nervous, as he had no idea how they were going to twist his memories into knots. The defence law firm was called the 'Right and Wong & Associates' who had employed Brisbane's slickest silk named Noah Lott. Noah, along with his instructing lawyer Dan Gleebitz, who just so happened to be an old mate of Donny's, bombarded him with questions. It felt like they were trying to pull a rabbit out of a hat.

'So, Detective Donny Wilson. That's your name, is it?'

'Yes,' replied Donny, trying to keep a straight face.

'Surely that can't be your real name. Let me guess, that's your undercover name, right? Like some sort of secret agent? Did you draw it out of a hat, or was it one of those names you give to yourself? First pet and first street you lived in, perhaps?'

'Yes,' Donny confirmed, feeling the heat rise.

'So, it's a fake name,' the barrister exclaimed, his voice booming like a bad karaoke singer in a pub. 'You live in a world of make-believe, pretending to be a criminal, and you basically lie all day, every day, as part of your job?'

'Essentially, yes.' Donny shrugged, trying to look casual, as though he hadn't just admitted to a life of deception.

'Do you think you're good at it?'

'Well, I suppose so,' Donny mumbled, feeling like a kid caught with his hand in the cookie jar.

'So good, in fact, that you don't even know when you're lying and when you're not!' And with that, the barrister pointed an accusatory finger at Donny.

'I...' Donny tried to interject, but the barrister was on a roll now.

'You've been doing this so long that you can't tell the difference between reality and a bad soap opera,' he yelled, his voice rising dramatically as if he were auditioning for a Shakespearean tragedy.

Donny glanced at the twelve jurors, heads down, scribbling like mad. They probably thought they'd stumbled into an episode of *Law & Order: Comedy Edition*. And this went on for hours, with Donny feeling like he was trapped in a never-ending loop of interrogation while the barrister revelled in his role as the villain of the piece. He smirked to himself, *Maybe I should change my name to Detective Donny the Delusional. At least that way, everyone would know what they're getting into.*

By the end of the day, Donny saw his mate Dan Gleebitz tug on Noah Lott's suit coat and motioned him to lean down. Donny was sure he could see Dan whisper 'He's had enough.' Donny had never expected to even get on the stand, so he hadn't bothered to read the fifty-five-page statement.

'Nothing more, Your Honour,' Mr Lott bellowed, and Donny gasped, relief flooding over him. He stepped down from the stand and headed home to drown his sorrows alone at his safe house. He knew it hadn't gone well. His evidence had been ripped to shreds, and he'd been made to look like he didn't have a clue what he was saying.

The next day, he staggered back into the Supreme Court with a belting hangover, or maybe he was still a bit tipsy. He couldn't quite tell. As fate would have it, the storm brewing over Donny's head suddenly dissipated. The Vietnamese Triad's hit on his life vanished into thin air after two simple words echoed through the courtroom.

'Not guilty.'

It wasn't just that Donny had failed as an undercover. He'd failed the team who'd trusted him. Months of work reduced to rubble, leaving him with nothing but the sour taste of disappointment and a brand that stuck like sweat: fuckup. His name had gone from penthouse to shithouse in the space of a verdict. Every sideways glance in the corridor, every silence in a briefing room, confirmed it. The only blessing? No one else was there to watch the verdict fall. Just me.

He had envisioned a very different ending. In some version of this, he walked out proud, maybe even respected—a bloke who risked everything and came out the other side with a collar and a war story. Instead, he stood on the edge of something that didn't feel like survival. It felt like a void. No fanfare, no closure. The thrill of dodging death, literally, should have felt like a second chance. But all it did was highlight the wreckage he'd walked away from. Then came the final insult. Wandering the corridors of the courthouse after the verdict was delivered, still simmering with rage and humiliation, Donny was ambushed by his old mate, Dan Gleebitz, who'd sat in court grinning like a cat who'd already swallowed the bird. He sidled up with the kind of smugness that only someone completely detached from consequence could carry.

'You won't believe this, mate,' Dan said, like he was about to share a juicy footy score. 'The fucking Tran's just put an extra hundred grand into my account for getting them off. It's just a game, mate, don't worry about it. How about I shout lunch?' Donny stared at him, stunned. The sheer casualness of it, the ease with which his mate laughed off blood money, it hit like a punch to the throat. And to think, it was probably the same money that would have been paid to someone who put a bullet in Donny's head.

Here was his mate, practically skipping with joy, basking in victory while Donny stood there with the aftertaste of failure in his mouth. It felt surreal. The entire system was crooked, and somehow, he'd been the only one that came out bruised.

'Lunch? Sure.' His voice felt flat—celebrating felt absurd. But he followed, unsure what else to do. He had no plan. No place to be. They ended up in one of those five-star joints near the Brisbane River, the kind of place where CEOs paid for thousand-dollar lunches and no one blinked. Plush velvet booths, dim lights, menus without prices—Donny looked wildly out of place in his crumpled suit, long, greasy hair, goatee and enough piercings to trigger a metal detector.

Then the wine came. Hundred-dollar steaks on the table, five-hundred-dollar bottles of merlot spinning in their glasses. The flavours did more than coat his tongue—they dulled the edges. Gran Patrón followed, shot after shot, each one sliding down easier, each one taking the sting out of reality. For a few hours it all blurred—the courtroom. The operation. Karen. Even the hit. None of it mattered in here. Laughter rolled, booze hit like morphine, and for a while he wasn't Donny the fuckup, or a ghost of a copper who'd gone too deep. He was just a bloke on the piss, pretending the world might still be alright. Either way, he really didn't give a fuck.

Then the bill landed—three grand. Dan didn't flinch. 'You weak cunt! It's only three grand. You're not going home until we do ten.' Donny forced a laugh, but inside, he felt hollow at the thought of having nowhere else to be. He didn't care about the money or the night or even what tomorrow looked like. The booze was working, and that was enough. The idea of drinking till dawn sounded alright—fuck it, why not? As the evening rolled on, the restaurant came alive. Conversations hummed. Bottles emptied. The air was thick with expensive perfume and false confidence. Every round felt like a tiny win over the darkness clawing inside him. With each clink of glass, Donny toasted the silence in his mind.

Time bent. The world outside vanished. This was no longer a meal. It was a bender disguised in white linen. A slow-motion collapse under chandeliers. And maybe, just maybe, the hit was lifted. Or maybe it never existed at all. Did the Detectives make it up? It didn't matter. What mattered was that something inside him was cracking, splinter by splinter. And while everyone else seemed to be playing some twisted game and laughing their arses off, Donny was starting to realise the real battle wasn't out there in the streets or the courtroom.

The war was inside his own head. He just didn't want to admit it yet.

So, he drank.

Donny didn't remember how he got home. The details were vague, a taxi maybe, or a long walk through the bones of a sleeping city. Either way, he ended up slumped on the couch, suit crumpled, head pounding, the bitter aftertaste of wine and self-loathing still clinging to his tongue. The silence was absolute. No Karen. No operation. No fucking purpose. He lit a smoke and stared at the ceiling, exhaling slowly. His phone buzzed once—some meaningless notification.

This was supposed to be the part where everything made sense. After the bust. After the trial. After the close call. He was supposed to feel something other than this ache in his chest that never left. Instead, all that was left was him, a bottle of something half-finished and the echo of a courtroom performance he didn't even believe in. He thought of the headlines that would never print his name. The people who'd forget what he risked. The Tran's walking free. His mate with his fat bonus. Everyone walked away with something. Everyone but him, apart from a lavish lunch.

Donny shuffled to the window, staring out at the empty street below. His reflection in the glass stared back—bloodshot eyes, gaunt face, hair that hadn't seen a brush in weeks. He barely recognised himself anymore. There was no gun to his head, no imminent threat. But that didn't make the war any quieter. It had just gone underground, burrowing deeper. And Donny? Well, Donny was still pretending it wasn't happening. Still chasing noise to drown it out.

But the silence was catching up.

# 30

# KING OF THE
# FABULOUS

After the West End job, I was put on 'downtime,' the polite term for 'go try to feel normal until we throw you back into the fire'. No target. No briefing. Just me—left alone with the ringing echo of what went down in Operation Nifty.

I spent some time with my family. Had a few quiet dinners with Mum and Dad, like old times. Mum would fuss over the dinner, act like she wasn't clocking the tiredness in my eyes. Dad would pour a glass of red, give me shit about looking tired, but there was always that look, the one that said, 'I don't know what you've seen, son, but I'm here when you want to stop pretending'. We didn't talk about the job. Not a word would be spoken.

They knew better than to ask, and I didn't have the words even if I wanted to tell them. But the smell of Mum's cooking, the click of Dad's knife against the plate, the quiet between sentences, that was home. That was safety. And for a moment or two, I could almost forget.

Then there was Peta. God, she was the only sparkle of normal I had left. We had a couple of date nights, one Italian and another Thai. Nothing fancy, just being together. Holding hands across the table, laughing, pretending we had a future I could actually show up for. She'd smile at me like I wasn't slipping away, like I hadn't become a ghost walking between two worlds. But deep down, I knew she could feel it. That I wasn't really in that restaurant with her. I was still wired for war. Still listening for the next threat. Still bracing for the bang. I wanted to be there. With her. I just didn't know how to stay.

So, when the itch got too loud and the mask too heavy, I bailed. Packed up and headed south—time to disappear for a bit. I shot down to the Gold Coast and bunked in with my old mate GG at Main Beach on The Fabulous French Toast. It felt like home away from home. Sun, surf and rum on repeat.

Mornings were spent soaking up the sun and surf, lunch beers at the Surf Club, then dinners along Tedder Avenue—overpriced steaks, cocktails served with a wink, rubbing shoulders with the beautiful people. When night fell, I chased whatever distraction fit—casino tables or strip clubs under neon lights. It was a fantasy, a fever dream, and I leaned in hard. One night, I hit it big at the casino, walked out ten grand heavier, chest out, eyes gleaming. By the time we hit the Crazy Horse, a popular showgirls joint in Surfer's Paradise, I was riding high and throwing money like I owned the place. Literal hundred-dollar notes flung into the air like wedding confetti.

'Oi! Can you buy me a lap dance?' one of the boys shouted, eyes wild as *Sandstorm* thumped through the speakers like a defibrillator for the soul. I laughed, licked my thumb like some cashed-up kingpin, sniffed the notes for good luck, and flicked two hundreds at him. 'Go on, have a ripper time, young fella,' I shouted, turning back to my Corona and letting the madness swirl around me. In that moment, I felt untouchable, like the undisputed King of The Fabulous ruling over a kingdom of tits, tequila and total detachment. *No wonder people get hooked on this lifestyle.*

But even then, somewhere under the noise and neon lights, I felt it, that nagging weight, that hollow thump in the chest that reminded me none of it was real. I could throw money, dance with strangers, drink myself into oblivion—but I couldn't shake the feeling that I was somewhere out there watching it all from behind a window. Locked out. Forgotten.

This wasn't Todd's world. This was Donny's—this chaos, this mask, this madness. I'd worn the cover for so long I didn't know how to take it off anymore. And the more I tried to drown it, the louder it got. The truth was, downtime wasn't rest. It was a drift. And I was miles from shore, holding a beer in one hand and a broken compass in the other.

# 31

# OPERATION FIDDLE

Sometimes, the real enemy is your own mind. It was April 2002 and I'd just come off a high. The Fabulous French Toast days, Crazy Horse nights and a binge that would make Keith Richards wince. But there was no time to unpack the mess. This next job came calling, and this one hit differently.

Caroline Stuttle was nineteen, English, bright-eyed and full of wonder. She had been travelling Australia with a friend on a gap year that was meant to be the adventure of a lifetime. Bundaberg was one of the final stops on her trip. A charming, quiet sugar town with backpacker charm, rum on tap and a reputation for being safe.

But one April night, everything changed.

Caroline was walking home across the Burnett Bridge when a desperate drug-addled thief tried to rip the handbag off her shoulder. In the struggle, she was pushed over the side and fell to her death. The story rocked the Bundaberg community to its core. The tight-knit, sun-soaked town became a global headline. What was once a safe haven for travellers was suddenly a crime scene, its heart cracked wide open by senseless violence.

The investigation fired up immediately, but answers were hard to come by. No witnesses. No clear suspects. Just whispers in the pubs about names that meant something to the wrong kind of people. Rumours swirled about local drug dealers, addicts and ghosts from the underworld floating just beneath the surface. But no one was talking. Not to the cops, anyway.

And that's where Donny came into the picture.

Like a thunderclap in a cloudless sky, the call came through from the Detective Inspector.

'Pack your bags. You're heading to Bundaberg,' he barked, his tone all business, no bullshit. 'Beardy's your controller. He'll brief you on the way.'

I barely had time to blink. I threw my gear in the car, clipped in my emotional seatbelt and hit the highway. The further I drove, the more the scenery changed. The glitter of the Gold Coast gave way to rolling cane fields and wide, empty skies. By the time I reached the small country town of Gympie, it felt like I was crossing some invisible line, leaving behind one kind of madness for another. Beardy was waiting just outside town. You couldn't miss him—fake tan, bleached tips, white teeth and a grin that said he knew ten jokes dirtier than yours. He briefed me like he was reading a menu, very casual, confident, peppered with gallows humour. That was Beardy.

Sharp as a tack, dry as dust and utterly unflappable. And fuck, I liked him.

We rolled into Bundaberg not long after. Quiet streets. Big sky. A main strip that looked like it hadn't changed since the '70s. I found a cheap motel on the main drag and checked in for what was supposed to be a week. The sheets smelt like bleach and sluts, but I wasn't there for a holiday. The goal was simple: infiltrate, blend, listen. I figured the best place to start was in the pubs. Every watering hole became a stage. I drank middies with fruit pickers and schooners with scaffies. I kept my ears open and my back to the wall. What I found was a town still bleeding. Locals were shaken, backpackers even more so. Everyone was on edge. The attack on Caroline had cracked something wide open, and in that crack, the names started surfacing.

Old faces from the Caboolture underworld. Drug dealers and users, I already knew by smell. Turns out Mad-Madden's grip stretched further than I'd thought. It didn't take long before Bundaberg started to feel familiar. The chaos was subtler here—less neon, more rust. But it was still chaos. Fights in the pub car park. Girls too young with eyes too old. It wasn't glamorous, but it was real. And then came the curveball: new job, new name.

I was being pulled out of Donny and reborn—again. Beardy broke it to me over a counter meal at the Bargara Beach Hotel.

'You'll be using a different name for this one. Fresh start. New crew. You're Jason Reynolds now. They'll call you Renno.'

I paused, steak knife mid-air. Renno? I'd just spent the better part of eighteen months becoming Donny. It felt second nature now. When someone shouted 'Donny!' across a crowded pub, I turned without thinking. I'd built a reputation on that name. I wore it like a jacket—frayed, grimy, but mine.

The decision to change the name was used as a lesser risky option. Everyone in Caboolture knew that an undercover named 'Donny' was responsible for bringing down Mad-Madden's crew and word was out. It was easier not to have that association.

Besides, orders were orders. So, I nodded and took a sip of my beer. 'Righto. Guess I'm Renno now.' And just like that, another mask slipped into place. A new name. A new story. A new town with old ghosts and a new set of rules. And if I wanted to find the bastard who pushed that girl off the bridge, I had to play by them. So, I rolled my shoulders, cracked another beer and started getting to know who Renno really was.

Fortunately, or so I thought, Beardy had arrived well prepared. Fresh ID, a stack of club memberships, even a fabricated paper trail so clean it would've fooled the taxation department. With those in hand, I managed to secure a beachside unit in Bargara. Fifth floor, ocean views, high-end security, the lot. A fortress in the sky. Perfect for a man trying to disappear in plain sight.

But safety's a funny thing when your own mind becomes the threat. The first few days in Bargara were manageable. I walked the foreshore, scoped out local watering holes, kept my ear to the ground. But when the sun dipped and the streets emptied, something shifted. My body stopped pretending. The nights were brutal. Lying in that sterile, well-secured unit, my mind couldn't rest; it roared. I would shut the blinds, double-check the locks and go through the same routine like some kind of obsessive ritual. But no matter how many deadbolts clicked, the fear came crawling in through the cracks. Was it because I had to carry a new persona? An identity I had not yet connected with? Was it the thought of leaving Donny behind?

I would lay in bed, heart thumping against my ribs like a drum line. Sometimes I would shake uncontrollably. Not from cold but from something deeper. The kind of fear that doesn't have a name, just a presence. Shadows danced in the corners of the room. I would see figures at the door that weren't there. Hear footsteps I knew didn't actually exist. But nothing compared to what happened when I rolled over. There, every night without fail, I would reach instinctively for the other side of the bed and find her. Karen. Pale. Still. A noose around her neck, staring straight through me. Crying. And just like that, the air would vanish from the room.

I would sit bolt upright, drenched in sweat, heart hammering. Every nerve screamed. *It's not real.* But knowing that didn't make it stop, and so I did what broken men do best.

I drank.

The bottles began piling up like trophies of defeat. The more I drank, the less I felt. The less I felt, the more I drank. It was a closed loop. A trap. And I walked into it willingly. I sought out a doctor in Bargara—well, Renno did. Told him I had trouble sleeping. The doctor didn't ask many questions, just scribbled out a script for temazepam and handed it over like it was Panadol. I was loaded. I popped the first one that night and washed it down with a glass of shiraz. Then two. Then three. And for a few hours… silence. While it offered temporary relief, it also led me down a path of dependency, creating a cycle that left me feeling trapped.

As I struggled with these issues, I realised that the façade of this new identity was crumbling under the strain of my mental health. The life I had hoped to build in Bundaberg was overshadowed by these escalating fears and the phantom images of my past. Haunted by Karen. Haunted by Donny. Haunted by everything I had seen and done. Each night became a battle against my own mind, and I knew I needed to confront the demons that haunted my soul if I ever hoped to find peace.

There was one constant for me in those days: Red Hot Chilli Peppers' *Dosed*. That track lived in the car, wedged between CDs of Nirvana and Pearl Jam. It cranked through the speakers every morning on the drive from Bargara to Bundaberg. My hope? That it would keep me tethered. It never really did, but I kept playing it anyway. That song understood something I myself couldn't explain. Sadness, you could hum. Heartbreak, you could almost survive if you let the melody do the bleeding for you. All I ever wanted was her to be alive.

And as the days rolled on, I knew the walls were starting to crack. My mask was slipping, and Renno's mask—slick, confident, in control—was paper-thin. Behind these masks, the truth was screaming to get out. But I wasn't ready to hear it. Not yet.

# 32

# CHASING SHADOWS

After doing a great job as a bar fly in just about every pub in Bundaberg and coming up with absolutely zip, Renno was finally thrown a lifeline, if you could call it that. His next assignment came in the form of a registered informant known only as 'The Worm'. The name fit. He was a sad sack of shit who was on the dole. A failed farmer, he was on the bones of his arse and hated everyone. He chose to be an informant for the QPS purely to make some money.

Renno had met The Worm a few times in town and said he could introduce Renno to Lance. Lance was a suspected drug dealer and a link in the Caroline Stuttle investigation. Detectives were sure Lance had something to do with it, but the details were murky. That's where Renno came in. The plan? The Worm would set up the buy by inviting Lance around. His task was clear: buy four ounces of speed from Lance, get friendly with him and see if he makes any admissions to murdering Caroline.

The Worm lived about forty-five minutes from Bundaberg, also known as 'Bundy', on some godforsaken bush block that looked like it had been plucked straight from a horror movie. No phone signal. No neighbours. Just trees, dust and the kind of silence that made your skin crawl. The dirt road out to the property felt like a warning in itself—narrow, rutted, endless. The kind of road where missing people posters should have lined the trees. The Worm's house was perched up on a slight hill at the end. Not a soul either side of it.

Renno made the trip anyway. He was already half-cut by the time he rolled up, having downed four cans of OP rum and Coke. Clarity? Gone. Nerves? Numbed just enough to keep his foot on the pedal. But the second Renno turned into the long driveway, all that bravado evaporated.

Four dark pit bull terriers confronted him. Each was chained to the same stake hammered into the ground—six-metre leads with the surrounding grass worn into a perfect circle from endless pacing and lunging. Musclebound demons frothing at the mouth like they'd been summoned straight out of *Mad Max: Rural Fury*. The moment they saw Renno, all hell broke loose—chains whipped taut, paws gouging trenches in the dirt, spinning and thrashing like they were trying to tear a hole in the universe just to get to him.

One locked eyes with Renno, head low, teeth bared, like it had just spotted lunch. 'Sweet Jesus,' Renno muttered, frozen behind the wheel. 'If this is the welcome party, what the fuck's waiting inside?' For a second, he genuinely thought the chains would snap. That he'd die out there in the dust, half drunk and half eaten, while The Worm sat inside scratching his balls and loading a bong. 'The black dog is not gonna take me.' Renno whispered to himself.

And still, he had to get out of the car.

The main game that day was to meet The Worm's mate Lance. Lance had clearly lost the plot because when he saw Renno's car drive up the long dirt driveway his paranoia got the better of him and he ran out the back of the house and into the scrub. He was shirtless, no shoes and hiding behind some trees. The Worm was yelling out to him to come back and that it was just Renno, who was his mate. 'Bullshit. It's the cops,' Lance yelled out.

After about 10 minutes of convincing him Renno wasn't a cop, Lance slowly headed back up to the house, yet still very wary. Sweat poured off him in sheets, his pupils two black holes swallowing what little reason he had left. In one hand, a machete—rusted, notched and swinging like an extension of his madness that he had used to cut through the bushes.

This was *Crocodile Dundee* meets *Wolf Creek*. As soon as he clocked Renno, Lance stopped dead. 'You're a fuckin' cop,' he screamed.

'Me? Dressed like this?' T-shirt. Thongs. Half a meat pie sweating on the dash. Not exactly cop material. For thirty long, breathless minutes, Renno stood there in the midday heat, getting grilled like a Bunnings sausage while Lance danced on the edge of full-blown psychosis. He waved the machete with wild flourishes, a conductor orchestrating madness, spit flying as he ranted about wiretaps, surveillance, demons in his TV.

Then—snap. He turned on The Worm. 'You lied to me, ya dog! You fuckin' lied!' Without warning, Lance lunged. The machete came within inches of The Worm's guts. The Worm stumbled back, hands up, trying to talk him down, but the bloodlust was already there, pulsing behind Lance's eyes. Renno barely breathed. Then Lance turned again. Now, it was Renno's turn.

The machete was suddenly at Renno's throat, cold steel pressing against his skin, the edge trembling in Lance's white-knuckled grip. Renno didn't flinch; he couldn't. His heart jackhammered in his chest, but his face stayed blank, calm. The only thing that moved was the bead of sweat trailing down his temple. Lance's eyes twitched.

'You're lying to me. I can *see* it.'

And then finally, The Worm stepped in. 'Oi! Calm down, Lance! He's my mate. He's not a fuckin' cop. You've gotta trust me.'

'Why would I trust you? You're a low dog cunt, you would sell your grandmother out.' Lance twitched again, eyes darting between them. Then he lowered the blade, slowly… but not all the way. Just enough for the two men to feel like they could breathe again. They sensed that they still weren't entirely out of the woods. Renno's pulse was still thundering in his ears. His neck burned where the machete had kissed his skin, and his brain was fizzing with fury and disbelief. The rules didn't matter anymore. His training? Gone. His cover? Who the fuck was Renno anyway?

Inside the house was a tomb of sweat and smoke, the curtains drawn tight like they were hiding something darker than sunlight. On the coffee table, a homemade bong fashioned from a sun-bleached juice bottle, its green hose trailing like a hospital line for addicts. The thing reeked of desperation and backyard engineering. Renno didn't hesitate. He dropped onto the crusty couch with the grace of a man completely over it, grabbed the bottle like it was a life saver, lit the scorched cone and drew deep. The water bubbled like a fountain of sin. Chemical, sharp, familiar. *Sweet. Fucking. Mercy.* He coughed it out, eyes watering, chest rattling like a kicked dog, then passed it wordlessly to Lance, who was still standing, twitching, eyes narrowed. He looked at Renno like he'd just been offered a truce in a language he barely understood. Finally, he took it out of Renno's hands. And hit it. Hard. The shift was subtle at first. A crack in the madness.

One cone turned into three. Then five. They passed the bottle back and forth like two twitchy Wimbledon players in a match no one wanted to win. Words slowed. The rants softened. Lance's jaw unclenched. At some point, the machete vanished from his hand, slipped away, forgotten, now resting like a sleeping dog beside the couch. Renno stared at it, blinking through the haze. He could still feel the steel on his throat, still hear Lance's voice echoing in his skull. But he didn't say a word. He just took another hit. He allowed the numbness in. Let the lines blur a little more. For now, he was alive. And in this world? That was enough.

Then it hit him. Like a gut punch from nowhere. A cold, sharp jolt to the chest. The wire. Still taped beneath his shirt. Still live. Renno froze. His skin crawled with the sudden weight of it, like it was glowing, pulsing, screaming. Every creaking floorboard sounded like boots. Every shadow twitched like it was holding a rifle. Any second now, the door would explode inward and tactical goggles would fill the room, barking orders, turning this paranoid sitcom into a bloodbath.

He stared at Lance, who was now deep into a slurry of word salad. Something about satellites. Or lizard people. No, that's right, it was about spacemen in silk tights. Or maybe it was the postman working for the police. Renno couldn't tell anymore. Finally, miraculously, Lance hit some kind of psychic timeout. He stared at Renno for a long, glassy second, then wandered out the front, still muttering about 'the good stuff' like a junkie prophet receiving messages from the spirit realm.

As Renno sank further into the couch, he realised it felt like being swallowed by a giant, over-affectionate, fluffy marshmallow—one that somehow also left you feeling like you'd just sprinted a marathon through a heatwave. That's when Renno realised: after chugging cone after cone, he was absolutely ripped. Not just stoned, he was so high he could have applied for citizenship on Mars.

He glanced at the bong and thought of another round. 'Jesus,' he muttered, 'any more baked and I'll be hosting a cooking show with Nigella!' The couch creaked beneath him, almost like it was in on the joke, and he cracked up, giggling into the cushions. The cushions were laughing back at him. And then, Lance was back, looking reborn. Lit up like he'd spoken to the angels—the angels of speed. He dropped a bag of whiz onto the table without a word.

After numerous attempts, Renno peeled himself off the couch with the grace of a crash test dummy and staggered back outside to his car. His brain was working at about a quarter of its normal speed. *Right, let's grab the dosh.* After fumbling around in the car for a minute or so, he finally unearthed the envelope of cash wedged under the seat.

He returned and handed it over to Lance. The exchange was silent. One nod. One bag. Lance was happy and the evidence was secured. And Renno, well, he felt like a ghost. A man floating somewhere between the badge and the abyss. Renno finally climbed back into his car, hands trembling as he fumbled with a battered pack of ciggies. He lit one with a shaky flick of the lighter, dragging smoke deep into his lungs like it might anchor him back to Earth.

Lance swanned over to Renno's car and started acting like they were best friends. 'Hey man, if you need anymore, just come to my place in town okay?' and handed Renno and piece of paper with his address on it.

'Will do man,' replied Renno.

Renno hit the accelerator and took off. 'Just another relaxing afternoon in the bush,' he muttered to himself. But the laughter died quickly. His fingers were still twitching. His skin felt like it was humming. His heartbeat thudded against his ribs like it was trying to break out. Adrenaline and green—two substances that were never meant to party together. One said 'run'. The other said 'melt'. His mind was a war zone, and he couldn't remember whose side he was supposed to be on.

The forty-five-minute drive back to Bundy took about ninety minutes. Renno, in his unhinged state, was unable to push the speedometer past twenty-five clicks. By the time he got home, the sun had dipped behind the scrub and the world outside had gone quiet. Too quiet.

The night ritual back in the unit resumed without ceremony, like muscle memory. Rum. A double shot, no mixer. Then another. Temazepam. One. Then two. Each tablet dissolved into his system like whispers of dreams. He chased them with the burning warmth of Bundaberg Rum, savouring the sensation as if it were a sacred communion, he leaned back, the world around him beginning to warp and shimmer. He pressed play on his favourite tunes, letting the melodies wash over him. The munchies crept in, insistent and demanding, and so Renno reached for two packets of Tim Tams, their chocolatey allure irresistible. Each bite was a revelation, a burst of flavour that sent ripples of ecstasy through his senses.

Sinking deeper into the plush embrace of the couch, Renno felt utterly wrecked. Time slowed to a crawl; every moment stretched and twisted. The music enveloped him, each note vibrating in harmony as if it were a symphony performed by fourteen different speakers, all conversing with one another in a cosmic dialogue.

He cranked up the volume, the sound cascading through the room like waves of colour. Laying back, he closed his eyes, surrendering to the kaleidoscope of sensations. Each breath was a journey, each heartbeat a reminder of the wonder swirling around him. Everything was alive, pulsing, breathing, dancing in the vibrant tapestry of his mind.

Finally, he collapsed into bed, the mattress cracking under his weight as he leaned over to flick off the lights. The room swallowed him whole. Darkness pressed in, thick and absolute. The ceiling fan ticked like a metronome for madness. Somewhere in the black, the shadows moved. Or maybe they didn't. But Renno saw it. Something.

A shape in the doorway. Still. Watching. Renno stared until his eyes burned, skin crawling under the weight of something unseen. Finally, he summoned the nerve to flick the light switch on. Nothing. The doorway was empty. Just a hole in the wall shaped like dread.

Flick. Off.

There. Again. The figure. A silhouette not shaped by chance.

Flick. On.

Gone.

It was like playing chicken with his own fear. Three, maybe four times Renno did that. Light on. Gone. Light off. Back again. His heart slammed against his ribs with each pass. He couldn't tell anymore if he was hallucinating, dreaming, or just unravelling completely. 'Come on, Temazepam,' Renno whispered. 'Do your thing.' And slowly, like thick fog rolling in from the cane fields, the pills took hold. The edges dulled. The panic numbed. His thoughts drifted like smoke, untethered and heavy. With a final breath, Renno gave in.

What came was a night of fractured dreams—scenes that felt more real than the waking world. Men with machetes. Dogs with human eyes. The sound of radios whispering his name from inside the walls. And always, that shadow in the doorway. Just watching and waiting.

# 33

# TWILIGHT ZONE TANGO

By the time Renno woke at ten the next morning, the sun was punching through his curtains like it had a personal vendetta against his hangover. His head throbbed and his mouth felt like it had been carpet-bombed with rum and ashtrays. His phone buzzed on the bedside table like a fly trapped in a jar. He cracked one eye open and squinted at the screen. Controller Beardy. The only bloke who could make a phone call feel like a summons to the principal's office.

'Oi, Renno,' Beardy's voice hit him like a slap. 'Get your lazy arse over to my unit. We need a serious chinwag.'

Renno groaned, rolling over. 'Yeah, nah, mate. I'm rooted. Got a date with my pillow and maybe six more hours of unconsciousness.'

'Nope! Listen here, you muppet,' Beardy snapped, full fire and brimstone now. 'If you don't waddle over here right this second, I swear I'll swing by your place, tip out every drop of rum you've got, and take a glorious piss all over your pillows and blankets.' He was laughing now, unhinged. 'And I'll tell everyone you were caught sipping a Bacardi Cruiser in a bubble bath with Enya playing in the background!'

Renno sighed. Beardy wasn't bluffing. The last time Renno ignored one of his 'urgent' calls, it ended with a karaoke machine, a spicy meat pie and a formal warning from the building manager.

'Okay, keep ya knickers on. I'll jump in the 'Eiffel Tower' and head straight over,' Renno said.

As he stumbled towards the shower, Renno shook his head, chuckling. Only Beardy could turn a wake-up call into a full-blown hostage negotiation. But that was just par for the course in their friendship—equal parts chaos, threats, rum and laughter. And honestly, he wouldn't have it any other way.

Beardy didn't waste time with pleasantries when Renno caught up with him and handed him the bag of speed he scored from Lance.

'We need to get those fuckin' guns back, Renno,' he said, beer in one hand, voice low and serious.

'What guns?'

The mood had shifted. It turned out that Lance and his merry band of drug-fuelled idiots had pulled off a break-in at the local gun shop. Word spread faster than a dose of herpes at schoolies week.

Twenty firearms gone. No suspects in custody. And the rumour mill? Spinning like a pokie machine on free play.

Everyone had a theory, from the bloke at the servo to the lady who walked her cat in a pram. Beardy didn't mince his words. 'HQ wants eyes on Lance. Today.' So much for easing into the day with a bit of greasy food and a few hours on the punt. Renno nodded, knowing full well this wasn't a choice. When the bosses said jump, you didn't ask how high—you just checked your shoelaces and prayed the landing wouldn't break you. He grabbed his keys and jumped into his Ford. A mixed cassette tape clicked into place, the speakers coughing to life with Slayer's *Dead Skin Mask*. The timing was poetic.

'*Dance with the dead in my dreams, Listen to their hallowed screams, The dead have taken my soul, Temptation's lost all control.*'

Renno smirked. The lyrics read like the pages of his life story.

Lance lived in a little two-bedroom unit in a rundown 1960s complex that looked as though it had been given up on decades ago. Peeling paint, rusted fly screens and a vibe that screamed 'you're gonna have a bad time'. Approaching the unit, Renno sighed and then knocked. The door creaked open and, standing there like a junkie scarecrow, was a fella named Drew P Balz—a local gun nut with the social graces of a pissed-off wombat. Most people just called him 'Droopy'. His pupils were doing laps; nose crusted and jaw ticking like a clock with bad wiring. And just to really kick things off, he had a handgun pointed directly at Renno's face.

From the look of him, Droopy had more than likely spent the night spooning the weapon after indulging in some of Lance's crooked product. His expression said one thing: Unhinged. Fully, completely, gloriously unhinged.

'What do you want, cunt?' Droopy barked, eyes wide and twitching like a bush wallaby frozen in the headlights at midnight. Renno's stomach dropped. The gun in Droopy's hand wasn't shaking. He opened his mouth, ready to talk his way out of it. And then, like some bizarre good fortune, Lance stumbled out of the back room, shirtless, eyes crusted, looking like he'd just crawled out of a three-day bender.

'Droopy, ya fuckwit,' Lance slurred, rubbing his face. 'That's Renno. He's cool, man.' This was a massive change in attitude from the last time Renno saw Lance. Obviously, he hadn't been using his own product. Reluctantly, Droopy lowered the gun and placed it on a coffee table. Renno then struck like a whip, his right hand clamping around Droopy's throat as he drove him hard against the wall. Droopy's breath caught mid-gasp, his hands twitching, caught somewhere between fight, freeze and fuck it. Renno didn't say a word. He just stared into Droopy's eyes menacingly. Twenty seconds of silence. No blink. No bluff. Just pressure and presence. Then, without a sound, Renno let go, turned and sat down on the couch like he was settling into his own lounge room. This wasn't planned it was a real response to having a gun in the face. Renno had been living that life so much that it was just natural.

The air was thick now. Tense. Sizzling. Like something could explode any second. Lance tried to cut the tension. 'Jesus, have you two girls had enough? Kiss and make up, will ya?' Droopy's stare didn't waver. Neither did Renno's. The whole room was stuck in a standoff until Renno, ever the wildcard, decided to break the silence his way. He whipped out his Japanese throwing knife. The blade caught the flickering fluorescent light, flashing like a predator's eye. He waved it around with the gleeful recklessness of a kid showing off his new toy, a wild grin plastered across his face. Droopy and Lance instinctively jumped back, eyes wide, faces pale. Renno's unpredictability had them rattled. 'Sharp as hell! Cop a look at this beauty,' Renno cackled, eyes dancing with mischief and madness. Then, thwack—he hurled the knife into the wall just behind Droopy's head.

Droopy froze for a beat, adrenaline still thumping, then stepped forward, curiosity pushing past fear. He plucked the knife from the wall and turned it over in his hands, inspecting it like he'd just stumbled onto buried treasure. His eyebrows shot up, impressed. The blade was immaculate. Razor-edged. A reflection of Renno's bizarre obsession with sharp, shiny, dangerous things. Then, in a move that twisted the tension even tighter, Renno snatched the knife out of Droopy's hands and handed it to Lance. His only weapon just handed over, no strings attached. It was either a wild gamble or a strange signal of trust.

'You sure about this?' Lance muttered, barely audible.

Renno just shrugged, grin unwavering. 'Mate, every time I use it, I deadset reckon I'm gonna lose the top of me thumb.'

He leaned in, voice causal now. 'Hey thanks for that stuff yesterday.'

'No probs man, All good hey?' replied Lance.

'Yeah man all good. I might get more next week hey.'

'Too easy.'

Lance gripped the knife by the handle gave it a go, throwing it twice into the wall. Hyped by the action, Droopy darted off to fetch a black pen to scrawl a crude target on the gyprock. The three of them started playing like bored kids stuck inside on a rainy day. All the tension had gone in the air and the room was filled with laughter.

Then Renno dropped it.

'But I need something better, mate. You know where I can get anything?' His tone was casual but direct.

Lance raised an eyebrow. 'Like what?'

Renno glanced left, then right, like they were in a crowded bar instead of a drug den. Then he shaped his hand into a mock pistol, thumb up, finger out.

'A bang bang.'

Silence. Heavy and long. Renno felt it in his chest. Fuck. Too much, too soon. Lance looked at Droopy, and Droopy looked back. Just the slightest nod between them.

'You got a car?' Lance asked, voice flat and serious now.

'Yeah, out front.'

'Let's go.'

They had fallen for it. Renno was feeling like he was unstoppable and had a very misguided thought to himself. *I'm too good for this job.*

Next thing, Renno was behind the wheel. Lance was in the passenger seat, fiddling with a police scanner he carried as if it were second nature to him. Droopy sat in the back, still gripping his pistol like it was the only thing keeping him tethered to this world.

The mood had shifted again. The game was over. No one said a word. Renno could see Lance feverishly texting on his phone.

'Where we going?' Renno asked.

'Just start driving. I'll direct you,' Lance snapped, barking orders like the captain of a sinking ship.

They were cruising through the chaos of Bundy's CBD when Renno slammed on the brakes so hard the tyres screamed. His head whipped around like it was on a swivel.

'What the fuck are you doing?' Lance shouted, gripping the dash like it might detach and rocket them out of there.

But Renno wasn't listening. He was somewhere else, eyes locked on the figure of a woman walking up the footpath in a blue sundress, long dark hair flowing behind her like something out of a dream. She slipped through the doors of the Old Bundy Tavern like she owned the joint.

'I gotta go back. I swear that was Karen!'

He flung himself out the door, seatbelt trying to choke him back into reality. Lance reeled. 'Mate, we don't have time for a bloody girl hunt! Jesus Christ, stay in the car!'

But Renno was already halfway to the pub, fired up on a mix of rum, temazepam and enough weed to make Snoop Dogg take a knee. His heart was pounding. It had to be her. It had to be. Maybe she'd faked her death, started fresh in Bundy, running a fruit stand by day and ruling the town by night. It didn't matter how insane it sounded. It felt real.

The car sat idling in the middle of the street, door wide open. But Renno didn't care. He burst through the tavern doors only to come face to face with a startled, blonde backpacker who was getting ready to open the pub.

'Where's Karen?'

'What?' The woman was clearly confused. 'I'm the only one here.'

Renno stared, dumbfounded. Shocked. Then, nothing. Just the hollow thud of reality hitting him in the chest. He trudged back to the car, shoulders sagging, feet dragging like he'd been shot in both legs. Lance was still frozen in place, knuckles white, shaking his head like he'd just seen the future and it looked bleak.

'You're off your fuckin' rocker, mate,' Lance muttered. 'We don't have all bloody day. Who the fuck was that?'

'Nah no one,' replied Renno.

Then after about 30 seconds of silence Renno thought he better explain. 'I thought it was some backpacker that I fucked a couple of weeks ago,' Renno blurted.

'Ah fucken soap dodgers,' laughed Droopy.

'Yeah they love diving off the bridge hey Droops?' Lance joined in laughing with Droopy as though it was a private joke.

Renno thought this would be a good time to quiz them about Caroline.

'I fucken heard about that pommy girl a couple of months ago, did she jump?' asked Renno.

Both blokes stopped laughing almost at the same time and then looked straight out the window.

Still looking out the window, Lance muttered, 'Just drive will ya.'

Renno slumped back in his seat, eyes glazed, still floating somewhere between his location and a fantasy where love could outlive a ghost. Because in Renno's world, anything was possible, logic had long since packed its bags and caught a bus out of town. Normal didn't exist anymore.

In his mind, Karen was still out there, alive and thriving, probably lounging on a beach somewhere, sipping a piña colada with that cheeky half smile she used to flash when things got weird. He just had to find her. Maybe convince her to ditch the imaginary fruit stand gig and ride shotgun on a real adventure. If only he could drag his head out of the clouds long enough to focus on the road in front of him.

By now, the day was slipping into late afternoon, and the sun was lying low, decorating the sky with streaks of pink and orange. *Perhaps a drunken artist has been let loose up there with a paintbrush.*

As the trio drove out of town, Renno noted that the backroads were getting narrower, more twisted. It felt like he was driving straight into a dead end. 'Turn left here,' Lance said suddenly, pointing at a gap in the pines. Renno flicked the wheel without a word, and

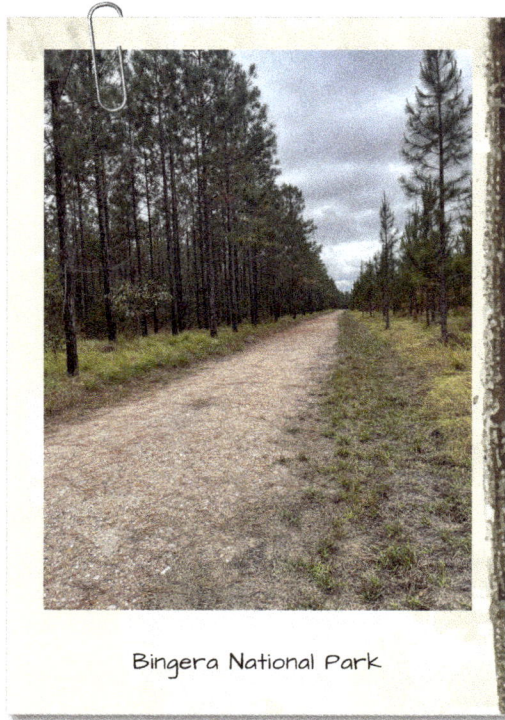

Bingera National Park

just like that, they slipped into Bingera National Park, a place Lance claimed was the burial ground for stolen guns. As the car edged deeper into the shadows, Renno felt his stomach drop. The track wound in a full kilometre from the main road, and before long, the last of the sunlight vanished behind the canopy. The bush was still, heavy and almost too quiet—like it was holding its breath. The trees closed in overhead, tall and skinny like silent spectators, watching everything unfold with knowing smirks. It was the kind of place where you don't just lose phone reception, you lose your grip on reality.

Renno scanned the darkness, heart thudding and mind reeling. *This has all the ingredients of a Friday the 13th movie. All we need now is Jason with his hockey mask to show up,* Renno thought to himself. 'Oh, brilliant,' he muttered out loud—sarcasm laced with dread. *This is how I go out. Seeya world… offed in the middle of the sticks by a bunch of loose units, playing Indiana Jones with buried rifles. Perfect.* Renno had seen some weird shit in his time, but this? This was next level.

As the car crunched to a stop on the dirt track, all three doors swung open.

Renno stepped out first and froze. A bloke emerged from behind a row of pine trees, shotgun in hand, cradled like a newborn. *Holy shit, this is a fuckin' setup.* The air was thick—quiet and eerie, as though the bush itself was holding its breath. Droopy climbed out next, hand hovering near his waistband. Lance strolled around casually, barely sparing the armed man a glance. 'That's just Kev. Kev the Head,' Lance said, waving it off like he was introducing a mate at the pub. 'He's with me.' He wasn't lying about Kev's name. The cunt had a massive noggin with a skinny body that reminded Renno of a Chuppa Chup. Renno didn't move. His heart was doing burnouts inside his chest. He glanced at the car. Door still open. Engine still ticking. *Could make a run for it. Nah, too late for that.*

As the shadows danced around him, he half expected to spot a sign that read: 'Welcome to the Twilight Zone.' And that's when it happened. Droopy jammed the gun against Renno's head, the cold metal pressing into his temple like a trigger warning from the universe. Renno thought about the recording device tucked deep inside his jeans. *Ha, a lot of good it will do now.*

There was only one way out of this: to reason with a bunch of gun-toting junkies. *Great.*

'Listen, fellas,' he began, trying to sound calm while sweat dripped down his chest. 'I probably don't need the gun anymore. I gotta head back.' He turned to walk to the car, trying to ignore the cold press of metal against his head. No one moved. They just stared him down, unmoving and threatening. Renno felt the paranoia crawl under his skin. This was it. The forest swallowed sound. Even the birds had gone quiet. There would be no finding him. *Well, if I'm going out, at least I'll have a cracking story for the big fella upstairs.*

Maybe a joke would ease the tension. No such luck. 'Oi, fellas. What do you reckon we crack a few tins instead? I've got an esky full of piss in the back. Still nothing. Lance was wandering through the trees, rustling like a bush pig on a scavenger hunt. Droopy and Kev

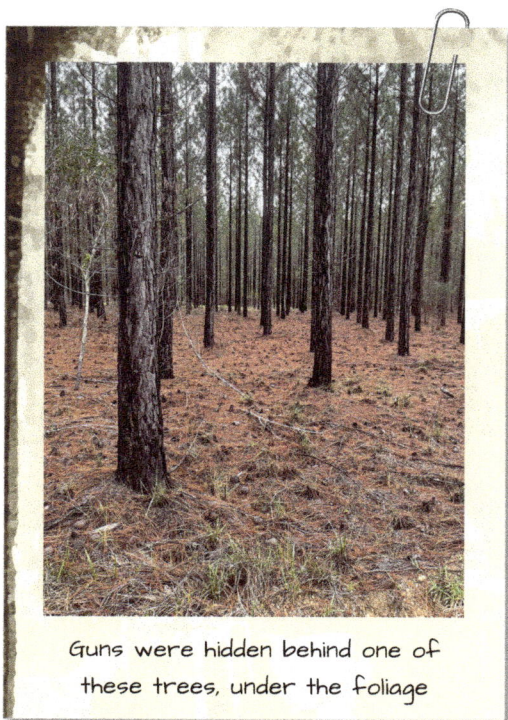

Guns were hidden behind one of these trees, under the foliage

the Head weren't biting. Twenty, thirty minutes dragged by with Renno trying to keep the mood from slipping into murder territory.

Then finally. A break in the stillness. 'Found it! Over here,' Lance called from deep in the trees.

Droopy cocked his head. 'Let's go.'

Renno followed, every step heavier than the last. His feet dragged. His brain screamed. His gut was numb. They were walking towards a massive pine trunk, and he was sure Lance had been digging his grave behind it. A strange calm settled over his mind and body. *Maybe this is it. Maybe someone's finally gonna put me out of my misery.*

Then came the panic. *What if no one finds my body?* He closed his eyes as they rounded the tree, bracing for the bang. Nothing. Renno opened his eyes. Lance was standing over a duffle bag full of guns, grinning. Droopy and Kev the Head were pissing themselves laughing.

'Nice one, fellas. You got me,' Renno said, half choking, half laughing.

'Fuckin' hell. That was a good one,' Lance howled, wiping tears from his eyes. 'So, which one do you want?'

Renno peered into the bag. 'How many are in there?'

Lance shrugged. 'Dunno. About twenty or so.'

Renno grinned. 'Fuck it. I'll take the lot.' Why not? Technically, recovering all the stolen firearms was just good police work.

Lance snorted. 'Nah, got a few buyers already lined up.'

Renno rummaged through the bag of weapons and pulled out two Rugers, still in their plastic cases. 'You've gotta be shitting me,' he said, holding them like buried treasure. 'These are gonna make a hell of a bang. How much?'

Lance didn't hesitate. 'Fifteen hundred each.'

'Sweet. Let me hit the ATM on the way back.'

As he steered the car back to town, Renno couldn't help but silently congratulate himself. The Rugers were tucked safely in the boot and AC/DC's *Moneytalks* was blaring through the speakers. The Bundy boys were in a good mood, laughing and hollering like they'd just pulled off the heist of the decade. They pulled up at Lance's place.

'Shit, I forgot to hit the ATM,' Renno swore.

Lance just waved it off. 'How much ya got on ya?'

Renno checked his pocket. 'Three hundred.'

'Ah, fuck it, that'll do today – but you owe me.'

'Bang. There ya go.' Renno grinned as he flicked the notes over. He jumped back into the driver's seat, slammed his foot on the accelerator and tore down the road towards Beardy's unit. When he arrived, he popped the boot and hauled out the two handguns. *What a legend.*

Inside, Beardy leant against the wall, unimpressed. And then he spotted the guns. His eyebrows shot up in surprise. He recovered quickly.

'That all you got, mate?'

'Yeah, mate,' Renno shrugged, trying to play it cool. 'That's all I could scrounge up. The rest were already snapped up.'

'For fuck's sake, Renno. We needed the whole bloody arsenal,' Beardy groaned, raking a hand through his mess of hair.

Renno held firm, still riding the high. 'Yeah, I know that. But it wasn't exactly a stroll through the fuckin' park,' he explained, launching into a rapid-fire rundown of Droopy, the gun to his head and the pine forest stunt that nearly left him six feet under. 'I thought I was a goner. You could have been out there digging up a shallow grave with my name on it!'

Beardy scratched at his head, clearly trying to process it all. 'Alright,' he muttered, 'but what the hell am I supposed to tell HQ?'

Renno just shrugged. 'Don't give a fuck.'

Beardy's eyes bulged. 'How much did this set us back, then?'

'Fifteen hundred each,' Renno said, deadpan.

Beardy nearly choked. 'You're fuckin' kidding me?'

Renno let the tension hang, then smirked. 'But… I have done something which will make you look good. I talked him down. Three hundred for both.'

Beardy blinked like he'd misheard. 'How the fuck did you manage that?'

Renno leaned back, cocky as ever. 'Mate, I keep tellin' ya, I'm the best in the game. I could sell a kebab to a Lebanese bloke at two in the morning after a night on the tins.'

With a triumphant laugh, he grabbed a forty-pound bottle of rum from the fridge. 'Time to head home and have a few. I need enough to pass out and forget this bloody day.'

As he walked out, Beardy just shook his head, muttering with a half-smile, 'You're a bloody legend, Renno.'

'I know, cunt,' replied Renno giggling his head off.

# 34

# DOGS ARE TALKIN'

As the chaos of Bundy brewed hotter, a storm arrived wearing mirrored sunglasses and a smirk. Detective Senior Sergeant Eric Pouch-House from the drug squad, known as 'The Gambler,' rolled into town like a dodgy Elvis impersonator—flashy, loud and impossible to ignore. Everyone knew his reputation: a chronic punter with a knack for losing houses and marriages like they were scratchies. Rumour had it that he had skimmed more from drug warrants than a pokie machine on a pension day, but no matter how dirty the whispers got, the bosses kept promoting him like he was next in line for sainthood. This name was familiar. For the life of him Renno couldn't place him. *Hang on… Oh no! Not the Detective from the pub!*

So, when he rocked up unannounced to The Worm's bush shack, the operation was as good as cooked. The Gambler swaggered across the dry dirt with all the subtlety of a parade float. The Worm watched from the back steps, lighting a rollie with shaking hands.

'Forget the local detectives,' The Gambler drawled. 'You work for me now.' Before The Worm could respond, the bloke slapped a crisp fifty into his hand like it was a golden ticket. 'Everyone's got a price, mate. Yours just got found.'

With that, he was gone, back in his car, trailing ego and exhaust. The Worm sat for a long while, staring at the fifty, wondering if it would catch fire in his hand. That night, the phone calls started, midnight threats that blurred the line between drunken rants and genuine menace. 'Oi, cunt,' The Gambler slurred down the line, laughter echoing behind him. 'Remember who's got the upper hand. Cross me, and you'll disappear.'

After a week of worry, The Worm rang Renno in a panic, words tumbling out like marbles on concrete.

'He's gonna kill me, mate! I can't handle this shit!'

'Relax,' came Renno's blunt reply. 'He's a pisshead playing tough guy. Let me sort it.'

Renno swung by Beardy's unit to debrief. Beardy scratched at his chin, muttering like a man trying to solve a puzzle with missing pieces.

'Fuck me. This is bad. That clown's untouchable.' He stood abruptly. 'Alright. I'm heading to Brissy. You go take The Worm out, get him back onside. Piss, pool, the works. Just keep the bastard from bolting.'

A happy informant is a useful informant.

Following orders, Renno scooped up The Worm and off they went to the neighbouring town of Gin Gin for a good ol' fashioned Friday blowout at the country pub. The joint was humming, schooners clinking, cane farmers swapping yarns under sweat-stained Akubras. Renno was that hungry he could have eaten a dead rat and made soup with the trap it was caught in. A bloke at the bar, who Renno dubbed the Bull, sat there, tattooed and terrifying. After a few beers and two thick T-bones that could double as pillows, Renno had the bar eating out of his hand. He cracked jokes, stirred the locals and played pool like a man on a mission. As he washed down the last bite of his steak with another mouthful of beer, he leaned back, letting out a satisfied sigh. 'This is living. I'm as full as a centipede's sock drawer. A T-bone, a couple of beers and the camaraderie of a good country pub, it doesn't get much better than this.'

And as the sun set outside, casting a golden glow through the pub windows, Renno couldn't help but feel grateful for that Aussie way of living. He wouldn't trade it for the world. 'How about some pool? My shout,' Renno grinned at The Worm, buying two double rums and dropping coins on the edge of the pool table. They faced off against two wiry farmhands from a local cane property. The blokes were downing rum like the best of them. One's name was Kane, so Renno dubbed him 'Kane Crusher'. The other was Frank, naturally nicknamed 'Fertiliser Frank'. Four games in, Renno and The Worm were up four to nil. The locals weren't thrilled. 'Nice shot, Crusher,' Renno jeered. 'Did your missus teach ya how to play?'

Game five, and the mood soured like a warm VB.

'You call that a shot?' Fertiliser yelled, flinging his cue like it was a sword. Crusher, eyes bulging and mullet flaring with fury, roared back, 'At least I'm not playing like a bloody girl!'

Then... snap. Like a gunshot in a cathedral, the cue shattered across Fertiliser's skull. All hell broke loose. In a split-second frenzy, fists erupted like fireworks. Crusher lunged for Renno, but he ducked low, the punch sailing past and smacking The Worm clean on the nose. Reeling back, The Worm crashed into a table, sending beer and chips flying across the pub floor.

Renno bounced up and drove a thunderous right hook into Crusher's face— cartilage cracked, blood sprayed like confetti. The crowd gasped and then roared.

'Oi! Watch it, mate,' a leather-clad bikie snarled, wiping Bundy rum from his beard.

'Not my fault, you muppet,' The Worm shot back, hurling a haymaker that missed everyone and splintered the bar. The publican's eyes bulged like those belonging to a cartoon character.

'Right, that's it,' he bellowed from behind the bar, reaching his limit and hurling a towel like a white flag. 'Settle it down or fuck off! I'm not running a bloody zoo!'

But the brawl had found its rhythm. Bull leapt in like it was State of Origin '89, spilling his beer and swinging wild. He caught a bikie with a sledgehammer punch that dropped him flat. The bar erupted. That was Fertiliser's cue. He swaggered up to Bull.

'You think you're tough, mate?'

'Only when I'm sober,' Bull retaliated, raising his glass. 'Which I'm bloody not.' They collided like freight trains. Renno, grabbing The Worm off the floor, made the executive decision: time to vanish.

'Exit, stage left,' he muttered, dragging The Worm out the side door.

As they bolted towards the car and peeled onto Gin Gin Road, both men laughed like lunatics, nursing bruises and spilt beers.

'Not bad for a quiet night,' Renno chuckled.

'Yeah, but I don't think I'll be popping my head in there anytime too soon,' The Worm replied with blood flowing from his nose.

'Let's hit Bundy tomorrow, lunch run. I'll pick you up,' Renno enthused.

'Can't. Gotta take the missus to the doc.'

'No worries. Gimme a bell when you're home.'

The car came to a stop in front of The Worm's house. Renno watched as his hopeless informant stumbled up the dusty drive. Once The Worm disappeared from view, Renno reached for his phone.

'The Worm is back on board. All good.'

'Yeah, well… not exactly,' came Beardy's uneasy reply. 'Look, I'm heading back from Brissy. We'll talk in the morning, alright.'

And with that, he hung up.

Back at his unit, Renno poured himself a glass of rum big enough to tranquilise livestock, downed two temazepam and collapsed.

The next morning, Beardy arrived looking like he'd bathed in bad news. Renno glanced up, a flicker of cautious optimism in his voice.

'How'd it go down there?'

Beardy let out a heavy sigh, sinking into the chair like he was carrying the weight of every bad decision made in the last week. 'Mate, it's a bloody disaster. The Gambler's gone and blown it wide open.'

Renno frowned. 'How?'

'He's been mouthing off to every crook in town,' Beardy said, rubbing his temples. 'Told 'em The Worm's a dog and you're a narc.'

Renno scoffed, but his tone was defiant. 'Yeah? So what? I've dealt with worse. I can clean this up. Been there, done that, got the T-shirt, twice.'

Beardy didn't smile. He leaned forward, voice low and grim. 'Yeah, I know you can. But the bosses… they're shitting themselves. They're not worried about your safety or how this mess affects you. They're worried you'll lawyer up. Maybe sue the department. That's what's keeping them awake at night, not you bleeding out in the cane fields.'

Renno let out a bitter chuckle, eyes narrowing. 'Yeah, I bloody know that. Feelings don't mean shit when it comes to politics.'

Beardy ran a hand through his beard, now wirier and wilder than ever, as if it had absorbed every ounce of stress he'd endured.

'And here's the kicker,' he said, pausing for dramatic effect. 'They've wrapped up the job. It's done. Shut down. No warning, no debrief. Just over. We're heading home tonight.'

Renno's shoulders stiffened, his heart thumping once in protest. 'What?'

'Witness protection's coming in to scoop up The Worm and his family,' Beardy said flatly. 'You and me, we pack up and piss off. This one's finished, mate.'

Renno stared at him for a bit, eyes wide, the words sinking in like stones. 'For fuck's sake.'

No one is getting charged as the whole job is now compromised and the informant's safety is paramount.

Beardy didn't say anything for a moment. He just sat there scratching at the greying bristle on his jaw like he was trying to dig an answer out of his own skin. Then he nudged Renno with an elbow and offered a sly grin.

'Oi, you still remember where those guns are stashed in the forest?'

Renno blinked, still processing the sudden implosion of the entire op.

'Shit. Sort of. Probably right next to the shallow grave I almost ended up in.'

Beardy chuckled in response. 'Perfect. We'll head out at midnight and grab 'em on the way home.'

Renno shook his head, running a hand through his hair. 'Great. Nothing like a midnight stroll through pitch-black bushland to really boost my confidence.'

Beardy shrugged like it was just another Tuesday. 'Oh well. Let's give it a red-hot crack.'

Renno's first step was to clear and clean out the unit. When he was finished, the place looked fit for a royal visit—bleached bathroom, straightened bed, even the fridge door had been wiped clean. Then, just for laughs, he paid two weeks' rent in advance. Why not? It wasn't his money. He tossed the keys to the manager and muttered something about 'moving on to bigger things.'

Just before midnight, he parked outside Beardy's unit—headlights off, engine idling. The two of them looked like dodgy night watchmen heading off to rob a cemetery—hoodies up, bags in the back, caffeine and stupidity coursing through their veins. Driving south in a convoy heading towards the Baringa National Park, the highway was lit only by the occasional sign and the eerie white of the moon. Renno suddenly veered left onto a rough dirt track. The tyres spat gravel and groaned as they dropped into ruts big enough to swallow a wheel.

'Bloody hell, it's dark,' he muttered, peering into the tree line like it might bite him. 'I'm never gonna remember where old mate stashed that bloody bag.' The further they drove in, the more the world fell away—no streetlights, no sign of human life, not even the chirp of crickets. Just thick black bushland and that strange, humming silence that makes your spine itch. Eventually, Renno rolled to a stop, headlights stabbing into the trees like searchlights. 'I reckon they're down there,' he said, pointing into a shadowy wall of pines and trying to sound more confident than he felt.

Beardy locked his own car doors with a definitive click and shook his head. 'Fuck that! Looks like a horror movie waiting to happen.

Are we about to meet Mike Myers and Freddy Krueger for a midnight barbie?'

Renno groaned. 'I'm tired, Beards. Let's just get this over with before I lose my nerve or the ghosts change their minds.'

With a final swig of lukewarm coffee, Renno stepped out, torch in hand, and disappeared into the dark.

'Mate,' Beardy whispered as they stepped over fallen branches and past towering trees, 'if a drop bear lands on me, I'm suing.' They pushed through the underbrush, swatting mozzies, ducking webs and cursing roots. Renno checked one tree and then the next, retracing steps burned into memory by adrenaline and panic. Then there it was, half-covered in a dusty tarp, just where he remembered. 'Fuck yeah!' he called out. 'Found 'em!'

Beardy nearly face-planted the ground in excitement. 'Quick, grab the bag before the forest decides to claim us both.' Renno slung the duffle over his shoulder, both of them legging it back to their vehicles like kids fleeing a busted party. They didn't stop until their tyres hit bitumen again.

Under the cover of early morning grey, they rolled into Brisbane's inner north. Renno turned off the highway and pulled into a deserted car park behind a government office block, the tyres crunching over loose gravel. With a grunt, he popped the boot, dragged out the duffel and tossed it into the back of Beardy's ute like it was full of dirty laundry instead of black-market handguns. 'There you go,' he muttered, wiping his hands on his jeans. 'The bosses will be thrilled.'

Beardy gave a slow nod, like he couldn't decide whether to laugh or light a cigarette. 'I'll lodge 'em at the exhibits facility and head back to head office. Good work up there, mate. Seriously. But just remember, sometimes the game doesn't go the way you want it to.'

Renno snorted. 'Yeah, yeah. Story of my life.'

He gave a half-hearted wave and turned back towards his own car, his voice trailing behind him. 'Right now, I couldn't give a stuff. I'm off to The Fabulous. Gonna get properly bent.' He didn't wait for Beardy's response.

As Renno drove off, the high of the operation's close started bleeding out of him like warmth from a bad wound. A bitter weight pressed in under his ribs, something darker, heavier than just exhaustion. Renno had gone to Bundaberg hoping for—no, needing—answers. Something to piece together what had happened to Caroline Stuttle. Nineteen. English. Full of dreams. Her life had been carved out of the world in the most senseless, brutal way imaginable. And now, months later, all Renno had was more noise. No justice. No clarity. Just rumours, silence and the kind of sadness that clung to your bones. He wanted to do right by Caroline Stuttle. For her family. For himself. But now, it all felt like a farce. Bundy had chewed him up and spat him out with little more than a couple of Rugers in the boot and another haunted look in the mirror.

Renno arrived on The Fabulous, parked at a mate's place, threw on his boardies and hit the surf like a man possessed. He punched through waves. Let the salt sting his eyes and the ocean knock the breath from his lungs.

That one schooner at the surf club turned into six. Then ten. Then who knows what. The night unravelled in a swirl of laughter, strangers, pool tables and neon haze. A twelve-hour bender that bent time and memory until nothing mattered except the next drink and the beat of the jukebox.

Because it was over.

Operation Fiddle—the chaos, the guns, the paranoia, the shadow play—had been wrapped. Tied off with bullshit, panic and a shallow grave of missed opportunities. Witness protection had swept up The Worm and his family like dust off the floor. The case files were boxed. The bosses at HQ had moved on. And so had Renno—at least on paper.

What followed was downtime. The blank space between operations. No briefings. No aliases. No threats. Just a temporary void. It was meant to be a time for recovery. But no one ever told him how exactly to recover. Time passed and the seasons shifted like smoke, dragging Caroline Stuttle further into memory. But some stories don't fade. They echo.

And then, finally, a break. A name. Ian Douglas Previte, 32, was charged with Caroline's murder. Previte had followed Caroline Stuttle that night across the Burnett Bridge. He'd tried to rip her handbag from her shoulder. She resisted. Fought. Screamed. And so, he'd pushed her. Over the edge. As if her life was worth no more than what she carried in her hands. The real twist came days later—a sucker punch Renno never saw coming. Lance and Droopy—those two cooked-out cockroaches from the gun drop and the machete circus. They'd been there, under the bridge that night. She died while they hid in the shadows, too stoned to move and too scared to matter.

And somehow, that felt like the perfect ending to such a goddamn mess—justice delayed, truth buried and the only people who cared left staring at the waves, trying to forget. Renno didn't know if he wanted to vomit or set something on fire. So instead, he cracked another beer. Because sometimes that's the only justice you get.

# 35

# OPERATION
# ALPHA YEW

The job was simple. Survive long enough to finish it. Operation Yew was a four-month undercover assignment targeting Jimmy Larson, a longstanding methamphetamine supplier deeply entrenched in the north Queensland regions of Mackay and Sarina. It was meant to be surgical—build rapport, make the buys, gather the evidence. But the job quickly spiralled into a psychological grind, stretched across the vast spine of Queensland from Brisbane to Townsville, with Mackay as the unpredictable heartbeat in between. Working under the alias again of Donny, the operation saw constant movement: long hauls up and down the Bruce Highway, meetings with targets in cane fields, sketchy motel rooms and tense dealings in pub car parks. The Marlborough Stretch became a second home to me—a ghost-ridden purgatory between danger and downtime.

# DONNY

The operation kicked off one month after the Bundy gig was closed down. When the bosses said it was time to bring Donny back from wherever he had been hiding, I felt a sense of relief. I knew this character. Knew him better than I knew my real self—whatever real was. More importantly, being Donny meant I could live recklessly under the guise of work—let the anger and frustration out while ignoring what was really going on inside my brain.

And so, I woke Donny up, pulled on his favourite pair of pluggers and got ready to play my part, happy to be tuning out from the shitshow that was my life. That was my specialty—pushing anything resembling reality as far down as I could. Ignorance is bliss, after all. Or so they say.

My point of contact was Rattlesnake, a registered informant from Brisbane with a knack for disappearing, drug binges and sowing suspicion. It was through Rattlesnake that I was introduced to Jimmy, a paranoid but influential dealer suspected of moving large quantities of methamphetamine (or speed, as it is commonly known) under the radar, possibly with protection from a corrupt Mackay-based detective.

For those four months, I survived on adrenaline and instinct, laced with a good dose of rum. I was constantly on the move, constantly lying and trying desperately to keep hold of the thin, fraying thread that still tied the real me back to my life. Peta, my family, my friends—all waiting, yet again, for the real Todd to come home.

The job consumed everything: sleep, sanity, even the shape of who I was. And yet, it worked. Well, it worked in the name of police work—not so much in my own game of life.

# 36

# SHAKY
# INTRODUCTIONS

**D**onny's phone blared to life, shattering the silence of his hangover-addled mind. He rolled over groggily to look at the time. Eight. *Who the hell is calling me at this time of the morning?*

'Hello,' he croaked, voice thick as fog.

'This is Detective Inspector Craven Morehead,' came the clipped voice. 'Donny, pack your bags. You're heading to Mackay today. Report to Detective Sergeant Door at your safe house by nine.'

The line went dead. Donny stared at the phone like it had grown legs and danced off the bedside table.

With a grunt, he rolled out of bed, last night's revelry clinging to him like a bali tattoo. He packed light—enough clothes for a week, a bottle of rum and a packet of smokes—then hit the road, leaving behind the neon haze of The Fabulous. At the safe house, he was greeted by Detective Sergeant Door, a bloke whose face could curdle milk. 'Listen up,' Door said, leaning in like he was passing on state secrets. 'The detectives in Sarina are in deep shit. As you already know, big Jimmy Larson's been running speed for the bikies for years. We've got an informant to introduce you, but here's the kicker—word is that a local detective's dirty. We tread carefully.'

'Great. Just bloody great. Another one,' Donny mumbled, already feeling the pressure. He was told to pick up the registered informant, Rattlesnake, from a house on Brisbane's north side. The drive was set for the next day. No one could tell him how long he would be away— could be two weeks, could be nine months. He packed accordingly.

At dawn, Donny rolled through the sleeping streets and scooped up Rattlesnake, a wiry twenty-year-old who'd spent more time inside than out. They cruised north. By the time they hit the Marlborough stretch, Rattlesnake was twitchy, eyes darting, legs bouncing. He had practically chain smoked White Ox rollies from Brisbane to Mackay.

'Hey,' Donny said, keeping it casual. 'Think you could give Jimmy a bell? Let him know we're rolling into town tonight?'

'Yeah, sure,' Rattlesnake said, voice shaky. He dialled. The phone rang and rang. Nothing. 'I'll try again later,' he mumbled, tossing the phone down like it had betrayed him.

Donny glanced at him. 'Just keep it cool, mate.'

As the highway stretched ahead and darkness closed in, Donny braced for the chaos Mackay had waiting. They rolled into town as the sun dipped low, casting long shadows over streets that smelled like sweat and secrets. Neon signs flickered outside motels and pubs, laughter and shouts spilling into the humid air. Rattlesnake tried Jimmy's number again. He answered, and after a brief chat, he hung up the phone.

'Head to the Austral Hotel,' he directed Donny.

As they steered into the car park, Donny took in the venue. It was the kind that fades into memory. 'Wait here,' Rattlesnake said, tone suddenly serious. 'I'll go in first. You stay put.'

Donny leaned back, eyeing the flickering neon and the shadows dancing beneath it. Time dragged like a bad movie. Then Rattlesnake came barrelling back out, panic etched across his face.

'Let's go. Jimmy's got a gun and he's pissed off!' Rattlesnake barked, diving into the car.

Donny raised an eyebrow. He'd seen this rodeo before, likely just another yarn. Still, he played along. 'Right. Let's go,' he said, firing up the engine and pulling away.

As they cruised through Mackay, Rattlesnake's speed-fuelled jitters gave him away. Donny could see it—he hadn't come down in the last shower. Rattlesnake had scored with the cash he'd been handed.

'I booked us into a seedy motel on the main strip,' Donny said, glancing sideways at the shaking Rattlesnake. 'Two rooms. Side by side. We lay low. We don't leave our rooms till the morning.'

# DONNY

Donny was wrecked. It had been a long drive, not just in terms of distance but in terms of the company. He collapsed into bed, the fluorescent lights buzzing overhead like angry bees. Sleep came fast—but not easy.

The next morning, sunlight sliced through the curtains. Donny, still groggy, knocked on Rattlesnake's door. He was greeted with silence. He knocked harder. Still nothing.

'Oi! You in there?' he called through the door.

Panic crept in. Donny dialled Rattlesnake's number. It went straight to voicemail.

'Fuck. I don't need this.' His anxiety was blooming. He considered his options, kick the door in or ask at the office. He chose the latter. No luck.

And so, his morning was spent scouring town cafés, skate parks and street corners until he finally spotted Rattlesnake swaggering along with two lads, laughing like he hadn't done the dodgy and disappeared. Donny slammed on the brakes, leapt from the car, and charged.

'Oi!' he bellowed, grabbing the snake by the hair and hauling him to the car. 'You can't grab me like that,' Rattlesnake snapped, wide-eyed.

'Yeah? Maybe think of that before going AWOL. You are lucky I didn't break your fuckin' jaw,' Donny shot back.

They drove in silence, the air tense and crackling. Rattlesnake squirmed, avoiding Donny's stare.

'Look. I made up the stuff about Jimmy and the gun,' Rattlesnake confessed. 'I just wanted some gear.'

'No shit, Sherlock,' Donny replied. 'Now ring Jimmy. Set up a meet. Tonight.'

That night, they headed to the Royal Hotel. The pokies whirred, laughter echoed. Rattlesnake spotted Jimmy, hunched at one of the poker machines, eyes locked intently on the screen.

'Oi, Jimmy!' Rattlesnake called out.

Jimmy looked up, wary. 'What do you want?'

'Need to talk. This is the bloke I mentioned. Let's step outside for a minute.'

Jimmy sighed. 'This better be good.'

Outside, under a flickering streetlight, Donny made his pitch. 'Word is, you're the man to talk to about… certain products.'

Jimmy didn't blink. He just stood there, considering Donny.

'I don't deal with just anyone,' he said finally. 'What's your angle?'

Rattlesnake jumped in, 'Donny's solid and got connections.'

'You better not being selling my shit here, I got this territory covered.' Jimmy said.

Donny had to think on his feet, 'Nah mate Brissy.'

Jimmy's dark eyes studied them a moment longer, then he shrugged. 'Alright. I'll give you a shot. Trust is earned. Screw me and you'll be swimming with the fish.'

'Understood,' Donny nodded. 'So, what's the next step?'

'Call next week. I'm waiting on a new batch.'

Donny and Rattlesnake jumped back in the car and started heading back to Brisbane.

# 37

# THE LIGHT CATCHES EVERYTHING

One week later Donny had set the wheels in motion to buy five ounces of speed from Jimmy. 'Meet me at the Caltex just before you hit Sarina,' Jimmy had said. 'I'll be lurking around the back.' His voice oozed calm, but it was the kind of calm that reeked of something wrong, like a snake basking in the sun.

'No worries, mate. I'll give you a bell when I'm an hour out,' Donny replied, masking the churn in his gut with bravado. He felt like a criminal mastermind. If only he had the blueprint.

The highway north was long and mean, and Donny knew it too well by now. The Marlborough stretch was a brutal, lonely expanse of the Bruce Highway that had chewed up better men than him. Nearly four hundred clicks of straight, soul-sapping bitumen, broken only by two 'blink and you'll miss 'em' towns—Marlborough and St Lawrence. Locals had nicknames for it. The Horror Stretch. The Crystal Highway. Names born from whispered stories about murders, disappearances and lights in the treetops that didn't belong to any man or machine. Some said windscreens shattered for no reason. Others swore that headlights blinked into existence from nowhere—only to vanish just as fast. Even wildlife seemed ghostly out there, like something in the trees was daring you to stop.

Donny didn't scare easily, but the Marlborough stretch got under his skin, especially at night. The sky stretched overhead, too wide and too quiet. The stars looked too close, and the darkness felt sentient. He pulled in at St Lawrence to fuel up and shoot the breeze with the servo locals. They spoke like characters from a horror flick.

'Never stop out there after dark,' one old-timer warned. 'Just keep your foot down. Don't look in the mirrors. And whatever you do, don't look back.'

Donny chuckled, but the back of his neck prickled. They told him about folks who hit a roo, pulled over to check the damage and never made it back behind the wheel. Stories of glowing orbs bouncing above the tree line, following drivers like ghosts that hadn't made peace. The Min Min lights, they said. Aboriginal legend. But legends usually didn't feel like they were watching you. Donny shook off the chill and kept rolling north, the highway a black ribbon unravelling into nowhere.

He stopped in Carmila, lit up just enough to feel real. There, under the hum of a streetlamp, he stashed the cash, tested his recording gear and made the necessary calls. Controller first. Then Peta. 'Hey, babe. I'm an hour out from Sarina. Meeting old mate soon. If you don't hear from me in a couple of hours, call the boss,' Donny said, trying to keep his voice light. But Peta's worry came through the line like static. Donny couldn't answer it. Couldn't let it in. He was too deep now and too close.

The trees seemed to lean in as he drove. The dark pressed harder. The road, once endless, now felt like a funnel—tightening with every passing kilometre. His gut clenched as he approached the servo in Sarina. Something felt off. He didn't feel fear exactly, more like being on stage with the spotlight too bright and the trapdoor already open. 'Where are you, you shady bastard?' Donny muttered, scanning the lot. Then he saw it—Jimmy's car, half hidden beneath a tree.

Donny parked, slid out and climbed into Jimmy's passenger seat. The overhead light clicked on bright, revealing way too much.

'Hey, Jimmy. How's it hanging?' he asked, casual as ever.

'Yeah, good. How was the drive?' Jimmy's eyes scanned Donny like he was doing a risk assessment.

'That Marlborough stretch is a fuckin' punish. Goes on forever,' Donny said, shaking his head.

'Doesn't it just,' Jimmy nodded.

Small talk flowed, but Donny's nerves frayed at the edges. Then he looked down. His blood iced over. Somehow, one of the recording wires had snaked down the inside of his black jeans, resting near the bridge of his foot, right where it could catch the light. Right next to his double pluggers.

His first instinct was to cover it. His second was to just let it ride.

Let's make this interesting, he thought. How good am I at bullshit?

He shifted just enough for Jimmy to get a peek, testing the tension like a man poking a crocodile. Jimmy broke the silence. 'I got ya four ounces, mate.'

Donny didn't blink. 'Thought we agreed on five?'

'Did we? Shit. Take it or leave it,' Jimmy shrugged like it was a Sunday market haggle.

Donny kept his tone easy, but his mind was racing. 'Alright, no dramas. Money's in the car. How much is the four? Twenty grand?'

'Five four for an ounce,' Jimmy replied.

'Twenty-one, six hundred.' Donny's answer was almost immediate, his maths riding the adrenaline.

Jimmy smirked. 'Look at you, schoolboy genius.'

'No discount for driving all the way up here?' Donny asked, hoping to squeeze a bit of sympathy from his dealer.

'That's your choice, mate. Go get the cash.'

Donny climbed out slowly, each step feeling like it might set off an alarm. Back at his car, he grabbed the cash, tucked the wire deeper into his jeans and returned to the passenger seat, praying nothing was showing. Common sense, it seemed, had prevailed—he no longer wanted to run the gauntlet with part of the recording device on show.

Donny handed the wad of cash over and forced a grin.

'Here ya go. I'll see you in a week.'

Jimmy took the money without a word, then handed Donny a plastic medicine bottle. Warm. Gooey. Brown. Donny popped the lid and sniffed. The unmistakable stench of methamphetamine—cat piss and battery acid.

'Well, here's to paradise,' he muttered, holding the bottle up to the dome light like it was vintage merlot. Who knew crime would smell this bad?

As Donny slid back into his own car, he rang his controller. 'Got it. I'll see ya in Townsville.' Then he hung up. The tension finally cracked. He revved the engine and Tom Cochrane's *Life is a Highway* blasted from the tape deck. Donny laughed hollow but real. His hands were still shaking. But the job was done—for now.

Heading north to Townsville, Donny figured he had better call Peta. He knew she cared more than he sometimes deserved, and after the night he'd just survived, hearing her voice felt like grabbing onto a rope in the dark. After checking into a low-rent hotel in Townsville, he handed the bottle of speed over to his controller, a quiet exchange that somehow made it feel more real. Evidence bagged and another crime documented and filed away.

For a brief, blissful moment, Donny collapsed onto the bed, letting the adrenaline bleed out of him. But it didn't last. Paperwork waited: notes, statements, transcripts from the recordings stitched to his jeans. It was like being back in high school, cramming for an exam, except the curriculum now was deceit, addiction and a growing taste for risk that Donny couldn't seem to shake. He stayed in Townsville for a week, lying low. Enough time to reset. Enough time, he thought, to let the dust settle. But under it all, the itch was there, and the job wasn't done yet. On the seventh day, he picked up the phone and dialled Jimmy, asking for another five ounces of 'cat's piss'. Jimmy's voice came through flat and sharp, 'Call me when you're an hour out. Meet me at the usual spot.' There was something in Jimmy's tone this time. A coldness and a distance that left Donny with a knot forming in his gut. Something wasn't right. But he told himself it was just paranoia, shrugged it off and rolled on.

Donny cruised back through Ayr, Home Hill, Bowen and Proserpine, the familiar graveyard towns slipping by like tombstones in the dark. Around four hours later, he pulled into Kuttabul to set up. As always, he checked his recording devices, counted out the cash with steady hands and made the obligatory calls—first to his controller and then to Peta. Six Bundy rum cans sat chilling in the esky on the passenger seat, a little liquid courage to ease the knot he couldn't shake. The sun dipped low as Donny rolled back into Mackay, the golden light bleeding out of the cane fields, leaving nothing but long shadows and silence.

When he pulled into the Caltex, Jimmy was nowhere to be found. Donny picked up his phone. 'Take the first dirt road west after the creek, into the cane fields,' Jimmy barked down the line. Donny didn't argue. He flicked the indicator and started driving, the rumble of his engine echoing off the empty buildings. He found the turn-off easily and began weaving deeper into the cane fields, away from the lights, away from witnesses. His every instinct screamed 'trap!'. In the rear-view mirror, an unfamiliar car loomed. Donny's hands tightened on the wheel. His mouth was dry. His heart was a drum in his ears. The car stopped, dust swirling around like shadowy ghosts, as Jimmy walked slowly over to Donny's parked vehicle.

Donny spotted something dark clutched in Jimmy's hand. *A gun?* He couldn't be sure. Jimmy leaned in, eyes drilling into Donny.

'G'day, Jimmy,' Donny forced out, trying his damned hardest to sound casual. 'What's the deal? Why aren't we at the servo?'

Jimmy's voice was a low growl. 'You seen Rattlesnake lately?'

Donny's gut dropped. 'Not for a while, mate. Why's that?'

Jimmy sniffed the air like a wolf catching a scent. 'He rang me the other night. Said to watch you. Said you're not what you claim to be. You're a cop, aren't ya? Setting me up?'

The words hung heavy in the air. And then, without pausing to think, Donny exploded. 'That cunt owes me five fucking grand!' he roared, smashing his fist into the dashboard for effect.

Jimmy flinched. Just a little. But it was enough.

'I've heard that shit before,' Donny continued with his rant. 'He tells people the same thing down in Brisbane. Bet he owes you too, eh?'

The air between them stretched taut, brittle as glass.

'Well? Does he?' Donny shouted, letting the madness pour out— the desperation, the rage.

For a moment, there was only silence, thick and suffocating. Then Jimmy cracked. 'Yeah,' he admitted, almost sheepishly. 'He does.'

Donny leaned forward, voice low and venomous. 'Mate, he said the same about you. I thought you were smarter than that. Maybe you're the liability here. Maybe I shouldn't be doing business with you.'

# DONNY

Donny casually fanned the twenty grand of cash sitting on his lap like a deck of playing cards. It was a not-so-subtle gesture. Jimmy's eyes narrowed and his posture stiffened.

'Nah, fuck that,' Donny snapped, turning the key like he was about to bolt. 'You can get fucked. I'm out.'

'Hold on! I just had to ask ya!' Jimmy blurted, half-panicked now.

Donny kept pushing. 'You didn't have to. I never asked you to disrespect me like that. I thought we had trust. You fucked that.'

Jimmy back-pedalled fast. 'Donny, buddy, it's all good! Here, here's the gear. I'll give you five ounces for twenty-one, six. That's a free one. No dramas, mate!'

Donny sat back, breathing hard, weighing it up. He always knew the risk when going undercover. He knew it could all come unstuck in an instant, but that was the job. And the lure of the score, the bust and the win was too strong to resist. Without a word, he handed over the cash and snatched the gear out of Jimmy's offered hand. The two men exchanged a grim handshake, each knowing they no longer trusted the other. Donny knew he had to lock Jimmy down— he didn't need a dealer on the streets spinning shit that he was a cop. He eased himself out of the car and squared up to Jimmy. Nose-to-nose, Donny stared him down. 'Don't you ever fucking accuse me of that shit again.'

Jimmy wilted under the stare. 'Yeah, buddy. Okay,' he mumbled.

As Donny drove back down the dirt track to safety, he felt like he'd just bluffed his way through a game of Russian roulette and won. This time. His thoughts swirled as he began the trek back down the dreaded Marlborough stretch. By the time he rolled into Rockhampton, four hours later and checked into a shitty hotel, it felt like crossing the finish line of a marathon he hadn't trained for. But in his gut, he knew the race was far from over. And next time, he might not be so lucky.

# 38

# WHITE KNUCKLES AND SEA BREEZES

**B**ack in Brisbane, I threw myself into the illusion of normal life—the illusion of Todd. Dinners with Peta and quiet drinks with his folks. Polite smiles, light chatter and long silences where no one dared ask what I'd been doing on the road. I tried to lean into the calm, but it was like trying to walk on legs that hadn't stopped shaking yet. The adrenaline crash hit hard. Not all at once but in slow, creeping waves that left my limbs heavy and my chest tight. My body had been running hot for weeks, wired for deception, danger and deals that could go sideways in a blink. With the job done for now, everything had shut down—mind and body. The result? I couldn't sit still, but I couldn't move either. Go figure.

Sleep came in jolts, sweat-soaked the sheets. Flashes of headlights in my dreams and the ghost of Jimmy's suspicion still clinging, festering in the back of my mind, much like a cigarette burn.

Desperate to escape the static in my skull, I booked a weekend at the good old sunny Sunshine Coast with Peta. I was grasping at anything that looked, sounded or felt like some form of freedom. *Surely, I can pretend to just be a bloke on holiday? Pretend that I can enjoy lapping up the sunshine, beers and surf.* I almost believed it myself until my phone rang. It was Jimmy.

'Donny! I'm flying down to Caboolture on Friday afternoon. Got another five ounces for ya, mate. No need to drive north.' Jimmy's voice was too cheerful. Like he was offering a lift to the airport, not a trunk full of felonies. I sighed, the image of our weekend plans flickering and dying in front of my eyes. Then I realised that I could make it work—do the deal and still spend my weekend with Peta. It would be a ten-minute detour off the highway. A quick pick-up, just like grabbing a loaf of bread. *I wonder if Peta will go for it?*

Jimmy suggested a hotel near the Bribie turnoff. So, off we set on our unusual getaway. *Where the sun meets sin.* As I pulled the car into the hotel car park, I could feel the tension radiating off Peta. She was gripping the armrest, her eyes scanning every shadow.

'Just… be careful, alright? You know how these things can go,' she said, voice low.

'Relax, babe,' I said, forcing a grin. 'It's just a quick pick-up. Watch the car. If anything looks off, give me a call.' My heart was pounding, but at that moment, I couldn't show it. Inside, the deal went smoothly. Too smoothly. Ten minutes later, I strolled back out—five ounces tucked neatly into my pocket—wearing the grin of a bloke who thought he'd just robbed the universe and got away with it.

'See! Easy as pie!' But Peta wasn't buying my bravado. She was still white-knuckling the door handle.

'Yeah, well, that pie could've been filled with fucking poison,' she snapped, her voice tight with anxiety.

I laughed loudly, adrenaline pumping through my veins. 'C'mon, it's all part of the game.' And, for that moment, I let myself believe that it was—that the game I was playing wasn't warped and fraught with danger. I was caught somewhere between fact and fantasy. *Just a guy on a weekend getaway, beers in the esky, girl by his side. Job well done.* I met up with the controller just up the road and handed over the exhibit without fanfare, as if it were nothing more than a parcel drop. Then, finally, I switched off my phone. No pings. No calls. No dealers. No shadows.

Even with the phone off and the world on mute, sitting there on the beach, something inside me kept humming. It wasn't just adrenaline anymore. It was something worse. Restlessness disguised as purpose. Guilt dressed up as duty. I had Peta beside me, sand between my toes, a cold beer in hand, and yet I still felt like I was watching my life through glass. Inside, I was more Donny than Todd. I knew Todd was in there somewhere, screaming to come home, but Donny kept the door locked. Truthfully, I no longer knew how to be the man I was born to be. The job had carved out too much of the real me—the man my family needed me to be. Peta deserved more, but I kept avoiding, trading away, the part of me that needed to be there for the future. I didn't do it for the money. Not even for the win. I did it because being Donny was the only thing that still made sense.

# 39

# GAME OVER

Four months of dirty deals, sketchy motels, half-truths and late-night drives where every set of headlights in the rear-view could have meant the end. Now, finally, it was time to pull the pin. A couple more buys, one final sting, and then it would all be over, one way or another. Jimmy told Donny he'd be in Brisbane again this weekend. 'Hey Jimmy, I'm holed up at a motel in Hamilton, Brisbane. Swing by when you can,' Donny said down the line, trying to sound like it was just another boring Saturday meeting, not the first move in the endgame.

Enter Detective Sergeant Badger, known to his mates as Mack. Mack was Donny's boss and he was being introduced as his uncle, the man with the money. The unit was a typical motel with two single beds and a mini kitchenette and a table and two chairs. When Jimmy walked through the hotel door, Donny was draped across one of the beds like some washed-up soapie actor, pretending to be relaxed while his heart hammered against the inside of his ribs.

Mack was at the table, stiff and sharp, eyes flicking to the door and back again, the tension in the room thick enough to drown in.

'Jimmy, meet Mack,' Donny said, his voice breezy, his palms sweating. After some awkward handshakes and small talk, Mack leaned in, dropping his voice to a growl.

'Listen here, Jimmy. I'm just the money behind this little venture. I don't touch the product. I don't want my face in your memory bank. After today, you won't see me again. And my name? You didn't hear it. You didn't say it. Capiche?'

Jimmy nodded too fast, too eager. The kind of nod you see from someone who's already halfway to running.

Mack popped open his briefcase, fished out an envelope thick with cash ($22,000 to be exact) and casually flung it towards Donny the whole time still in small talk with Jimmy. Except his aim was catastrophic. The envelope dropped like a brick straight into Donny's lap, slamming square into the crown jewels. Whack! Donny let out a strangled, wounded bellow, doubling over in agony. He writhed across the bed, clutching himself like he'd just been shot. Mack and Jimmy barely noticed. They were too busy locking in the deal, leaving Donny to fight for his life in the background like an extra nobody had scripted.

Somehow, through a blur of tears and curses, Donny snatched up the envelope and passed it to Jimmy, who took it with the careful, confused expression of a man wondering if he'd just signed up for a gig as an extra on Home and Away. Jimmy left, probably thinking he'd just navigated a clean easy sale. He had no idea the jaws were already closing.

Donny was still curled up on the bed, cradling what was left of his manhood, trying to explain between gasps of laughter and pain. When Mack finally worked out what had happened he laughed so hard he nearly fell off his chair, slapping his thigh like he was at the goddamn Melbourne Comedy Festival. Later, when people called Donny 'ballsy,' there was a reason, and it wasn't just about courage.

And then came the final setup.

With the operation winding down, Mack hatched a plan that was equal parts tactical and bat shit. 'Let's move it up to Airlie Beach. Get a unit loaded with enough piss to float a battleship. Charter a boat. Bring Jimmy up from Mackay, it's not far for him to travel. We'll get the final buy on tape and then drop the hammer. Big finale, boys!' It sounded mad. But it was the kind of mad that just might work.

Two weeks had passed, Donny picked up the phone. 'Oi, Jimmy! Me and Mack are kicking back at Airlie Beach. Got a fridge full of piss, boat booked, couple of topless girls joining us later for a bit of a party. Mack wants to say thanks for all the business, mate.'

Jimmy hesitated. Donny could hear it—a flicker of fear crackling down the line.

'Yeah... sounds good. I'll be there tomorrow around twelve,' Jimmy said, masking nerves behind fake cheer.

'Bring your drinking boots and ten ounces of the good stuff, eh?' Donny ordered.

'Done,' Jimmy replied, sealing his own fate.

# DONNY

The next twenty-four hours dragged by. Donny and Mack sat in the bugged-out unit, pounding beers to kill the nerves. Every clink of the bottle caps felt like a drumbeat leading towards execution. Outside, the detectives were posted up, eyes on the clock, ready to spring. Inside, Donny paced the room like a lion in a shrinking cage.

Midday came.

No Jimmy.

Half-past and still no Jimmy. Donny's skin itched. His hands shook. The walls felt like they were closing in. As the clock ticked over to one, he cracked and reached for his phone.

'Hey mate,' Donny barked to Jimmy. 'You get lost?'

'Nah, just round the corner. Something feels off.' Jimmy's voice was brittle, frayed at the edges.

Donny's heart dropped. He forced a laugh—loud, fake and desperate. 'Mate, you're just being paranoid. We've been chilling here all week! Nothing's going on. Get your arse here.'

A pause. Then, 'Alright. Be there soon.' But it didn't sound like a promise. It sounded like a man walking himself into a trap.

Finally, after what felt like a lifetime, there was a knock. Donny yanked the door open with a grin nailed to his face. There was Jimmy, pale, sweat beading his forehead and eyes darting like a trapped rat.

'G'day mate,' Donny boomed, practically dragging him inside. 'Beer's cold, sun's out, the girls are on their way. Life's good, brother.'

Jimmy tried to smile but failed miserably.

Mack waved him over, gesturing out the window towards the sparkling ocean.

'See that boat, Jimmy? That's ours for the arvo. Nothing dodgy. Just good times. Let's square up, then hit the water.'

Jimmy fumbled out the four ounces of meth. His hands were shaking. Donny counted out the usual sum—twenty-one, six—slow and deliberate, stretching the seconds like piano wire. Every note, every breath in the room hung sharp, waiting for the crash.

And then, boom! The front door exploded inward.

'This is a raid! Don't move!'

Two detectives stormed in like they were kicking off a war. Before Donny could even blink, he was slammed against the wall, cuffed tight, while Jimmy hit the floor hard beside him.

'Don't say a word, Donny!' Jimmy shouted in pure panic.

'I won't,' Donny snapped back, playing the part with venom. The cops dragged Donny out the door, straight next door and dumped him on the bed. The room erupted. Detectives laughing until they were breathless, tears streaming, fists banging the walls.

'How'd that look?' one gasped between fits.

'Oscar-worthy,' another barked, slapping Donny hard on the back.

'Someone unclip these bloody cuffs, would ya,' roared Donny. Donny pushed himself upright, buzzing with a wild, manic energy.

He was alive. And he was fuckin' king! A roar tore from his throat, guttural and savage. They'd done it.

They'd taken Jimmy down, clean as a whistle, and Donny had played him like a fiddle. Sure, a flicker of guilt nipped at the back of Donny's mind. Jimmy had trusted him, he had bought the lies. But fuck it. That was the job. Donny cracked a can of beer, foam spraying across the room, and raised it high. 'To the fuckin' win!' he bellowed, grinning so hard it hurt. The adrenaline was surging, hot and endless, turning his veins into fire.

He felt invincible, untouchable, riding a wave so high it would take days to come down. And deep down, he knew he wasn't coming down anytime soon. The party was just getting started.

The next day, it was time for Donny to face off against Jimmy at the local Police Station. Now, Jimmy wasn't buying it for a second that Donny was an undercover cop. 'Yeah, right, mate,' he said to the Detective. 'Next, you'll tell me you're a bloody astronaut.' So, a face-to-face was necessary, and the detectives were keen to reel him in as their next informant.

Jimmy had been shuttled from the watchhouse cell to an interview room, looking more like a disgruntled shopper than a hardened criminal. The fluorescent lights flickered above him, casting a harsh glare, but he didn't care. He was too busy staring at the floor, contemplating his predicament—or maybe just the scuff marks on the tiles.

In walked Donny, looking like he'd just stepped off a fashion magazine cover for *Undercover Cops Monthly*.

'Hi, Jimmy,' he said, trying for a friendly tone, like a barista offering a free coffee.

Jimmy didn't so much as glance up. The silence stretched out longer than a line at a nightclub on Friday night. Finally, Donny broke the ice, 'Yes, Jimmy, I'm an undercover cop. All the deals you did are recorded and will be used against you in court. I suggest you cooperate with the detectives.'

Still no response from Jimmy. The silence hung in the air, thick enough to cut with a knife. After what felt like an eternity, Jimmy slowly lifted his gaze, locking eyes with Donny. 'Well, I have to give it to you, you're fucken good,' he said, a smirk creeping onto his face.

Donny shrugged, trying to play it cool. 'It's my job, mate.'

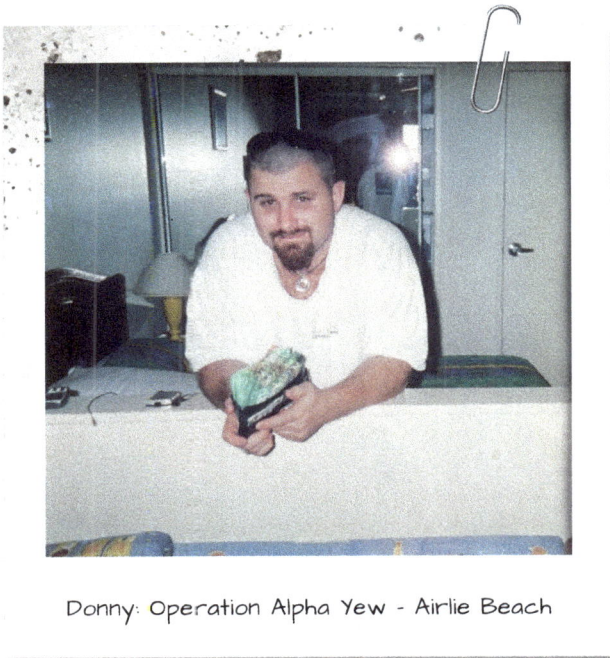

Donny: Operation Alpha Yew - Airlie Beach

Jimmy leaned back, crossing his arms. 'I suppose you're right. You had a job to do. But I'm still not talking to the jacks.'

Donny leaned in closer, his voice dropping to a conspiratorial whisper. 'That's your choice, mate. Good luck with that.'

And just like that, Jimmy, stubborn as a mule, decided to plead guilty and ended up with a nice ten-year holiday in the slammer. As he was led away, he couldn't help but chuckle to himself. 'At least I won't have to listen to any more of your drivel!'

Donny shook his head with a laugh, knowing he'd just scored another win. Who knew being an undercover cop could be such a laugh?

# 40

# NOT EVEN WORTH THE BULLETS

Sometimes you don't survive on your training. You survive on your bullshit.

Donny was back from Airlie Beach and was hoping for some down time, but this was never gonna happen. He was getting stretched thinner than cheap cling wrap. The QPS were squeezing him dry. As his phone buzzed, he squinted at the screen and saw it was his controller. 'Oi, Donny, we've got a quick job. Southern outskirts of Brisbane tomorrow night. Hit the safe house by four, sharp.' Donny tossed the phone down and laughed. Since when did crooks or undercovers give a shit about being on time.

The next afternoon, Donny rolled into the safe house just after half-past, scratching at the stubble on his chin, playing it casual. His controller glared at him. 'Tonight. Weasels' clubhouse. You're going in. Intel recon only. We want to know who's there and what's happening. We think there's likely a bit of prostitution going on. And let us know if there's any drug dealing.'

Donny raised an eyebrow. 'And how exactly am I supposed to waltz into a bikie clubhouse?'

The controller grinned like he was offering candy to a baby. 'Just knock on the door.'

*Fuck me dead! Here we go again,* Donny thought, shaking his head. *These old-school detectives are living in a bloody fantasy.*

'Are you serious?' Donny said out loud. 'You reckon they'll just let some random bloke waltz in?'

The controller smirked and pulled out a flimsy flyer, crumpled and dog-eared, advertising some sort of local shindig at The Weasels' clubhouse. 'Look at this. Tattoo Show. They're inviting the locals for a good time.'

Donny took the flyer, giving it a once over. 'Well, I'll be. Doesn't look half bad. Might have to stay longer than planned. You might struggle to drag me out of there.'

'Just keep it cool, yeah?' his controller sighed. 'Stay till midnight, and we'll scoop you up in the shopping centre car park across the road.'

'Right,' Donny nodded, a mix of dread and excitement bubbling in his gut. 'What's the worst that could happen?' He pocketed the flyer, flashing a grin that didn't quite reach his eyes. It was going to be a long night, and the last thing he needed was to end up on the wrong side of a bunch of bikies. But then again, that was just another day in the life of Donny, a bloke who'd learned to roll with the punches, even when the odds were stacked against him. Not every job took Donny away for months at a time. Sometimes it was like this one, a random call, a flyer shoved in his hand, and off he went, no backup, no briefing, no real plan. Just a pawn the QPS could move wherever they liked. Disposable and forgettable. And tonight, that meant walking blindly into a bikie clubhouse with nothing but a grin, a gut full of beer and whatever bullshit he could spin to stay alive.

Donny figured he'd better have a solid pre-game warmup, so he swung by the local pub for six schooners before strolling over to the Weasels. He felt loose and bulletproof. Just enough booze to numb the part of his brain that told him it was a bad idea. The Weasels' clubhouse sat tucked in an industrial wasteland. It was nothing more than a battered corrugated shed with floodlights buzzing like angry wasps. Donny knocked once. The door cracked open and a slab of muscle the size of a fridge glared down at him. 'Yeah, cunt, what do you want?' the giant barked.

Donny lifted the flyer. 'Heard there's a party tonight. I got this from the local mechanics.'

The scowl broke into a grin. 'Fuck yeah. Get in here.'

Well, that was easy, Donny thought, stepping inside.

It was chaos. A biker's wet dream—Harleys gleaming in the corner, strippers grinding on makeshift stages, pool tables swamped by mountains of meathead bikies. The air stank of sweat, smoke, cheap beer and something darker. Every second bloke wore cuts that screamed prison time, not fashion. Donny drifted through the crowd, soaking it in. All five foot eleven of him wedged between monsters, blokes six foot five and up, necks thicker than most blokes' thighs. Everyone was having a ripper of a time. Drinks were cheap, food was on the grill and a stripper was putting on a show that could make Pamela Anderson blush.

Feeling a bit cheeky, Donny sauntered over to one of the pool tables, slapping two bucks on the edge like he owned the joint. As soon as the game wrapped up, it was his turn to take on the winner. His competitor was Shorty, the Weasels' Sergeant at Arms. At nearly seven foot, he would have tipped the scales at around one hundred and fifty kilos. Donny cruised through the first game without trying too hard. Shorty barely potted two balls. His face twisted like he'd been forced to eat his own jocks.

'Best of three, cunt,' Shorty snapped, grabbing the break.

'Fuckin' oath,' Donny smirked. Shorty sunk four balls off the break, playing like a man possessed. Donny let him have the next two games, swallowing the urge to win. Tonight, survival meant losing with a smile. During the game Donny was having a good old chat with Shorty. Shorty was just an old softy, he just didn't like losing pool in his own club to a nobody.

Before he knew it, midnight rolled around. There he slouched, propped up at the bar, passing joints down the line with a gaggle of bikies. Beer flowed like water and arms draped around shoulders in a show of camaraderie. One of the blokes let out a laugh, 'This is pretty good shit!'

Another chimed in, 'Shit yeah! I'm starting to laugh at the peanuts because I'm so stoned!' Their laughter roared like thunder, and

Donny couldn't help but join in, knowing they were all giggling over absolutely nothing.

Just then, his phone buzzed, breaking the spell. It was his controller. 'Midnight, mate. Time to leave. Shopping centre carpark now.'

'Nah, fuck that! I'm staying.' And with that, Donny grabbed his beer and the pool cue. One more game, he told himself. One more for the road. Lining up a shot, he felt a presence too close. Someone was standing over his shoulder. 'G'day, Todd! Thought that was you!' The voice was clear as day over the noise.

Donny froze mid-stroke. Heart slamming. Brain screaming. Slowly, he turned. Some half-cut clown, big grin, pointing at him.

'Tugun, mate! You played A-grade. I was in reserve. You smashed it back then!'

Panic ripped through Donny's gut. He'd changed but not enough. He forced a lazy laugh. 'Tugun? Mate, where the fuck's Tugun? I'm from Sydney.'

The bloke wasn't having it. 'Nah! Mate, you carved 'em up! And weren't you a cop back then?' The word *cop* dropped into the room like a live grenade. The music hiccupped, voices dulled and heads turned. In that heartbeat, Donny knew: act or die. He dropped the cue. Stepped in and belted the bloke across the chin with everything he had. The guy dropped like a sandbag. Dead silent. Three Weasels rushed over and grabbed the idiot on the floor. They hauled him off towards a back room without a second glance at Donny.

Donny bent, picked up the cue and took his next shot as if nothing had happened. Inside, he was drowning in adrenaline. Had he just got away with that? How close a call had it been?

Donny had spent many months going through different scenarios in his mind and how he would deal with this sort of encounter. Some was making up rehearsed stories, but some meant using plain violence. This time, Donny chose violence.

Deciding it was time to split before things turned sour, he took off to the bathroom to take a piss before bailing. As he was finishing washing his hands, about ten Weasels barged in. This was going to be tricky. One bloke, bigger than the rest, snarled, 'Oi, cunt. That's my brother you just decked.'

'Ah, fuck. Really?' Donny laughed, dry-mouthed. 'Mate, sorry to break it to ya, but he grabbed me cock. He's a poof, I had to straighten him out.'

The bikies shifted, their smiles fading. 'He's fuckin' done *what*?' the big bloke thundered.

'Yeah, mate,' Donny said, hands raised, playing it cool. 'Gay. Surprised you didn't know.'

The bikies stared. A moment stretched longer than life itself.

Then came the shotgun. From behind the group, one Weasel levelled a pump action at Donny's face. 'And you're a cop, hey?' he growled. For half a heartbeat, Donny stared death in the eyes. He was wearing a wire, but it had stopped hours ago. If they patted him down, it was game over. 'Too right I am. Call me Sergeant Donny. You're all under arrest. Hands behind ya back, boys.'

'Don't you believe me? I'm a cop, here's my badge.' Donny said and started checking every one of his pockets. 'Fuck I must have left it at home.' 'Oh well, it looks like you blokes are off the hook now.' Donny continued.

Silence fell like a thick fog. Thirty seconds ticked by. Donny held his breath and it looked like the game was finally up. 'Go on. Okay, get it over with. Pull the trigger,' Donny said, his voice steady, masking the fear inside.

Then, one by one, the Weasels burst into laughter, clapping Donny on the back like old mates. 'We don't even know who that cunt was,' one of them howled. 'We were gonna turf him before you dropped him. Figured we'd fuck with ya a bit first. Bit of a laugh, eh?' Donny noticed a few of them were the ones he was at the bar with passing the joint along the line.

As they filed out, Donny caught snippets of their chatter. 'We got the cunt! Did you see his face?' one snorted.

'Priceless,' another added. 'You're not even worth the bullets.' More laughter.

Relief washed over Donny. He was lucky he'd taken that piss; otherwise, there would have been a massive puddle at his feet. With adrenaline pumping through his veins like a double shot of espresso, he made a beeline for the exit, eager to leave the chaos of the night behind. The wild escapades were fun and all, but he had a more pressing mission: the shopping centre. He needed to check if his controller was still there, waiting like a loyal dog for its owner to return.

'You stupid prick,' the controller roared, punching the dashboard, as Donny sidled into the passenger seat. 'When I say leave, you fucking leave!'

Donny wiped the sweat off his brow and grinned. 'Couldn't help it, mate. Was onto something big.'

'Yeah?' the controller sneered. 'What, exactly?'

Donny leaned back, letting the madness of the night wash over him. 'Turns out they're just a bunch of top blokes who love a beer and a joint. Didn't see a thing.'

The controller shook his head, muttering curses under his breath.

Donny just laughed, staring out the window into the night.

# 41

# OPERATION
# ALPHA AARON

Operation Alpha Aaron saw Donny tasked with hitting the Brisbane Fortitude Valley nightclubs to score as many ecstasy pills as possible. They called it a cold start, but for Donny, it felt more like a bloody ice bath. Of course, Donny was sporting a look that screamed 'bikie' louder than a revving Harley. He stood out like a sore thumb in The Valley's trendy scene. Picture this: Donny hitting up hundreds of punters for pills, and his efforts were about as fruitful as a dry cactus. It looked dodgy as hell, like a sheepdog trying to herd a group of headless chickens. Desperate, Donny pitched a wild idea to his controller: bring in a female undercover as his 'girlfriend'.

Enter Liz.

Liz was a stunner with dark hair, curves that could cause a traffic accident and a presence that drew eyes.

On night one, Donny and Liz strutted into The Beat. Liz went to work, shoving her assets in everyone's face and charming punters like she'd been born for it. Meanwhile, Donny nursed a Corona in the corner, playing the tough, silent type. Every twenty minutes, Liz waltzed back over, a massive bag of pills in hand, pocketing more cash before heading back out. By the end of the night, they'd racked up around four hundred MDMA pills. Easy money. And Liz had scored every seller's phone number too, probably for more than just pills. In the world of dodgy dealings, Donny was starting to think he might actually have a knack for this.

MDMA, Ecstasy, Molly, Pingas, whatever you want to call it, hit Queensland in the late '90s like a freight train. Most came from Holland, stamped with logos like Mitsubishi and Crown. Rewind to 1912, when German pharmaceutical company Merck allegedly cooked up the first MDMA (that's 3,4-methylenedioxymethamphetamine for those playing at home) to develop the world's first appetite suppressor. According to reports, Merck studied the effects of MDMA pharmacologically, but not on humans or animals, in both 1927 and 1959. Other than that, the drug sat relatively unnoticed until it was introduced as a street drug in the late '60s. By the time the '80s rolled around, it was the drug of choice for raves, where beats pumped and kids melted into bliss. It became the darling of the dance scene, where it was all about euphoric vibes and nonstop partying.

Then, in 1985, the US Drug Enforcement Administration killed the buzz, declaring it a Schedule I drug, where it stays alongside heroin and LSD. But by the 2000s, scientists began to peek back into its therapeutic potential, looking at how it could help with PTSD, anxiety and depression. And guess what? The results of MDMA-assisted therapy were promising. Organisations like the Multidisciplinary Association for Psychedelic Studies jumped in, waving the flag for research and funding.

Now, in the 2020s, MDMA is back in the spotlight, undergoing clinical trials for its therapeutic uses, especially in treating PTSD. MDMA's journey has been a wild ride from being an obscure lab creation to a controversial party drug, and now a serious contender in the therapeutic arena.

But, back in the early 2000s, Donny and Liz were focused on one thing—hauling in the ecstasy dealers. And so, they became the dynamic duo of the nightlife scene, cleaning up every Friday and Saturday night, usually 'working' till the sun was coming up. They'd clock off at dawn, only to shimmy over to the day clubs like a couple of university students after too many No-Doz. The QPS moved them into a flash unit at Kangaroo Point. A six-month lease, unlimited budgets and an endless stream of 'friends' pouring through their door every weekend. Pre-drinks, fake engagement party—they played the part perfectly. All the gifts, all the evidence logged. Well, mostly.

They became fixtures at all the hottest clubs, blending into Fortitude Valley's nightlife like old pros. Donny drifted deeper into the role until it stopped feeling like a role. They met wonderful people like Sugar Marie. Six foot four and queen of the showgirls. Sugar Marie took them in like family. The smell backstage was part lavender, part rough sex, and Liz loved it, always sneaking into the change rooms, soaking up the raw, electric life of it all. The nights blurred with drinks, hugs and wild laughter. It was the kind of living that made you forget what side you were really on. Sugar Marie and her mates became Donny and Liz's personal security.

Then there was Lorenzo, an Italian fella. A decade older, fresh out of a divorce, knee-deep in the party scene and making a few bucks slinging pills. But Lorenzo wasn't a hardened crim. He was a bloke whose heart hadn't caught up to his bad decisions. He latched onto Donny and Liz like a drowning man to driftwood. Pints poured, secrets spilled, stories of heartbreak and of being hollowed out by life's quiet betrayals. Donny liked the guy, and Lorenzo trusted Donny. And that made it worse because Lorenzo was selling. And Donny was buying. And that evidence was piling up just like the rest. When the hammer dropped and Lorenzo's world caved in, he didn't call his family. He didn't call a lawyer. He called Donny. The bloke who'd helped put him there.

Donny and Liz knowingly built the case against Lorenzo—every bag, every pill and every phone number pocketed and logged. Every drunken conversation laughed off—all nails driven into Lorenzo's coffin. It was the classic betrayal of undercover work: befriend them, drink with them, laugh with them and then hand them over to the wolves. Lorenzo got pinched hard and faced serious time. And out of all the blokes in the world he could have called while teetering on the edge of the New Farm cliffs, ready to end it all, he called Donny. Donny tore across Brisbane like a madman, heart hammering faster than a kid who'd just discovered his dad's *Penthouse* stash. The river was quiet and eerie, and there, perched like a ghost against the sky, was Lorenzo. One step away from becoming just another tragic news story.

'Oi, mate!' Donny hollered, striding over with the swagger of a man who'd just won a pub brawl. He could see it in Lorenzo's eyes—the dead, hollow stare of someone ready to let go. Nope, not happening. Donny needed to bring him back down to Earth. With a few classic Aussie one-liners, Donny did his best to bring Lorenzo through the darkness. It was the only way he knew to help—with laughter, bullshit and madness. He stepped closer to the edge, close enough to smell his own fear.

'Alright, on the count of three… you ready?' Donny called out, mischief dripping off every word. Lorenzo blinked at him, stunned.

'What?'

'Don't be a failure at this too, mate! Come on, let's jump together!' Donny grinned, part madman, part saviour. Lorenzo just stared, slack-jawed, disbelief plastered on his face.

'Surely you're not afraid of dying,' Donny barked, tone rising. 'Maybe the afterlife's the real paradise, and we're the mugs stuck here!'

Still no answer, just the broken repetition: 'What?'

'If life's eternal, why are we only doing it once?' Donny pressed, reckless now. He grabbed Lorenzo's hand and yelled, 'Okay, on three! One… two…'

Panic broke through. Lorenzo yanked back, dragging Donny with him, the two of them tumbling away from the edge in a chaotic flurry of limbs and curses. They hit the ground hard, sprawled and breathless, staring up at the empty sky above them. 'Right,' Donny panted, grinning like a lunatic. 'That was either the worst plan ever or the best laugh I've had all week.' Lorenzo cracked a smile, the first real one Donny had seen in months. And just like that, the weight started to lift a little. Two broken bastards lying on their backs on the cliff edge, laughing at how close they'd come to losing it all.

They ended up sitting on a park bench for hours after that, in a deep, bonded chat that would make a grown man weep. Somewhere between the laughing and the crying, Lorenzo opened. And what really knocked Donny for six was realising Lorenzo was an old Paduan from his school days. They'd roamed the same halls. Probably pissed off the same teachers and, more than likely, sat in the same bloody detention room. Two kids from the same place, and look how far they'd fallen in different ways. While Lorenzo had been ready to end it all on a cliff, Donny was out there playing the part of the reluctant therapist, proving that sometimes you just need a mate to pull you back from the edge—literally and figuratively.

Donny headed home and sat in the suffocating quiet of his safe house, where it really hit him. *Fuck.* Lorenzo's family, his kids, his mates—they would have been left carrying the same unbearable pain, guilt and suffering Donny knew all too well. Donny had heard it said a thousand times: Suicide doesn't end the pain, it just passes it on to the ones who stay behind. And now, he could feel it. All of it.

Donny just sat there staring at the wall. So many thoughts, flashbacks, pain and heartache. It was like stepping back through that sliding door, back to Karen, back to the wreckage he thought he could outrun. He didn't know it yet, but everyone else around him could already see it clear as day. The volcano inside him was finally cracking. Donny broke down like he never had before. It had been building up in him for months and months. Months of running, months of lying and months of laughing to hide the bleeding underneath—to hide the real person inside. It all came roaring out of him at once, and it was unstoppable.

# 42

# OPERATION WATTLES

One sweltering afternoon, Donny was summoned into the boss's office, a cramped box that smelled like stale coffee and bureaucracy. Detective Sergeant Keith Naracott, a grizzled veteran with a gut that suggested he loved more than just coffee, waved him in. 'Donny, listen up,' Naracott said, voice gravelly. 'Your time's almost up. You can wrap things up and waltz back to normal policing or stick around for one last job.'

Donny leaned forward. 'Yeah? I'm in. What's the gig?'

Naracott raised a hand, cutting him off. 'Hold your horses. You need to hear what it entails first.'

'Don't care, mate. I'm ready. Just tell me.'

Naracott leaned back, arms crossed. 'The job's in Sydney. New South Wales cops are involved.'

Donny's excitement deflated like a popped footy. He slumped back, hands in his face. 'You're not fuckin' serious.'

'Dead serious,' Naracott replied. The brief was clear: Two New South Wales coppers were suspected of having a pill press, colluding with nightclub bouncers to flood Sydney's streets with Mitsubishi-stamped MDMA.

Donny's mind raced. Crooks in uniform. Worse than anything he'd faced. He weighed it up. Becoming Todd once more and opting for a boring Crime Stoppers desk job or one last dive headfirst into hell. 'Alright. I'm in.' His fists clenched under the desk. 'Fuck those dogs.'

Before he knew it, he was on a plane to Sydney, diving into the city's underbelly with a fake name, a fat budget and a high-rise apartment overlooking Hyde Park. One last mission. One last chance to lose himself all over again.

Donny hit Sydney running. Met the New South Wales Internal Affairs crew, a strange mix of hardened veterans and rookie dreamers. They handed him the keys to the apartment and a BMW parked underground. Life was good. Life was dangerous. The first step was to meet Ghosty, an informant who'd connect him to the crooks. The first play? Ghosty was to introduce Donny to Ollie, a massive roided-up freak—all muscle and menace. He was working for the crooked cops. And the first buy? One thousand pills. No small stuff this time.

The meeting went down in a Darlinghurst pub, dark and sticky with secrets. The pub was crawling with undercover couples at every table. There were tactical squads parked around the corner and a white van out front jammed with listening cops. Compared to Donny's old QPS operations, it was like trading in a tricycle for a V8. The deal slid through like butter. Twenty-two grand and one thousand Mitsubishi pills. Easy. Too easy.

Donny, now rocking a bleached blonde buzz cut, black leather jacket and a rogue's tickler under his lip, strutted through Sydney's nightlife like he owned it. Another buy with Ollie went down smoothly, another thousand pills stacked on the evidence pile. The New South Wales cops weren't just selling, they were manufacturing. And Donny, well, he was one handshake away from burning them all down. He couldn't help but chuckle to himself. What an easy job this was. The whole affair felt like a walk in the park, cash in hand, no worries. Just as the New South Wales Internal Affairs were scratching their heads, concocting a plan to rope in the local cops on the drug scene, Donny's phone buzzed, jolting him from his thoughts.

The call came from Ollie. 'Massive party, Donny. Superyacht. Sydney Harbour. Saturday night. You've gotta come.'

A superyacht party would be a different league of glitz, glamour and connections that could very well include the cops he was chasing.

Donny played it cool. 'Nah, got a date with a stripper from the Honey Pot, mate. Might give it a miss,' he said, feigning nonchalance. His Saturday night was emptier than a pub at dawn, but he had to keep up appearances. 'Come on, mate, you know you want to,' Ollie coaxed. 'Think of the connections. This isn't just any party. It's where deals get made and fortunes change hands. Bring your date if you want.'

Donny smirked. 'Alright, I'm in.'

He called the detectives to casually tip them off about the invite. From the way they exchanged glances, they were already clocking that something bigger was brewing. A few days later, word came down: the New South Wales police targets would be there too. It was clear the walls had ears. *Ah, now we're getting somewhere,* Donny thought, that familiar smirk tugging at his mouth. This wasn't just a piss-up, it was a goldmine waiting to be tapped.

At Circular Quay, the sunset glistened across the harbour like a thousand scattered diamonds. Two security guards, sharp-suited and stone-faced, stood checking names. 'Donny?' one called out, eyeing him up.

'That's me.' Donny puffed his chest slightly, savouring the rare feeling of being on the guest list. His name was crossed off, and a cold beer found its way into his hand courtesy of a passing waiter.

Stepping onto the yacht, Donny's jaw nearly hit the deck. This wasn't a boat. This was a bloody floating palace. Three opulent lounges, glittering chandeliers, king-size suites with spa baths, even a bubbling jacuzzi and a helipad hanging overhead like a crown jewel. *At least ten mill worth,* he thought, shaking his head.

'Donny! You made it!' Ollie bellowed, waving him over like a long-lost mate. 'Where's ya date?' he teased, his eyes gleaming.

'She got called into work. She'll spew when she hears about this tinnie,' Donny replied, grinning and sweeping his hand at the floating mansion. 'Tinnie,' Ollie laughed, slapping his back. 'Biggest tinnie I've ever seen!'

They meandered the decks. There were models in designer bikinis splashing in the spa, rugby league stars swanning about and TV-familiar faces mingling with minor celebs. The air was thick with champagne spray and the kind of easy arrogance money buys.

'Bet they've got more champagne on this thing than the Queen's birthday,' Ollie marvelled.

'Hope they've got a bloody steak, too. I'm starving,' Donny quipped.

They grabbed fresh beers and played it cool, but under the easy banter, Donny's senses sharpened. Tonight wasn't just about the party. It was about getting the upper hand. Soon enough, Donny was introduced to two important faces.

'Donny, this is Craig and Brett,' Ollie said, clapping both men on the back. Donny plastered on his best easy grin, shaking hands firmly. Craig's eyes flicked over him, sceptical. Brett? All business.

'How do you know Donny, Ollie?' Craig asked, casual but sharp-edged.

'Met him through Ghosty down in Darlinghurst. Good bloke. He's been around a while.'

Craig and Brett exchanged the smallest glance, enough to make Donny's stomach tighten. *Sizing me up,* he thought. *Deciding whether I'm worth trusting... or worth burying.*

'Alright, we're heading to the bar. Catch ya later, boys,' Brett said with a flat smile, the two moving off like sharks into deeper water.

Donny turned to Ollie. 'What's their deal?'

'Cops, mate. Always twitchy,' Ollie shrugged. 'Just keep it cool.'

*Right,* Donny thought. *Keep it cool.*

The party was lifting now—loud laughter, drinks flowing and bodies looser. But Donny was working. Scanning faces, eavesdropping, piecing together the scene like a jigsaw puzzle made of cocaine and fake smiles.

'Let's sit,' Ollie said, leading him to a plush corner booth. As they settled in, Ollie leaned in low. 'You alright? You seem off.'

Donny forced a grin. 'Mate, not real keen on you being mates with these cops. It's a bit close to home, don't ya think?'

'Nah, mate! That's why you needed to meet 'em,' Ollie insisted, grinning wide. 'They're the ones making the Mitsubishis.'

Donny blinked. 'You fuckin' serious?' he hissed.

'Dead set! If they weren't doing it, some other greasy cunt would be. And besides...' Ollie lowered his voice even more, 'they're looking after us.'

Donny nodded slowly, swallowing down the rising unease. 'Alright,' he said finally, raising his beer. 'To new connections.'

They clinked glasses, but Donny's eyes never stopped scanning. Craig and Brett were back at the bar, talking low, heads close.

*Business,* Donny thought. *The kind that doesn't end in a tax return.* He needed to get closer. 'Oi, I'll be back in a tick,' he said, sliding out of the booth. 'Just going to grab a drink.'

He sidled up to the bar, acting casual. Close enough to hear Craig mutter: '...play it right, we'll have the market cornered.'

'Need to move fast,' came Brett's reply. 'Last thing we need is someone sniffin' around.' Donny's blood thrummed. *Gotcha.* But before he could soak up more, Ollie's voice cut through the noise.

'Oi, Donny! You coming?'

'Yeah, mate! Just ordering!' Donny turned, feeling Craig and Brett's eyes burn holes in his back. Back at the booth, Donny kept his smile loose, but inside, he was grinding gears. The stakes had just gone up.

The party boiled over. Girls topless in the jacuzzi. Men and women gliding past Donny, touching his arms, gazing wide-eyed. Everyone was swimming in MDMA, love and laughter dripping off them like sweat. 'Mate, hitting the pisser,' Donny said, swaggering towards the back.

Ollie tossed him a small bag of pingas. 'Drop a few while you're in there, mate!'

Donny grinned. 'Beauty.' With the bag tucked discreetly into his pocket, he disappeared into the crowd. In this game, loyalty was tested one pill at a time, and Donny just swallowed the loaded chamber. After a quick pit stop, he swung open the door and ran straight into Brett and Craig, posted outside like two bad bouncers on a worse night.

'G'day, fellas!' Donny barked, forcing a casual grin. 'How's the night treating ya?'

Brett shot him a look that could curdle milk. 'How the fuck do you know Ghosty, mate?' he snapped, arms folding across his chest.

'Just a bloke I know around the pubs,' Donny replied, keeping his tone loose.

'Bullshit!' Craig growled, stepping in closer. 'What the fuck are you doing here?'

Donny kept his voice steady, but the unease in his gut was growing.

'Just hanging with Ollie. He invited me, that's all.'

'No, fuckhead. I mean, what the fuck are you doing in Sydney?' Brett pushed. 'This ain't Brisbane. You got some explaining to do.'

Donny shrugged. 'Had to get out of Brissy, mate. Few people wanted money off me.'

Brett leaned in, breath hot with contempt. 'I don't like you. Ghosty is a New South Wales cop who just got charged with corruption. And he's gonna dog, mark my words.'

'You're a fuckin' narc, aren't ya?' Craig added, his face inches from Donny's.

Donny shook his head hard. 'Mate, I didn't even know he was a bloody cop! Didn't know you two were either! I came down here to lay low just trying to make a few bucks, for fucks sake!'

Before Donny could react, Brett shoved him backwards into the cramped toilet cubicle. Craig slammed the door shut behind them.

'Take your clothes off. You wearing a wire?' Brett barked, voice low and venomous.

'A fucking what?' Donny stammered, eyes wide.

'Are you recording us, you cunt?' Brett roared, nose to nose with him.

'No way! What the hell is going on?' Donny protested, heart hammering against his ribs.

'Shirt. Jeans. Now,' Brett ordered, his tone leaving no room for negotiation.

Hands trembling, Donny stripped down. He emptied his pockets onto the floor—wallet, loose change, the works. They rifled through it all—his licence, bank cards, Video Ezy membership—making sure nothing looked out of place. Then Brett pulled the bag of pingas from Donny's jeans.

'Whose are these?' he demanded, narrowing his eyes.

Donny swallowed. 'Just holding 'em for Ollie. He told me to have a couple.'

'Well, have ya?' Brett pushed, voice dripping with menace.

'Not yet,' Donny replied, a flash of defiance cutting through the fear.

Craig grinned, a cruel glint in his eye. 'Well, now's your fuckin' chance. We know narcs don't use.'

And just like that, Donny's world tilted. He thought of Karen, the drug that had taken her away still haunting him. He thought of the job, the Hyde Park apartment, the BMW, the life he was carving out. He thought of everything he stood to lose. He had two choices: swallow the pills or blow his cover wide open. With a deep breath, Donny convinced himself this was for the job. This was for Karen. He popped two Mitsubishis into his mouth and chased them down with tap water, grimacing at the taste. Tastes like bloody hairspray, he thought.

Brett burst out laughing. 'Well, well. Maybe we were wrong about you.'

Craig clapped him on the back as the door swung open. 'Stick around, mate. You're in for one hell of a night.'

Donny: 2002 Operation Wattles Sydney

They strolled out, laughing like they'd just pulled off the prank of the century. Donny stood alone in the cubicle, heart pounding, regret pooling in his gut alongside the bitter aftertaste of betrayal. He was in for a long night.

Back out on deck, Donny found Ollie in stitches, laughing with Brett and Craig like a pack of drunken teenagers. Donny chuckled, sliding a fresh beer across to Ollie. 'Top up, mate. The night's young. Let's see where it goes.'

'Fuck yeah,' Brett chimed in, shooting Donny a mischievous grin. 'Can't wait to see how you handle it!'

Donny forced a grin back, feeling like the punchline to a joke he hadn't heard yet. He sipped his beer, waiting for the MDMA to kick in. Twenty minutes ticked by. Nothing. Another twenty. Still nothing. Maybe they're duds, he thought, starting to relax slightly. Bloody typical.

And then, bam. It hit like a Mack truck. First, a tingle, then a thumping heartbeat and then the world swirled into chaos. The music cranked to eleven. Lights pulsed like lightning strikes. The deck beneath his feet pitched and rolled. Donny's hands rubbed unconsciously down his thighs, trying to ground himself, but he was already gone, gliding through the crowd like a feather in a cyclone. Time melted. He could have danced for minutes or hours. As *Murder on the Dancefloor* blared from the speakers, Donny let go. *I'm murdering it on the dancefloor with these moves*, he thought busily to himself. Two stunning women pulled him into their orbit, matching his wild energy beat for beat.

'How 'bout the jacuzzi, girls?' he shouted, grinning like a loon. The next thing he knew, they were all stripped down to their underwear, splashing around like overgrown kids at a pool party. Donny leapt out dripping wet, grabbed an older woman by the hand, and spun her across the deck in a mad, laughing dance. Still in his jocks with no shame in sight. 'Look at us!' he howled, chest out, arms flailing. King of the fuckin' world.

By two in the morning, the party had started to wind down like a cheap Bali watch. Brett appeared at Donny's elbow, buzzing like a kid at a theme park.

'Where we going now, Donny? Show us those joints you were banging on about!'

At this point, Donny was on fire, barking orders like he was Moses parting the Red Sea. 'Let's keep it rolling, boys!' he hollered, waving his arms theatrically.

Ollie tried to pull the pin. 'Mate, I gotta work tomorrow. I'm out.'

'Bullshit,' Donny fired back, swaggering hard. 'If you're gonna run with the pack, don't piss like a puppy! Thought you had some go in ya. Maybe I was wrong.'

Ollie hesitated, pride warring with exhaustion, and then he grinned and gave in. 'Alright, I'm coming.' 'That's the spirit,' Donny crowed, slapping him on the back. 'I'll even shout ya a lap dance if you like!' And with that, the ragtag gang spilled into the Sydney night, chasing trouble into the small hours, Donny right at the front, running on nothing but adrenaline, bad decisions and a couple of very powerful little pills.

# 43

# CRASH LANDING

Donny led the crew—Ollie, Brett, Craig and a few other stragglers—down the street like he was leading a victory parade. They swaggered towards the Honey Pot, the neon buzzing like a wasp nest. At the door, Donny spotted the bouncer—a brick wall with arms like tree trunks. 'Hey, mate,' Donny bellowed, throwing out a hand like they were long-lost cousins. The bouncer rolled his eyes but cracked a grin. Clearly, he'd seen Donny's type before. After shouting the entire crew into the club, Donny strutted inside like he owned the joint. He snagged a prime spot at the bar, slapped down a card to kick off a tab and started ordering lap dances for Brett and Craig, sliding the girls a few extra notes for the 'special treatment'.

He chuckled to himself. *All being paid for by the New South Wales police force,* he thought with a laugh. *Cheers to the boys in blue.* Just as he was raising an imaginary glass, Ollie piped up. 'Oi, where's your date?'

Donny blinked, struggling to focus. 'My what? What the fuck are you on about, ya big puffed-up galah?'

'The girl you were supposed to take to the tinnie,' Ollie pressed, suspicious.

'Oh, fuck, that's right,' Donny slapped his forehead theatrically. 'Fucks me. She must've finished work early.'

Ollie gave him a sharp look, scanning the room like a hawk. 'You reckon?' he asked, voice dropping.

'Must have,' Donny laughed, oblivious to the unease knotting in Ollie's gut. The night rolled on. The drinks flowed like a river after a storm. Donny was raising hell, spinning yarns that could've made a sailor blush. Lap dancers twirled around, and everyone was laughing like there wasn't a care in the world. Then the door swung open.

And in strolled two real coppers—the kind who didn't just play dress up. Their eyes swept the room like predators. Donny's heart skipped a beat, but he slapped Ollie on the back and boomed, 'Look, mate! Entertainment's here. Just like I ordered!'

Ollie went white as a sheet. 'That's not the sort of entertainment I want,' he muttered. The cops made a beeline for them.

'Evening, gentlemen,' one said, deadpan. 'Mind if we have a chat?'

Donny, still running hot on ego and bravado, flashed a grin that could charm the pants off a statue. 'Of course, officers! We were just discussing ways to support our local law enforcement. Right, boys?' The laughter dried up like a puddle in the desert. Tension thickened the air.

Ollie leaned in, whispering urgently. 'You're not seriously thinking of trying to bribe them, are ya?'

Donny winked. 'What's a little generosity among friends?'

He pulled out a fat wad of cash, fanned it like playing cards. The lead cop arched an eyebrow. 'You boys realise this isn't how you win friends in the force, right?'

Donny froze mid grin, caught like a possum in a spotlight. 'Ah, come on, mate. We're just having a laugh.'

The officers weren't laughing. 'We'll need to see some ID. And we'll be having a chat about your... generosity.'

Donny, sensing the floor slipping out from under him, threw out another Hail Mary. 'Ladies and gentlemen! I think there's been a misunderstanding. All part of the entertainment!'

The cops started pulling out their notepads. Donny's mind raced. Time to do what he did best. He leaned in close to the nearest cop, plastering on his most charming, drunken grin. 'How 'bout we settle this over a few cold ones? On me?'

For a second, just a second, he thought he saw one of them fight back a smirk. And then, Brett strolled up, leaned in and whispered something in the cop's ear. Whatever magic words he used, it worked. The officers snapped their notebooks shut, straightened up and strutted out the door like they'd just won the bloody lottery. The room exhaled as one. The buzz of the night deflated faster than a cheap blow-up mattress. One by one, the blokes peeled off, heading into the Sydney dawn. Before he knew it Donny was the only one left. Donny stumbled out, blinking into the brutal sunrise that felt like God himself was swinging a spotlight straight into his hungover skull. He flagged a cab with all the grace of a three-legged donkey and collapsed into the back seat.

Back at his unit, sleep was playing hard to get, like a cat that just wouldn't come when called. Donny cranked up the stereo like it owed him money, poured a frosty beer that glistened like it was blessed by the beer gods and let the thumping bass drown out the last remnants of the night's chaotic adventures. It was time for a one-man rave! As Pennywise blasted out *Fuck Authority*, Donny once again felt like the king of the world, well at least the king of his living room, which was a modest throne made of mismatched furniture and the odd pizza box. *How good,* he thought, nodding along as if he were in a rock concert instead of a small apartment.

Then came Alien Ant Farm crooning about being a *Smooth Criminal*, and Donny couldn't help but channel his inner Michael Jackson, complete with some moonwalking. By the time Basement Jaxx chimed in with *Where's Your Head At,* he was convinced his head was somewhere between the fridge and the front door, probably lost in search of more snacks. As the clock approached midday, Donny realised it was time to call it a night, or was it a day? Who even knew anymore? He plopped down on his couch, surrounded by empty bottles, pondering whether he should go to bed or just embrace the chaos and order a pizza. After all, at this hour, it was practically brunch!

Only when the sun was high and merciless did he finally crash, face-planting into bed like a sack of wet cement. He slept like the dead until morning. And when he woke, it took a full five minutes of staring at the ceiling to remember where the hell he even was.

The phone shattered the silence. Donny squinted at the screen. It was one of the Sydney detectives. 'We need to meet. Today at midday, same place,' the voice said. It was all business and no pleasantries.

'Okay,' Donny croaked, dragging himself out of bed, his head still stuffed with cotton wool. By the time he pulled into the shopping centre car park, the sun was punishing, beating down like a cop's flashlight on a guilty man. He spotted the detectives loitering by their car, looking like they were on an extended smoko. Donny slid into the back seat of the detective's car. The engine hummed to life. As they cruised out, one detective shot him a smirk.

'We had Brett and Craig's phones tapped,' he said, almost laughing. 'They didn't buy it. They reckon you're a cop. And mate, they were *pissing themselves* about you having to take those pills. Said you really played it up.'

Donny groaned, dragging a hand through his hair. 'Shit. Thought I sold it pretty well. But yeah, I was wasted. No choice, really.'

The detective chuckled. 'Yeah, we know. We heard the whole thing.'

The second detective, voice harder, cut in. 'Well, anyway. Thanks for your help. But you'll be heading back to Queensland tomorrow.'

Donny stared out the window, the words sinking in like stones. 'Fuck,' he muttered, the weight of it all crashing down.

Later, standing at the Qantas check-in desk, Donny stared at his boarding pass: 'Donald Wilson'. It felt like a name tag at the world's shittiest reunion. As he pocketed the ticket, he turned for one last look out at Sydney. He could almost hear the echoes of the yacht party, the thump of bass, the fake laughter, the deals whispered in the dark. All swallowed now. Gone.

Donny hated a lot of things, but crooked cops pretending they were any better than the scum they hunted that cut deepest. He hated that he hadn't been able to finish the job. Hated that, like most things in this world, the truth would rot in the shadows, never seeing the light. He never asked what happened to Brett and Craig. Didn't need to. In this life, justice was just a story you told yourself to sleep at night. Most of the time, the good guys didn't win. Most of the time, survival was the only prize.

When Donny boarded that flight back to Brisbane, he wasn't just leaving Sydney behind. He was leaving another piece of himself buried in the wreckage. No medals. No parades. Just another mask peeled away, leaving the man underneath a little more frayed, a little hollower. But he was still standing.

# 44

# WHAT WAS LEFT OF ME

Undercover gave me everything I didn't know I needed. It let me be reckless and gave me a way to bleed in plain sight without anyone really noticing. I could fight, lie, vanish, drink too much, feel nothing and no one called it broken. They called it brave. Donny didn't flinch. He walked into rooms thick with threat, where deals were sealed with shotguns on the table and a nod meant life or death. He made killers laugh. Took punches and threw them back. He could lie to your face, shake your hand and walk out smiling, all without losing control. I loved it.

I was stabbed at. Held at gunpoint. Surrounded in forests with a gun pointed at my head and no backup on the way. I bought from people who buried problems in cane fields and bragged about it later. I wore wires and recording devices that slipped with sweat during high-risk buys, not knowing if anyone would notice. I was followed and recognised in pubs by people I'd burned in other lives. I trusted informants who could've flipped me in a heartbeat. One night, I stood on a cliff beside a man ready to jump and realised part of me wanted to go with him. I infiltrated meth labs, heroin kitchens, nightclub syndicates and police corruption rings. I lived under fake names, staged identities and rented apartments wired for betrayal. And somewhere in all that, a one-hundred-thousand-dollar bounty on my head.

Surveillance failed me more than once. My name, my real one, was nearly spoken too many times. And every time I stepped into a deal, I did it knowing full well: no one was coming to save me. But the weapons weren't the real danger. It was the erosion. The slow, silent disappearance of who I was. The longer I lived as Donny, the less of Todd remained. The edge became home. The lies became easier than the truth. And when it was finally over, I didn't know how I would ever come back.

# PART 3

'When life dropped me to my knees, purpose was
the only thing I found worth standing up for.'

— Todd Maguire

Undercover work ended. But the danger didn't. What came after was quieter but far more brutal. The mission changed from staying alive as Donny to staying sane as Todd. They told me to 'reintegrate'. To sit at desks, answer phones, nod politely, wear a uniform again. But after two years of walking into rooms where people might kill me, how was I expected to care about petty tips and community barbecues? I'd lived too long on adrenaline, in shadows, in lies. I couldn't just switch it off. The ghosts didn't leave when the ops ended; they followed me into train carriages, offices, bedrooms. I picked fights without meaning to. My only coping strategy was my continued drinking. I lashed out, then numbed out. The world had moved on, but I hadn't.

Therapy didn't work—talking only made it worse. The system wanted me compliant, stable and quiet. But I was none of those things. I was angry, hollow, exhausted and still playing the part, they needed me to play, albeit a different one. Smiling. Passing tests. Pretending I was okay when I wasn't. The truth is, I survived undercover, but I didn't come out clean. I came out cracked down the middle, worse than I had ever been. Karen's death had ripped me wide open, and the undercover life had deepened that divide. Sadly, no one could see how bad I was because I didn't let them.

Part two was about surviving the underbelly of society. Part three is about surviving myself.

# 45

# CULTURE SHOCK

**D**onny Wilson had been shelved reluctantly like a dodgy relic from another life. He was a ghost rattling the halls of a world that no longer made sense. The QPS rolled out a six-month reintegration program, dragging me step by step towards some imagined version of normal. Truth is, I didn't want out. I'd just hit my stride in the undercover game and I loved it. Every chaotic, lawless, adrenaline-drenched second of it. It fed my inner demons and left no room for grief.

So when I was ordered to report to Crime Stoppers HQ in Brisbane at eight o'clock sharp on a Monday morning, I rocked up at quarter past nine. Immediately, I felt like I'd been tossed back into a world that no longer spoke my language. As I strolled past reception, I sensed the eyes on my back. Maybe they thought I'd just crawled out of a drainpipe or wandered in from the set of *Who Wants to Be a Cop*. Spoiler alert: I wasn't winning any prizes.

# DONNY

'Oi, Maguire! You're late,' barked the Senior Sergeant, a bloke who looked like he'd been steeped in old coffee for a decade. His uniform hung like a curtain, and his frown could clear a paddock of crows.

'Yeah, well, traffic was a nightmare, and this is the earliest I've been up in two years,' I said, slinging on a grin that had worked better on criminals than coppers. He crossed his arms and rolled his eyes hard enough to spot his own spine.

'Just get in there, Maguire. We've got a class on being a decent citizen. You'll need it.'

The training room had the vibe of a funeral wake. I grabbed a seat, wondering if snacks were allowed or if this was one of those dry, no-fun affairs. The Sergeant piped up: 'Welcome to Crime Stoppers. Today we're going to talk about community engagement and the importance of being a responsible citizen.' I stifled a laugh, thinking about all the lines I'd crossed in the name of duty. *But hey, at least I'm here and trying.* The whole place felt off, like stepping into an alternate reality. I half expected to see aliens by the water cooler. Eight hours in the same cramped room? Fuck that. I was sure I'd suffocate by lunch.

They gave me a few menial tasks: answer a call, take notes, punch it into the system. For those not familiar, Crime Stoppers is a hotline for anonymous dibber dobbers, a real-life game of Spot the Snitch. Well, at least, that's how I saw it back then. The calls trickled in. Petty complaints.

'I saw a cat in a tree.'

'Neighbour's barbecue is too loud.'

My brain was turning to soup. Then, a call came through that yanked me back to life. 'Hello, you've got Crime Stoppers. What would you like to report?'

I said, trying to sound halfway professional. 'I just wanna report my neighbour smoking dope,' said the voice on the other end, serious as a heart attack. I blinked.

'Are you bloody serious, mate? You wanna dog your neighbour over a bit of green?'

'Yeah…'

'Mate, worry about your own backyard, hey? You know what happens to snitches… snitches get stitches.' My voice was sharp, maybe a little too sharp. I could feel the old heat boiling over.

Right then, the Inspector, built like a fridge and twice as charming, stormed over and snatched the phone from me like I was holding a live grenade. He handed it off to a calm-looking woman at the next desk who probably knew how to handle humans without starting fires.

'Alright, Todd, let's go for a walk. Cool down a bit,' he said, motioning to the hallway. As we strolled out, I couldn't help myself.

'What a bloody dog! Doesn't he know he could get himself into serious trouble with that sort of carry on? There are fuckin' rules out there!'

The boss gave me a sideways glance, a faint smirk on his lips. 'I think we might find another job for you, mate. This might not be your scene.'

And just like that, reality punched me in the face. The world was moving on. But I was still stuck dragging the weight of an identity that didn't quite fit anymore. Turns out, coming back to the land of the living was going to be a lot messier than I'd bargained for.

# 46

# THE MAN NO
# ONE SEES

I lasted in Crime Stoppers for two of the longest months of my life, they then shipped me off to Dutton Park Police Station to finish my so-called reintegration into 'normal' general duties policing. Back then, coppers could ride the train in full uniform and no one blinked. I was on a late shift. On my way to work in the middle of the day. I took a seat down the back of the carriage, the kind of spot where you can watch everyone, but no one is watching you. Old undercover habits die hard. I never liked having people behind me. It was quiet, too quiet. Just a few scattered commuters with blank faces, bags on laps, all pretending the world was fine. But I wasn't pretending. I was scanning, clocking shoes, body language and eye movements. I didn't know how to sit still anymore. Not really. Then the door slid open.

A bloke stepped through from the next carriage, walking towards me. I blinked twice, then three more times. My gut dropped before my brain caught up. It was Marshall from Caboolture. The violent, unpredictable, loose unit with a blade fetish and no fear of consequence. Last I'd heard, he was inside for stabbing Krystal. And now here he was, walking towards me like a ghost through fog. My heart thumped once real loud. My pulse spiked, hot and fast, I knew I wasn't Donny anymore, but he didn't. He was staring straight at me. I didn't flinch, didn't blink, but was locked on and ready.

He kept walking slowly and deliberately towards me with his eyes flicking from the windows to me and back again like he was trying to place me. His head tilted and his brows tightened. I shifted slightly to balance myself and then clenched my fists. If he recognised me, the carriage would turn into a fucking crime scene. He reached my row, paused for a second, turned and stared at me. I stared back. And then, just like that, he turned, opened the door to the next carriage, and walked on. Didn't say a word. Didn't recognise me. I exhaled slow and tight like defusing a bomb.

In that moment, it hit me all at once: Donny was invisible now. He was gone. Whatever version of me Marshall had known, whatever mask I'd worn back then, it was dust. And maybe that was good. But sitting there, alone on that rattling train, I didn't feel free. I felt erased. Like I'd become a man who could vanish in plain sight. And no one would notice.

Finally, the six months of reintegration came to an end. I'd passed every random piss test, every psychometric quiz, every tedious sit down with psychologists trying to crack the surface. Hell, I even saw straight through a textbook Crime and Misconduct Commission setup—an abandoned car, a bag of speed on the front seat. I seized it, logged it and booked it as evidence without blinking. They wanted to test the ex-undercover and let me tell you, it was a piss-weak effort. After two years of living in lies, I'd become an expert in the art of performance. And I wasn't about to let that show. Not to them. Not yet. I had the system figured out. I knew the rules, and I knew the cost of breaking them. The last thing I was going to do was open up to the QPS or any shrink they paid by the hour. No way I was handing them the keys to my damage.

So, I played the part. I smiled and nodded, threw out the right buzzwords and said the things they wanted to hear. Meanwhile, inside, I was barely holding it together. But they didn't see that. They never do. Because the moment you admit you're injured psychologically or emotionally, you're done. They slap a label on you. Liability. Weak. Broken. The camaraderie, the brotherhood, the quiet trust between coppers, all gone right before your eyes. One confession and you're on the outer. I'd seen it happen too many times. And I wasn't about to be next.

So, I kept the mask on. I played the good little soldier and walked the line like it wasn't razor-thin. I pretended everything was fine while the real me, the frayed and fragile version, hid behind my eyes, waiting for a crack to open. It was a dangerous game. But I was good at it. Maybe too good.

And as the months dragged on, I couldn't shake the feeling that the whole performance was about to implode. Like I was one wrong move away from everything I'd buried crashing back to the surface.

# 47

# THE COMEDOWN

Adjusting back to normal life after undercover was like an AFL midfielder packing into the front row of a rugby league scrum. I was in the game, sure. But it wasn't the right one. Every hit felt wrong. Every move felt offbeat. After the Crime Stoppers disaster and the ghost train run-in with Marshall, I was meant to be finding my footing. Reintegration. Re-entry. All those fancy terms they used to make it sound like we were astronauts returning from space, not broken cops crawling out of the underworld. But truthfully, I wasn't ready to retire from being Donny, and Todd wasn't ready to take his place.

Donny had been my armour, sharp, dangerous, unfeeling. He could lie without flinching, charm the violent, drink with killers and sleep beside death like it was a warm blanket. He didn't cry, didn't hope and didn't need. He just survived, and I'd worn him so well, I didn't know how to take the mask off—to put him away for good. The job was over, but the wiring was still hot. My brain didn't trust safety.

My body didn't recognise calm. So I found myself continuing to search for the edge, for noise, chaos and numbness.

Enter MDMA.

The lure of the escape was too strong. I felt like I was continuously floating through a Queen of the Stone Age track—*Feel Good Hit of the Summer*. I was one pill away from liking techno, and I hated myself for it. But I kept going because sober meant feeling, and I wasn't ready for that. I had been told to go back to work life and be a normal person. Wear the uniform. Catch the train. Push paper and smile, but I rebelled harder than a second-hand lawn mower coughing up its last breath. I was seething and full of rage I couldn't name, drowning my grief in beers and pills, all while hating the world with a passion that burned hotter than the bitumen in January. What I truly craved more than the noise, more than the high, was connection. Just like I felt in the two years I was Donny. What I got was the cold shoulder.

People looked at me like I was radioactive. Like they could smell the violence on me; like I was some kind of monster. They didn't recognise this version of me and to be honest, neither did I. The anger had changed me. It had sunk into my bones and twisted my grin into a sneer. People judged me for what they saw in the moment—the short fuse, the flat eyes, the bitterness. They couldn't see the ghost underneath, the storm still swirling inside. And they couldn't see the man still wearing Donny like a second skin.

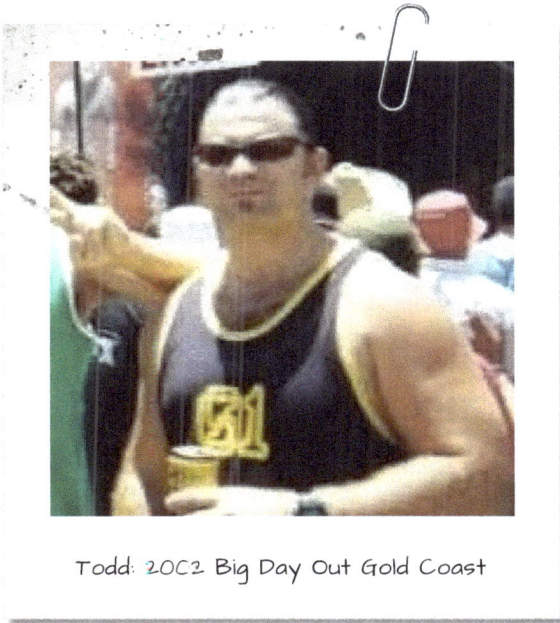

Todd: 2002 Big Day Out Gold Coast

But I felt it. Every day, Donny had kept me alive. But now, he was killing me slowly.

# 48

# THE FLICKER

realise the anger, the hatred, the binge drinking were not the core wounds. Just symptoms and Band-Aids on bullet holes. The real damage ran deeper, and I was a walking injury, limping through a world that had moved on, bleeding from places no one could see. And because I didn't know how to sit with it, with the grief, the guilt, the years of pretending, I tried to burn it out of myself. Tried to outdrink it, outfight it, outrun it. The funny thing is pain doesn't work like that. It just sits and waits, it watches, and it grows.

Through all that chaos Peta was my rock the only one who didn't flinch. She saw something in me, not Donny the chameleon, not the bitter, fire eyed version of Todd. But me. The man underneath. The flicker of something good. A trace of who I used to be, or maybe who I could become. She didn't try to fix me and didn't ask for explanations or timelines. She just stood beside me, steadfast, unshaken and unconditional. To be honest that terrified me. Because for someone like me, someone who'd built a life on lies and masks real connection felt like standing at the edge of a cliff. When we eventually moved in together, it was a minefield of emotion I didn't know how to navigate. Living with her sister added a layer of pressure, two caring women watching me tiptoe around the wreckage of my own identity. But still, Peta was steady. She didn't crowd me and didn't demand more than I could give. She just cared and that made me pull away, not because I didn't love her but because I did. The more I felt for her, the more afraid I became.

Because if it went south, if I failed, I wouldn't just lose her I'd lose the last thread tying me to the man I was still trying to claw back. Donny didn't know how to love. He was built for survival, not intimacy. He could fake connection, mirror emotion, even charm people into trusting him but it was all for the job. All part of the act. But this wasn't a job. This was real.

And Todd—the fractured, struggling version of me trying to remerge—wanted this. I wanted her and wanted a life that wasn't built on manipulation or fear. The trouble was, Donny never truly left. He lingered, just under the surface. He was the voice in my head when I wanted to run, the old reflex when I flinched at closeness. The pull towards self-destruction every time love felt too good to be true and I couldn't kill him. Not without killing the parts of me that had kept me alive.

But I could try to choose differently.

Every day with Peta was a choice to stay, to be honest, to risk being seen. It wasn't easy and it wasn't clean. But she made it possible, she made me want to fight not only to survive, but to belong. Brick by brick, life was trying to rebuild itself around me. But rebuilding only works if the foundation isn't still on fire.

# 49

# A REASON TO
# COME HOME

Things were finally starting to line up on the work front as I landed a spot in the State Flying Squad, then switched over to Property Crime, a job that had me bouncing around the state, staying sharp but grounded, less undercover chaos and more good old-fashioned detective work.

In 2003, Peta and I bought our first home together. That was one of the only real upsides of undercover work—I'd squirrelled away enough cash to help us get a proper place, a roof and a future. For the first time in a long time, I started to imagine what life might look like if I stuck around long enough to enjoy it. The kind of life where I wasn't always looking over my shoulder. The kind of life where maybe, just maybe, I wasn't completely broken.

In 2004, we tied the knot. It was real, and it was fun. It wasn't any Hollywood production, just us, surrounded by family and friends. There were no grand speeches or fairy-tale moments, but there was a quite promise exchanged that day. A promise that despite the chaos I'd come from and the chaos still buried inside me, maybe I could still be something more than just the guy who survived. I loved Peta and somehow through it all she still loved me back.

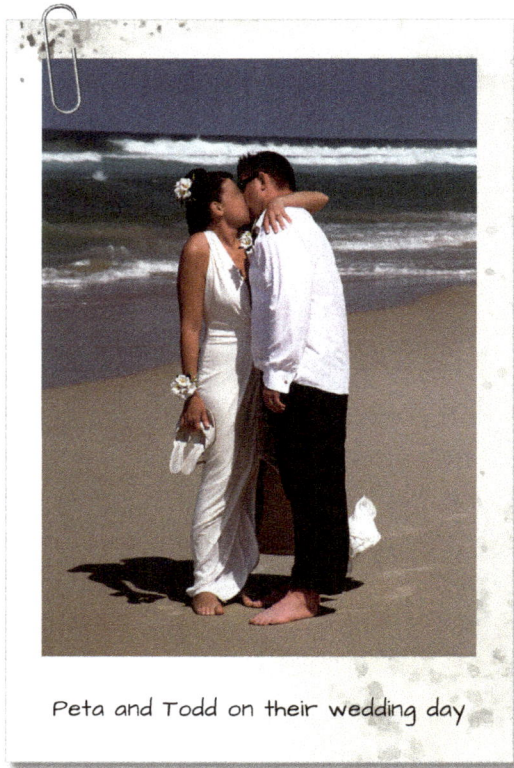

Peta and Todd on their wedding day

Then in October 2005, our son Fletcher came screaming into the world red faced and just perfect. In that moment, life cracked open. The walls I had built to keep everything out, grief, guilt and fear all started to crumble. Suddenly, I wasn't just a copper or a husband,

I was someone's dad. Holding Fletcher for the first time felt like gripping something both terrifying and sacred. Here was this tiny, fragile little bloke who didn't care about my past or what I'd seen; he just wanted warmth, safety and love. I'd spent years surrounded by death and violence, thinking I'd already seen the extremes of life. But this, this was life. This was purpose. Life suddenly felt whole, like for once, the universe handed me something not to fight or flee from, but to nurture and a real reason to show up. A reason to come home.

Fletcher didn't fix me as that wasn't his job. But he cracked me open in a way I didn't know was possible, and for the first time in a long time, I didn't just want to live I wanted to *be better*.

For him.

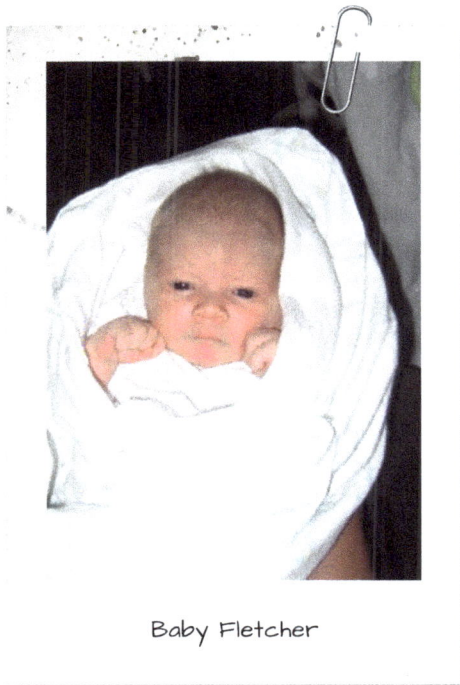

Baby Fletcher

I transferred to Fortitude Valley CIB and traded the travelling for routine, the 7:07am train, *The Courier-Mail* in hand, shoulder to shoulder with other public servants in their shiny shoes and stiff collars. It felt foreign at first, like I was wearing someone else's life, but I got used to it.

In 2005, I wandered down to the local footy field just to see if the old engine still ran. The Samford Stags were giving it a solid crack in the Brisbane Second Division. The team was a mashup of BRL veterans, young guns with something to prove, and washed-up blokes like me trying to outrun the past. And let's be honest, I was in my thirties and built more like a bar fridge than an athlete. That first game nearly killed me. I felt like I'd been run over by a cattle truck. But stubbornness is a hell of a thing, and I kept turning up, kept pushing and I kept proving to myself that there was still fight in the tank. My first milestone was lasting fifteen minutes on the field without gasping for a durrie.

Three seasons later, I was still lacing up the boots. Still charging into contact like it owed me money. Sure, I broke my forearm in my first year and needed a plate, the whole works. Classic freight train, I'd lined up in the second row, looked at the bloke next to me and said, 'You go low, I'm taking this cu**'s head off.' Turns out, he ducked, and I clocked the top of his skull with my arm instead. I staggered back, proud as hell. 'Did you hear that crack? Reckon I got him!' My mate just stared at my arm. 'Yeah… not sure about him, but you're cooked, mate.' I looked down. There it was a dent in my forearm the size of his head. That's when the pain caught up. I raised my other hand for a sub, trying not to black out.

But it didn't stop me, not a chance.

Next season, I strapped on a foam pad over my 'Warwick Farm' like Big Mal Meninga in the'90s, my childhood hero. He was massive, fast, fearless and I wore that pad like a badge of honour. A reminder that I was still in the fight, that I still had more to give. Footy never became a job and that's what I loved about it. It was fun. It was freedom. It was something I chose, not something I had to survive. It was the people I met along the way, the stories we shared, the places it took me that stitched something back into the fabric of my life. Something solid and something true.

I wasn't healed, not even close. But I was moving and breathing and showing up every day and that counted for something. Because now I wasn't just playing life for myself, I was playing for Fletcher and for Peta. For a life I never thought I'd live long enough to want.

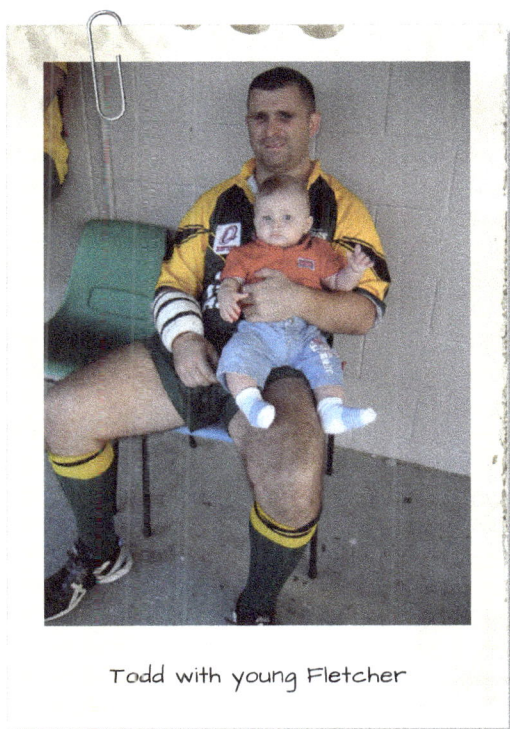

Todd with young Fletcher

# 50

# BEING DAD

A way from footy, I thought I was making progress. Life had structure now—a steady job, a house, a beautiful wife, an amazing son who thought the sun rose and set with me. On paper, I was back on track. But inside, I was still burning. The anger hadn't left; it had just found new places to hide. I was snapping at the littlest things, knocking back beers like they were water and burying myself in work, in anything loud enough to drown the silence. I was a textbook case of PTSD, but too stubborn or too scared to admit it.

And beneath all that rage, restlessness and exhaustion was the grief. Still there, still sharp and still echoing from the day Karen died. I never really gave that pain a place to live. I just carried it like a silent fracture in my chest. I'd been so deep in survival mode, during undercover I was disconnected, half feral, that I never let myself feel it. Not properly. I couldn't, because feeling it meant accepting it and if I accepted it, I might never get up again. So, I continued to try to outrun it.

I chased distraction and adrenaline. I chased anything that made me feel something or nothing. I thought that was strength. That if I kept moving fast enough, grief couldn't catch me. But grief doesn't chase. It waits.

Having a son changed everything. Fletcher wasn't just a baby; he was a mirror I couldn't avoid. A tiny heartbeat walking around outside my body. Proof that something good could still come from someone like me. He didn't know about Karen, or Donny, or the lies I'd lived. He didn't care about the damage or the darkness. He just knew I was Dad, his anchor, his safe place, his whole world and that lit a fire in me, not the reckless kind I'd been burning in for years, but something steadier. A fire that said *stay, fight, be better*. This little boy didn't need a ghost for a father. He needed someone solid. And I needed to become that man not just for him, but to prove to myself that I still could.

I knew I needed help, so I threw myself into therapy sessions sitting across from professionals; I tried to talk it out. But this was the early 2000s and mental health support back then was about as user friendly as a VHS player with no remote. There were no podcasts. No Instagram reels normalising trauma. No online communities of other broken men learning how to be whole. It wasn't like now where you can hear a bloke on a podcast talk about PTSD and suddenly realise, *shit, that's me*. Back then, mental health was a closed room with bad lighting and a cheap plastic chair. You walked in, ticked boxes on a clipboard, and got told to breathe deeply and go for a jog. It wasn't built for someone like me. The system didn't speak my language, and it didn't know what to do with a copper who'd worn a wire through speed deals, had a shotgun pointed at his head, and still couldn't talk about the day he cradled the woman he loved when she died.

Every good day felt like luck. I was trying to be a father, a husband, a man, all while wrestling with a version of me that wouldn't let go. Some days I was fine. Other days, I wanted to punch walls or drink myself stupid, or just simply disappear. But I didn't. I had two reasons to keep getting out of bed: Peta and Fletcher.

Peta never flinched, I knew she saw through it all—the fire, the fear, the fractured edges—and loved me anyway the best way she knew how. And Fletcher, my boy, gave me something I didn't know I was still allowed to have: hope and unconditional love. I had to figure it out. Not for me. For them.

I just had to keep going.

# 51

# BEIGE COUCHES

Everyone said the same thing, on repeat. *You need to talk to someone.* But talking never worked for me. I didn't like pouring my guts out to a stranger with a clipboard and a clock. I didn't want to offload it onto my mates or dump it all on Peta, although I did. Some people would use my anger and grief against me, and others I could tell were just over it. Burned out on my pain, and honestly, thinking about it made it worse. Digging it up only buried me deeper. So yeah, I tried therapy, over and over again, sitting on beige couches, answering the questions, even playing along for a while. But the truth was it didn't ease the ache, it didn't quiet the rage, and it sure as hell didn't bring Karen back.

What I hated most was sitting across from some therapist who couldn't even remember her name, who'd glance at the clock more than at me. Just when I'd work up the courage to open up, to finally say the unsayable, they'd cut me off. *'Time's up.'* No shit it was. Then I'd walk out $180 poorer, only to see them greet the next poor bastard like it was speed dating for the soul. They all said therapy would make me 'normal' again. But what the hell was *normal* after what I'd lived through. The broken sleep, the outbursts, the weight in my chest, this was my new normal. Trying to go back to the person I was before Karen died was like trying to glue back a shattered mirror and pretend it never cracked. And the worst part, I resented anyone who tried to help, especially the ones who'd never seen real shit. I'd sit there thinking, *What the fuck would you know?* It's like a bloke explaining the pain of childbirth—you just don't get to speak on what you haven't lived.

Everyone had answers but none of them fit, and that's what no one tells you about trauma. It doesn't respond to logic. It's not a maths equation you can solve with breathing exercises and polite affirmations. It lives in your bones. And it doesn't let go just because you pay someone to listen.

# 52

# THE LONG
# WAY BACK

Years had passed before I finally saw it: if anything was going to change, it had to start with me. No therapist was going to fix it. No program. No second chance served up on a silver platter. Just me staring down at my own reflection, asking the kind of questions that make your stomach turn. Sure, the anger still simmered, but I'd gone soft too, in ways that didn't sit right. Somewhere between the politics of policing, the pressure to keep peace at home, and friendships that expected loyalty without truth, I'd become a yes man. Nodding along, biting my tongue and avoiding conflict because I couldn't stomach another loss. I wasn't the rock anymore. I was the cushion, soft around the edges, built to absorb everyone else's shit. I smoothed things over, swallowed words, avoided the hard conversations. Always worried that if I pushed back, if I stood my ground, I'd lose someone. Again!

# DONNY

Years of grinding pressure had stripped me down. Bit by bit, I'd shaped myself to fit what others needed at work, at home, with mates until I couldn't even recognise the original blueprint. My masculinity didn't vanish all at once. It leaked out slowly, like air from a punctured tyre. Eventually, I couldn't tell if I was standing firm… or just standing still. I started to see it in the younger blokes on the footy field, in the ones I coached. They were fighting the same internal war, told to be strong, but not show it. To lead but not dominate. To care but never crack. And I realised this wasn't just my struggle. It was bigger than that. We'd lost sight of what masculinity and strength really meant. Not bravado. Not control. But that steady kind of masculinity that shows up, speaks the truth, and doesn't flinch when the wind howls. And I wanted it back.

I learnt to understand and accept that the pain was a gift. It was the pathway to gain power over my thoughts. Everyone in the world will experience pain in their life, and in fact more pain than pleasure. Because life is a struggle. Embracing pain as part of your journey makes life just that little bit easier.

I had learnt over the years, to me, being a man meant staying calm under pressure, owning my emotions, speaking up when it mattered and standing my ground when it counted. Not because it was easy, but because someone had to. And being a loving partner, well that wasn't about flowers or sweet words. It was about creating safety, real safety: physical, emotional and mental. Now, I understood that in theory but putting it into practice was a war. Some days, I felt like I was making real progress. Then, bang, a setback would hit, and I'd spiral back to square one. Like riding a rollercoaster in the dark, blindfolded, no brakes. And it would take months to crawl out of those holes. Alcohol had always been there since I was fourteen, part rite of passage, part rebellion. But after Karen died, it changed. It wasn't just a crutch. I wasn't drinking to unwind. I was drinking to disappear and to numb the relentless ache in my chest. I told myself I wasn't an alcoholic. I was just addicted to escape.

There were stretches where I gave it up just to prove I could. And I could. Those weeks felt lighter, clearer, almost like I could breathe properly again. But even now, that whisper still creeps in: *Just one more, mate. You've earned it.* And sometimes, I listen. Not because I want to but because guilt, weirdly, feels easier than grief. So, I kept walking that tightrope somewhere between the man I wanted to be, and the shadow I couldn't quite shake. I knew what I had to do. But bridging that gap, it felt like trying to leap a canyon with no rope, no safety net and no guarantee. This loop played out for years. I fell, got up again and fell again over and over. But through it all, Peta stood by me steadier than I ever deserved; she was my anchor in the storm and she copped more than anyone should have.

And for that, I'll be forever grateful.

# 53

# ACCEPTANCE

As I step into my fifties, the truth hits harder than ever: time is no longer an endless runway. The reality of mortality, of lost years and the scars they left behind have become impossible to ignore. With this realisation, a quiet urgency has crept in, a need to make peace with what's gone, and to make something out of what's left. I've learned a few things along the way, real hard lessons most of them. Lessons earned in blood, silence and late-night spirals. So, here's what I know now, or at least what I'm starting to understand.

## Let go of the need for answers.

For years I chased meaning like a dog chasing headlights; desperate, blinded, and getting nowhere. I wanted to know *why* things happened the way they did. Why Karen died. Why I became Donny. Why I couldn't sleep, couldn't feel, couldn't talk without boiling over. But some questions don't have answers. Or if they do, they don't come with clarity or closure, and so I've had to let go, slowly and painfully accepting that not everything needs to be solved and not everything does have a reason. Some pain just needs to be carried, not cured, and in that surrender, I've found moments of peace; tiny, hard earned breaths of calm.

## Embrace life's fragility.

In twenty-seven years of policing, I've seen hundreds of dead bodies, from the young to the elderly. I've knelt beside families who lost children, parents, partners. I've seen lives ended in ways that defy reason. But nothing—*nothing*—compares to the helpless agony of watching someone you love die in front of you. Fighting for them, begging and losing them anyway. It rewires you and breaks the illusion that life is fair or predictable. In that devastation, I've come to cherish the small things more fiercely: a morning coffee, a laugh with Fletcher, the way Peta still shakes her head when I'm being an idiot. This world is brutal but it's also breathtaking, if you let it be.

## Focus on what you can control.

Reflecting on the chaos and mistakes I made during those years, it's tempting to package my experiences into tidy advice and say, 'Here's what you should do.' But that would be bullshit. I'm not here to preach as I don't have the answers. This book isn't a guide to getting life right in a few simple steps; it's a raw, honest account of how badly it can go when you don't. A map of missteps. A record of the hard lessons I had to learn the painful way. It's less a blueprint and more a cautionary tale. A reminder that even when you lose yourself, it's still possible to claw something back.

## Learn to love yourself.

Learn to enjoy your own company. Do not rely on or expect anyone to fill that space. Solitude is not a prison, it's where you get stronger. The man that can truly be alone and happy in his own skin is somebody that no one can control.

It took me a long time to realise, but I had to turn Karen's rejection into fuel, a reason to grow stronger. And I began to see her choice for what it was—hers alone. Not mine to carry.

Everyone's storm is different. Your pain, your grief, your darkness won't look like mine. But the feeling of being lost is universal, and while I can't walk your path for you, I can offer something I learned along mine: when everything else feels out of control, focus on what you can. You can't undo the past. You can't fix other people and you can't guarantee anything. But you can choose how you respond. You can decide moment by moment whether you're going to show up bitter or calm. Whether you're going to lash out or lean in. Whether you're going to let the pain define you or shape you into something stronger. You can start small, choose honesty over silence and grace over rage, action over avoidance. Surround yourself with people who lift you, not drain you and learn to say no when it matters, and yes when it's right. It won't solve everything, but it will start something. Something real. Something within reach.

When you're ready, and I mean really ready, that's where healing begins.

## The therapy myth.

When I tell you I tried, I really did. I sat in those sterile rooms, poured my guts out to strangers with degrees on the wall and clocks on their desks. I left those sessions hollower than when I walked in. I don't fault them, some people find healing there, but for me, talking didn't loosen the knots. It tightened them and thinking made it worse. Feeling made it dangerous. Therapy didn't ease the ache in my heart or the grief of not being able to change that fateful day and my decisions in the years to follow. It didn't make the nightmares stop or explain the guilt that still punches me in the ribs some nights. These sessions felt like I was renting compassion by the hour and that kind of help doesn't stick for me.

What I finally learned was this: therapy wasn't going to rescue me, and no one else was either. I had to stop outsourcing my survival. The answers weren't in their questions or their notebooks—they had to come from me. The day I stopped expecting someone else to fix me was the first day I actually began to heal.

## The fight for sleep and sanity.

Even now, sleep's a cruel joke. Twenty-seven years of shift work, trauma, and meds have shredded my body clock. After leaving the QPS in late 2023, I figured I'd feel better. Lighter. Rested. But I was still dragging my arse through each day like a zombie with a hangover. Eventually, I saw a sleep specialist. They hooked me up with more wires than an FBI sting and ran two full tests. The result: Hyperarousal. Apparently, my brain never truly switches off. Even when I'm asleep, it's still running sprints. A classic trauma response, they said. I asked, 'What's the fix?' The Doc shrugged. 'A lobotomy?'

The Doc laughed and said, 'Not that serious but along those lines. Good luck, mate.'

So now I'm in the deep end of the experimental pool chasing relief through Ketamine therapy. Hospitals call it pain relief. Dealers call it Special K. I just call it a gamble. I'm hoping not to vanish into a K-hole, but after everything, that risk feels almost clean compared to the slow rot of doing nothing. If you've made it this far, you already know—conventional paths were never going to save me.

The truth is, PTSD isn't leaving my life. It's stitched into me. But I'll keep searching, keep testing whatever edges science or medicine put on the table. Because if there's even a sliver of something that can ease the weight, I'll take it. I'm not done fighting for a better way to live.

And still, I keep going.

Because this isn't just a survival story; it's a rebuilding one. I've been the ghost, the actor, the fighter, the failure, the husband and the father. I've clawed back bits of myself from the wreckage, ever so slowly and at times brutally. If there's anything I've learned from the edge, it's this. Healing doesn't always look like healing. Sometimes it looks like showing up when you don't want to. Holding your kid's hand when your own hands are shaking. Letting your wife love you, even when you're not sure you deserve it. I don't have it all figured out. I never will. But I'm still here. Still trying. Still learning. And that, finally, is enough.

# Epilogue

# WHAT MY MUM TAUGHT ME

In October 2023, I faced an unimaginable loss: my greatest supporter, my mum. She went into hospital with a chest infection, and before we knew it, she was gone. When she was first admitted to the hospital, we thought it was just a minor setback, but reality sank in fast. The doctor sat us down for *that* conversation, the one that pulls the rug out from under you. There was nothing more they could do.

From that moment, we moved into a kind of vigil. My sister and her daughters came first, then my brother, then Dad. Finally, it was my turn. I arrived at the hospital, heart heavy but steady. I pulled up a chair beside her bed and held her hand. We sat together and watched TV just like old times, grasping at whatever normalcy we could.

# DONNY

As the hours passed, the air changed. Something shifted. The nurse came in and quietly nodded. 'This is it. Hold her hand tightly.' So, I did. I gripped her hand with everything I had, pouring all my love and strength into that final moment. As she took her last breath, I felt something I didn't expect. I felt honour. I'd been her safe place till the end. I like to think she knew that. That she trusted I could carry her through.

And this happened on the very first day of my new job after QPS.

In the weeks that followed, I made a vow: to honour her life, to carry her strength and spirit with me. To do better. And I meant it. But there was a thought that wouldn't leave me: *Would Karen have been proud of how I handled her death?* Deep down, I know the answer. And it hurts. I think not. I failed her, and I certainly didn't handle her loss with grace or strength. That truth sits heavy. The regret still stings. It's taken me twenty-five years to get here, to face that truth fully. To say out loud: 'I wish I'd done better. I'm sorry I didn't save you.'

My mum's memory is now my compass. Her love is the measure. Life is far too short to stay stuck in the dark. It's time to step into the light and start making every moment count. Take your time, wherever you are on your own journey. There's no race. But with resilience and the right people by your side, healing will come.

To sign off with a quote from Les Norton, 'Know everyone – trust no one – and paddle your own canoe.'

As you were…

# FROM ONE
# SURVIVOR TO
# ANOTHER

*'One day you will tell your story of how
you overcame what you went through, and
it will be someone else's survival guide.'*

–Brené Brown

Living with what the medical world calls PTSD has always felt wrong to me. 'Disorder' makes it sound like I'm broken beyond repair. I don't buy that. I call it Post-Traumatic Stress *Injury* (PTSI)—because that's what it feels like: an injury to the brain. And I've had plenty of injuries before. Footy left me with a busted eye, and an arm and knee full of pins and plates. None of them ever healed perfectly, but they healed enough to keep me moving. My mind is no different, just no plates and screws yet.

Most injuries mend if you give them time, treatment, and grit. The scars never disappear—but scars aren't weakness. They're the proof that you took the hit, and you're still here.

For me, PTSI is an ongoing journey. It doesn't just fade into the background; it's something I manage every day. There are moments when the shadows creep in, when triggers blindside me, when the nights stretch long and anxious. The difference now is that I can see the signs. I can feel myself pulling back, snapping at people, drowning. And when I do, I know it's time to claw my way back to the things that keep me steady and reconnect with the grounding forces in my life. I don't wait for someone else to fix me anymore—I keep searching, keep working, because healing might be slow, but it's still possible.

Like I have said, for me, solace doesn't come from traditional therapy sessions. Instead, I find strength and healing in the unwavering support of my family and, more recently, putting pen to paper. This has allowed me to process emotions and experiences that were once too painful to confront. Writing this book, in particular, has been the most therapeutic endeavour I've undertaken. It has allowed me to express aloud my deepest, darkest thoughts and moments in time without breaking down.

If you've made it this far, thank you for walking this road with me. Maybe you've seen parts of your own story in mine. Maybe not. But if this book has done anything, I hope it's cracked open the door to a conversation about trauma, about grief, about identity and about what it means to rebuild when everything inside you feels like rubble.

I used to think healing meant fixing myself. That I had to be the man I was before it all fell apart. But I've learned that healing isn't about going back—it's about going forward with what you've got left. And sometimes, that's enough. So, if you're still in the thick of it, still fighting your own demons, just know this: you're not alone. Keep showing up. Keep fighting. Not to survive but to live. Because one day, someone might need your story to survive their own.

Thank you for allowing me to share my story.

Yours in healing, Todd.

# LEGAL INDEMNITY

A lot of people warned me about the legal ramifications of writing this book. As I've said all names have been changed. I have been very vague about the methodologies that we used as undercover agents to record and obtain evidence from the crooks. In saying that I hope they are not using the same devices because in 2001 they were outdated. And for extra piece of mind, I got solicitor Dan Gleebitz from Right and Wong & Associates to run a bloodshot eye across the content. And I can gladly say that it was all ok. Then we went to lunch.

# ABOUT THE AUTHOR

Todd Maguire's retirement from the Queensland Police Service (QPS) in 2023 marked the end of a remarkable twenty-seven-year career dedicated to serving his community. His extensive experience included deep undercover operations, serious criminal investigations, bomb detection, counter-terrorism and tactical crime operations, where he served across the state. As a Detective, Todd was notably the lead investigator for Operation Echo Shine, the response to forty-three women in southeast Queensland being sexually assaulted while on running trails and bikeways in 2006. Further notable investigations were the tomato poisoning in Bowen, which caused fifty million dollars damage to the farming industry in 2010. QPS issued a two-hundred-thousand-dollar reward.

Todd has positively impacted countless lives, particularly through his efforts to combat dangerous drugs and organised crime. Through his commitment and bravery, Todd Maguire made significant contributions public safety and the fight against crime in Queensland. His legacy is one of resilience and dedication in the face of adversity, reflecting the vital role that law enforcement plays in protecting communities.

## Recognitions and commendations

The following awards were presented to the author by Commissioner Bob Atkinson in recognition of his dedication, bravery and significant contributions to the investigation and prosecution of major criminal activity in Queensland.

### Certificate of Recognition 2004

*'In recognition of your contribution to the investigation and detection of significant criminal history in the state of Queensland.'*

### Commissioners Citation 2004

*'Senior Constable Todd John Maguire performed duties as a covert police operative during the period of 31 January 2001 and 31 January 2003.*

*During this period Senior Constable Maguire performed covert duties in Controlled Operations known as AXIL, ICEPICK, SPENT, SHINE, TALARA, NIFTY, THORPE, YEW, AARON, SWAN and WATTLES.*

*A total of 52 persons were charged with 530 offences, including 15 for Trafficking in Dangerous Drugs a consequence of these operations.*

*Senior Constable Maguire infiltrated criminal networks to gather evidence and intelligence used in the arrest and prosecution of individuals involved in major and organised criminal activity. Senior Constable Maguire also gathered evidence and intelligence used for restraint and forfeiture of assets.*

*Senior Constable Maguire, whilst displaying dedication, resourcefulness and initiative in the performance of his duties as a covert police operative, made significant contributions to the investigation and detection of major and organised crime in Queensland.'*

## Commissioner's Certificate of Service

### Detective Sergeant

# Todd John Maguire

*Registered Number: 4010502*

Sergeant Maguire commenced as a Recruit with the Queensland Police Service on 7 October 1996. He served as a Police Officer from 26 April 1997 to 20 October 2023 and resigned after 27 years and 1 month of dedicated service to the community of Queensland.

### Awards Granted

| | |
|---|---|
| Queensland Police Service Medal | 2007 |
| 2010 - 2011 Queensland Flood and Cyclone Citation | 2011 |
| 15 Year Clasp to the Queensland Police Service Medal | 2012 |
| National Medal | 2012 |
| Queensland Police 150 Years Citation | 2014 |
| National Police Service Medal | 2015 |
| G20 Citation | 2016 |
| 20 Year Clasp to the Queensland Police Service Medal | 2017 |
| XXI Commonwealth Games Citation | 2019 |
| 25 Year Clasp to the Queensland Police Service Medal | 2022 |
| 1st Clasp to the National Medal | 2023 |

### Ranks & Appointment

| | |
|---|---|
| Recruit | 7 October 1996 |
| Constable | 26 April 1997 |
| Senior Constable | 1 October 2003 |
| Detective | 3 November 2006 |
| Sergeant | 25 March 2013 |

### Stations / Establishments

| | |
|---|---|
| Queensland Police Academy (Recruit) | 7 October 1996 |
| Gold Coast District (Training) | 26 April 1997 |
| Broadbeach Station | 1 May 1998 |
| Indooroopilly Station | 25 March 2000 |
| Crime Operations Branch | 8 January 2001 |
| North Brisbane District Criminal Investigation Branch, Fortitude Valley | 26 September 2005 |
| Mackay Whitsunday District Criminal Investigation Branch, Bowen | 23 December 2008 |
| Sunshine Coast District Tactical Crime Squad, Kawana | 14 January 2012 |
| Crime and Corruption Commission, Crime Group | 14 February 2022 |
| Operational Policy and Improvement, Project Officer | 25 September 2023 |

KATARINA CARROLL APM
COMMISSIONER

# Donny The Soundtrack

**CD 1**

1. The Screaming Jets - Shivers
2. Paul Kelly – I've done all the dumb things
2. Celibate Rifles – It's a Wonderful Life
3. TISM - I'm on the Drug
4. Right Said Fred - I'm Too Sexy
5. Bondi Cigars – Howlin at the moon
6. Regurgitator – (I sucked a lot of Cock)
7. Better than Ezra - Good
8. Sister Hazel - All For You
9. Prince - Party like its 1999
10. Blink-182 - Adams Song
11. System of a Down - Lonely Day
12. The Corrs – Forgiven not Forgotten
13. Puddle of Mud - She Hates Me
14. The Verve Pipe - The Freshman
15. Evanescence - My Immortal
16. Powderfinger - Lost and Running
17. Corey Taylor - Snuff (Live)
18. Clutch - Gone Cold
19. Five Finger Death Punch - Jekyll and Hyde
20. Birds of Tokyo - The Greatest Mistakes
21. Lenny Kravits - Fly Away

**CD2**

21. Slipknot - People = Shit
22. Eminem – The Real Slim Shady
23. Slipknot - The Heretic Anthem
24. Metallica – Creeping Death
25. Motorhead – Ace of Spades
26. Slayer – Raining Blood
27. Pantera – Walk
28. Slayer – Disciple (God Hates us all)
29. Beasts of Burbon – I Don't Care 'bout Nothin Anymore
30. Rose Tattoo – We Can't be Beaten
31. Janes Addiction – Been Caught Stealing
32. Red Hot Chilli Peppers – Dosed
33. Rage Against the Machine – Killing in the Name of
34. Hatebreed - Looking Down the Barrell
35. V Spy V Spy – Don't Tear it Down
36. Harvey Danger - Flagpole Sitter
37. Pennywise – Fuck Authority
38. Alien Ant Farm – Smooth Criminal
39. Basement Jax – Where's you head at?
40. Queens of the Stone Age – Feel Good Hit of the Summer
41. Jet - Are you gonna be my Girl
42. Clutch - Gone Cold

Spotify

www.ingramcontent.com/pod-product-compliance
Lightning Source LLC
Chambersburg PA
CBHW051242020426

42333CB00025B/3022

# TRANZLATY

## La lingua è per tutti

## A nyelv mindenkié

# Il richiamo della foresta

## A vadon hívó szava

Jack London

Italiano / Magyar

# Nel primitivo
## A primitívbe

**Buck non leggeva i giornali.**
Buck nem olvasott újságot.
**Se avesse letto i giornali avrebbe saputo che i guai si stavano avvicinando.**
Ha olvasta volna az újságokat, tudta volna, hogy baj van készülőben.
**Non erano guai solo per lui, ma per tutti i cani da caccia.**
Nemcsak őrá, hanem minden dagályvízi kutyára is várt a baj.
**Ogni cane con muscoli forti e pelo lungo e caldo sarebbe stato nei guai.**
Minden erős izmú és meleg, hosszú szőrű kutya bajba kerülhet.
**Da Puget Bay a San Diego nessun cane poteva sfuggire a ciò che stava per accadere.**
Puget-öböltől San Diegóig egyetlen kutya sem menekülhetett a közelgő események elől.
**Gli uomini, brancolando nell'oscurità artica, avevano trovato un metallo giallo.**
A sarkvidéki sötétségben tapogatózó férfiak sárga fémre bukkantak.
**Le compagnie di navigazione a vapore e di trasporto erano alla ricerca della scoperta.**
Gőzhajózási és közlekedési vállalatok üldözték a felfedezést.
**Migliaia di uomini si riversarono nel Nord.**
Több ezer férfi rohant be Északföldre.
**Questi uomini volevano dei cani, e i cani che volevano erano cani pesanti.**
Ezek az emberek kutyákat akartak, és a kutyák, amiket akartak, nehéz kutyák voltak.
**Cani dotati di muscoli forti per lavorare duro.**
Erős izmokkal rendelkező kutyák, amelyekkel megdolgozhatnak.
**Cani con il pelo folto che li protegge dal gelo.**
Szőrös bundájú kutyák, hogy megvédjék őket a fagytól.

**Buck viveva in una grande casa nella soleggiata Santa Clara Valley.**

Buck egy nagy házban lakott a napsütötte Santa Clara-völgyben.

**La casa del giudice Miller era chiamata così.**

Miller bíró lakása, az ő házát hívták.

**La sua casa era nascosta tra gli alberi, lontana dalla strada.**

A háza az úttól beljebb állt, félig elrejtve a fák között.

**Si poteva intravedere l'ampia veranda che circondava la casa.**

Megpillanthatták a házat körülvevő széles verandát.

**Si accedeva alla casa tramite vialetti ghiaiosi.**

A házat kavicsos kocsifelhajtók közelítették meg.

**I sentieri si snodavano attraverso ampi prati.**

Az ösvények széles gyepen kanyarogtak.

**In alto si intrecciavano i rami degli alti pioppi.**

Magas nyárfák összefonódó ágai hajoltak a fejük felett.

**Nella parte posteriore della casa le cose erano ancora più spaziose.**

A ház hátsó részében még tágasabbak voltak a dolgok.

**C'erano grandi scuderie, dove una dozzina di stallieri chiacchieravano**

Voltak ott nagy istállók, ahol egy tucat lovász beszélgetett

**C'erano file di cottage per i servi ricoperti di vite**

Sorokban álltak a szőlővel befuttatott cselédkunyhók

**E c'era una serie infinita e ordinata di latrine**

És végtelen és rendezett sora volt a melléképületeknek

**Lunghi pergolati d'uva, pascoli verdi, frutteti e campi di bacche.**

Hosszú szőlőlugasok, zöld legelők, gyümölcsösök és bogyóskertek.

**Poi c'era l'impianto di pompaggio per il pozzo artesiano.**

Aztán ott volt az artézi kút szivattyútelepe.

**E c'era la grande cisterna di cemento piena d'acqua.**

És ott volt a nagy cementtartály, tele vízzel.

**Qui i ragazzi del giudice Miller hanno fatto il loro tuffo mattutino.**

Itt tették meg reggeli csobbanásukat Miller bíró fiai.

E lì si rinfrescavano anche nel caldo pomeriggio.

És ott hűsöltek is a forró délutánon.

E su questo grande dominio, Buck era colui che lo governava tutto.

És e hatalmas birtok felett Buck uralkodott.

Buck nacque su questa terra e visse qui tutti i suoi quattro anni.

Buck ezen a földön született, és itt élt mind a négy évében.

C'erano effettivamente altri cani, ma non avevano molta importanza.

Valóban voltak más kutyák is, de azok nem igazán számítottak.

In un posto vasto come questo ci si aspettava la presenza di altri cani.

Más kutyákra is számítottak egy ekkora helyen.

Questi cani andavano e venivano oppure vivevano nei canili affollati.

Ezek a kutyák jöttek-mentek, vagy a forgalmas kennelekben éltek.

Alcuni cani vivevano nascosti in casa, come Toots e Ysabel.

Néhány kutya elrejtve élt a házban, mint például Toots és Ysabel.

Toots era un carlino giapponese, Ysabel una cagnolina messicana senza pelo.

Toots egy japán mopsz, Ysabel egy mexikói szőrtelen kutya volt.

Queste strane creature raramente uscivano di casa.

Ezek a különös lények ritkán léptek ki a házból.

Non toccarono terra né annusarono l'aria esterna.

Nem érintették a földet, és nem szagolgatták a szabad levegőt sem.

C'erano anche i fox terrier, almeno una ventina.

Ott voltak a foxterrierek is, legalább húszan.

Questi terrier abbaiavano ferocemente a Toots e Ysabel in casa.

Ezek a terrierek vadul ugatott Tootsra és Ysabelre bent.

Toots e Ysabel rimasero dietro le finestre, al sicuro da ogni pericolo.

Toots és Ysabel ablakok mögött maradtak, biztonságban a bajtól.

Erano sorvegliati da domestiche armate di scope e stracci.

Seprűkkel és felmosórongyokkal felfegyverzett szobalányok őrizték őket.

Ma Buck non era un cane da casa e nemmeno da canile.

De Buck nem volt házkutya, és nem is kennelkutya.

L'intera proprietà apparteneva a Buck come suo legittimo regno.

Az egész birtok Bucké volt, mint jogos birodalma.

Buck nuotava nella vasca o andava a caccia con i figli del giudice.

Buck a tartályban úszott, vagy a Bíró fiaival vadászott.

Camminava con Mollie e Alice nelle prime ore del mattino o tardi.

Mollie-val és Alice-szel sétált a kora reggeli vagy a késői órákban.

Nelle notti fredde si sdraiava davanti al fuoco della biblioteca insieme al giudice.

Hideg éjszakákon a könyvtár kandallója előtt feküdt a bíróval.

Buck accompagnava i nipoti del giudice sulla sua robusta schiena.

Buck erős hátán lovagolta a Bíró unokáit.

Si rotolava nell'erba insieme ai ragazzi, sorvegliandoli da vicino.

A fiúkkal hempergett a fűben, és szorosan őrizte őket.

Si avventurarono fino alla fontana e addirittura oltre i campi di bacche.

Elmerészkedtek a szökőkúthoz, sőt, még a bogyósföldek mellett is elhaladtak.

Tra i fox terrier, Buck camminava sempre con orgoglio regale.

A foxterrierek között Buck mindig királyi büszkeséggel sétált.

Ignorò Toots e Ysabel, trattandoli come se fossero aria.

Nem törődött Tootsszal és Ysabellel, úgy kezelte őket, mintha levegő lenne.

**Buck governava tutte le creature viventi sulla terra del giudice Miller.**

Buck uralkodott Miller bíró földjén élő összes élőlény felett.

**Dominava gli animali, gli insetti, gli uccelli e perfino gli esseri umani.**

Uralkodott állatok, rovarok, madarak és még emberek felett is.

**Il padre di Buck, Elmo, era un enorme e fedele San Bernardo.**

Buck apja, Elmo egy hatalmas és hűséges bernáthegyi volt.

**Elmo non si allontanò mai dal Giudice e lo servì fedelmente.**

Elmo soha nem hagyta el a Bíró oldalát, és hűségesen szolgálta őt.

**Buck sembrava pronto a seguire il nobile esempio del padre.**

Buck láthatóan kész volt követni apja nemes példáját.

**Buck non era altrettanto grande: pesava sessanta chili.**

Buck nem volt egészen olyan nagy, száznegyven fontot nyomott.

**Sua madre, Shep, era una splendida cagnolina da pastore scozzese.**

Az anyja, Shep, kiváló skót juhászkutya volt.

**Ma nonostante il suo peso, Buck camminava con una presenza regale.**

De még ekkora súly mellett is Buck királyi tekintéllyel járt.

**Ciò derivava dal buon cibo e dal rispetto che riceveva sempre.**

Ez a jó ételnek és a mindig kapott tiszteletnek volt köszönhető.

**Per quattro anni Buck aveva vissuto come un nobile viziato.**

Buck négy éven át úgy élt, mint egy elkényeztetett nemesember.

**Era orgoglioso di sé stesso e perfino un po' egocentrico.**

Büszke volt magára, sőt, kissé egoista is.

**Quel tipo di orgoglio era comune tra i signori delle campagne remote.**

Az efféle büszkeség gyakori volt a távoli vidéki urak körében.

**Ma Buck si salvò dal diventare un cane domestico viziato.**

De Buck megmentette magát attól, hogy elkényeztetett
házkutyává váljon.

**Rimase snello e forte grazie alla caccia e all'esercizio fisico.**

Vadászat és testmozgás közben is karcsú és erős maradt.

**Amava profondamente l'acqua, come chi si bagna nei laghi
freddi.**

Mélyen szerette a vizet, mint azok az emberek, akik hideg
tavakban fürödnek.

**Questo amore per l'acqua mantenne Buck forte e molto sano.**

A víz iránti szeretete erőssé és egészségessé tette Buckot.

**Questo era il cane che Buck era diventato nell'autunno del
1897.**

Ez volt az a kutya, amivé Buck 1897 őszén vált.

**Quando lo sciopero del Klondike spinse gli uomini verso il
gelido Nord.**

Amikor a Klondike-i sztrájk a fagyos Északra húzta az
embereket.

**Da ogni parte del mondo la gente accorse in massa verso la
fredda terra.**

Az emberek a világ minden tájáról özönlöttek a hideg vidékre.

**Buck, tuttavia, non leggeva i giornali e non capiva le notizie.**

Buck azonban nem olvasott újságot, és nem értette a híreket
sem.

**Non sapeva che Manuel fosse una persona cattiva con cui
stare.**

Nem tudta, hogy Manuel rossz ember a társasága.

**Manuel, che aiutava in giardino, aveva un grosso problema.**

Manuelnek, aki a kertben segített, komoly problémával kellett
szembenéznie.

**Manuel era dipendente dal gioco d'azzardo alla lotteria
cinese.**

Manuel rabja volt a kínai lottójátékoknak.

**Credeva fermamente anche in un sistema fisso per vincere.**

Ő is erősen hitt egy fix győzelmi rendszerben.

**Questa convinzione rese il suo fallimento certo e inevitabile.**

Ez a hite tette a kudarcát biztossá és elkerülhetetlenné.

Per giocare con un sistema erano necessari soldi, soldi che a Manuel mancavano.

Egy rendszerhez pénz kell, ami Manuelnek hiányzott.

Il suo stipendio bastava a malapena a sostenere la moglie e i numerosi figli.

A fizetéséből alig tudta eltartani feleségét és számos gyermekét.

La notte in cui Manuel tradì Buck, tutto era normale.

Azon az éjszakán, amikor Manuel elárulta Buckot, minden normális volt.

Il giudice si trovava a una riunione dell'Associazione dei coltivatori di uva passa.

A bíró a Mazsolás Termesztők Egyesületének ülésén volt.

A quel tempo i figli del giudice erano impegnati a fondare un club sportivo.

A bíró fiai akkoriban egy atlétikai klub megalapításával voltak elfoglalva.

Nessuno vide Manuel e Buck uscire dal frutteto.

Senki sem látta Manuelt és Buckot távozni a gyümölcsösön keresztül.

Buck pensava che questa fosse solo una semplice passeggiata notturna.

Buck azt hitte, hogy ez a séta csak egy egyszerű éjszakai séta.

Incontrarono un solo uomo alla stazione della bandiera, a College Park.

Csak egyetlen férfival találkoztak a College Parkban lévő zászlóállomáson.

Quell'uomo parlò con Manuel e si scambiarono i soldi.

Az a férfi beszélt Manuellel, és pénzt váltottak.

"Imballa la merce prima di consegnarla", suggerì.

„Csomagold be az árut, mielőtt kiszállítod" – javasolta.

La voce dell'uomo era roca e impaziente mentre parlava.

A férfi hangja rekedt és türelmetlen volt, miközben beszélt.

Manuel legò con cura una corda spessa attorno al collo di Buck.

Manuel gondosan vastag kötelet kötött Buck nyaka köré.

"Se giri la corda, lo strangolerai di brutto"

„Csavard meg a kötelet, és alaposan megfojtod"

**Lo straniero emise un grugnito, dimostrando di aver capito bene.**

Az idegen felnyögött, jelezve, hogy jól érti a dolgot.

**Quel giorno Buck accettò la corda con calma e silenziosa dignità.**

Buck nyugodt és csendes méltósággal fogadta el a kötelet aznap.

**Era un atto insolito, ma Buck si fidava degli uomini che conosceva.**

Szokatlan tett volt, de Buck megbízott az ismerőseiben.

**Credeva che la loro saggezza andasse ben oltre il suo pensiero.**

Úgy hitte, bölcsességük messze túlmutat az övéin.

**Ma poi la corda venne consegnata nelle mani dello straniero.**

De aztán a kötelet az idegen kezébe adták.

**Buck emise un ringhio basso che suonava come un avvertimento e una minaccia silenziosa.**

Buck halk, fenyegető morgást hallatott.

**Era orgoglioso e autoritario e intendeva mostrare il suo disappunto.**

Büszke és parancsoló volt, és szándékosan kimutatta nemtetszését.

**Buck credeva che il suo avvertimento sarebbe stato interpretato come un ordine.**

Buck úgy gondolta, hogy a figyelmeztetését parancsnak fogják értelmezni.

**Con suo grande stupore, la corda si strinse rapidamente attorno al suo grosso collo.**

Legnagyobb meglepetésére a kötél erősen megfeszült vastag nyaka körül.

**Gli mancò l'aria e cominciò a lottare in preda a una rabbia improvvisa.**

Elállt a lélegzete, és hirtelen dühében harcolni kezdett.

**Si lanciò verso l'uomo, che si lanciò rapidamente contro Buck a mezz'aria.**

Ráugrott a férfira, aki gyorsan eltalálta Buckot a levegőben.

L'uomo afferrò Buck per la gola e lo fece ruotare abilmente in aria.

A férfi megragadta Buck torkát, és ügyesen megcsavarta a levegőben.

Buck venne scaraventato a terra con violenza, atterrando sulla schiena.

Buckot keményen a földre zuhanták, és hanyatt esett.

La corda ora lo strangolava crudelmente mentre lui scalciava selvaggiamente.

A kötél most kegyetlenül fojtogatta, miközben vadul rúgkapált.

La sua lingua cadde fuori, il suo petto si sollevò, ma non riprese fiato.

Kiesett a nyelve, fel-le rándult a mellkasa, de nem kapott levegőt.

Non era mai stato trattato con tanta violenza in vita sua.

Életében nem bántak vele ilyen erőszakkal.

Non era mai stato così profondamente invaso da una rabbia così profonda.

Soha ezelőtt nem töltött el ilyen mély düh.

Ma il potere di Buck svanì e i suoi occhi diventarono vitrei.

De Buck ereje elhalványult, és tekintete üvegessé vált.

Svenne proprio mentre un treno veniva fermato lì vicino.

Épp akkor vesztette el az eszméletét, amikor egy vonatot leintettek a közelben.

Poi i due uomini lo caricarono velocemente nel vagone bagagli.

Aztán a két férfi gyorsan bedobta a poggyászkocsiba.

La cosa successiva che Buck sentì fu dolore alla lingua gonfia.

Buck ezután fájdalmat érzett a feldagadt nyelvében.

Si muoveva su un carro traballante, solo vagamente cosciente.

Egy remegő kocsiban mozgott, csak homályosan volt eszméleténél.

Il fischio acuto di un treno rivelò a Buck la sua posizione.

Egy vonatsíp éles sivítása elárulta Bucknak a hollétét.

Aveva spesso cavalcato con il Giudice e conosceva quella sensazione.

Gyakran lovagolt már a Bíróval, és ismerte az érzést.

Fu un'esperienza unica viaggiare di nuovo in un vagone bagagli.

Megint az a különleges rázkódtatás volt, hogy egy poggyászkocsiban utaztam.

Buck aprì gli occhi e il suo sguardo ardeva di rabbia.

Buck kinyitotta a szemét, és tekintete dühtől égett.

Questa era l'ira di un re orgoglioso detronizzato.

Ez egy büszke király haragja volt, akit elmozdítottak trónjáról.

Un uomo allungò la mano per afferrarlo, ma Buck colpì per primo.

Egy férfi nyúlt, hogy megragadja, de Buck csapott le először.

Affondò i denti nella mano dell'uomo e la strinse forte.

A férfi kezébe mélyesztette a fogait, és szorosan megszorította.

Non mi lasciò andare finché non svenne per la seconda volta.

Nem engedte el, míg másodszor is el nem ájult.

"Sì, ha degli attacchi", borbottò l'uomo al facchino.

– Aha, rohamai vannak – motyogta a férfi a poggyászkezelőnek.

Il facchino aveva sentito la colluttazione e si era avvicinato.

A poggyászos meghallotta a dulakodást, és közelebb jött.

"Lo porto a Frisco per conto del capo", spiegò l'uomo.

– Friscóba viszem a főnök miatt – magyarázta a férfi.

"C'è un bravo dottore per cani che dice di poterli curare."

„Van ott egy kiváló kutyadoktor, aki azt mondja, meg tudja gyógyítani őket."

Più tardi quella notte l'uomo raccontò la sua versione completa.

Később aznap este a férfi részletesen beszámolt az esetről.

Parlava da un capannone dietro un saloon sul molo.

Egy kikötői kocsma mögötti fészerből beszélt.

"Mi hanno dato solo cinquanta dollari", si lamentò con il gestore del saloon.

„Csak ötven dollárt kaptam" – panaszkodott a kocsmárosnak.

"Non lo rifarei, nemmeno per mille dollari in contanti."

„Nem tenném meg újra, még ezerért sem készpénzben."

La sua mano destra era strettamente avvolta in un panno insanguinato.

Jobb kezét szorosan becsavarta egy véres kendő.

La gamba dei suoi pantaloni era completamente strappata dal ginocchio al piede.

A nadrágszára térdtől talpig teljesen szétszakadt.

"Quanto è stato pagato l'altro tizio?" chiese il gestore del saloon.

„Mennyit fizettek a másik korsónak?" – kérdezte a kocsmáros.

«Cento», rispose l'uomo, «non ne accetterebbe uno in meno».

– Százat – felelte a férfi –, egy centtel sem fogadna el kevesebbet.

"Questo fa centocinquanta", disse il gestore del saloon.

– Ez százötvenet tesz ki – mondta a kocsmáros.

"E lui li merita tutti, altrimenti non sono meglio di uno stupido."

„És megéri az egészet, különben én sem leszek jobb egy ostobánál."

L'uomo aprì gli involucri per esaminarsi la mano.

A férfi kibontotta a csomagolást, hogy megvizsgálja a kezét.

La mano era gravemente graffiata e ricoperta di croste di sangue secco.

A kéz csúnyán el volt szakadva és be volt száradva a vérrel.

"Se non mi viene l'idrofobia..." cominciò a dire.

„Ha nem leszek hidrofóbiás…" – kezdte mondani.

"Sarà perché sei nato per impiccarti", giunse una risata.

– Azért leszel, mert arra születtél, hogy lógj – hallatszott egy nevetés.

"Aiutami prima di partire", gli chiesero.

„Gyere, segíts, mielőtt elindulsz" – kérték fel.

Buck era stordito dal dolore alla lingua e alla gola.

Buckot teljesen elkábulta a nyelvében és a torkában érzett fájdalom.

Era mezzo strangolato e riusciva a malapena a stare in piedi.

Félig megfojtották, és alig tudott lábra állni.

Ciononostante, Buck cercò di affrontare gli uomini che lo
avevano ferito così duramente.
Buck mégis megpróbált szembenézni azokkal az emberekkel,
akik annyira megbántották.
Ma lo gettarono a terra e lo strangolarono ancora una volta.
De azok ismét letaszították és megfojtották.
Solo allora riuscirono a segargli il pesante collare di ottone.
Csak ezután tudták lefűrészelni a nehéz rézgallért.
Tolsero la corda e lo spinsero in una cassa.
Elhúzták a kötelet és egy ládába lökték.
La cassa era piccola e aveva la forma di una gabbia di ferro
grezza.
A láda kicsi volt, és egy durva vasketrec alakú.
Buck rimase lì per tutta la notte, pieno di rabbia e di
orgoglio ferito.
Buck egész éjjel ott feküdt, tele haraggal és sértett
büszkeséggel.
Non riusciva nemmeno a capire cosa gli stesse succedendo.
Fel sem foghatta, mi történik vele.
Perché quegli strani uomini lo tenevano in quella piccola
cassa?
Miért tartották őt ezek a furcsa emberek ebben a kis ládában?
Cosa volevano da lui e perché questa crudele prigionia?
Mit akartak tőle, és miért ez a kegyetlen fogság?
Sentì una pressione oscura e la sensazione che il disastro si
avvicinasse.
Sötét nyomást érzett; a katasztrófa közeledtének érzése.
Era una paura vaga, ma si impadronì pesantemente del suo
spirito.
Homályos félelem volt, de erősen nehezedett a lelkére.
Diverse volte sobbalzò quando la porta del capanno
sbatteva.
Többször is felugrott, amikor a fészer ajtaja zörgött.
Si aspettava che il giudice o i ragazzi apparissero e lo
salvassero.
Azt várta, hogy a Bíró vagy a fiúk megjelennek és megmentik.

Ma ogni volta solo la faccia grassa del gestore del saloon faceva capolino all'interno.

De minden alkalommal csak a kocsmáros kövér arca kukucskált be.

Il volto dell'uomo era illuminato dalla debole luce di una candela di sego.

A férfi arcát egy faggyúgyertya halvány fénye világította meg.

Ogni volta, il latrato gioioso di Buck si trasformava in un ringhio basso e arrabbiato.

Buck örömteli ugatása minden alkalommal halk, dühös morgásba váltott.

Il gestore del saloon lo ha lasciato solo per la notte nella cassa

A kocsmáros magára hagyta az éjszakára a ládában

Ma quando si svegliò la mattina seguente, altri uomini stavano arrivando.

De amikor reggel felébredt, egyre több férfi jött.

Arrivarono quattro uomini e, con cautela, sollevarono la cassa senza dire una parola.

Négy férfi jött, és óvatosan, szó nélkül felkapták a ládát.

Buck capì subito in quale situazione si trovava.

Buck azonnal tudta, milyen helyzetbe került.

Erano ulteriori tormentatori che doveva combattere e temere.

További kínzók voltak, akikkel harcolnia és akikkel félnie kellett.

Questi uomini apparivano malvagi, trasandati e molto mal curati.

Ezek a férfiak gonosznak, rongyosnak és nagyon rosszul ápoltnak tűntek.

Buck ringhiò e si lanciò contro di loro con furia attraverso le sbarre.

Buck vicsorgott, és vadul rájuk rontott a rácsokon keresztül.

Si limitarono a ridere e a colpirlo con lunghi bastoni di legno.

Csak nevettek és hosszú fapálcákkal piszkálták.

Buck morse i bastoncini, poi capì che era quello che gli piaceva.

Buck beleharapott a botokba, aztán rájött, hogy pont ezt szeretik.

Così si sdraiò in silenzio, imbronciato e acceso da una rabbia silenziosa.

Így hát csendben lefeküdt, mogorván és csendes dühtől égve.

Caricarono la cassa su un carro e se ne andarono con lui.

Felemelték a ládát egy szekérre, és elhajtottak vele.

La cassa, con Buck chiuso dentro, cambiò spesso proprietario.

A láda, amiben Buck volt bezárva, gyakran cserélt gazdát.

Gli impiegati dell'ufficio espresso presero in mano la situazione e si occuparono di lui per un breve periodo.

Az expressz irodai tisztviselők vették át az irányítást, és röviden intézkedtek.

Poi un altro carro trasportò Buck attraverso la rumorosa città.

Aztán egy másik szekér vitte Buckot a zajos városon át.

Un camion lo portò con sé scatole e pacchi su un traghetto.

Egy teherautó dobozokkal és csomagokkal együtt vitte fel egy kompra.

Dopo l'attraversamento, il camion lo scaricò presso un deposito ferroviario.

Miután átkelt, a teherautó egy vasútállomáson lerakta.

Alla fine Buck venne fatto salire a bordo di un vagone espresso in attesa.

Vvégre Buckot betették egy várakozó expresszkocsiba.

Per due giorni e due notti i treni trascinarono via il vagone espresso.

Két napon és két éjszakán át a vonatok elhúzták a gyorskocsit.

Buck non mangiò né bevve durante tutto il doloroso viaggio.

Buck sem evett, sem ivott az egész fáradságos út alatt.

Quando i messaggeri cercarono di avvicinarlo, lui ringhiò.

Amikor a gyorshírnökök megpróbáltak közeledni hozzá, morgott.

Risposero prendendolo in giro e prendendolo in giro crudelmente.

Válaszul gúnyolták és kegyetlenül ugratták.

**Buck si gettò contro le sbarre, schiumando e tremando**

Buck a rácsoknak vetette magát, habzott és remegett

**risero sonoramente e lo presero in giro come i bulli della scuola.**

Hangosan nevettek, és úgy gúnyolódtak vele, mint az iskolai zaklatók.

**Abbaiavano come cani finti e agitavano le braccia.**

Úgy ugattak, mint a műkutyák, és csapkodtak a karjukkal.

**Arrivarono persino a cantare come galli, solo per farlo arrabbiare ancora di più.**

Még kakasként is kukorékoltak, hogy még jobban felbosszantsák.

**Era un comportamento sciocco e Buck sapeva che era ridicolo.**

Ostoba viselkedés volt, és Buck tudta, hogy nevetséges.

**Ma questo non fece altro che accrescere il suo senso di indignazione e vergogna.**

De ez csak elmélyítette benne a felháborodást és a szégyent.

**Durante il viaggio la fame non lo disturbò molto.**

Az út során nemigen gyötörte az éhség.

**Ma la sete portava con sé dolori acuti e sofferenze insopportabili.**

De a szomjúság éles fájdalmat és elviselhetetlen szenvedést okozott.

**La sua gola secca e infiammata e la lingua bruciavano per il calore.**

Száraz, gyulladt torka és nyelve égett a forróságtól.

**Questo dolore alimentava la febbre che cresceva nel suo corpo orgoglioso.**

Ez a fájdalom táplálta a büszke testében egyre erősödő lázat.

**Durante questa prova Buck fu grato per una sola cosa.**

Buck egyetlen dologért volt hálás a tárgyalás alatt.

**Gli avevano tolto la corda dal grosso collo.**

A kötelet lehúzták vastag nyakáról.

**La corda aveva dato a quegli uomini un vantaggio ingiusto e crudele.**

A kötél tisztességtelen és kegyetlen előnyt biztosított azoknak az embereknek.

**Ora la corda non c'era più e Buck giurò che non sarebbe mai più tornata.**

Most a kötél eltűnt, és Buck megesküdött, hogy soha többé nem tér vissza.

**Decise che nessuna corda gli sarebbe mai più passata intorno al collo.**

Elhatározta, hogy soha többé nem tekeredik kötél a nyakába.

**Per due lunghi giorni e due lunghe notti soffrì senza cibo.**

Két hosszú napon és éjszakán át szenvedett étel nélkül.

**E in quelle ore, accumulò dentro di sé una rabbia enorme.**

És ezekben az órákban hatalmas dühöt halmozott fel magában.

**I suoi occhi diventarono iniettati di sangue e selvaggi per la rabbia costante.**

Szeme vérben forgó és vad lett az állandó dühtől.

**Non era più Buck, ma un demone con le fauci che schioccavano.**

Már nem Buck volt, hanem egy csattogó állkapcsú démon.

**Nemmeno il Giudice avrebbe potuto riconoscere questa folle creatura.**

Még a Bíró sem ismerte volna fel ezt az őrült teremtményt.

**I messaggeri espressi tirarono un sospiro di sollievo quando giunsero a Seattle**

A gyorshírnökök megkönnyebbülten felsóhajtottak, amikor megérkeztek Seattle-be

**Quattro uomini sollevarono la cassa e la portarono in un cortile sul retro.**

Négy férfi felemelte a ládát, és bevitték a hátsó udvarba.

**Il cortile era piccolo, circondato da mura alte e solide.**

Az udvar kicsi volt, magas és masszív falak vették körül.

**Un uomo corpulento uscì dalla stanza con una scollatura larga e una camicia rossa.**

Egy nagydarab férfi lépett ki egy megereszkedett piros pulóveringben.

Firmò il registro delle consegne con una calligrafia spessa e decisa.

Vastag, merész kézzel írta alá a szállítókönyvet.

Buck intuì subito che quell'uomo era il suo prossimo aguzzino.

Buck azonnal megérezte, hogy ez a férfi a következő kínzója.

Si lanciò violentemente contro le sbarre, con gli occhi rossi di rabbia.

Hevesen a rácsoknak vetette magát, dühtől vörös szemekkel.

L'uomo si limitò a sorridere amaramente e andò a prendere un'ascia.

A férfi csak sötéten elmosolyodott, és odament egy baltáért.

Teneva anche una mazza nella sua grossa e forte mano destra.

Vastag és erős jobb kezében egy botot is hozott.

"Lo porterai fuori adesso?" chiese l'autista preoccupato.

„Most kiviszed?" – kérdezte a sofőr aggódva.

"Certo", disse l'uomo, infilando l'ascia nella cassa come se fosse una leva.

– Persze – mondta a férfi, és a baltát emelőként a ládába szegezte.

I quattro uomini si dileguarono all'istante, saltando sul muro del cortile.

A négy férfi azonnal szétszéledt, és felugrottak az udvar falára.

Dai loro punti sicuri in alto, aspettavano di ammirare lo spettacolo.

Biztonságos helyeikről, fentről várták, hogy szemtanúi lehessenek a látványosságnak.

Buck si lanciò contro il legno scheggiato, mordendolo e scuotendolo violentemente.

Buck a szilánkos fára vetette magát, vadul harapdálva és remegve.

Ogni volta che l'ascia colpiva la gabbia, Buck era lì pronto ad attaccarla.

Valahányszor a baltával eltalálták a ketrecet, Buck ott volt, hogy megtámadja.

**Ringhiò e schioccò le dita in preda a una rabbia selvaggia, desideroso di essere liberato.**

Vad dühvel morgott és csattant, alig várta, hogy szabadulhasson.

**L'uomo all'esterno era calmo e fermo, concentrato sul suo compito.**

A kint álló férfi nyugodt és kiegyensúlyozott volt, elszántan végezte a feladatát.

**"Bene allora, diavolo dagli occhi rossi", disse quando il buco fu grande.**

– Akkor hát, te vörös szemű ördög – mondta, amikor a lyuk már nagyra nyílt.

**Lasciò cadere l'ascia e prese la mazza nella mano destra.**

Eldobta a baltát, és jobb kezébe vette a botot.

**Buck sembrava davvero un diavolo: aveva gli occhi iniettati di sangue e fiammeggianti.**

Buck tényleg úgy nézett ki, mint egy ördög; vérben forgó, lángoló szemei voltak.

**Il suo pelo si rizzò, la schiuma gli salì alla bocca e gli occhi brillarono.**

Felborzolta a bundáját, hab gomolygott a szája körül, szeme csillogott.

**Lui tese i muscoli e si lanciò dritto verso il maglione rosso.**

Megfeszítette izmait, és egyenesen a piros pulóverre vetette magát.

**Centoquaranta libbre di furia si riversarono sull'uomo calmo.**

Száznegyven fontnyi düh csapott a nyugodt férfira.

**Un attimo prima che le sue fauci si chiudessero, un colpo terribile lo colpì.**

Mielőtt még összeszorult volna az állkapcsa, szörnyű ütés érte.

**I suoi denti si schioccarono insieme solo sull'aria**

Fogai összecsattantak, semmi mást nem látott, csak a levegőt.

**una scossa di dolore gli risuonò nel corpo**

fájdalomlökés visszhangzott végig a testén

**Si capovolse a mezz'aria e cadde sulla schiena e su un fianco.**

A levegőben megpördült, és a hátára, illetve az oldalára zuhant.

**Non aveva mai sentito prima un colpo di mazza e non riusciva a sostenerlo.**

Még soha nem érzett botütést, és nem tudta felfogni.

**Con un ringhio acuto, in parte abbaio, in parte urlo, saltò di nuovo.**

Egy sikító vicsorgással, részben ugatással, részben sikolysal ismét ugrott.

**Un altro colpo violento lo colpì e lo scaraventò a terra.**

Egy újabb brutális ütés érte, és a földre repítette.

**Questa volta Buck capì: era la pesante clava dell'uomo.**

Buck ezúttal megértette – a férfi nehéz bunkója volt az.

**Ma la rabbia lo accecò e non pensò minimamente di ritirarsi.**

De a düh elvakította, és esze ágában sem volt visszavonulni.

**Dodici volte si lanciò e dodici volte cadde.**

Tizenkétszer vetette magát előre, és tizenkétszer esett el.

**La mazza di legno lo colpiva ogni volta con una forza spietata e schiacciante.**

A fabáb minden alkalommal könyörtelen, zúzó erővel csapott le rá.

**Dopo un colpo violento, si rialzò barcollando, stordito e lento.**

Egyetlen heves ütés után kábultan és lassan talpra állt.

**Il sangue gli colava dalla bocca, dal naso e perfino dalle orecchie.**

Vér folyt a szájából, az orrából, sőt még a füléből is.

**Il suo mantello, un tempo bellissimo, era imbrattato di schiuma insanguinata.**

Egykor gyönyörű kabátját véres hab maszatosa volt.

**Poi l'uomo si fece avanti e gli sferrò un violento colpo al naso.**

Aztán a férfi odalépett, és egy gonosz ütést mért az orrára.

**L'agonia fu più acuta di qualsiasi cosa Buck avesse mai provato.**

A fájdalom élesebb volt, mint amit Buck valaha is érzett.

Con un ruggito più da bestia che da cane, balzò di nuovo all'attacco.

Egy vadállatiasabb üvöltéssel, mint kutyaszerűséggel, ismét támadásra ugrott.

Ma l'uomo gli afferrò la mascella inferiore e la torse all'indietro.

De a férfi megragadta az alsó állkapcsát, és hátracsavarta.

Buck si girò a testa in giù e cadde di nuovo violentemente al suolo.

Buck fejjel előre fordult, és ismét keményen a földre zuhant.

Un'ultima volta, Buck si lanciò verso di lui, ormai a malapena in grado di reggersi in piedi.

Buck még utoljára rárontott, alig bírva megállni a lábán.

L'uomo colpì con sapiente tempismo, sferrando il colpo finale.

A férfi szakértő időzítéssel csapott le, megadva az utolsó ütést.

Buck crollò a terra, privo di sensi e immobile.

Buck mozdulatlanul, eszméletlenül rogyott össze.

"Non è uno stupido ad addestrare i cani, ecco cosa dico io", urlò un uomo.

„Nem hanyagolja a kutyabetörést, ezt mondom én is!" – kiáltotta egy férfi.

"Druther può spezzare la volontà di un segugio in qualsiasi giorno della settimana."

„Druther a hét bármely napján képes megtörni egy kutya akaratát."

"E due volte di domenica!" aggiunse l'autista.

„És kétszer egy vasárnap!" – tette hozzá a sofőr.

Salì sul carro e tirò le redini per partire.

Felmászott a szekérre, és megrántotta a gyeplőt, hogy elinduljon.

Buck riprese lentamente il controllo della sua coscienza

Buck lassan visszanyerte az öntudatát.

ma il suo corpo era ancora troppo debole e rotto per muoversi.

de a teste még túl gyenge és törött volt a mozgáshoz.

Rimase lì dove era caduto, osservando l'uomo con il maglione rosso.

Ott feküdt, ahol eleset, és a vörös pulóveres férfit figyelte.

"Risponde al nome di Buck", disse l'uomo, leggendo ad alta voce.

– Buck nevére hallgat – mondta a férfi, miközben hangosan olvasott.

Citò la nota inviata con la cassa di Buck e i dettagli.

Idézett a Buck ládájával és a részletekkel küldött üzenetből.

"Bene, Buck, ragazzo mio", continuò l'uomo con tono amichevole,

– Nos hát, Buck, fiam – folytatta a férfi barátságos hangon –,

"Abbiamo avuto il nostro piccolo litigio, e ora tra noi è finita."

„Levettünk egy kis veszekedést, és most vége van közöttünk."

"Tu hai imparato qual è il tuo posto, e io ho imparato qual è il mio", ha aggiunto.

„Megtanultad a helyed, és én is a sajátomat" – tette hozzá.

"Sii buono e tutto andrà bene e la vita sarà piacevole."

„Légy jó, és minden jól fog menni, és az élet kellemes lesz."

"Ma se sei cattivo, ti spaccherò a morte, capito?"

„De ha rossz vagy, akkor agyonverlek, érted?"

Mentre parlava, allungò la mano e accarezzò la testa dolorante di Buck.

Miközben beszélt, kinyújtotta a kezét, és megsimogatta Buck fájó fejét.

I capelli di Buck si rizzarono al tocco dell'uomo, ma lui non oppose resistenza.

Buck haja felállt a férfi érintésére, de nem ellenkezett.

L'uomo gli portò dell'acqua e Buck la bevve a grandi sorsi.

A férfi vizet hozott neki, amit Buck nagy kortyokban ivott meg.

Poi arrivò la carne cruda, che Buck divorò pezzo per pezzo.

Aztán jött a nyers hús, amit Buck darabonként felfalt.

Sapeva di essere stato sconfitto, ma sapeva anche di non essere distrutto.

Tudta, hogy megverték, de azt is tudta, hogy nincs megtörve.

Non aveva alcuna possibilità contro un uomo armato di manganello.

Esélye sem volt egy bunkóval felfegyverzett férfival szemben.

Aveva imparato la verità e non dimenticò mai quella lezione.

Megtanulta az igazságot, és soha nem felejtette el ezt a leckét.

Quell'arma segnò l'inizio della legge nel nuovo mondo di Buck.

Ez a fegyver jelentette a jog kezdetét Buck új világában.

Fu l'inizio di un ordine duro e primitivo che non poteva negare.

Ez egy kemény, primitív rend kezdete volt, amelyet nem tagadhatott.

Accettò la verità: i suoi istinti selvaggi erano ormai risvegliati.

Elfogadta az igazságot; vad ösztönei most már felébredtek.

Il mondo era diventato più duro, ma Buck lo affrontò coraggiosamente.

A világ egyre keményebbé vált, de Buck bátran szembenézett vele.

Affrontò la vita con una nuova cautela, astuzia e una forza silenziosa.

Új óvatossággal, ravaszsággal és csendes erővel fogadta az életet.

Arrivarono altri cani, legati con corde o gabbie, come era successo a Buck.

Több kutya is érkezett, kötelekhez vagy ládákhoz kötözve, mint Buck.

Alcuni cani procedevano con calma, altri si infuriavano e combattevano come bestie feroci.

Néhány kutya nyugodtan jött, mások dühöngtek és vadállatok módjára verekedtek.

Tutti loro furono sottoposti al dominio dell'uomo con il maglione rosso.

Mindannyiukat a vörös pulóveres férfi uralma alá vonták.

Ogni volta Buck osservava e vedeva svolgersi la stessa lezione.

Buck minden alkalommal ugyanazt a tanulságot látta kibontakozni.

**L'uomo con la clava era la legge: un padrone a cui obbedire.**

A bottal járó férfi maga volt a törvény; egy úr, akinek engedelmeskedni kellett.

**Non era necessario che gli piacesse, ma che gli si obbedisse.**

Nem kellett kedvelni, de engedelmeskedni kellett neki.

**Buck non si è mai mostrato adulatore o scodinzolante come facevano i cani più deboli.**

Buck soha nem hízelgett vagy csóválta a kezét, mint a gyengébb kutyák.

**Vide dei cani che erano stati picchiati e che continuavano a leccare la mano dell'uomo.**

Látott megvert kutyákat, amelyek mégis nyalogatták a férfi kezét.

**Vide un cane che non obbediva né si sottometteva affatto.**

Látott egy kutyát, amely egyáltalán nem engedelmeskedett, és egyáltalán nem volt hajlandó meghajolni.

**Quel cane ha combattuto fino alla morte nella battaglia per il controllo.**

A kutya addig küzdött, amíg el nem pusztult az irányításért folytatott csatában.

**A volte degli sconosciuti venivano a trovare l'uomo con il maglione rosso.**

Idegenek néha meglátogatták a vörös pulóveres férfit.

**Parlavano con toni strani, supplicando, contrattando e ridendo.**

Furcsa hangon beszéltek, könyörögtek, alkudoztak és nevetgéltek.

**Dopo aver scambiato i soldi, se ne andavano con uno o più cani.**

Amikor pénzt váltottak, egy vagy több kutyával távoztak.

**Buck si chiese dove andassero questi cani, perché nessuno faceva mai ritorno.**

Buck azon tűnődött, hová tűntek ezek a kutyák, mert soha egy sem tért vissza.

la paura dell'ignoto riempiva Buck ogni volta che un uomo
sconosciuto si avvicinava

Az ismeretlentől való félelem töltötte el Buckot minden
alkalommal, amikor egy idegen férfi jött

era contento ogni volta che veniva preso un altro cane, al
posto suo.

Minden alkalommal örült, amikor egy másik kutyát vittek el,
nem pedig őt.

Ma alla fine arrivò il turno di Buck con l'arrivo di uno strano
uomo.

De végül Buckra került a sor egy különös férfi érkezésével.

Era piccolo, nervoso e parlava un inglese stentato e
imprecava.

Alacsony volt, inas, törött angolsággal és káromkodásokkal
beszélt.

"Sacredam!" urlò quando vide il corpo di Buck.

„Szent isten!" – kiáltotta, amikor meglátta Buck alakját.

"Che cane maledetto e prepotente! Eh? Quanto costa?" chiese
ad alta voce.

„Ez aztán egy átkozott zsarnokkutya! Hű? Mennyibe kerül?" –
kérdezte hangosan.

"Trecento, ed è un regalo a quel prezzo",

„Háromszáz, és ennyiért igazi ajándék."

"Dato che sono soldi del governo, non dovresti lamentarti,
Perrault."

„Mivel állami pénzről van szó, nem kell panaszkodnod,
Perrault."

Perrault sorrise pensando all'accordo che aveva appena
concluso con quell'uomo.

Perrault elvigyorodott az egyezségen, amit az előbb kötött a
férfival.

Il prezzo dei cani è salito alle stelle a causa della domanda
improvvisa.

A kutyák ára a hirtelen megnövekedett kereslet miatt az
egekbe szökött.

Trecento dollari non erano ingiusti per una bestia così bella.

Háromszáz dollár nem volt igazságtalan egy ilyen jószágért.

**Il governo canadese non perderebbe nulla dall'accordo**
A kanadai kormány semmit sem veszítene a megállapodással
**Né i loro comunicati ufficiali avrebbero subito ritardi nel trasporto.**
A hivatalos küldeményeiket sem késlekednék az út során.
**Perrault conosceva bene i cani e capì che Buck era una rarità.**
Perrault jól ismerte a kutyákat, és látta rajta, hogy Buck valami különleges.
**"Uno su dieci diecimila", pensò, mentre studiava la corporatura di Buck.**
„Tízből egy, tízezerhez egy" – gondolta, miközben Buck testalkatát vizsgálgatta.
**Buck vide il denaro cambiare di mano, ma non mostrò alcuna sorpresa.**
Buck látta, hogy a pénz gazdát cserél, de nem mutatott meglepetést.
**Poco dopo lui e Curly, un gentile Terranova, furono portati via.**
Hamarosan elvezették őt és Göndört, a szelíd újfundlandit.
**Seguirono l'omino dal cortile della casa con il maglione rosso.**
Követték a kis embert a piros pulóveres udvaráról.
**Quella fu l'ultima volta che Buck vide l'uomo con la mazza di legno.**
Buck utoljára látta a fabotos férfit.
**Dal ponte del Narwhal guardò Seattle svanire in lontananza.**
A Narvál fedélzetéről nézte, ahogy Seattle a távolba vesz.
**Fu anche l'ultima volta che vide le calde terre del Sud.**
Ez volt az utolsó alkalom is, hogy a meleg Délvidéket látta.
**Perrault li portò sottocoperta e li lasciò con François.**
Perrault levitte őket a fedélzet alá, és François-nál hagyta.
**François era un gigante con la faccia nera e le mani ruvide e callose.**
François egy fekete arcú óriás volt, durva, kérges kezekkel.
**Era un uomo dalla carnagione scura e dalla carnagione scura, un meticcio franco-canadese.**
Sötét bőrű és barna bőrű volt; egy félvér francia-kanadai.

**Per Buck, quegli uomini erano come non li aveva mai visti prima.**

Buck számára ezek az emberek olyanok voltak, amilyeneket még soha nem látott.

**Nei giorni a venire avrebbe avuto modo di conoscere molti di questi uomini.**

Sok ilyen emberrel fog megismerkedni az elkövetkező napokban.

**Non cominciò ad affezionarsi a loro, ma finì per rispettarli.**

Nem szerette meg őket, de tisztelni kezdte őket.

**Erano giusti e saggi e non si lasciavano ingannare facilmente da nessun cane.**

Szépek és bölcsek voltak, és egyetlen kutya sem könnyen becsaphatta őket.

**Giudicavano i cani con calma e punivano solo quando meritavano.**

Nyugodtan ítélték meg a kutyákat, és csak akkor büntették meg őket, ha megérdemelték.

**Sul ponte inferiore del Narwhal, Buck e Curly incontrarono due cani.**

A Narvál alsó fedélzetén Buck és Göndör két kutyával találkoztak.

**Uno era un grosso cane bianco proveniente dalle lontane e gelide isole Spitzbergen.**

Az egyik egy nagy fehér kutya volt a távoli, jeges Spitzbergákról.

**In passato aveva navigato su una baleniera e si era unito a un gruppo di ricerca.**

Egyszer vitorlázott egy bálnavadászhajóval, és csatlakozott egy felderítő csoporthoz.

**Era amichevole, ma astuto, subdolo e subdolo.**

Sunyi, alattomos és ravasz módon barátságos volt.

**Al loro primo pasto, rubò un pezzo di carne dalla padella di Buck.**

Az első étkezésükkor ellopott egy darab húst Buck serpenyőjéből.

Buck saltò per punirlo, ma la frusta di François colpì per prima.

Buck felugrott, hogy megbüntesse, de François ostora lecsapott előbb.

Il ladro bianco urlò e Buck reclamò l'osso rubato.

A fehér tolvaj felkiáltott, Buck pedig visszaszerezte az ellopott csontot.

Questa correttezza colpì Buck e François si guadagnò il suo rispetto.

Ez a pártatlanság lenyűgözte Buckot, és François kiérdemelte a tiszteletét.

L'altro cane non lo salutò e non volle nessuno in cambio.

A másik kutya nem köszöntötte, és viszonzást sem várt.

Non rubava il cibo, né annusava con interesse i nuovi arrivati.

Nem lopott ételt, és nem szaglászott érdeklődéssel az újonnan érkezők után.

Questo cane era cupo e silenzioso, cupo e lento nei movimenti.

Ez a kutya komor és csendes, komor és lassú mozgású volt.

Avvertì Curly di stargli lontano semplicemente lanciandole un'occhiata fulminante.

Egyszerűen csak dühösen meredt rá, és figyelmeztette Göndört, hogy maradjon távol.

Il suo messaggio era chiaro: lasciatemi in pace o saranno guai.

Az üzenete világos volt: hagyj békén, különben baj lesz.

Si chiamava Dave e non faceva quasi caso a ciò che lo circondava.

Dave-nek hívták, és alig vette észre a környezetét.

Dormiva spesso, mangiava tranquillamente e sbadigliava di tanto in tanto.

Gyakran aludt, csendben evett, és időnként ásított is.

La nave ronzava costantemente con il rumore dell'elica sottostante.

A hajó folyamatosan zümmögött, miközben lent dübörgött a légcsavar.

**I giorni passarono senza grandi cambiamenti, ma il clima si fece più freddo.**

A napok változatlanul teltek, de az idő egyre hidegebb lett.

**Buck se lo sentiva nelle ossa e notò che anche gli altri lo sentivano.**

Buck a csontjaiban érezte, és észrevette, hogy a többiek is.

**Poi una mattina l'elica si fermò e tutto rimase immobile.**

Aztán egy reggel megállt a légcsavar, és minden elcsendesedett.

**Un'energia percorse la nave: qualcosa era cambiato.**

Energia söpört végig a hajón; valami megváltozott.

**François scese, li mise al guinzaglio e li portò su.**

François lejött, pórázt kötött rájuk, és felhozta őket.

**Buck uscì e trovò il terreno morbido, bianco e freddo.**

Buck kilépett, és a talajt puhának, fehérnek és hidegnek találta.

**Lui fece un balzo indietro allarmato e sbuffò in preda alla confusione più totale.**

Riadtan hátraugrott, és teljes zavarodottságában felhorkant.

**Una strana sostanza bianca cadeva dal cielo grigio.**

Furcsa fehér anyag hullott a szürke égből.

**Si scosse, ma i fiocchi bianchi continuavano a cadergli addosso.**

Megrázta magát, de a fehér pelyhek továbbra is ráhullottak.

**Annusò attentamente la sostanza bianca e ne leccò alcuni pezzetti ghiacciati.**

Óvatosan megszagolta a fehér cuccot, és lenyalogatott néhány jeges darabkát.

**La polvere bruciò come il fuoco e poi svanì subito dalla sua lingua.**

A por tűzként égett, majd eltűnt a nyelvéről.

**Buck ci riprovò, sconcertato dallo strano freddo che svaniva.**

Buck újra próbálkozott, zavarba ejtve a furcsa, eltűnő hidegségtől.

**Gli uomini intorno a lui risero e Buck si sentì in imbarazzo.**

A körülötte álló férfiak nevettek, Buck pedig zavarba jött.

**Non sapeva perché, ma si vergognava della sua reazione.**
Nem tudta, miért, de szégyellte a reakcióját.

**Era la sua prima esperienza con la neve e la cosa lo confuse.**
Ez volt az első találkozása a hóval, és ez összezavarta.

## La legge del bastone e della zanna
A buzogány és agyar törvénye

**Il primo giorno di Buck sulla spiaggia di Dyea è stato un terribile incubo.**

Buck első napja a Dyea strandon egy szörnyű rémálomnak tűnt.

**Ogni ora portava con sé nuovi shock e cambiamenti inaspettati per Buck.**

Minden óra új megrázkódtatásokat és váratlan változásokat hozott Buck számára.

**Era stato strappato alla civiltà e gettato nel caos più totale.**

Kiragadták a civilizációból, és vad káoszba taszították.

**Questa non era una vita soleggiata e pigra, fatta di noia e riposo.**

Ez nem egy napsütéses, lustálkodós élet volt unalommal és pihenéssel.

**Non c'era pace, né riposo, né momento senza pericolo.**

Nem volt béke, nem volt pihenés, és nem volt pillanat sem veszélytelenül.

**La confusione regnava su tutto e il pericolo era sempre vicino.**

Zűrzavar uralkodott mindenen, és a veszély mindig közel leselkedett.

**Buck doveva stare attento perché quegli uomini e quei cani erano diversi.**

Bucknak ébernek kellett maradnia, mert ezek a férfiak és kutyák mások voltak.

**Non provenivano da città; erano selvaggi e spietati.**

Nem városiak voltak; vadak és könyörtelenek voltak.

**Questi uomini e questi cani conoscevano solo la legge del bastone e della zanna.**

Ezek a férfiak és kutyák csak a bunkó és az agyar törvényét ismerték.

**Buck non aveva mai visto dei cani combattere come questi feroci husky.**

Buck még soha nem látott kutyákat így verekedni, mint ezeket a vad huskykat.

**La sua prima esperienza gli insegnò una lezione che non avrebbe mai dimenticato.**

Az első élménye egy olyan leckét adott neki, amit soha nem fog elfelejteni.

**Fu una fortuna che non fosse lui, altrimenti sarebbe morto anche lui.**

Szerencséje volt, hogy nem ő volt, különben ő is meghalt volna.

**Curly era quello che soffriva, mentre Buck osservava e imparava.**

Göndör szenvedett, míg Buck figyelte és tanult.

**Si erano accampati vicino a un deposito costruito con tronchi.**

Egy rönkökből épült bolt közelében vertek tábort.

**Curly cercò di essere amichevole con un grosso husky simile a un lupo.**

Göndör megpróbált barátságos lenni egy nagy, farkasszerű huskyval.

**L'husky era più piccolo di Curly, ma aveva un aspetto selvaggio e cattivo.**

A husky kisebb volt, mint Göndör, de vadnak és gonosznak tűnt.

**Senza preavviso, lui saltò su e le tagliò il viso.**

Figyelmeztetés nélkül felugrott, és felhasította az arcát.

**Con un solo movimento i suoi denti le tagliarono l'occhio fino alla mascella.**

Fogai egyetlen mozdulattal vágtak le a szemétől az állkapcsáig.

**Ecco come combattevano i lupi: colpivano velocemente e saltavano via.**

Így harcoltak a farkasok – gyorsan csaptak és elugrottak.

**Ma c'era molto di più da imparare da quell'unico attacco.**

De többet lehetett tanulni ebből az egyetlen támadásból.

**Decine di husky si precipitarono dentro e formarono un cerchio silenzioso.**

Több tucat husky rohant be, és néma kört alkottak.
**Osservavano attentamente e si leccavano le labbra per la fame.**
Figyelmesen nézték, és éhesen nyalogatták az ajkukat.
**Buck non capiva il loro silenzio né i loro occhi ansiosi.**
Buck nem értette a hallgatásukat vagy a kíváncsi tekintetüket.
**Curly si lanciò ad attaccare l'husky una seconda volta.**
Göndör másodszor is a husky megtámadására rohant.
**Usò il suo petto per buttarla a terra con un movimento violento.**
Egy erős mozdulattal a mellkasával lökte fel.
**Cadde su un fianco e non riuscì più a rialzarsi.**
Az oldalára esett, és nem tudott felkelni.
**Era proprio quello che gli altri aspettavano da tempo.**
Erre vártak a többiek egész végig.
**Gli husky le saltarono addosso, guaindo e ringhiando freneticamente.**
A huskyk ráugrottak, őrjöngve ugattak és vicsorogtak.
**Lei urlò mentre la seppellivano sotto una pila di cani.**
Felsikoltott, miközben egy kutyakupac alá temették.
**L'attacco fu così rapido che Buck rimase immobile per lo shock.**
A támadás olyan gyors volt, hogy Buck a döbbenettől megdermedt.
**Vide Spitz tirare fuori la lingua in un modo che sembrava una risata.**
Látta, hogy Spitz kinyújtja a nyelvét, ami úgy hangzott, mintha nevetne.
**François afferrò un'ascia e corse dritto verso il gruppo di cani.**
François megragadott egy fejszét, és egyenesen a kutyák csoportjába rohant.
**Altri tre uomini hanno usato dei manganelli per allontanare gli husky.**
Három másik férfi botokkal verte el a huskykat.
**In soli due minuti la lotta finì e i cani se ne andarono.**
Alig két perc múlva vége volt a harcnak, és a kutyák eltűntek.

**Curly giaceva morta nella neve rossa calpestata, con il corpo fatto a pezzi.**

Göndör holtan feküdt a vörös, letaposott hóban, teste szétszaggatva.

**Un uomo dalla pelle scura era in piedi davanti a lei, maledicendo la scena brutale.**

Egy sötét bőrű férfi állt fölötte, és átkozta a brutális jelenetet.

**Il ricordo rimase con Buck e ossessionò i suoi sogni notturni.**

Az emlék Buckban maradt, és álmaiban kísértette éjszaka.

**Ecco come funzionava: niente equità, niente seconda possibilità.**

Ez volt itt a helyzet: nincs igazságosság, nincs második esély.

**Una volta caduto un cane, gli altri lo uccidevano senza pietà.**

Ha egy kutya elesett, a többi könyörtelenül ölte.

**Buck decise allora che non si sarebbe mai lasciato cadere.**

Buck ekkor eldöntötte, hogy soha többé nem engedi meg magának, hogy elessen.

**Spitz tirò fuori di nuovo la lingua e rise guardando il sangue.**

Spitz ismét kinyújtotta a nyelvét, és nevetett a véren.

**Da quel momento in poi, Buck odiò Spitz con tutto il cuore.**

Attól a pillanattól kezdve Buck teljes szívéből gyűlölte Spitzet.

**Prima che Buck potesse riprendersi dalla morte di Curly, accadde qualcosa di nuovo.**

Mielőtt Buck magához térhetett volna Göndör halálából, valami új történt.

**François si avvicinò e legò qualcosa attorno al corpo di Buck.**

François odajött, és valamit Buck köré tekert.

**Era un'imbracatura simile a quelle usate per i cavalli al ranch.**

Olyan hám volt, amilyet a tanyán a lovakon használnak.

**Così come Buck aveva visto lavorare i cavalli, ora era costretto a lavorare anche lui.**

Ahogy Buck látta a lovakat dolgozni, most neki is dolgoznia kellett.

**Dovette trascinare François su una slitta nella foresta vicina.**

Szánkón kellett húznia François-t a közeli erdőbe.

**Poi dovette trascinare indietro un pesante carico di legna da ardere.**

Aztán vissza kellett húznia egy rakomány nehéz tűzifát.

**Buck era orgoglioso e gli faceva male essere trattato come un animale da lavoro.**

Buck büszke volt, ezért fájt neki, hogy úgy bántak vele, mint egy munkásállattal.

**Ma era saggio e non cercò di combattere la nuova situazione.**

De bölcs volt, és nem próbált megküzdeni az új helyzettel.

**Accettò la sua nuova vita e diede il massimo in ogni compito.**

Elfogadta az új életet, és minden feladatban a legjobb tudása szerint dolgozott.

**Tutto di quel lavoro gli risultava strano e sconosciuto.**

A munkában minden furcsa és ismeretlen volt számára.

**François era severo e pretendeva obbedienza senza indugio.**

François szigorú volt, és késedelem nélkül engedelmességet követelt.

**La sua frusta garantiva che ogni comando venisse eseguito immediatamente.**

Ostorával gondoskodott arról, hogy minden parancsot azonnal végrehajtsanak.

**Dave era il timoniere, il cane più vicino alla slitta dietro Buck.**

Dave volt a kerekes kutya, a kutya állt legközelebb a szánhoz Buck mögött.

**Se commetteva un errore, Dave mordeva Buck sulle zampe posteriori.**

Dave megharapta Buck hátsó lábait, ha hibázott.

**Spitz era il cane guida, abile ed esperto nel ruolo.**

Spitz volt a vezető kutya, képzett és tapasztalt volt a szerepben.

**Spitz non riusciva a raggiungere Buck facilmente, ma lo corresse comunque.**

Spitz nem tudta könnyen elérni Buckot, de azért kijavította.

**Ringhiava aspramente o tirava la slitta in modi che insegnavano a Buck.**

Keményen morgott, vagy olyan módon húzta a szánt, ami Buckot is tanította.

**Grazie a questo addestramento, Buck imparò più velocemente di quanto tutti si aspettassero.**

A képzés során Buck gyorsabban tanult, mint bármelyikük várta.

**Lavorò duramente e imparò sia da François che dagli altri cani.**

Keményen dolgozott, és tanult mind François-tól, mind a többi kutyától.

**Quando tornarono, Buck conosceva già i comandi chiave.**

Mire visszatértek, Buck már tudta a legfontosabb parancsokat.

**Imparò a fermarsi al suono della parola "oh" di François.**

François-tól tanulta meg, hogy a „ho" hangjára megálljon.

**Imparò quando era il momento di tirare la slitta e correre.**

Megtanulta, mikor kellett húznia a szánt és futnia.

**Imparò a svoltare senza problemi nelle curve del sentiero.**

Megtanulta, hogy gond nélkül szélesre kanyarodjon az ösvény kanyarulataiban.

**Imparò anche a evitare Dave quando la slitta scendeva velocemente.**

Azt is megtanulta, hogy kerülje el Davet, amikor a szán gyorsan gurult lefelé.

**"Sono cani molto buoni", disse orgoglioso François a Perrault.**

„Nagyon jó kutyák" – mondta François büszkén Perrault-nak.

**"Quel Buck tira come un dannato, glielo insegno subito."**

„Ez a Buck iszonyatosan jól húz – én gyorsan megtanítom."

**Più tardi quel giorno, Perrault tornò con altri due husky.**

Később aznap Perrault még két husky kutyával tért vissza.

**Si chiamavano Billee e Joe ed erano fratelli.**

Billee és Joe volt a nevük, és testvérek voltak.

**Provenivano dalla stessa madre, ma non erano affatto simili.**

Ugyanattól az anyától származtak, de egyáltalán nem voltak hasonlóak.

**Billee era un tipo dolce e molto amichevole con tutti.**

Billee kedves természetű és túlságosan barátságos volt mindenkivel.

**Joe era l'opposto: silenzioso, arrabbiato e sempre ringhiante.**

Joe az ellentéte volt – csendes, dühös és mindig vicsorgó.

**Buck li salutò amichevolmente e si mantenne calmo con entrambi.**

Buck barátságosan üdvözölte őket, és nyugodt volt mindkettőjükkel.

**Dave non prestò loro attenzione e rimase in silenzio come al solito.**

Dave nem figyelt rájuk, és szokásához híven csendben maradt.

**Spitz attaccò prima Billee, poi Joe, per dimostrare la sua superiorità.**

Spitz először Billee-t, majd Joe-t támadta meg, hogy megmutassa dominanciáját.

**Billee scodinzolava e cercava di essere amichevole con Spitz.**

Billee csóválta a farkát, és megpróbált barátságos lenni Spitzhez.

**Quando questo non funzionò, cercò di scappare.**

Amikor ez nem sikerült, inkább megpróbált elmenekülni.

**Pianse tristemente quando Spitz lo morse forte sul fianco.**

Szomorúan sírt, amikor Spitz erősen megharapta az oldalát.

**Ma Joe era molto diverso e si rifiutava di farsi prendere in giro.**

De Joe egészen más volt, és nem hagyta magát zaklatni.

**Ogni volta che Spitz si avvicinava, Joe si girava velocemente per affrontarlo.**

Valahányszor Spitz a közelébe ért, Joe gyorsan megfordult, hogy szembenézzen vele.

**La sua pelliccia si drizzò, le sue labbra si arricciarono e i suoi denti schioccarono selvaggiamente.**

Felborzolta a bundáját, felkunkorodott az ajka, és vadul csattogtak a fogai.

Gli occhi di Joe brillavano di paura e rabbia, sfidando Spitz a colpire.

Joe szeme félelemtől és dühtől csillogott, ahogy Spitzet lecsapásra sürgette.

Spitz abbandonò la lotta e si voltò, umiliato e arrabbiato.

Spitz feladta a harcot, és megalázva, dühösen elfordult.

Sfogò la sua frustrazione sul povero Billee e lo cacciò via.

Szegény Billee-n vezette le a dühét, és elkergette.

Quella sera Perrault aggiunse un altro cane alla squadra.

Azon az estén Perrault még egy kutyával bővítette a csapatot.

Questo cane era vecchio, magro e coperto di cicatrici di battaglia.

Ez a kutya öreg, sovány volt, és harci sebek borították.

Gli mancava un occhio, ma l'altro brillava di potere.

Az egyik szeme hiányzott, de a másik erőtől csillogott.

Il nome del nuovo cane era Solleks, che significa "l'Arrabbiato".

Az új kutya neve Solleks volt, ami a Mérges Embert jelentette.

Come Dave, Solleks non chiedeva nulla agli altri e non dava nulla in cambio.

Dave-hez hasonlóan Solleks sem kért semmit másoktól, és semmit sem adott cserébe.

Quando Solleks entrò lentamente nell'accampamento, persino Spitz rimase lontano.

Amikor Solleks lassan bevonult a táborba, még Spitz is távol maradt.

Aveva una strana abitudine che Buck ebbe la sfortuna di scoprire.

Volt egy furcsa szokása, amit Buck balszerencséjére felfedezett.

Solleks detestava essere avvicinato dal lato in cui era cieco.

Solleks utálta, ha arról az oldalról közelítették meg, ahol vak volt.

Buck non lo sapeva e commise quell'errore per sbaglio.

Buck ezt nem tudta, és véletlenül követte el ezt a hibát.

Solleks si voltò di scatto e colpì la spalla di Buck in modo profondo e rapido.

Solleks megpördült, és mélyen, gyorsan megvágta Buck vállát.
**Da quel momento in poi, Buck non si avvicinò mai più al
lato cieco di Solleks.**
Attól a pillanattól kezdve Buck soha többé nem került Solleks
szem elől.
**Non ebbero mai più problemi per il resto del tempo che
trascorsero insieme.**
Az együtt töltött idejük hátralévő részében soha többé nem
volt bajuk.
**Solleks voleva solo essere lasciato solo, come il tranquillo
Dave.**
Solleks csak arra vágyott, hogy békén hagyják, mint a csendes
Dave.
**Ma Buck avrebbe scoperto in seguito che ognuno di loro
aveva un altro obiettivo segreto.**
De Buck később megtudta, hogy mindkettőjüknek volt egy
másik titkos célja is.
**Quella notte Buck si trovò ad affrontare una nuova e
preoccupante sfida: come dormire.**
Azon az éjszakán Buck egy új és nyugtalanító kihívással nézett
szembe – hogyan aludjon el.
**La tenda era illuminata caldamente dalla luce delle candele
nel campo innevato.**
A sátor melegen világított a gyertyafényben a havas mezőn.
**Buck entrò, pensando che lì avrebbe potuto riposare come
prima.**
Buck belépett, és arra gondolt, hogy ott is ugyanúgy
kipihenheti magát, mint azelőtt.
**Ma Perrault e François gli urlarono contro e gli tirarono delle
padelle.**
De Perrault és François ráordítottak és serpenyőket dobáltak.
**Sconvolto e confuso, Buck corse fuori nel freddo gelido.**
Buck megdöbbenve és zavartan kirohant a dermesztő hidegbe.
**Un vento gelido gli pungeva la spalla ferita e gli congelava
le zampe.**
Keserű szél csípte sebesült vállát és megdermedtették a
mancsait.

**Si sdraiò sulla neve e cercò di dormire all'aperto.**
Lefeküdt a hóba, és megpróbált kint aludni a szabadban.
**Ma il freddo lo costrinse presto a rialzarsi, tremando forte.**
De a hideg hamarosan arra kényszerítette, hogy felkeljen, és
erősen remegett.
**Vagò per l'accampamento, cercando di trovare un posto più
caldo.**
Átbotorkált a táboron, melegebb helyet keresve.
**Ma ogni angolo era freddo come quello precedente.**
De minden sarok ugyanolyan hideg volt, mint az előző.
**A volte dei cani feroci gli saltavano addosso dall'oscurità.**
Néha vad kutyák ugrottak rá a sötétségből.
**Buck drizzò il pelo, scoprì i denti e ringhiò in tono
ammonitore.**
Buck felborzolta a bundáját, kivillantotta a fogát, és
figyelmeztetően vicsorgott.
**Lui stava imparando in fretta e gli altri cani si sono subito
tirati indietro.**
Gyorsan tanult, a többi kutya pedig gyorsan hátrált.
**Tuttavia, non aveva un posto dove dormire e non aveva idea
di cosa fare.**
Mégis, nem volt hol aludnia, és fogalma sem volt, mitévő
legyen.
**Alla fine gli venne in mente un pensiero: andare a dare
un'occhiata ai suoi compagni di squadra.**
Végre eszébe jutott egy gondolat – megnézni, hogy vannak-e a
csapattársai.
**Ritornò nella loro zona e rimase sorpreso nel constatare che
non c'erano più.**
Visszatért a környékükre, és meglepődve látta, hogy eltűntek.
**Cercò di nuovo nell'accampamento, ma ancora non riuscì a
trovarli.**
Újra átkutatta a tábort, de még mindig nem találta őket.
**Sapeva che loro non potevano stare nella tenda, altrimenti ci
sarebbe stato anche lui.**
Tudta, hogy nem lehetnek a sátorban, különben ő is ott lenne.

**E allora, dove erano finiti tutti i cani in quell'accampamento ghiacciato?**

Hová tűntek a kutyák ebben a fagyos táborban?

**Buck, infreddolito e infelice, girò lentamente intorno alla tenda.**

Buck, fázva és nyomorultan, lassan körözött a sátor körül.

**All'improvviso, le sue zampe anteriori sprofondarono nella neve soffice e lo spaventarono.**

Hirtelen mellső lábai a puha hóba süllyedtek, és megijesztették.

**Qualcosa si mosse sotto i suoi piedi e lui fece un salto indietro per la paura.**

Valami megmozdult a lába alatt, és ijedtében hátraugrott.

**Ringhiava e ringhiava, non sapendo cosa si nascondesse sotto la neve.**

Morgott és vicsorgott, fogalma sem volt, mi rejlik a hó alatt.

**Poi udì un piccolo abbaio amichevole che placò la sua paura.**

Aztán egy barátságos kis ugatást hallott, ami enyhítette a félelmét.

**Annusò l'aria e si avvicinò per vedere cosa fosse nascosto.**

Beleszimatolt a levegőbe, és közelebb jött, hogy lássa, mi rejtőzik.

**Sotto la neve, rannicchiata in una calda palla, c'era la piccola Billee.**

A hó alatt, meleg gombóccá összegömbölyödve feküdt a kis Billee.

**Billee scodinzolò e leccò il muso di Buck per salutarlo.**

Billee farkcsóválva megnyalta Buck arcát, hogy üdvözölje.

**Buck vide come Billee si era costruito un posto per dormire nella neve.**

Buck látta, hogyan készített Billee magának alvóhelyet a hóban.

**Aveva scavato e sfruttato il suo calore per scaldarsi.**

Leásta magát, és a saját hőjét használta fel melegen.

**Buck aveva imparato un'altra lezione: ecco come dormivano i cani.**

Buck egy újabb leckét tanult meg – így aludtak a kutyák.

Scelse un posto e cominciò a scavare la sua buca nella neve.

Kiválasztott egy helyet, és elkezdte ásni a saját gödrét a hóban.

All'inizio si muoveva troppo e sprecava energie.

Először túl sokat mozgott, és ezzel energiát pazarolt.

Ma ben presto il suo corpo riscaldò lo spazio e si sentì al sicuro.

De hamarosan a teste felmelegítette a teret, és biztonságban érezte magát.

Si rannicchiò forte e poco dopo si addormentò profondamente.

Szorosan összegömbölyödött, és nemsokára mélyen elaludt.

La giornata era stata lunga e dura e Buck era esausto.

Hosszú és nehéz nap volt, Buck pedig kimerült.

Dormì profondamente e comodamente, anche se fece sogni selvaggi.

Mélyen és kényelmesen aludt, bár álmai vadul teltek voltak.

Ringhiava e abbaiava nel sonno, contorcendosi mentre sognava.

Morgott és ugatott álmában, fészkelődve álmodás közben.

Buck non si svegliò finché l'accampamento non cominciò a prendere vita.

Buck csak akkor ébredt fel, amikor a tábor már életre kelt.

All'inizio non sapeva dove si trovasse o cosa fosse successo.

Először azt sem tudta, hol van, vagy mi történt.

La neve era caduta durante la notte e aveva seppellito completamente il suo corpo.

Az éjszaka folyamán hó esett, és teljesen eltemette a testét.

La neve lo circondava, fitta su tutti i lati.

A hó minden oldalról szorosan körülvette.

All'improvviso un'ondata di paura percorse tutto il corpo di Buck.

Hirtelen félelemhullám söpört végig Buck egész testén.

Era la paura di rimanere intrappolati, una paura che proveniva da istinti profondi.

A csapdába eséstől való félelem volt, mélyen gyökerező ösztönökből fakadó félelem.

**Sebbene non avesse mai visto una trappola, la paura era viva dentro di lui.**

Bár még soha nem látott csapdát, a félelem benne élt.

**Era un cane addomesticato, ma ora i suoi vecchi istinti selvaggi si stavano risvegliando.**

Szelíd kutya volt, de most régi, vad ösztönei kezdtek felébredni.

**I muscoli di Buck si irrigidirono e il pelo gli si rizzò su tutta la schiena.**

Buck izmai megfeszültek, és a hátán felállt a szőre.

**Ringhiò furiosamente e balzò in piedi nella neve.**

Vadul felvicsorgott, és egyenesen felugrott a hóba.

**La neve volava in ogni direzione mentre lui irrompeva nella luce del giorno.**

Hó repült minden irányba, ahogy kitört a napfényre.

**Ancora prima di atterrare, Buck vide l'accampamento disteso davanti a lui.**

Még a partraszállás előtt Buck látta maga előtt a szétterülő tábort.

**Ricordò tutto del giorno prima, tutto in una volta.**

Egyszerre mindenre emlékezett az előző napról.

**Ricordava di aver passeggiato con Manuel e di essere finito in quel posto.**

Emlékezett rá, ahogy Manuellel sétáltunk, és végül itt kötöttünk ki.

**Ricordava di aver scavato la buca e di essersi addormentato al freddo.**

Emlékezett rá, hogy megásta a gödröt, és elaludt a hidegben.

**Ora era sveglio e il mondo selvaggio intorno a lui era limpido.**

Most már ébren volt, és a körülötte lévő vad világ tiszta volt.

**Un grido di François annunciò l'improvvisa apparizione di Buck.**

François kiáltása üdvözölte Buck hirtelen megjelenését.

**"Cosa ho detto?" gridò a gran voce il conducente del cane a Perrault.**

– Mit mondtam? – kiáltotta hangosan Perrault-nak a kutyahajcsár.

**"Quel Buck impara sicuramente in fretta", ha aggiunto François.**

„Az a Buck tényleg gyorsan tanul, mint bármi más" – tette hozzá François.

**Perrault annuì gravemente, visibilmente soddisfatto del risultato.**

Perrault komolyan bólintott, láthatóan elégedett volt az eredménnyel.

**In qualità di corriere del governo canadese, trasportava dispacci.**

A kanadai kormány futárjaként küldeményeket kézbesített.

**Era ansioso di trovare i cani migliori per la sua importante missione.**

Alig várta, hogy megtalálja a legjobb kutyákat fontos küldetéséhez.

**Ora si sentiva particolarmente contento che Buck facesse parte della squadra.**

Különösen örült most, hogy Buck a csapat tagja lett.

**Nel giro di un'ora, alla squadra furono aggiunti altri tre husky.**

Egy órán belül további három husky került a csapatba.

**Ciò ha portato il numero totale dei cani della squadra a nove.**

Ezzel a csapatban lévő kutyák teljes száma kilencre emelkedett.

**Nel giro di quindici minuti tutti i cani erano imbracati.**

Tizenöt percen belül az összes kutya a hámjában volt.

**La squadra di slitte stava risalendo il sentiero verso Dyea Cañon.**

A szánkócsapat Dyea Cañon felé döcögött felfelé az ösvényen.

**Buck era contento di andarsene, anche se il lavoro che lo attendeva era duro.**

Buck örült, hogy elmehet, még ha nehéz is volt a munka.

**Scoprì di non disprezzare particolarmente né il lavoro né il freddo.**

Rájött, hogy nem utálta különösebben a munkát vagy a hideget.

**Fu sorpreso dall'entusiasmo che pervadeva tutta la squadra.**

Meglepte a lelkesedés, ami az egész csapatot eltöltötte.

**Ancora più sorprendente fu il cambiamento avvenuto in Dave e Solleks.**

Még meglepőbb volt a változás, ami Dave-vel és Solleksszel történt.

**Questi due cani erano completamente diversi quando venivano imbrigliati.**

Ez a két kutya teljesen más volt, amikor befogták őket.

**La loro passività e la loro disattenzione erano completamente scomparse.**

Passzivitásuk és közönyük teljesen eltűnt.

**Erano attenti e attivi, desiderosi di svolgere bene il loro lavoro.**

Éberek és aktívak voltak, és igyekeztek jól elvégezni a munkájukat.

**Si irritavano ferocemente per qualsiasi cosa provocasse ritardi o confusione.**

Hevesen ingerültek lettek bármitől, ami késedelmet vagy zavart okozott.

**Il duro lavoro sulle redini era il centro del loro intero essere.**

A gyeplőn végzett kemény munka volt egész lényük középpontjában.

**Sembrava che l'unica cosa che gli piacesse davvero fosse tirare la slitta.**

Úgy tűnt, a szánhúzás az egyetlen dolog, amit igazán élveztek.

**Dave era in fondo al gruppo, il più vicino alla slitta.**

Dave a csoport hátulján volt, legközelebb magához a szánhoz.

**Buck fu messo davanti a Dave e Solleks superò Buck.**

Buckot Dave elé ültették, Solleks pedig Buck elé húzott.

**Il resto dei cani era disposto in fila indiana davanti a loro.**

A többi kutya egyetlen sort alkotva terelődött előre.

**La posizione di testa in prima linea era occupata da Spitz.**

Az élvonalban a vezető pozíciót Spitz töltötte be.

**Buck era stato messo tra Dave e Solleks per essere istruito.**

Buckot Dave és Solleks közé helyezték oktatás céljából.

**Lui imparava in fretta e gli insegnanti erano risoluti e capaci.**

Gyorsan tanult, a tanárok pedig határozottak és rátermettek voltak.

**Non permisero mai a Buck di restare a lungo nell'errore.**

Soha nem engedték, hogy Buck sokáig tévedésben maradjon.

**Quando necessario, impartivano le lezioni con denti affilati.**

Éles fogakkal tanították a leckéiket, ha kellett.

**Dave era giusto e dimostrava una saggezza pacata e seria.**

Dave igazságos volt, és csendes, komoly bölcsességről tanúskodott.

**Non mordeva mai Buck senza una buona ragione.**

Soha nem harapta meg Buckot alapos ok nélkül.

**Ma non mancava mai di mordere quando Buck aveva bisogno di essere corretto.**

De sosem mulasztotta el a harapást, amikor Bucknak helyreigazításra volt szüksége.

**La frusta di François era sempre pronta e sosteneva la loro autorità.**

François ostora mindig készen állt, és alátámasztotta tekintélyüket.

**Buck scoprì presto che era meglio obbedire che reagire.**

Buck hamarosan rájött, hogy jobb engedelmeskedni, mint visszatámadni.

**Una volta, durante un breve riposo, Buck rimase impigliato nelle redini.**

Egyszer, egy rövid pihenő alatt, Buck beleakadt a gyeplőbe.

**Ritardò la partenza e confuse i movimenti della squadra.**

Késleltette a kezdést és összezavarta a csapat mozgását.

**Dave e Solleks si avventarono su di lui e lo picchiarono duramente.**

Dave és Solleks rárontottak, és durván megverték.

**La situazione peggiorò ulteriormente, ma Buck imparò bene la lezione.**

A gubanc csak rosszabb lett, de Buck jól megtanulta a leckét.

**Da quel momento in poi tenne le redini tese e lavorò con attenzione.**

Ettől kezdve feszesen tartotta a gyeplőt, és óvatosan dolgozott.

**Prima che la giornata finisse, Buck aveva portato a termine gran parte del suo compito.**

Mire a nap véget ért, Buck már nagyrészt elsajátította a feladatát.

**I suoi compagni di squadra quasi smisero di correggerlo o di morderlo.**

A csapattársai szinte abbahagyták a firtatását vagy a harapdálását.

**La frusta di François schioccava nell'aria sempre meno spesso.**

François ostora egyre ritkábban csattant a levegőben.

**Perrault sollevò addirittura i piedi di Buck ed esaminò attentamente ogni zampa.**

Perrault még Buck lábait is felemelte, és gondosan megvizsgálta mindegyik mancsot.

**Era stata una giornata di corsa dura, lunga ed estenuante per tutti loro.**

Kemény, hosszú és kimerítő futásnap volt ez mindannyiuk számára.

**Risalirono il Cañon, attraversarono Sheep Camp e superarono le Scales.**

Felmentek a Cañonon, át Sheep Campen, és elhaladtak a Scales-hegység mellett.

**Superarono il limite della vegetazione arborea, poi ghiacciai e cumuli di neve alti diversi metri.**

Átlépték az erdőhatárt, majd gleccsereket és több méter mély hótorlaszokat.

**Scalarono il grande e freddo Chilkoot Divide.**

Megmászták a nagy hideget és a félelmetes Chilkoot-hágót.

**Quella cresta elevata si ergeva tra l'acqua salata e l'interno ghiacciato.**

Az a magas gerinc a sós víz és a fagyott belső tér között állt.

**Le montagne custodivano il triste e solitario Nord con ghiaccio e ripide salite.**

A hegyek jéggel és meredek emelkedőkkel őrizték a szomorú és magányos Északot.

Scesero rapidamente lungo una lunga catena di laghi sotto la dorsale.

Jól haladtak lefelé a vízválasztó alatti hosszú tóláncon.

Questi laghi riempivano gli antichi crateri di vulcani spenti.

Ezek a tavak kialudt vulkánok ősi krátereit töltötték meg.

Quella notte tardi raggiunsero un grande accampamento presso il lago Bennett.

Késő este elérték a Bennett-tónál lévő nagy tábort.

Migliaia di cercatori d'oro erano lì, intenti a costruire barche per la primavera.

Több ezer aranyásó volt ott, csónakokat építettek a tavaszra.

Il ghiaccio si sarebbe presto rotto e dovevano essere pronti.

A jég hamarosan felszakadozott, és készen kellett állniuk.

Buck scavò la sua buca nella neve e cadde in un sonno profondo.

Buck ásta a gödröt a hóban, és mély álomba zuhant.

Dormiva come un lavoratore, esausto dopo una dura giornata di lavoro.

Úgy aludt, mint egy munkásember, kimerülten a kemény munkanaptól.

Ma venne strappato al sonno troppo presto, nell'oscurità.

De túl korán a sötétben, felrángatták álmából.

Fu nuovamente imbrigliato insieme ai suoi compagni e attaccato alla slitta.

Újra befogták a társaival, és a szánhoz erősítették.

Quel giorno percorsero quaranta miglia, perché la neve era ben calpestata.

Azon a napon negyven mérföldet tettek meg, mivel a hó alaposan le volt taposva.

Il giorno dopo, e per molti giorni a seguire, la neve era soffice.

Másnap, és még sok-sok azután is, a hó puha volt.

Dovettero farsi strada da soli, lavorando di più e muovendosi più lentamente.

Maguknak kellett megtenniük az utat, keményebben dolgozva és lassabban haladva.

**Di solito, Perrault camminava davanti alla squadra con le ciaspole palmate.**

Perrault általában úszóhártyás hótalpakkal haladt a csapat előtt.

**I suoi passi compattavano la neve, facilitando lo spostamento della slitta.**

Léptei belenyomták a havat, megkönnyítve ezzel a szán mozgását.

**François, che era al timone della barca a vela, a volte prendeva il comando.**

François, aki a gearboomról kormányzott, néha átvette az irányítást.

**Ma era raro che François prendesse l'iniziativa**

De ritkán fordult elő, hogy François átvette a vezetést.

**perché Perrault aveva fretta di consegnare le lettere e i pacchi.**

mert Perrault sietett a levelek és csomagok kézbesítésével.

**Perrault era orgoglioso della sua conoscenza della neve, e in particolare del ghiaccio.**

Perrault büszke volt a hóval, és különösen a jéggel kapcsolatos ismereteire.

**Questa conoscenza era essenziale perché il ghiaccio autunnale era pericolosamente sottile.**

Ez a tudás elengedhetetlen volt, mivel az őszi jég veszélyesen vékony volt.

**Dove l'acqua scorreva rapidamente sotto la superficie non c'era affatto ghiaccio.**

Ahol a víz gyorsan áramlott a felszín alatt, ott egyáltalán nem volt jég.

**Giorno dopo giorno, la stessa routine si ripeteva senza fine.**

Napról napra ugyanaz a rutin ismétlődött vég nélkül.

**Buck lavorava senza sosta con le redini, dall'alba alla sera.**

Buck hajnaltól estig szüntelenül gürcölt a gyeplőben.

**Lasciarono l'accampamento al buio, molto prima che sorgesse il sole.**

Sötétben hagyták el a tábort, jóval napkelte előtt.

Quando spuntò l'alba, avevano già percorso molti chilometri.

Mire megvirradt, már sok kilométert maguk mögött hagytak.

Si accamparono dopo il tramonto, mangiando pesce e scavando buche nella neve.

Sötétedés után vertek tábort, halat ettek és a hóba ásták magukat.

Buck era sempre affamato e non era mai veramente soddisfatto della sua razione.

Buck mindig éhes volt, és soha nem volt igazán elégedett az adagjával.

Riceveva ogni giorno mezzo chilo di salmone essiccato.

Naponta másfél font szárított lazacot kapott.

Ma il cibo sembrò svanire dentro di lui, lasciandogli solo la fame.

De az étel mintha eltűnt volna belőle, hátrahagyva az éhséget.

Soffriva di continui morsi della fame e sognava di avere più cibo.

Állandó éhség gyötörte, és arról álmodozott, hogy több ételt kap.

Gli altri cani hanno ricevuto solo mezzo chilo di cibo, ma sono rimasti forti.

A többi kutya csak egy fontnyi ételt kapott, de erősek maradtak.

Erano più piccoli ed erano nati in una società nordica.

Kisebbek voltak, és az északi életbe születtek.

Perse rapidamente la pignoleria che aveva caratterizzato la sua vecchia vita.

Gyorsan elvesztette azt a finnyásságot, ami régi életét jellemezte.

Fino a quel momento era stato un mangiatore prelibato, ma ora non gli era più possibile.

Régen ínycsiklandó evő volt, de most ez már nem volt lehetséges.

I suoi compagni arrivarono primi e gli rubarono la razione rimasta.

A társai végeztek először, és elrabolták a megmaradt adagját.

**Una volta cominciati, non c'era più modo di difendere il cibo da loro.**

Miután elkezdték, nem volt módja megvédeni az ételét tőlük.

**Mentre lui lottava contro due o tre cani, gli altri rubarono il resto.**

Míg ő két-három kutyát elűzött, a többiek ellopták a többit.

**Per risolvere il problema, cominciò a mangiare velocemente come mangiavano gli altri.**

Hogy ezt helyrehozza, olyan gyorsan kezdett enni, mint a többiek.

**La fame lo spingeva così forte che arrivò persino a prendere del cibo non suo.**

Az éhség annyira hajtotta, hogy még a saját ételét is elfogyasztotta.

**Osservò gli altri e imparò rapidamente dalle loro azioni.**

Figyelte a többieket, és gyorsan tanult a tetteikből.

**Vide Pike, un nuovo cane, rubare una fetta di pancetta a Perrault.**

Látta, ahogy Pike, az új kutya, ellop egy szelet szalonnát Perrault-tól.

**Pike aveva aspettato che Perrault gli voltasse le spalle per rubare la pagnotta.**

Pike megvárta, amíg Perrault hátat fordít, hogy ellopja a szalonnát.

**Il giorno dopo, Buck copiò Pike e rubò l'intero pezzo.**

Másnap Buck lemásolta Pike-ot, és ellopta az egészet.

**Seguì un gran tumulto, ma Buck non fu sospettato.**

Nagy felfordulás támadt, de Buckot senki sem gyanúsította.

**Al suo posto venne punito Dub, un cane goffo che veniva sempre beccato.**

Ehelyett Dubot, az ügyetlen kutyát büntették meg, akit mindig elkaptak.

**Quel primo furto fece di Buck un cane adatto a sopravvivere al Nord.**

Az első lopás Buckot olyan kutyává tette, aki képes túlélni az északi vidéket.

**Ha dimostrato di sapersi adattare alle nuove condizioni e di saper imparare rapidamente.**

Megmutatta, hogy gyorsan tud alkalmazkodni az új körülményekhez és tanul.

**Senza tale adattabilità, sarebbe morto rapidamente e gravemente.**

Ilyen alkalmazkodóképesség nélkül gyorsan és rosszul halt volna meg.

**Segnò anche il crollo della sua natura morale e dei suoi valori passati.**

Ez erkölcsi természetének és múltbeli értékeinek összeomlását is jelentette.

**Nel Southland aveva vissuto secondo la legge dell'amore e della gentilezza.**

Délvidéken a szeretet és a kedvesség törvénye szerint élt.

**Lì aveva senso rispettare la proprietà e i sentimenti degli altri cani.**

Ott volt értelme tiszteletben tartani a tulajdont és más kutyák érzéseit.

**Ma i Northland seguivano la legge del bastone e la legge della zanna.**

De Északföld a bunkó és az agyar törvényét követte.

**Chiunque rispettasse i vecchi valori era uno sciocco e avrebbe fallito.**

Aki itt a régi értékeket tisztelte, az ostoba volt, és el fog bukni.

**Buck non rifletté su tutto questo nella sua mente.**

Buck mindezt nem gondolta végig magában.

**Era in forma e quindi si adattò senza pensarci due volte.**

Fitt volt, így gondolkodás nélkül alkalmazkodott.

**In tutta la sua vita non era mai fuggito da una rissa.**

Egész életében soha nem futott el harc elől.

**Ma la mazza di legno dell'uomo con il maglione rosso cambiò la regola.**

De a piros pulóveres férfi fa bunkója megváltoztatta ezt a szabályt.

**Ora seguiva un codice più profondo e antico, inscritto nel suo essere.**

Most egy mélyebb, régebbi, a lényébe bevésődött kódot
követett.

**Non rubava per piacere, ma per il dolore della fame.**

Nem élvezetből lopott, hanem az éhség kínjától.

**Non rubava mai apertamente, ma rubava con astuzia e
attenzione.**

Soha nem rabolt nyíltan, hanem ravaszul és körültekintően
lopott.

**Agì per rispetto verso la clava di legno e per paura delle
zanne.**

A fabáb iránti tiszteletből és az agyartól való félelemből
cselekedett.

**In breve, ha fatto ciò che era più facile e sicuro che non farlo.**

Röviden, azt tette, ami könnyebb és biztonságosabb volt, mint
a meg nem tétele.

**Il suo sviluppo, o forse il suo ritorno ai vecchi istinti, fu
rapido.**

A fejlődése – vagy talán a régi ösztöneihez való visszatérése –
gyors volt.

**I suoi muscoli si indurirono fino a diventare forti come il
ferro.**

Izmai addig keményedtek, amíg olyan erősnek nem érezték
magukat, mint a vas.

**Non gli importava più del dolore, a meno che non fosse
grave.**

Már nem törődött a fájdalommal, kivéve, ha komoly volt.

**Divenne efficiente dentro e fuori, senza sprecare nulla.**

Kívül-belül hatékony lett, semmit sem pazarolt.

**Poteva mangiare cose disgustose, marce o difficili da
digerire.**

Képes volt undorító, romlott vagy nehezen emészthető
dolgokat enni.

**Qualunque cosa mangiasse, il suo stomaco ne sfruttava ogni
singolo pezzetto di valore.**

Bármit is evett, a gyomra az utolsó morzsáig felhasználta.

**Il suo sangue trasportava i nutrienti in tutto il suo potente
corpo.**

Vére messzire szállította a tápanyagokat erős testében.
**Ciò gli ha permesso di sviluppare tessuti forti che gli hanno conferito un'incredibile resistenza.**
Ez erős szöveteket épített ki, amelyek hihetetlen kitartást biztosítottak számára.
**La sua vista e il suo olfatto diventarono molto più sensibili di prima.**
A látása és a szaglása sokkal érzékenyebbé vált, mint korábban.
**Il suo udito diventò così acuto che riusciva a percepire anche i suoni più deboli durante il sonno.**
A hallása annyira kiélesedett, hogy álmában is halvány hangokat tudott hallani.
**Nei sogni sapeva se quei suoni significavano sicurezza o pericolo.**
Álmaiban tudta, hogy a hangok biztonságot vagy veszélyt jelentenek.
**Imparò a mordere con i denti il ghiaccio tra le dita dei piedi.**
Megtanulta, hogyan harapja a fogaival a jégbe a lábujjai között.
**Se una pozza d'acqua si ghiacciava, lui rompeva il ghiaccio con le gambe.**
Ha egy itatóhely befagyott, a lábaival törte fel a jeget.
**Si impennò e colpì duramente il ghiaccio con gli arti anteriori rigidi.**
Felágaskodott, és merev mellső lábaival keményen a jégre csapódott.
**La sua abilità più sorprendente era quella di prevedere i cambiamenti del vento durante la notte.**
Legfeltűnőbb képessége az éjszakai szélváltozások előrejelzése volt.
**Anche quando l'aria era immobile, sceglieva luoghi riparati dal vento.**
Még szélcsendben is szélvédett helyeket választott.
**Ovunque scavasse il nido, il vento del giorno dopo lo superava.**
Ahol fészket ásott, a másnapi szél elsuhant mellette.

**Alla fine si ritrovava sempre al sicuro e protetto, al riparo dal vento.**

Mindig kényelmesen és védve feküdt, a szellő elől védve.

**Buck non solo imparò dall'esperienza: anche il suo istinto tornò.**

Buck nemcsak tapasztalatból tanult – az ösztönei is visszatértek.

**Le abitudini delle generazioni addomesticate cominciarono a scomparire.**

A megszelídített generációk szokásai elkezdtek hanyatlani.

**Ricordava vagamente i tempi antichi della sua razza.**

Homályosan emlékezett fajtája ősi időire.

**Ripensò a quando i cani selvatici correvano in branco nelle foreste.**

Visszagondolt azokra az időkre, amikor a vadkutyák falkákban szaladgáltak az erdőkben.

**Avevano inseguito e ucciso la loro preda mentre la inseguivano.**

Üldözték és megölték prédájukat, miközben lefuttatták.

**Per Buck fu facile imparare a combattere con forza e velocità.**

Bucknak könnyű volt megtanulnia, hogyan kell foggal és gyorsan harcolni.

**Come i suoi antenati, usava tagli, squarci e schiocchi rapidi.**

Vágásokat, vágásokat és gyors csettintéseket használt, akárcsak ősei.

**Quegli antenati si risvegliarono in lui e risvegliarono la sua natura selvaggia.**

Azok az ősök megmozdultak benne, és felébresztették vad természetét.

**Le loro vecchie abilità gli erano state trasmesse attraverso la linea di sangue.**

Régi képességeik vérvonalon keresztül öröklődtek át rá.

**Ora i loro trucchi erano suoi, senza bisogno di pratica o sforzo.**

A trükkjeik most már az övéi voltak, gyakorlás vagy erőfeszítés nélkül.

**Nelle notti fredde e tranquille, Buck sollevava il naso e ululò.**

Csendes, hideg éjszakákon Buck felemelte az orrát és vonyított.

**Ululò a lungo e profondamente, come facevano i lupi tanto tempo fa.**

Hosszan és mélyen vonyított, ahogy a farkasok tették régesrégen.

**Attraverso di lui, i suoi antenati defunti puntarono il naso e ulularono.**

Rajta keresztül halott ősei orrukat hegyezve üvöltöttek.

**Hanno ululato attraverso i secoli con la sua voce e la sua forma.**

Hangján és alakján keresztül üvöltöttek lefelé az évszázadokon.

**Le sue cadenze erano le loro, vecchi gridi che parlavano di dolore e di freddo.**

A hangja az övék volt, régi kiáltások, melyek a bánatról és a hidegről árulkodtak.

**Cantavano dell'oscurità, della fame e del significato dell'inverno.**

A sötétségről, az éhségről és a tél jelentéséről énekeltek.

**Buck ha dimostrato come la vita sia plasmata da forze che vanno oltre noi stessi,**

Buck bebizonyította, hogy az életet rajtunk kívül álló erők alakítják,

**l'antico canto risuonò nelle vene di Buck e si impadronì della sua anima.**

Az ősi dal felszállt Buckból, és megragadta a lelkét.

**Ritrovò se stesso perché gli uomini avevano trovato l'oro nel Nord.**

Azért találta meg önmagát, mert az emberek aranyat találtak Északon.

**E lo trovò perché Manuel, l'aiutante giardiniere, aveva bisogno di soldi.**

És azért találta magát, mert Manuelnek, a kertész segédjének, pénzre volt szüksége.

## La Bestia Primordiale Dominante
### Az uralkodó ősállat

**La bestia primordiale dominante era più forte che mai in Buck.**
A domináns ősállat Buckban ugyanolyan erős volt, mint valaha.
**Ma la bestia primordiale dominante era rimasta dormiente in lui.**
De az uralkodó ősállat szunnyadt benne.
**La vita sui sentieri era dura, ma rafforzava la bestia che era in Buck.**
Az ösvényen töltött élet kemény volt, de megerősítette Buckban a benne rejlő vadállatot.
**Segretamente la bestia diventava sempre più forte ogni giorno.**
Titokban a szörnyeteg minden egyes nappal erősebb és erősebb lett.
**Ma quella crescita interiore è rimasta nascosta al mondo esterno.**
De ez a belső fejlődés rejtve maradt a külvilág számára.
**Una forza primordiale calma e silenziosa si stava formando dentro Buck.**
Egy csendes és nyugodt, ősi erő épült Buckban.
**Una nuova astuzia diede a Buck equilibrio, calma e compostezza.**
Az új ravaszság egyensúlyt, nyugodt önuralom és higgadtságot kölcsönzött Bucknak.
**Buck si concentrò molto sull'adattamento, senza mai sentirsi completamente rilassato.**
Buck erősen az alkalmazkodásra koncentrált, sosem érezte magát teljesen ellazultnak.
**Evitava i conflitti, non iniziava mai litigi e non cercava mai guai.**
Kerülte a konfliktusokat, soha nem kezdett verekedéseket, és nem kereste a bajt.

**Ogni mossa di Buck era scandita da una riflessione lenta e costante.**

Buck minden mozdulatát lassú, de biztos megfontolás jellemezte.

**Evitava scelte avventate e decisioni improvvise e sconsiderate.**

Kerülte a meggondolatlan döntéseket és a hirtelen, meggondolatlan döntéseket.

**Sebbene Buck odiasse profondamente Spitz, non gli mostrò alcuna aggressività.**

Bár Buck mélységesen gyűlölte Spitzet, nem mutatott vele szemben agressziót.

**Buck non provocò mai Spitz e mantenne le sue azioni moderate.**

Buck soha nem provokálta Spitzet, és visszafogottan cselekedett.

**Spitz, d'altro canto, percepì il pericolo crescente in Buck.**

Spitz viszont érezte a Buckban növekvő veszélyt.

**Vedeva Buck come una minaccia e una seria sfida al suo potere.**

Buckot fenyegetésnek és hatalma komoly kihívásának tekintette.

**Coglieva ogni occasione per ringhiare e mostrare i suoi denti aguzzi.**

Minden alkalmat megragadott, hogy vicsorogjon és megmutassa éles fogait.

**Stava cercando di dare inizio allo scontro mortale che sarebbe dovuto avvenire.**

Megpróbálta megkezdeni a halálos harcot, amelynek el kellett jönnie.

**All'inizio del viaggio, tra loro scoppiò quasi una lite.**

Az út elején majdnem verekedés tört ki közöttük.

**Ma un incidente inaspettato impedì che il combattimento avesse luogo.**

Ám egy váratlan baleset megakadályozta a verekedést.

**Quella sera si accamparono sul gelido lago Le Barge.**

Azon az estén tábort vertek a keservesen hideg Le Barge-tavon.

**La neve cadeva fitta e il vento era tagliente come una lama.**

Keményen esett a hó, a szél pedig késként vágott.

**La notte era scesa troppo in fretta e l'oscurità li aveva avvolti.**

Túl gyorsan leszállt az éjszaka, és sötétség vette körül őket.

**Difficilmente avrebbero potuto scegliere un posto peggiore per riposare.**

Aligha választhattak volna rosszabb helyet a pihenésre.

**I cani cercavano disperatamente un posto dove sdraiarsi.**

A kutyák kétségbeesetten kerestek egy helyet, ahol lefeküdhetnek.

**Dietro il piccolo gruppo si ergeva un'alta parete rocciosa.**

Egy magas sziklafal emelkedett meredeken a kis csoport mögött.

**Per alleggerire il carico, la tenda era stata lasciata a Dyea.**

A sátrat Dyeában hagyták, hogy könnyítsenek a terhen.

**Non avevano altra scelta che accendere il fuoco direttamente sul ghiaccio.**

Nem volt más választásuk, mint hogy magukon a jégen tüzet gyújtsanak.

**Stendevano i loro accappatoi direttamente sul lago ghiacciato.**

Hálóruháikat közvetlenül a befagyott tóra terítették.

**Qualche pezzo di legno galleggiante dava loro un po' di fuoco.**

Néhány uszadékfa-rúd adott nekik egy kis tüzet.

**Ma il fuoco è stato acceso sul ghiaccio e attraverso di esso si è scongelato.**

De a tűz a jégen rakódott, és azon keresztül olvadt el.

**Alla fine cenarono al buio.**

Végül sötétben ették meg a vacsorájukat.

**Buck si rannicchiò accanto alla roccia, al riparo dal vento freddo.**

Buck összegömbölyödött a szikla mellett, védve a hideg széltől.

**Il posto era così caldo e sicuro che Buck non voleva andarsene.**

A hely olyan meleg és biztonságos volt, hogy Buck nem szívesen mozdult el onnan.

**Ma François aveva scaldato il pesce e stava distribuendo le razioni.**

De François már megmelegítette a halat, és már osztotta az élelmet.

**Buck finì di mangiare in fretta e tornò a letto.**

Buck gyorsan befejezte az evést, és visszafeküdt az ágyába.

**Ma Spitz ora giaceva dove Buck aveva preparato il suo letto.**

De Spitz most ott feküdt, ahol Buck megágyazott.

**Un ringhio basso avvertì Buck che Spitz si rifiutava di muoversi.**

Egy halk vicsorgás figyelmeztette Buckot, hogy Spitz nem hajlandó mozdulni.

**Finora Buck aveva evitato lo scontro con Spitz.**

Buck eddig elkerülte a Spitz-csel vívott harcot.

**Ma nel profondo di Buck la bestia alla fine si liberò.**

De Buck legbelül végre elszabadult a szörnyeteg.

**Il furto del suo posto letto era troppo da tollerare.**

A hálóhelyének ellopása túl sok volt ahhoz, hogy elviselje.

**Buck si lanciò contro Spitz, pieno di rabbia e furore.**

Buck dühösen és dühösen Spitzre vetette magát.

**Fino a quel momento Spitz aveva pensato che Buck fosse solo un grosso cane.**

Spitz eddig csak egy nagy kutyának gondolta Buckot.

**Non pensava che Buck fosse sopravvissuto grazie al suo spirito.**

Nem gondolta, hogy Buck a szelleme révén élte túl.

**Si aspettava paura e codardia, non furia e vendetta.**

Félelemre és gyávaságra számított, nem dühre és bosszúra.

**François rimase a guardare mentre entrambi i cani schizzavano fuori dal nido in rovina.**

François bámulta, ahogy mindkét kutya előtört a romos fészekből.

**Capì subito cosa aveva scatenato quella violenta lotta.**

Azonnal megértette, mi indította el a vad küzdelmet.

**"Aa-ah!" gridò François in sostegno del cane marrone.**

„Ááá!" – kiáltotta François, támogatva a barna kutyát.

**"Dategli una bella lezione! Per Dio, punite quel ladro furbo!"**

„Adj neki egy verést! Istenre, büntesse meg azt a sunyi tolvajt!"

**Spitz dimostrò altrettanta prontezza e fervore nel combattere.**

Spitz egyenlő készenlétet és vad harci vágyat mutatott.

**Gridò di rabbia mentre girava velocemente in tondo, cercando un varco.**

Dühösen felkiáltott, miközben gyorsan körözött, rést keresve.

**Buck mostrò la stessa fame di combattere e la stessa cautela.**

Buck ugyanazt a harci vágyat és ugyanazt az óvatosságot mutatta.

**Anche lui girò intorno al suo avversario, cercando di avere la meglio nella battaglia.**

Ő is megkerülte ellenfelét, próbálva fölénybe kerülni a csatában.

**Poi accadde qualcosa di inaspettato e cambiò tutto.**

Aztán történt valami váratlan, és mindent megváltoztatott.

**Quel momento ritardò l'eventuale lotta per la leadership.**

Ez a pillanat késleltette a vezetésért folytatott végső küzdelmet.

**Ci sarebbero ancora molti chilometri di sentiero e di lotta da percorrere prima della fine.**

Még sok kilométernyi út és küzdelem várt a végére.

**Perrault urlò un'imprecazione mentre una mazza colpiva l'osso.**

Perrault egy káromkodást kiáltott, amikor egy bunkó csontnak csapódott.

**Seguì un acuto grido di dolore, poi il caos esplose tutt'intorno.**

Éles, fájdalmas sikoly következett, majd mindenütt káosz tört ki.

**Forme scure si muovevano nell'accampamento: husky selvatici, affamati e feroci.**

Sötét alakok mozogtak a táborban; vad, kiéhezett és vadak kutyák.

**Quattro o cinque dozzine di husky avevano fiutato l'accampamento da molto lontano.**

Négy-öt tucat husky szaglászott már messziről a tábor körül.

**Si erano introdotti furtivamente mentre i due cani litigavano lì vicino.**

Csendben lopakodtak be, miközben a két kutya a közelben verekedett.

**François e Perrault si lanciarono all'attacco, colpendo con i manganelli gli invasori.**

François és Perrault rohamra indultak, botokkal lendítve a támadókat.

**Gli husky affamati mostrarono i denti e si dibatterono freneticamente.**

Az éhező huskyk kivillantották a fogaikat, és dühösen visszavágtak.

**L'odore della carne e del pane li aveva fatti superare ogni paura.**

A hús és a kenyér illata minden félelmüktől megfosztotta őket.

**Perrault picchiò un cane che aveva nascosto la testa nella buca delle vivande.**

Perrault megvert egy kutyát, amely a fejét az eleségdobozba dugta.

**Il colpo fu violento e la scatola si ribaltò, facendo fuoriuscire il cibo.**

Az ütés erős volt, a doboz felborult, és étel ömlött ki belőle.

**Nel giro di pochi secondi, una ventina di bestie feroci si avventarono sul pane e sulla carne.**

Másodpercek alatt egy tucat vadállat tépte szét a kenyeret és a húst.

**I bastoni degli uomini sferrarono un colpo dopo l'altro, ma nessun cane si allontanò.**

A férfiütők ütésről ütésre érkeztek, de egyetlen kutya sem fordult el.

**Urlavano di dolore, ma continuarono a lottare finché non rimase più cibo.**

Fájdalmukban üvöltöttek, de addig küzdöttek, amíg el nem fogyott az élelmük.

**Nel frattempo i cani da slitta erano saltati giù dalle loro culle innevate.**

Eközben a szánhúzó kutyák kiugrottak havas ágyaikból.

**Furono immediatamente attaccati dai feroci e affamati husky.**

Azonnal megtámadták őket a veszett, éhes huskyk.

**Buck non aveva mai visto prima creature così selvagge e affamate.**

Buck még soha nem látott ilyen vad és kiéhezett teremtményeket.

**La loro pelle pendeva flaccida, nascondendo a malapena lo scheletro.**

Bőrük lazán lógott, alig rejtve a csontvázukat.

**C'era un fuoco nei loro occhi, per fame e follia**

Tűz égett a szemükben az éhségtől és az őrülettől

**Non c'era modo di fermarli, di resistere al loro assalto selvaggio.**

Nem lehetett őket megállítani; nem lehetett ellenállni vad rohamuknak.

**I cani da slitta vennero spinti indietro e premuti contro la parete della scogliera.**

A szánhúzó kutyákat hátralökték, a sziklafalhoz nyomták.

**Tre husky attaccarono Buck contemporaneamente, lacerandogli la carne.**

Három husky támadt rá Buckra egyszerre, és a húsába tépték a húsát.

**Il sangue gli colava dalla testa e dalle spalle, dove era stato tagliato.**

Vér ömlött a fejéből és a vállából, ahol megvágták.

**Il rumore riempì l'accampamento: ringhi, guaiti e grida di dolore.**

A zaj betöltötte a tábort; morgás, visítás és fájdalmas kiáltások.

**Billee pianse forte, come al solito, presa dal panico e dalla mischia.**

Billee hangosan sírt, mint általában, a pánik és a csetepaté közepette.

**Dave e Solleks rimasero fianco a fianco, sanguinanti ma con aria di sfida.**

Dave és Solleks egymás mellett álltak, vérezve, de dacosan.

**Joe lottava come un demonio, mordendo tutto ciò che gli si avvicinava.**

Joe démonként harcolt, mindent megharapott, ami a közelébe került.

**Con un violento schiocco di mascelle schiacciò la zampa di un husky.**

Egyetlen brutális állkapocs-csattanással szétzúzta egy husky lábát.

**Pike saltò sull'husky ferito e gli ruppe il collo all'istante.**

Pike ráugrott a sebesült huskyra, és azonnal eltörte a nyakát.

**Buck afferrò un husky per la gola e gli strappò la vena.**

Buck elkapott egy huskyt a torkánál, és átszakította az erét.

**Il sangue schizzò e il sapore caldo mandò Buck in delirio.**

Vér fröccsent, és a meleg íz őrületbe kergette Buckot.

**Si lanciò contro un altro aggressore senza esitazione.**

Gondolkodás nélkül rávetette magát egy másik támadóra.

**Nello stesso momento, denti aguzzi si conficcarono nella gola di Buck.**

Ugyanebben a pillanatban éles fogak vájtak Buck torkába.

**Spitz aveva colpito di lato, attaccando senza preavviso.**

Spitz oldalról csapott le, előzetes figyelmeztetés nélkül támadva.

**Perrault e François avevano sconfitto i cani rubando il cibo.**

Perrault és François legyőzték az élelmet lopó kutyákat.

**Ora si precipitarono ad aiutare i loro cani a respingere gli aggressori.**

Most siettek, hogy segítsenek kutyáiknak visszaverni a támadókat.

**I cani affamati si ritirarono mentre gli uomini roteavano i loro manganelli.**

Az éhező kutyák visszavonultak, miközben a férfiak meglendítették a bunkóikat.

**Buck riuscì a liberarsi dall'attacco, ma la fuga fu breve.**
Buck kiszabadult a támadás elől, de a menekülés rövid volt.
**Gli uomini corsero a salvare i loro cani e gli husky tornarono ad attaccarli.**
A férfiak a kutyáik megmentésére rohantak, de a huskyk ismét ellepték őket.
**Billee, spaventato e coraggioso, si lanciò nel branco di cani.**
Billee, akit félelemmel rémített a bátorság, beugrott a kutyák falkájába.
**Ma poi fuggì attraverso il ghiaccio, in preda al terrore e al panico.**
De aztán átmenekült a jégen, nyers rettegésben és pánikban.
**Pike e Dub li seguirono da vicino, correndo per salvarsi la vita.**
Pike és Dub szorosan a nyomukban követték őket, életüket mentve futva.
**Il resto della squadra si disperse e li inseguì.**
A csapat többi tagja szétszóródott, és a nyomukban követte őket.
**Buck raccolse le forze per correre, ma poi vide un lampo.**
Buck összeszedte minden erejét, hogy elfusson, de ekkor egy villanást látott.
**Spitz si lanciò verso Buck, cercando di buttarlo a terra.**
Spitz Buck oldalára vetette magát, és megpróbálta a földre lökni.
**Sotto quella banda di husky, Buck non avrebbe avuto scampo.**
Azzal a husky csapattal szemben Bucknak nem volt menekvés.
**Ma Buck rimase fermo e si preparò al colpo di Spitz.**
De Buck szilárdan állt és felkészült Spitz csapására.
**Poi si voltò e corse sul ghiaccio con la squadra in fuga.**
Aztán megfordult, és a menekülő csapattal együtt kirohant a jégre.

**Più tardi i nove cani da slitta si radunarono al riparo del bosco.**

Később a kilenc szánhúzó kutya összegyűlt az erdő menedékében.

**Nessuno li inseguiva più, ma erano malconci e feriti.**

Senki sem üldözte őket már, de összetörtek és megsebesültek.

**Ogni cane presentava delle ferite: quattro o cinque tagli profondi su ogni corpo.**

Minden kutyán sebek voltak; négy vagy öt mély vágás mindegyik testén.

**Dub aveva una zampa posteriore ferita e ora faceva fatica a camminare.**

Dubnak megsérült az egyik hátsó lába, és most már nehezen tudott járni.

**Dolly, l'ultimo cane arrivato da Dyea, aveva la gola tagliata.**

Dollynak, Dyea legújabb kutyájának elvágták a torkát.

**Joe aveva perso un occhio e l'orecchio di Billee era stato tagliato a pezzi**

Joe elvesztette az egyik szemét, Billee füle pedig darabokra tört.

**Tutti i cani piansero per il dolore e la sconfitta durante la notte.**

Az összes kutya fájdalmasan és legyőzötten sírt egész éjjel.

**All'alba tornarono lentamente all'accampamento, doloranti e distrutti.**

Hajnalban visszaosontak a táborba, fájóan és összetörve.

**Gli husky erano scomparsi, ma il danno era fatto.**

A huskyk eltűntek, de a kár már megtörtént.

**Perrault e François erano di pessimo umore e osservavano le rovine.**

Perrault és François rosszkedvűen álltak a romok felett.

**Metà del cibo era sparito, rubato dai ladri affamati.**

Az élelem fele eltűnt, az éhes tolvajok elrabolták.

**Gli husky avevano strappato le corde e la tela della slitta.**

A huskyk elszakították a szánkó kötözését és a vásznat.

**Tutto ciò che aveva odore di cibo era stato divorato completamente.**

Mindent, aminek ételszaga volt, teljesen felfaltak.

**Mangiarono un paio di stivali da viaggio in pelle di alce di Perrault.**

Megették Perrault egy pár jávorszarvasbőr utazócsizmáját.

**Hanno masticato le pelli e rovinato i cinturini rendendoli inutilizzabili.**

Bőr reiseket rágcsáltak, és használhatatlanná tették a szíjakat.

**François smise di fissare la frusta strappata per controllare i cani.**

François abbahagyta a tépett korbács bámulását, hogy ellenőrizze a kutyákat.

**«Ah, amici miei», disse con voce bassa e preoccupata.**

– Ó, barátaim – mondta halk, aggodalommal teli hangon.

**"Forse tutti questi morsi vi trasformeranno in bestie pazze."**

„Talán ezek a harapások őrült fenevadakká változtatnak benneteket."

**"Forse tutti cani rabbiosi, sacredam! Che ne pensi, Perrault?"**

„Talán mind veszett kutyák, szent ég! Mit gondolsz, Perrault?"

**Perrault scosse la testa, con gli occhi scuri per la preoccupazione e la paura.**

Perrault a fejét rázta, szeme elkomorult az aggodalomtól és a félelemtől.

**C'erano ancora quattrocento miglia tra loro e Dawson.**

Még négyszáz mérföld választotta el őket Dawsontól.

**La follia dei cani potrebbe ormai distruggere ogni possibilità di sopravvivenza.**

A kutyaőrület most már minden esélyt tönkretehet a túlélésre.

**Hanno passato due ore a imprecare e a cercare di riparare l'attrezzatura.**

Két órát töltöttek káromkodással és a felszerelés megjavításával.

**La squadra ferita alla fine lasciò l'accampamento, distrutta e sconfitta.**

A sebesült csapat végül megtörve és legyőzve elhagyta a tábort.

**Questo è stato il sentiero più duro finora e ogni passo è stato doloroso.**

Ez volt a legnehezebb út, és minden lépés fájdalmas volt.

**Il fiume Thirty Mile non era ghiacciato e scorreva impetuoso.**

A Harminc Mérföld folyó nem fagyott be, és vadul sebesen hömpölygött.

**Soltanto nei punti calmi e nei vortici il ghiaccio riusciva a resistere.**

Csak a nyugodt helyeken és az örvénylő területeken sikerült a jégnek megállnia.

**Trascorsero sei giorni di duro lavoro per percorrere le trenta miglia.**

Hat nap kemény munka telt el, mire megtették a harminc mérföldet.

**Ogni miglio del sentiero porta con sé pericoli e minacce di morte.**

Az ösvény minden egyes mérföldje veszélyt és a halál fenyegetését hordozta magában.

**Uomini e cani rischiavano la vita a ogni passo doloroso.**

A férfiak és a kutyák minden fájdalmas lépéssel kockáztatták az életüket.

**Perrault riuscì a superare i sottili ponti di ghiaccio una dozzina di volte.**

Perrault tucatszor tört át vékony jéghidakon.

**Prese un palo e lo lasciò cadere nel buco creato dal suo corpo.**

Magához vett egy rudat, és leejtette azzal a lyukat, amit a teste ejtett.

**Quel palo salvò Perrault più di una volta dall'annegamento.**

Az a rúd többször is megmentette Perrault-t a fulladástól.

**L'ondata di freddo persisteva, la temperatura era di cinquanta gradi sotto zero.**

A hideg kitartott, a levegő ötven fok mínuszban volt.

**Ogni volta che cadeva, Perrault era costretto ad accendere un fuoco per sopravvivere.**

Valahányszor beleesett, Perrault-nak tüzet kellett gyújtania a túléléshez.

Gli abiti bagnati si congelavano rapidamente, perciò li faceva asciugare vicino al calore cocente.

A vizes ruhák gyorsan megfagytak, ezért perzselő hőségben szárította őket.

**Perrault non provava mai paura, e questo faceva di lui un corriere.**

Perrault-t soha nem fogta el a félelem, és ez tette őt futárrá.

**Fu scelto per affrontare il pericolo e lo affrontò con silenziosa determinazione.**

A veszélyre választották, és csendes elszántsággal fogadta.

**Si spinse in avanti controvento, con il viso raggrinzito e congelato.**

Szélbe szorította magát, összeaszott arca jégcsípte.

**Perrault li guidò in avanti dall'alba al tramonto.**

Halvány pirkadattól estig Perrault vezette őket előre.

**Camminava sul ghiaccio sottile che scricchiolava a ogni passo.**

Keskeny, peremén, jégen járt, ami minden lépésnél megrepedt.

**Non osavano fermarsi: ogni pausa rischiava di provocare un crollo mortale.**

Nem mertek megállni – minden szünet halálos összeomlást kockáztatott.

**Una volta la slitta si ruppe, trascinando dentro Dave e Buck.**

Egyszer a szán áttört, és magával rántotta Dave-et és Buckot.

**Quando furono liberati, entrambi erano quasi congelati.**

Mire kiszabadították őket, mindketten majdnem megfagytak.

**Gli uomini accesero rapidamente un fuoco per salvare Buck e Dave.**

A férfiak gyorsan tüzet raktak, hogy életben tartsák Buckot és Dave-et.

**I cani erano ricoperti di ghiaccio dal naso alla coda, rigidi come legno intagliato.**

A kutyákat orruktól farkukig jég borította, olyan merevek voltak, mint a faragott fa.

**Gli uomini li fecero correre in cerchio vicino al fuoco per scongelarne i corpi.**

A férfiak körbe-körbe futtatták őket a tűz közelében, hogy felolvasztsák a testüket.

**Si avvicinarono così tanto alle fiamme che la loro pelliccia rimase bruciacchiata.**

Olyan közel kerültek a lángokhoz, hogy a bundájuk megpörkölődött.

**Spitz ruppe poi il ghiaccio, trascinando dietro di sé la squadra.**

Spitz törte át legközelebb a jeget, maga után vonszolva a csapatot.

**La frenata arrivava fino al punto in cui Buck stava tirando.**

A törés egészen odáig ért, ahol Buck húzta.

**Buck si appoggiò bruscamente allo schienale, con le zampe che scivolavano e tremavano sul bordo.**

Buck erősen hátradőlt, mancsai megcsúsztak és remegtek a szélén.

**Anche Dave si sforzò all'indietro, proprio dietro Buck sulla linea.**

Dave is hátrafeszítette a labdát, közvetlenül Buck mögött a vonalon.

**François tirava la slitta e i suoi muscoli scricchiolavano per lo sforzo.**

François húzta a szánt, izmai ropogtak az erőfeszítéstől.

**Un'altra volta, il ghiaccio del bordo si è crepato davanti e dietro la slitta.**

Egy másik alkalommal a peremjég megrepedt a szánkó előtt és mögött.

**Non avevano altra via d'uscita se non quella di arrampicarsi su una parete ghiacciata.**

Nem volt más kiútjuk, mint megmászni egy befagyott sziklafalat.

**In qualche modo Perrault riuscì a scalare il muro: un miracolo lo tenne in vita.**

Perrault valahogyan átmászott a falon; egy csoda tartotta életben.

**François rimase sottocoperta, pregando che gli capitasse la stessa fortuna.**

François lent maradt, és hasonló szerencséért imádkozott.

**Legarono ogni cinghia, legatura e tirante in un'unica lunga corda.**

Minden szíjat, rögzítőelemet és vezetőszárat egyetlen hosszú kötéllé kötöttek.

**Gli uomini trascinarono i cani uno alla volta fino in cima.**

A férfiak egyesével húzták fel a kutyákat a tetejére.

**François salì per ultimo, dopo la slitta e tutto il carico.**

François mászott fel utoljára, a szánkó és az egész rakomány után.

**Poi iniziò una lunga ricerca di un sentiero che scendesse dalle scogliere.**

Aztán hosszas keresés kezdődött egy ösvény után, ami levezet a sziklákról.

**Alla fine scesero utilizzando la stessa corda che avevano costruito.**

Végül ugyanazzal a kötéllel ereszkedtek le, amit maguk készítettek.

**Scese la notte mentre tornavano al letto del fiume, esausti e doloranti.**

Leszállt az éj, mire kimerülten és fájdalmasan visszatértek a folyómederbe.

**Avevano impiegato un giorno intero per percorrere solo un quarto di miglio.**

Az egész nap mindössze negyed mérföldnyi előnyt hozott nekik.

**Quando giunsero all'Hootalinqua, Buck era sfinito.**

Mire elérték a Hootalinquát, Buck teljesen kimerült volt.

**Anche gli altri cani soffrivano le stesse condizioni del sentiero.**

A többi kutya ugyanúgy szenvedett az ösvényviszonyoktól.

**Ma Perrault aveva bisogno di recuperare tempo e li spingeva avanti giorno dopo giorno.**

De Perraultnak időt kellett nyernie, ezért minden nap hajtotta őket.

**Il primo giorno percorsero trenta miglia fino a Big Salmon.**

Az első napon harminc mérföldet utaztak Big Salmonba.

**Il giorno dopo percorsero trentacinque miglia fino a Little Salmon.**

Másnap harmincöt mérföldet utaztak Little Salmonba.

**Il terzo giorno percorsero quaranta miglia ghiacciate.**

A harmadik napon negyven hosszú, fagyott mérföldet nyomtak át.

**A quel punto si stavano avvicinando all'insediamento di Five Fingers.**

Addigra már közeledtek Öt Ujj településhez.

**I piedi di Buck erano più morbidi di quelli duri degli husky autoctoni.**

Buck lábai puhábbak voltak, mint a bennszülött huskyk kemény lábai.

**Le sue zampe erano diventate tenere nel corso di molte generazioni civilizzate.**

Mancsai sok civilizált generáció alatt érzékennyé váltak.

**Molto tempo fa, i suoi antenati erano stati addomesticati dagli uomini del fiume o dai cacciatori.**

Réges-régen folyami emberek vagy vadászok szelídítették meg őseit.

**Ogni giorno Buck zoppicava per il dolore, camminando con le zampe screpolate e doloranti.**

Buck minden nap fájdalmasan sántított, sebes, sajgó mancsain járt.

**Giunto all'accampamento, Buck cadde come un corpo senza vita sulla neve.**

A táborban Buck élettelen alakként zuhant a hóba.

**Sebbene fosse affamato, Buck non si alzò per consumare il pasto serale.**

Bár Buck éhes volt, mégsem kelt fel, hogy megegye a vacsoráját.

**François portò la sua razione a Buck, mettendogli del pesce vicino al muso.**

François odahozta Bucknak az adagját, miközben a halakat az orránál fogva tolta.

Ogni notte l'autista massaggiava i piedi di Buck per mezz'ora.

A sofőr minden este fél órán át dörzsölgette Buck lábát.

François arrivò persino a tagliare i suoi mocassini per farne delle calzature per cani.

François még a saját mokaszinjait is felszabdalta, hogy kutyalábbelit készítsen belőle.

Quattro scarpe calde diedero a Buck un grande e gradito sollievo.

Négy meleg cipő nagy és üdvözlendő megkönnyebbülést hozott Bucknak.

Una mattina François dimenticò le scarpe e Buck si rifiutò di alzarsi.

Egyik reggel François elfelejtette a cipőket, és Buck nem volt hajlandó felkelni.

Buck giaceva sulla schiena, con i piedi in aria, e li agitava in modo pietoso.

Buck a hátán feküdt, lábait a levegőbe emelve, és szánalmasan hadonászott velük.

Persino Perrault sorrise alla vista dell'appello drammatico di Buck.

Még Perrault is elvigyorodott Buck drámai könyörgése láttán.

Ben presto i piedi di Buck diventarono duri e le scarpe poterono essere tolte.

Buck lábai hamarosan megkeményedtek, és a cipőket el lehetett dobni.

A Pelly, durante il periodo in cui veniva imbrigliata, Dolly emise un ululato terribile.

Pellynél, hámozás közben Dolly rettenetes vonyítást hallatott.

Il grido era lungo e pieno di follia, e fece tremare tutti i cani.

A kiáltás hosszú volt és őrülettel teli, minden kutyát megremegtetett.

Ogni cane si rizzava per la paura, senza capirne il motivo.

Minden kutya félelmében felborzolta a dühét, anélkül, hogy tudta volna az okát.

Dolly era impazzita e si era scagliata contro Buck.

Dolly megőrült, és egyenesen Buckra vetette magát.

**Buck non aveva mai visto la follia, ma l'orrore gli riempì il cuore.**

Buck még soha nem látott őrültséget, de a szívét betöltötte a rémület.

**Senza pensarci due volte, si voltò e fuggì in preda al panico più assoluto.**

Gondolkodás nélkül megfordult és teljes pánikban elmenekült.

**Dolly lo inseguì, con gli occhi selvaggi e la saliva che le colava dalle fauci.**

Dolly üldözőbe vette, tekintete vad volt, szájából folyt a nyál.

**Si tenne sempre dietro a Buck, senza mai guadagnare terreno e senza mai indietreggiare.**

Közvetlenül Buck mögött maradt, soha nem előzte meg, és soha nem hátrált meg.

**Buck corse attraverso i boschi, giù per l'isola, sul ghiaccio frastagliato.**

Buck erdőn át futott, le a szigeten, át a csipkézett jégen.

**Attraversò un'isola, poi un'altra, per poi tornare indietro verso il fiume.**

Átkelt egy szigetre, majd egy másikra, és visszakerült a folyóhoz.

**Dolly continuava a inseguirlo, ringhiando sempre più forte a ogni passo.**

Dolly továbbra is üldözte, minden lépésnél morgással a nyomában.

**Buck poteva sentire il suo respiro e la sua rabbia, anche se non osava voltarsi indietro.**

Buck hallotta a lélegzetét és a dühét, bár nem mert hátranézni.

**François gridò da lontano e Buck si voltò verso la voce.**

François messziről kiáltotta, mire Buck a hang felé fordult.

**Ancora senza fiato, Buck corse oltre, riponendo ogni speranza in François.**

Buck, még mindig levegőért kapkodva, elfutott mellettük, minden reményét François-ba vetve.

**Il conducente del cane sollevò un'ascia e aspettò che Buck gli passasse accanto.**

A kutyahajcsár felemelte a fejszéjét, és megvárta, amíg Buck elrepült mellette.

**L'ascia calò rapidamente e colpì la testa di Dolly con forza mortale.**

A fejsze gyorsan lecsapott, és halálos erővel csapódott Dolly fejébe.

**Buck crollò vicino alla slitta, ansimando e incapace di muoversi.**

Buck a szán közelében rogyott össze, zihálva és mozdulni sem tudott.

**Quel momento diede a Spitz la possibilità di colpire un nemico esausto.**

Ez a pillanat lehetőséget adott Spitznek, hogy lecsapjon a kimerült ellenfélre.

**Morse Buck due volte, strappandogli la carne fino all'osso bianco.**

Kétszer megharapta Buckot, a húsát egészen a fehér csontig feltépve.

**La frusta di François schioccò, colpendo Spitz con tutta la sua forza, con furia.**

François ostora csattant, teljes, dühös erővel csapva le Spitzre.

**Buck guardò con gioia Spitz mentre riceveva il pestaggio più duro fino a quel momento.**

Buck örömmel nézte, ahogy Spitz élete eddigi legkeményebb verését kapja.

**«È un diavolo, quello Spitz», borbottò Perrault tra sé e sé.**

„Egy ördög ez a Spitz" – motyogta Perrault komoran magában.

**"Un giorno o l'altro, quel cane maledetto ucciderà Buck, lo giuro."**

„Hamarosan az az átkozott kutya megöli Buckot – esküszöm."

**«Quel Buck ha due diavoli dentro di sé», rispose François annuendo.**

– Két ördög lakozik abban a Buckban – felelte François bólogatva.

**"Quando osservo Buck, so che dentro di lui si cela qualcosa di feroce."**

„Amikor Buckot nézem, tudom, hogy valami vadság vár rá."

"Un giorno, si infurierà come il fuoco e farà a pezzi Spitz."

„Egy nap úgy megőrül, mint a tűz, és darabokra tépi Spitzet."

"Masticherà quel cane e lo sputerà sulla neve ghiacciata."

„Összerágja azt a kutyát, és a fagyott hóra köpi."

"Certo, lo so fin nel profondo."

„Biztosan tudom ezt a csontjaim mélyén."

Da quel momento in poi, i due cani furono in guerra tra loro.

Attól a pillanattól kezdve a két kutya háborúban állt.

Spitz guidava la squadra e deteneva il potere, ma Buck lo sfidava.

Spitz vezette a csapatot és birtokolta a hatalmat, de Buck ezt megkérdőjelezte.

Spitz si rese conto che il suo rango era minacciato da questo strano straniero del Sud.

Spitz rangját fenyegetve látta ezt a különös délvidéki idegent.

Buck era diverso da tutti i cani del sud che Spitz aveva conosciuto fino ad allora.

Buck minden déli kutyától különbözött, amit Spitz korábban ismert.

La maggior parte di loro fallì: troppo deboli per sopravvivere al freddo e alla fame.

Legtöbbjük kudarcot vallott – túl gyengék voltak ahhoz, hogy túléljék a hideget és az éhséget.

Morirono rapidamente a causa del lavoro, del gelo e del lento bruciare della carestia.

Gyorsan haltak a munka, a fagy és az éhínség lassú pusztítása alatt.

Buck si distingueva: ogni giorno più forte, più intelligente e più selvaggio.

Buck kitűnt a tömegből – napról napra erősebb, okosabb és vadabb lett.

Ha prosperato nonostante le difficoltà, crescendo al pari degli husky del nord.

A nehézségeken is boldogult, és egyre jobban felnőve versenyre kelhetett az északi huskykkal.

**Buck era dotato di forza, abilità straordinaria e un istinto paziente e letale.**

Bucknak ereje, vad ügyessége és türelmes, halálos ösztöne volt.

**L'uomo con la mazza aveva annientato Buck per fargli perdere la temerarietà.**

A bunkós férfi kiverte Buckból a meggondolatlanságot.

**La furia cieca se n'era andata, sostituita da un'astuzia silenziosa e dal controllo.**

A vak düh eltűnt, helyét csendes ravaszság és önuralom vette át.

**Attese, calmo e primordiale, in attesa del momento giusto.**

Várt, nyugodtan és őszintén, a megfelelő pillanatot keresve.

**La loro lotta per il comando divenne inevitabile e chiara.**

A parancsnokságért folytatott harcuk elkerülhetetlenné és egyértelművé vált.

**Buck desiderava la leadership perché il suo spirito la richiedeva.**

Buck vezetésre vágyott, mert a lelke ezt követelte.

**Era spinto da quello strano orgoglio che nasceva dal sentiero e dall'imbracatura.**

Az ösvény és a hám szülte különös büszkeség hajtotta.

**Quell'orgoglio faceva sì che i cani tirassero fino a crollare sulla neve.**

Ez a büszkeség arra késztette a kutyákat, hogy addig húzzák őket, amíg össze nem rogytak a hóban.

**L'orgoglio li spinse a dare tutta la forza che avevano.**

A büszkeség arra csábította őket, hogy minden erejüket beleadják.

**L'orgoglio può trascinare un cane da slitta fino al punto di ucciderlo.**

A büszkeség akár a haláláig is elcsábíthat egy szánhúzó kutyát.

**Perdere l'imbracatura rendeva i cani deboli e senza scopo.**

A hám elvesztése miatt a kutyák összetörtek és céltalanok voltak.

**Il cuore di un cane da slitta può essere spezzato dalla vergogna quando va in pensione.**

Egy szánhúzó kutya szívét összetörheti a szégyen, amikor nyugdíjba vonul.

**Dave viveva con questo orgoglio mentre trascinava la slitta da dietro.**

Dave ezt a büszkeséget vallotta, miközben maga mögött húzta a szánt.

**Anche Solleks diede il massimo con cupa forza e lealtà.**

Solleks is mindent beleadott komor erővel és hűséggel.

**Ogni mattina l'orgoglio li trasformava da amareggiati a determinati.**

A büszkeség minden reggel keserűségből eltökéltséggé változtatta őket.

**Spinsero per tutto il giorno, poi tacquero una volta giunti alla fine dell'accampamento.**

Egész nap nyomultak, aztán a tábor végében elcsendesedtek.

**Quell'orgoglio diede a Spitz la forza di mettere in riga i fannulloni.**

Ez a büszkeség erőt adott Spitznek ahhoz, hogy rendbe tegye a lustálkodókat.

**Spitz temeva Buck perché Buck nutriva lo stesso profondo orgoglio.**

Spitz félt Bucktól, mert Buckban is ott volt ez a mély büszkeség.

**L'orgoglio di Buck ora si agitò contro Spitz, ma lui non si fermò.**

Buck büszkesége most Spitz ellen fordult, és nem állt meg.

**Buck sfidò il potere di Spitz e gli impedì di punire i cani.**

Buck dacolt Spitz hatalmával, és megakadályozta, hogy kutyákat büntessen.

**Quando gli altri fallivano, Buck si frapponeva tra loro e il loro capo.**

Amikor mások kudarcot vallottak, Buck közéjük és vezetőjük közé lépett.

**Lo fece con intenzione, rendendo la sua sfida aperta e chiara.**

Szándékosan tette ezt, nyíltan és világosan fogalmazva meg a kihívást.

**Una notte una forte nevicata coprì il mondo in un profondo silenzio.**

Egyik éjjel sűrű hó borította be a világot mély csenddel.

**La mattina dopo, Pike, pigro come sempre, non si alzò per andare al lavoro.**

Másnap reggel Pike, aki továbbra is lustán viselkedett, nem kelt fel dolgozni.

**Rimase nascosto nel suo nido sotto uno spesso strato di neve.**

A fészkében rejtőzött egy vastag hóréteg alatt.

**François gridò e cercò, ma non riuscì a trovare il cane.**

François kiáltott és kereste a kutyát, de nem találta.

**Spitz si infuriò e si scagliò contro l'accampamento coperto di neve.**

Spitz dühbe gurult, és áttört a hófödte táboron.

**Ringhiò e annusò, scavando freneticamente con gli occhi fiammeggianti.**

Morgott és szimatolt, lángoló szemekkel, őrülten ásott.

**La sua rabbia era così violenta che Pike tremava sotto la neve per la paura.**

Olyan vad volt a dühe, hogy Pike félelmében reszketett a hó alatt.

**Quando finalmente Pike fu trovato, Spitz si lanciò per punire il cane nascosto.**

Amikor Pike-ot végre megtalálták, Spitz előrerontott, hogy megbüntesse a bujkáló kutyát.

**Ma Buck si scagliò tra loro con una furia pari a quella di Spitz.**

De Buck Spitzéhez hasonló dühvel ugrott közéjük.

**L'attacco fu così improvviso e astuto che Spitz cadde a terra.**

A támadás olyan hirtelen és okos volt, hogy Spitz a lábáról leesett.

**Pike, che tremava, trasse coraggio da questa sfida.**

Pike, aki eddig reszketett, bátorságot merített ebből a dacból.

**Seguendo l'audace esempio di Buck, saltò sullo Spitz caduto.**

Ráugrott a földön fekvő Spitzre, Buck merész példáját követve.

**Buck, non più vincolato dall'equità, si unì allo sciopero di Spitz.**

Buck, akit már nem kötött a tisztesség, csatlakozott a Spitz elleni sztrájkhoz.

**François, divertito ma fermo nella disciplina, agitò la sua pesante frusta.**

François, szórakozottan, mégis fegyelmezetten, lesújtott nehéz korbácsával.

**Colpì Buck con tutta la sua forza per interrompere la rissa.**

Teljes erejével Buckra ütött, hogy véget vessen a küzdelemnek.

**Buck si rifiutò di muoversi e rimase in groppa al capo caduto.**

Buck nem volt hajlandó megmozdulni, és a ledőlt vezető tetején maradt.

**François allora usò il manico della frusta e colpì Buck con violenza.**

François ezután az ostor nyelével keményen megütötte Buckot.

**Barcollando per il colpo, Buck cadde all'indietro sotto l'assalto.**

Buck megtántorodott az ütéstől, és hátraesett a roham alatt.

**François colpì più volte mentre Spitz puniva Pike.**

François újra és újra ütött, miközben Spitz megbüntette Pike-ot.

**Passarono i giorni e Dawson City si avvicinava sempre di più.**

Teltek a napok, és Dawson City egyre közelebb ért.

**Buck continuava a intromettersi, infilandosi tra Spitz e gli altri cani.**

Buck folyton közbeszólt, Spitz és más kutyák közé osonva.

**Sceglieva bene i suoi momenti, aspettando sempre che François se ne andasse.**

Jól választotta meg a pillanatait, mindig megvárta, míg François elmegy.

**La ribellione silenziosa di Buck si diffuse e il disordine prese piede nella squadra.**

Buck csendes lázadása elterjedt, és a csapatban rendetlenség vert gyökeret.

**Dave e Solleks rimasero leali, ma altri diventarono indisciplinati.**

Dave és Solleks hűségesek maradtak, de mások engedetlenné váltak.

**La squadra peggiorò: divenne irrequieta, litigiosa e fuori luogo.**

A csapat egyre rosszabb lett – nyugtalanok, veszekedősek és kilógtak a sorból.

**Ormai niente filava liscio e le liti diventavano all'ordine del giorno.**

Semmi sem működött többé simán, és a verekedések mindennapossá váltak.

**Buck rimase sempre al centro dei guai, provocando disordini.**

Buck a bajok középpontjában maradt, mindig nyugtalanságot szítva.

**François rimase vigile, temendo la lotta tra Buck e Spitz.**

François éber maradt, félt Buck és Spitz verekedésétől.

**Ogni notte veniva svegliato da zuffe e temeva che finalmente fosse arrivato l'inizio.**

Minden éjjel dulakodás ébresztette fel, attól tartva, hogy végre elérkezik a kezdet.

**Balzò fuori dalla veste, pronto a interrompere la rissa.**

Leugrott a köntöséből, készen arra, hogy megszakítsa a harcot.

**Ma il momento non arrivò mai e alla fine raggiunsero Dawson.**

De a pillanat sosem jött el, és végre megérkeztek Dawsonba.

**La squadra entrò in città in un pomeriggio cupo, teso e silenzioso.**

A csapat egy komor délutánon érkezett a városba, feszülten és csendesen.

**La grande battaglia per la leadership era ancora sospesa nell'aria gelida.**

A vezetésért folytatott nagy csata még mindig a fagyos levegőben lógott.

**Dawson era piena di uomini e cani da slitta, tutti impegnati nel lavoro.**

Dawson tele volt férfiakkal és szánhúzó kutyákkal, akik mind munkával voltak elfoglalva.

**Buck osservava i cani trainare i carichi dalla mattina alla sera.**

Buck reggeltől estig nézte, ahogy a kutyák húzzák a terheket.

**Trasportavano tronchi e legna da ardere e spedivano rifornimenti alle miniere.**

Rönköt és tűzifát szállítottak, ellátmányt szállítottak a bányákba.

**Nel Southland, dove un tempo lavoravano i cavalli, ora lavoravano i cani.**

Ahol egykor lovak dolgoztak Délvidéken, ma kutyák fáradoznak.

**Buck vide alcuni cani provenienti dal Sud, ma la maggior parte erano husky simili a lupi.**

Buck látott néhány délről származó kutyát, de a legtöbbjük farkasszerű husky volt.

**Di notte, puntuali come un orologio, i cani alzavano la voce e cantavano.**

Éjszaka, mint óramű, a kutyák felemelték a hangjukat dalra fakadva.

**Alle nove, a mezzanotte e di nuovo alle tre, il canto cominciò.**

Kilenckor, éjfélkor, majd ismét háromkor elkezdődött az éneklés.

**Buck amava unirsi al loro canto inquietante, selvaggio e antico nel suono.**

Buck imádott csatlakozni a hátborzongató, vad és ősi hangzású kántáláshoz.

**L'aurora fiammeggiava, le stelle danzavano e la neve ricopriva la terra.**

Az aurora lángolt, a csillagok táncoltak, és hó borította a földet.

**Il canto dei cani si elevava come un grido contro il silenzio e il freddo pungente.**

A kutyák dala kiáltásként harsant fel a csend és a keserves hideg ellen.

**Ma il loro urlo esprimeva tristezza, non sfida, in ogni lunga nota.**

De üvöltésük minden hosszú hangjában szomorúság, nem pedig dac volt.

**Ogni lamento era pieno di supplica: il peso stesso della vita.**

Minden jajgató kiáltás könyörgésből állt; magából az élet terhéből.

**Quella canzone era vecchia, più vecchia delle città e più vecchia degli incendi**

Az a dal régi volt – régebbi, mint a városok, és régebbi, mint a tüzek

**Quel canto era più antico perfino delle voci degli uomini.**

Az a dal még az emberi hangoknál is ősibb volt.

**Era una canzone del mondo dei giovani, quando tutte le canzoni erano tristi.**

Egy dal volt a fiatal világból, amikor minden dal szomorú volt.

**La canzone porta con sé il dolore di innumerevoli generazioni di cani.**

A dal számtalan kutyageneráció bánatát hordozta magában.

**Buck percepì profondamente la melodia, gemendo per un dolore radicato nei secoli.**

Buck mélyen érezte a dallamot, a korokba gyökerező fájdalomtól nyögött.

**Singhiozzava per un dolore antico quanto il sangue selvaggio nelle sue vene.**

Olyan bánattól zokogott, amely olyan régi volt, mint az ereiben csörgedező vér.

**Il freddo, l'oscurità e il mistero toccarono l'anima di Buck.**

A hideg, a sötétség és a rejtély megérintette Buck lelkét.

**Quella canzone dimostrava quanto Buck fosse tornato alle sue origini.**

Ez a dal bizonyította, mennyire visszatért Buck a gyökereihez.

Tra la neve e gli ululati aveva trovato l'inizio della sua vita.

Hóesésben és üvöltésben találta meg saját élete kezdetét.

**Sette giorni dopo l'arrivo a Dawson, ripartirono.**

Hét nappal Dawsonba érkezésük után ismét útra keltek.

**La squadra si è lanciata dalla caserma fino allo Yukon Trail.**

A csapat a laktanyából leugrott a Yukon ösvényre.

**Iniziarono il viaggio di ritorno verso Dyea e Salt Water.**

Megkezdték útjukat vissza Dyea és Sósvíz felé.

**Perrault trasmise dispacci ancora più urgenti di prima.**

Perrault még sürgősebb szállítmányokat szállított, mint
korábban.

**Era anche preso dall'orgoglio per la corsa e puntava a
stabilire un record.**

Emellett elfogta a túraösvényekre való odafigyelés, és
rekordot akart felállítani.

**Questa volta Perrault aveva diversi vantaggi.**

Ezúttal számos előny Perrault oldalán állt.

**I cani avevano riposato per un'intera settimana e avevano
ripreso le forze.**

A kutyák egy teljes hetet pihentek és visszanyerték erejüket.

**La pista che avevano tracciato era ora battuta da altri.**

Az általuk kitaposott ösvényt most mások tömörítették
keményre.

**In alcuni punti la polizia aveva immagazzinato cibo sia per i
cani che per gli uomini.**

Helyenként a rendőrök kutyáknak és férfiaknak egyaránt
tároltak élelmet.

**Perrault viaggiava leggero, si muoveva velocemente e aveva
poco a cui aggrapparsi.**

Perrault könnyen utazott, gyorsan mozgott, kevés teher
nehezedett rá.

**La prima sera raggiunsero la Sixty-Mile, una corsa lunga 50
miglia.**

Az első éjszakára elérték a Hatvan Mérföldet, egy ötven
mérföldes futást.

**Il secondo giorno risalirono rapidamente lo Yukon in direzione di Pelly.**

A második napon rohantak felfelé a Yukonon Pelly felé.

**Ma questi grandi progressi comportarono anche molta fatica per François.**

De ez a szép előrehaladás nagy megterheléssel járt François számára.

**La ribellione silenziosa di Buck aveva infranto la disciplina della squadra.**

Buck csendes lázadása megrengette a csapat fegyelmét.

**Non si univano più come un'unica bestia al comando.**

Már nem húzódtak össze, mint egy fenevad a gyeplőben.

**Buck aveva spinto altri alla sfida con il suo coraggioso esempio.**

Buck merész példájával másokat is dacolásra késztetett.

**L'ordine di Spitz non veniva più accolto con timore o rispetto.**

Spitz parancsát már nem fogadták félelemmel vagy tisztelettel.

**Gli altri persero ogni timore reverenziale nei suoi confronti e osarono opporsi al suo governo.**

A többiek elvesztették iránta való félelmüket, és szembe mertek szállni az uralmával.

**Una notte, Pike rubò mezzo pesce e lo mangiò sotto gli occhi di Buck.**

Egyik este Pike ellopott egy fél halat, és Buck szeme láttára megette.

**Un'altra notte, Dub e Joe combatterono contro Spitz e rimasero impuniti.**

Egy másik este Dub és Joe megküzdöttek Spitz-cel, és büntetlenül maradtak.

**Anche Billee gemette meno dolcemente e mostrò una nuova acutezza.**

Még Billee is kevésbé édesen nyafogott, és új élességet mutatott.

**Buck ringhiava a Spitz ogni volta che si incrociavano.**

Buck minden alkalommal Spitzre vicsorgott, valahányszor keresztezték egymás útját.

L'atteggiamento di Buck divenne audace e minaccioso, quasi come quello di un bullo.

Buck viselkedése merész és fenyegető lett, szinte zsarnoki.

Camminava avanti e indietro davanti a Spitz con un'andatura spavalda e piena di minaccia beffarda.

Hencegve, gúnyos fenyegetéssel járkált Spitz előtt.

Questo crollo dell'ordine si diffuse anche tra i cani da slitta.

A rend felbomlása a szánhúzó kutyák között is elterjedt.

Litigarono e discussero più che mai, riempiendo l'accampamento di rumore.

Többet veszekedtek és vitatkoztak, mint valaha, zajongással töltve meg a tábort.

Ogni notte la vita nel campeggio si trasformava in un caos selvaggio e ululante.

A tábori élet minden este vad, üvöltő káoszba fordult.

Solo Dave e Solleks rimasero fermi e concentrati.

Csak Dave és Solleks maradtak nyugodtak és koncentráltak.

Ma anche loro diventarono irascibili a causa delle continue risse.

De még ők is dühösek lettek az állandó verekedésektől.

François imprecò in lingue strane e batté i piedi per la frustrazione.

François furcsa nyelveken káromkodott és dühösen toporgott.

Si strappò i capelli e urlò mentre la neve gli volava sotto i piedi.

A haját tépte és kiabált, miközben a hó repült a lába alatt.

La sua frusta schioccò contro il gruppo, ma a malapena riuscì a tenerli in riga.

Ostorával átcsapott a csapat, de alig tartotta őket egy vonalban.

Ogni volta che voltava le spalle, la lotta ricominciava.

Valahányszor hátat fordított, újra kitört a harc.

François usò la frusta per Spitz, mentre Buck guidava i ribelli.

François korbácsütést mért Spitzre, míg Buck vezette a lázadókat.

**Ognuno conosceva il ruolo dell'altro, ma Buck evitava di addossare ogni colpa.**

Mindketten tudták a másik szerepét, de Buck kerülte a hibáztatást.

**François non ha mai colto Buck mentre iniziava una rissa o si sottraeva al suo lavoro.**

François soha nem kapta rajta Buckot verekedés kezdeményezésén vagy a munkájának elhanyagolásán.

**Buck lavorava duramente ai finimenti: la fatica ora gli dava entusiasmo.**

Buck keményen dolgozott hámban – a fáradság most már a lelkét is felpezsdítette.

**Ma trovava ancora più gioia nel fomentare risse e caos nell'accampamento.**

De még nagyobb örömet talált a táborban zajló verekedések és káosz szításában.


**Una sera, alla foce del Tahkeena, Dub spaventò un coniglio.**

Egyik este a Tahkeena torkolatánál Dub megijesztett egy nyulat.

**Mancò la presa e il coniglio con la racchetta da neve balzò via.**

Elvétette a fogást, és a hótalpas nyúl elszaladt.

**Nel giro di pochi secondi, l'intera squadra di slitte si lanciò all'inseguimento, gridando a squarciagola.**

Másodperceken belül az egész szánkócsapat vad kiáltásokkal üldözőbe vette őket.

**Nelle vicinanze, un accampamento della polizia del nord-ovest ospitava cinquanta cani husky.**

A közelben egy északnyugati rendőrségi tábor ötven husky kutyát tartott fenn.

**Si unirono alla caccia, scendendo insieme il fiume ghiacciato.**

Csatlakoztak a vadászathoz, együtt hömpölyögtek lefelé a befagyott folyón.

**Il coniglio lasciò il fiume e fuggì lungo il letto ghiacciato di un ruscello.**

A nyúl letért a folyóról, és egy befagyott patakmederben menekült felfelé.

**Il coniglio saltellava leggero sulla neve mentre i cani si facevano strada a fatica.**

A nyúl könnyedén szökdécselt a havon, miközben a kutyák küzdöttek vele.

**Buck guidava l'enorme branco di sessanta cani attorno a ogni curva tortuosa.**

Buck a hatvan kutyából álló hatalmas csapatot minden kanyarban körbevezette.

**Si spinse in avanti, basso e impaziente, ma non riuscì a guadagnare terreno.**

Alacsonyan és lelkesen nyomult előre, de nem tudott előrébb jutni.

**Il suo corpo brillava sotto la pallida luna a ogni potente balzo.**

Teste minden erőteljes ugrásnál megcsillant a sápadt holdfényben.

**Davanti a loro, il coniglio si muoveva come un fantasma, silenzioso e troppo veloce per essere catturato.**

Előttük a nyúl szellemként mozgott, hangtalanul és túl gyorsan ahhoz, hogy elkapják.

**Tutti quei vecchi istinti, la fame, l'eccitazione, attraversarono Buck.**

Azok a régi ösztönök – az éhség, az izgalom – végigsöpörtek Buckon.

**A volte gli esseri umani avvertono questo istinto e sono spinti a cacciare con armi da fuoco e proiettili.**

Az emberek időnként érzik ezt az ösztönt, és fegyverrel, golyóval vadásznak.

**Ma Buck provava questa sensazione a un livello più profondo e personale.**

De Buck ezt az érzést mélyebb és személyesebb szinten érezte.

**Non riuscivano a percepire la natura selvaggia nel loro sangue come Buck.**

Nem érezték a vadságot a vérükben úgy, ahogy Buck érezte.

**Inseguiva la carne viva, pronto a uccidere con i denti e ad assaggiare il sangue.**

Élő húst kergetett, készen arra, hogy fogaival öljön és vért kóstoljon.

**Il suo corpo si tendeva per la gioia, desiderando immergersi nel caldo rosso della vita.**

Teste örömtől feszült, meleg, vörös életben akart fürödni.

**Una strana gioia segna il punto più alto che la vita possa mai raggiungere.**

Egy különös öröm jelzi az élet legmagasabb pontját.

**La sensazione di raggiungere un picco in cui i vivi dimenticano di essere vivi.**

Egy olyan csúcs érzése, ahol az élők elfelejtik, hogy egyáltalán élnek.

**Questa gioia profonda tocca l'artista immerso in un'ispirazione ardente.**

Ez a mély öröm megérinti a lángoló ihletben elveszett művészt.

**Questa gioia afferra il soldato che combatte selvaggiamente e non risparmia alcun nemico.**

Ez az öröm elfogja a katonát, aki vadul harcol és nem kíméli az ellenséget.

**Questa gioia ora colpì Buck mentre guidava il branco in preda alla fame primordiale.**

Ez az öröm most Buckot ragadta magával, miközben ősi éhséggel vezette a falkát.

**Ululò con l'antico grido del lupo, emozionato per l'inseguimento.**

Az ősi farkaskiáltással vonyított, izgatottan az élő üldözéstől.

**Buck fece appello alla parte più antica di sé, persa nella natura selvaggia.**

Buck önmaga legősibb részét fedezte fel, elveszve a vadonban.

**Scavò in profondità dentro di sé, oltre la memoria, fino al tempo grezzo e antico.**

Mélyen belülre nyúlt, az emlékeken túlra, a nyers, ősi időbe.

**Un'ondata di vita pura pervase ogni muscolo e tendine.**

A tiszta élet hulláma áradt szét minden izmában és ínjában.

Ogni salto gridava che viveva, che attraversava la morte.
Minden ugrás azt üzente, hogy él, hogy átjutott a halálon.
Il suo corpo si librava gioioso su una terra immobile e
fredda che non si muoveva mai.
Teste vidáman szállt a mozdulatlan, hideg, meg sem rezdült
föld felett.
Spitz rimase freddo e astuto anche nei suoi momenti più
selvaggi.
Spitz még a legvadabb pillanataiban is hideg és ravasz
maradt.
Lasciò il sentiero e attraversò un terreno dove il torrente
formava una curva ampia.
Letért az ösvényről, és átkelt egy olyan területen, ahol a patak
szélesre kanyarodott.
Buck, ignaro di ciò, rimase sul sentiero tortuoso del coniglio.
Buck, mit sem sejtve erről, a nyúl kanyargós ösvényén maradt.
Poi, mentre Buck svoltava dietro una curva, il coniglio
spettrale si trovò davanti a lui.
Aztán, ahogy Buck befordult egy kanyarban, a szellemszerű
nyúl ott termett előtte.
Vide una seconda figura balzare dalla riva precedendo la
preda.
Látta, hogy egy második alak ugrik le a partról, megelőzve a
zsákmányt.
La figura era Spitz, atterrato proprio sulla traiettoria del
coniglio in fuga.
Az alak Spitz volt, aki pont a menekülő nyúl útjába landolt.
Il coniglio non riuscì a girarsi e incontrò le fauci di Spitz a
mezz'aria.
A nyúl nem tudott megfordulni, és a levegőben Spitz
állkapcsába ütközött.
La spina dorsale del coniglio si spezzò con un grido acuto
come il grido di un essere umano morente.
A nyúl gerince egy haldokló ember kiáltásához hasonló éles
sikoly kíséretében eltört.
A quel suono, il passaggio dalla vita alla morte, il branco
ululò forte.

Arra a hangra – az életből a halálba zuhanásra – a falka
hangosan felüvöltött.

**Un coro selvaggio si levò da dietro Buck, pieno di oscura
gioia.**

Egy vad kórus emelkedett fel Buck mögött, tele sötét
gyönyörűséggel.

**Buck non emise alcun grido, nessun suono e si lanciò dritto
verso Spitz.**

Buck nem kiáltott, egyetlen hangot sem adott ki, egyenesen
Spitznek rohant.

**Mirò alla gola, ma colpì invece la spalla.**

A torkot célozta meg, de ehelyett a vállát találta el.

**Caddero nella neve soffice, i loro corpi erano intrappolati in
un combattimento.**

Puha hóban bukfenceztek; testük harcba merült.

**Spitz balzò in piedi rapidamente, come se non fosse mai
stato atterrato.**

Spitz gyorsan felugrott, mintha soha nem is döngölték volna
le.

**Colpì Buck alla spalla e poi balzò fuori dalla mischia.**

Megvágta Buck vállát, majd kiugrott a küzdelemből.

**Per due volte i suoi denti schioccarono come trappole
d'acciaio, e le sue labbra si arricciarono e si fecero feroci.**

Kétszer is csattant a foga, mint az acélcsapda, ajkai vadra
húzódtak.

**Arretrò lentamente, cercando un terreno solido sotto i piedi.**

Lassan hátrált, szilárd talajt keresve a lába alatt.

**Buck comprese il momento all'istante e pienamente.**

Buck azonnal és teljesen megértette a pillanatot.

**Il momento era giunto: la lotta sarebbe stata una lotta
all'ultimo sangue.**

Elérkezett az idő; a harc élet-halál harc lesz.

**I due cani giravano in cerchio, ringhiando, con le orecchie
piatte e gli occhi socchiusi.**

A két kutya morogva, lelapult fülekkel, összeszűkült
szemekkel körözött.

Ogni cane aspettava che l'altro mostrasse debolezza o facesse un passo falso.

Mindegyik kutya arra várt, hogy a másik gyengeséget vagy hibát mutasson.

Buck percepiva quella scena come stranamente nota e profondamente ricordata.

Buck számára a jelenet hátborzongatóan ismerősnek és mélyen emlékezetesnek tűnt.

I boschi bianchi, la terra fredda, la battaglia al chiaro di luna.

A fehér erdők, a hideg föld, a holdfényben vívott csata.

Un silenzio pesante, profondo e innaturale riempiva la terra.

Nehéz csend töltötte be a tájat, mély és természetellenes csend.

Nessun vento si alzava, nessuna foglia si muoveva, nessun suono rompeva il silenzio.

Szél sem rezdült, levél sem mozdult, hang sem törte meg a csendet.

Il respiro dei cani si levava come fumo nell'aria gelida e silenziosa.

A kutyák lehelete füstként emelkedett a fagyos, csendes levegőben.

Il coniglio era stato dimenticato da tempo dal branco di animali selvatici.

A nyulat rég elfelejtette a vadállatok falkája.

Questi lupi semiaddomesticati ora stavano fermi in un ampio cerchio.

Ezek a félig megszelídített farkasok most mozdulatlanul álltak széles körben.

Erano silenziosi, solo i loro occhi luminosi rivelavano la loro fame.

Csendben voltak, csak izzó szemük árulkodott az éhségükről.

Il loro respiro saliva, mentre osservavano l'inizio dello scontro finale.

Felfelé lélegzetelállítóan nézték a végső küzdelem kezdetét.

Per Buck questa battaglia era vecchia e attesa, per niente strana.

Buck számára ez a csata régi és várható volt, egyáltalán nem furcsa.

**Era come il ricordo di qualcosa che doveva accadere da sempre.**

Olyan volt, mint valaminek az emléke, aminek mindig is meg kellett történnie.

**Spitz era un cane da combattimento addestrato, affinato da innumerevoli risse selvagge.**

Spitz egy kiképzett harci kutya volt, akit számtalan vad verekedés csiszolt.

**Dallo Spitzbergen al Canada, aveva sconfitto molti nemici.**

A Spitzbergáktól Kanadáig számos ellenféllel győzött le.

**Era pieno di rabbia, ma non cedette mai il controllo alla rabbia.**

Tele volt dühvel, de sosem adta át az irányítást a dühöngésnek.

**La sua passione era acuta, ma sempre temperata dal duro istinto.**

Szenvedélye éles volt, de mindig kemény ösztön mérsékelte.

**Non ha mai attaccato finché non ha avuto la sua difesa pronta.**

Soha nem támadott, amíg a saját védekezése a helyén nem volt.

**Buck provò più volte a raggiungere il collo vulnerabile di Spitz.**

Buck újra meg újra megpróbálta elérni Spitz sebezhető nyakát.

**Ma ogni colpo veniva accolto da un fendente dei denti affilati di Spitz.**

De minden csapást Spitz éles fogai hasítással fogadtak.

**Le loro zanne si scontrarono ed entrambi i cani sanguinarono dalle labbra lacerate.**

Agyarak összecsaptak, és mindkét kutya vérzett a felszakadt ajkakból.

**Nonostante i suoi sforzi, Buck non riusciva a rompere la difesa.**

Hiába tört rá Buck, nem tudta áttörni a védelmet.

**Divenne sempre più furioso e si lanciò verso di lui con violente esplosioni di potenza.**

Egyre dühösebb lett, vad erőkitörésekkel rohant előre.

Buck colpì ripetutamente la bianca gola di Spitz.

Buck újra meg újra Spitz fehér torkára csapott le.

Ogni volta Spitz schivava e contrattaccava con un morso tagliente.

Spitz minden alkalommal kitért, és egy metsző harapással vágott vissza.

Poi Buck cambiò tattica, avventandosi di nuovo come se volesse colpirlo alla gola.

Aztán Buck taktikát váltott, és úgy rohant, mintha ismét a torkának csapna.

Ma a metà attacco si è ritirato, girandosi per colpire di lato.

De támadás közben visszahúzódott, és oldalról támadott.

Colpì Spitz con una spallata, con l'intento di buttarlo a terra.

A vállával Spitznek vágta, azzal a céllal, hogy leüsse.

Ogni volta che ci provava, Spitz lo schivava e rispondeva con un fendente.

Spitz minden alkalommal kitért, amikor megpróbálta, és egy csapással válaszolt.

La spalla di Buck si faceva scorticare mentre Spitz si liberava dopo ogni colpo.

Buck válla felsírt, ahogy Spitz minden ütés után elhúzódott.

Spitz non era stato toccato, mentre Buck sanguinava dalle numerose ferite.

Spitzhez senki sem nyúlt, míg Buck számos sebből vérzett.

Il respiro di Buck era affannoso e pesante, il suo corpo era viscido di sangue.

Buck lélegzete gyors és nehéz volt, teste vértől ázott.

La lotta diventava più brutale a ogni morso e carica.

A harc minden egyes harapással és rohammal egyre brutálisabbá vált.

Attorno a loro, sessanta cani silenziosi aspettavano che il primo cadesse.

Körülöttük hatvan néma kutya várta az első elesést.

Se un cane fosse caduto, il branco avrebbe posto fine alla lotta.

Ha egy kutya elesik, a falka befejezi a harcot.

Spitz vide Buck indebolirsi e cominciò ad attaccare.

Spitz látta, hogy Buck gyengül, és támadásba lendült.

**Mantenne Buck sbilanciato, costringendolo a lottare per restare in piedi.**

Kibillentette az egyensúlyából Buckot, ami miatt küzdenie kellett a talpon maradásért.

**Una volta Buck inciampò e cadde, e tutti i cani si rialzarono.**

Buck egyszer megbotlott és elesett, mire az összes kutya felállt.

**Ma Buck si raddrizzò a metà caduta e tutti ricaddero.**

De Buck zuhanás közben kiegyenesedett, és mindenki visszasüppedt.

**Buck aveva qualcosa di raro: un'immaginazione nata da un profondo istinto.**

Bucknak volt valami ritka tulajdonsága – mély ösztönből született képzelőereje.

**Combatté per istinto naturale, ma combatté anche con astuzia.**

Természetes ösztönnel harcolt, de ravaszsággal is.

**Tornò ad attaccare come se volesse ripetere il trucco dell'attacco alla spalla.**

Újra rohamra kelt, mintha megismételné a válltámadás trükkjét.

**Ma all'ultimo secondo si abbassò e passò sotto Spitz.**

De az utolsó pillanatban leugrott, és Spitz alá került.

**I suoi denti si bloccarono sulla zampa anteriore sinistra di Spitz con uno schiocco.**

Fogai egy csattanással akadtak össze Spitz bal mellső lábán.

**Spitz ora era instabile e il suo peso gravava solo su tre zampe.**

Spitz most bizonytalanul állt, testsúlya mindössze három lábon nyugodott.

**Buck colpì di nuovo e tentò tre volte di atterrarlo.**

Buck ismét lecsapott, háromszor próbálta leteríteni.

**Al quarto tentativo ha usato la stessa mossa con successo**

A negyedik próbálkozásra ugyanazt a mozdulatot alkalmazta sikerrel.

**Questa volta Buck riuscì a mordere la zampa destra di Spitz.**

Ezúttal Bucknak sikerült Spitz jobb lábát megharapnia.
**Spitz, benché storpio e in agonia, continuò a lottare per sopravvivere.**
Spitz, bár nyomorék és kínok között volt, továbbra is küzdött a túlélésért.
**Vide il cerchio degli husky stringersi, con le lingue fuori e gli occhi luminosi.**
Látta, ahogy a huskyk köre egyre szorosabbra húzódik, kinyújtott nyelvekkel, izzó szemekkel.
**Aspettarono di divorarlo, proprio come avevano fatto con gli altri.**
Arra vártak, hogy felfalhassák, ahogyan másokkal is tették.
**Questa volta era lui al centro, sconfitto e condannato.**
Ezúttal középen állt; legyőzötten és kudarcra ítélve.
**Ormai il cane bianco non aveva più alcuna possibilità di fuga.**
A fehér kutyának most már nem volt lehetősége elmenekülni.
**Buck non mostrò alcuna pietà, perché la pietà non era a posto nella natura selvaggia.**
Buck nem mutatott irgalmat, mert az irgalom nem a vadonban való.
**Buck si mosse con cautela, preparandosi per la carica finale.**
Buck óvatosan mozgott, felkészülve az utolsó rohamra.
**Il cerchio degli husky si stringeva; lui sentiva i loro respiri caldi.**
A huskyk köre egyre közelebb ért; érezte meleg leheletüket.
**Si accovacciarono, pronti a scattare quando fosse giunto il momento.**
Leguggoltak, készen arra, hogy ugorjanak, ha eljön a pillanat.
**Spitz tremava nella neve, ringhiando e cambiando posizione.**
Spitz remegett a hóban, vicsorgott és változtatott az állásán.
**I suoi occhi brillavano, le labbra si arricciavano, i denti brillavano in un'espressione disperata e minacciosa.**
Szemei lángoltak, ajkai felkunkorodtak, fogai kétségbeesett fenyegetésként villogtak.

**Barcollò, cercando ancora di resistere al freddo morso della morte.**

Megtántorodott, még mindig próbálta visszatartani a halál hideg csípését.

**Aveva già visto situazioni simili, ma sempre dalla parte dei vincitori.**

Látott már ilyet korábban, de mindig a győztes oldalról.

**Ora era dalla parte perdente; lo sconfitto; la preda; la morte.**

Most a vesztes oldalon állt; a legyőzött; a préda; a halál.

**Buck si preparò al colpo finale, mentre il cerchio dei cani si faceva sempre più stretto.**

Buck az utolsó csapásra várva körözött, a kutyák gyűrűje egyre közelebb nyomult.

**Poteva sentire i loro respiri caldi; erano pronti a uccidere.**

Érezte forró leheletüket; készen álltak a gyilkolásra.

**Calò il silenzio; tutto era al suo posto; il tempo si era fermato.**

Csend lett; minden a helyén volt; megállt az idő.

**Persino l'aria fredda tra loro si congelò per un ultimo istante.**

Még a köztük lévő hideg levegő is megfagyott egy utolsó pillanatra.

**Soltanto Spitz si mosse, cercando di trattenere la sua fine amara.**

Csak Spitz mozdult, próbálta visszafogni keserű végét.

**Il cerchio dei cani si stava stringendo attorno a lui, come era suo destino.**

A kutyák köre egyre szűkült körülötte, ahogy a sorsa is.

**Ora era disperato, sapendo cosa stava per accadere.**

Most már kétségbeesett volt, tudta, mi fog történni.

**Buck balzò dentro e la sua spalla incontrò la sua spalla per l'ultima volta.**

Buck előreugrott, válla még utoljára összeért.

**I cani si lanciarono in avanti, nascondendo Spitz nell'oscurità della neve.**

A kutyák előretörtek, fedezve Spitzet a havas sötétségben.

**Buck osservava, eretto e fiero; il vincitore in un mondo selvaggio.**

Buck egyenesen állva figyelte őket; a győztes egy vad
világban.
**La bestia primordiale dominante aveva fatto la sua
uccisione, e la aveva fatta bene.**
Az uralkodó ősállat begyűjtette a zsákmányát, és ez jó volt.

## Colui che ha conquistato la maestria
### Aki elnyerte a mesteri címet

"Eh? Cosa ho detto? Dico la verità quando dico che Buck è un diavolo."

„Hé? Mit mondtam? Igazat mondok, amikor azt mondom, hogy Buck egy ördög."

**François raccontò questo la mattina dopo aver scoperto la scomparsa di Spitz.**

François ezt másnap reggel mondta, miután Spitz eltűntnek bizonyult.

**Buck rimase lì, coperto di ferite causate dal violento combattimento.**

Buck ott állt, tele sebekkel a kegyetlen küzdelem nyomaiból.

**François tirò Buck vicino al fuoco e indicò le ferite.**

François a tűzhöz húzta Buckot, és a sérüléseire mutatott.

«Quello Spitz ha combattuto come il Devik», disse Perrault, osservando i profondi tagli.

– Az a Spitz úgy harcolt, mint a Devik – mondta Perrault, a mély sebeket nézve.

«E quel Buck si batteva come due diavoli», rispose subito François.

– És hogy Buck úgy harcolt, mint két ördög – felelte azonnal François.

"Ora faremo buon passo; niente più Spitz, niente più guai."

„Most már jó úton haladunk; nincs több Spitz, nincs több baj."

**Perrault stava preparando l'attrezzatura e caricò la slitta con cura.**

Perrault pakolgatta a felszerelést, és gondosan megrakta a szánt.

**François bardò i cani per prepararli alla corsa della giornata.**

François befogta a kutyákat, hogy felkészüljön a napi futásra.

**Buck trotterellò dritto verso la posizione di testa, precedentemente occupata da Spitz.**

Buck egyenesen a Spitz által korábban megtartott vezető pozícióba ügetett.

**Ma François, senza accorgersene, condusse Solleks in prima linea.**

De François, mit sem törődve ezzel, előre vezette Solleks-et.

**Secondo François, Solleks era ora il miglior cane da corsa.**

François megítélése szerint Solleks volt most a legjobb vezetőkutya.

**Buck si scagliò furioso contro Solleks e lo respinse indietro in segno di protesta.**

Buck dühösen ráugrott Solleksre, és tiltakozásul visszaverte.

**Si fermò dove un tempo si era fermato Spitz, rivendicando la posizione di comando.**

Ott állt, ahol egykor Spitz állt, és átvette a vezető pozíciót.

**"Eh? Eh?" esclamò François, dandosi una pacca sulle cosce divertito.**

– Hé? Hé? – kiáltotta François, és szórakozottan a combjára csapott.

**"Guarda Buck: ha ucciso Spitz, ora vuole prendersi il posto!"**

„Nézd csak Buckot! Ő ölte meg Spitzet, most meg el akarja vállalni a munkát!"

**"Vattene via, Chook!" urlò, cercando di scacciare Buck.**

„Menj el, Chook!" – kiáltotta, miközben megpróbálta elkergetni Buckot.

**Ma Buck si rifiutò di muoversi e rimase immobile nella neve.**

De Buck nem volt hajlandó megmozdulni, és szilárdan állt a hóban.

**François afferrò Buck per la collottola e lo trascinò da parte.**

François megragadta Buckot a tarkójánál fogva, és félrerántotta.

**Buck ringhiò basso e minaccioso, ma non attaccò.**

Buck halkan és fenyegetően morgott, de nem támadott.

**François rimette Solleks in testa, cercando di risolvere la disputa**

François visszaszerezte a vezetést Solleksnek, megpróbálva rendezni a vitát

**Il vecchio cane mostrò paura di Buck e non voleva restare.**

Az öreg kutya félt Bucktól, és nem akart maradni.

Quando François gli voltò le spalle, Buck scacciò di nuovo Solleks.

Amikor François hátat fordított, Buck ismét kiűzte Solleks-et.

Solleks non oppose resistenza e si fece di nuovo da parte in silenzio.

Solleks nem ellenkezett, és csendben ismét félreállt.

François si arrabbiò e urlò: "Per Dio, ti sistemo!"

François dühös lett, és felkiáltott: „Istenemre, meggyógyítalak!"

Si avvicinò a Buck tenendo in mano una pesante mazza.

Egy nehéz bunkót tartva a kezében, Buck felé közeledett.

Buck ricordava bene l'uomo con il maglione rosso.

Buck jól emlékezett a piros pulóveres férfira.

Si ritirò lentamente, osservando François ma ringhiando profondamente.

Lassan hátrált, François-t figyelve, de mélyet morgott.

Non si affrettò a tornare indietro, nemmeno quando Solleks si mise al suo posto.

Nem sietett vissza, még akkor sem, amikor Solleks állt a helyén.

Buck si girò in cerchio, appena fuori dalla sua portata, ringhiando furioso e protestando.

Buck elérhetetlen távolságban körözött, dühösen és tiltakozva vicsorgott.

Teneva gli occhi fissi sulla mazza, pronto a schivare il colpo se François l'avesse lanciata.

A klubra szegezte a szemét, készen arra, hogy kitérjen, ha François dobna.

Era diventato saggio e cauto nei confronti degli uomini che maneggiavano le armi.

Bölcs és óvatos lett a fegyveres emberekkel szemben.

François si arrese e chiamò di nuovo Buck al suo vecchio posto.

François feladta, és visszahívta Buckot a korábbi helyére.

Ma Buck fece un passo indietro con cautela, rifiutandosi di obbedire all'ordine.

De Buck óvatosan hátrébb lépett, és nem volt hajlandó engedelmeskedni a parancsnak.

**François lo seguì, ma Buck indietreggiò solo di pochi passi.**

François követte, de Buck csak néhány lépést hátrált még.

**Dopo un po' François gettò a terra l'arma, frustrato.**

Egy idő után François dühösen elhajította a fegyvert.

**Pensava che Buck avesse paura di essere picchiato e che avrebbe fatto lo stesso senza far rumore.**

Azt gondolta, Buck fél a veréstől, és csendben fog jönni.

**Ma Buck non stava evitando la punizione: stava lottando per ottenere un rango.**

De Buck nem a büntetés elől menekült – a rangjáért küzdött.

**Si era guadagnato il posto di capobranco combattendo fino alla morte**

Halálos küzdelemmel érdemelte ki a vezető kutya pozíciót

**non si sarebbe accontentato di niente di meno che di essere il leader.**

Nem fog megelégedni kevesebbel, mint hogy vezető legyen.


**Perrault si unì all'inseguimento per aiutare a catturare il ribelle Buck.**

Perrault besegített az üldözésbe, hogy segítsen elkapni a lázadó Buckot.

**Insieme lo portarono in giro per l'accampamento per quasi un'ora.**

Együtt futkostak vele a táborban közel egy órán át.

**Gli scagliarono contro dei bastoni, ma Buck li schivò abilmente uno per uno.**

Bunkókkal dobálták meg, de Buck ügyesen kikerülte mindegyiket.

**Maledissero lui, i suoi antenati, i suoi discendenti e ogni suo capello.**

Átkozták őt, őseit, leszármazottait és minden egyes hajszálát.

**Ma Buck si limitò a ringhiare e a restare appena fuori dalla loro portata.**

De Buck csak vicsorgott vissza, és pont annyira maradt, hogy ne érhessék el.

**Non cercò mai di scappare, ma continuò a girare intorno all'accampamento deliberatamente.**

Soha nem próbált elfutni, hanem szándékosan körbejárta a tábort.

**Disse chiaramente che avrebbe obbedito una volta ottenuto ciò che voleva.**

Világossá tette, hogy engedelmeskedni fog, amint megkapja, amit akar.

**Alla fine François si sedette e si grattò la testa, frustrato.**

François végül leült, és dühösen megvakarta a fejét.

**Perrault controllò l'orologio, imprecò e borbottò qualcosa sul tempo perso.**

Perrault ránézett az órájára, káromkodott, és az elvesztegetett időről motyogott.

**Era già trascorsa un'ora, mentre avrebbero dovuto essere sulle tracce.**

Már eltelt egy óra, amikor már az ösvényen kellett volna lenniük.

**François alzò le spalle timidamente, guardando il corriere, che sospirò sconfitto.**

François szégyenlősen vállat vont a futár felé, aki legyőzötten felsóhajtott.

**Poi François si avvicinò a Solleks e chiamò ancora una volta Buck.**

Aztán François odament Sollekshez, és ismét Buckot szólította.

**Buck rise come ride un cane, ma mantenne una cauta distanza.**

Buck úgy nevetett, mint egy kutya, de óvatos távolságot tartott.

**François tolse l'imbracatura a Solleks e lo rimise al suo posto.**

François levette Solleks hámját, és visszavitte a helyére.

**La squadra di slittini era completamente imbracata, con un solo posto libero.**

A szánkócsapat teljes felszerelésben állt, csak egy hely volt betöltetlen.

**La posizione di comando rimase vuota, chiaramente riservata solo a Buck.**

A vezető pozíció üresen maradt, egyértelműen csak Bucknak szánták.

**François chiamò di nuovo e di nuovo Buck rise e mantenne la sua posizione.**

François újra szólt, Buck pedig ismét nevetett és kitartott.

**«Gettate giù la mazza», ordinò Perrault senza esitazione.**

– Dobd le a botot! – parancsolta Perrault habozás nélkül.

**François obbedì e Buck si lanciò subito avanti con orgoglio.**

François engedelmeskedett, Buck pedig azonnal büszkén előreügetett.

**Rise trionfante e assunse la posizione di comando.**

Diadalmasan felnevetett, és átvette a vezető helyet.

**François fissò le corde e la slitta si staccò.**

François biztosította a nyomait, és a szánt elengedték.

**Entrambi gli uomini corsero fianco a fianco mentre la squadra si lanciava lungo il sentiero del fiume.**

Mindkét férfi egymás mellett futott, miközben a csapat a folyó menti ösvényre rohant.

**François aveva avuto una grande stima dei "due diavoli" di Buck,**

François nagyra tartotta Buck „két ördögét",

**ma ben presto si rese conto di aver in realtà sottovalutato il cane.**

de hamarosan rájött, hogy valójában alábecsülte a kutyát.

**Buck assunse rapidamente la leadership e si comportò in modo eccellente.**

Buck gyorsan átvette a vezetést, és kiválóan teljesített.

**Buck superò Spitz per capacità di giudizio, rapidità di pensiero e rapidità di azione.**

Ítéletben, gyors gondolkodásban és gyors cselekvésben Buck felülmúlta Spitzet.

**François non aveva mai visto un cane pari a quello che Buck mostrava ora.**

François még soha nem látott olyan kutyát, mint amilyennek Buck most mutatta magát.

**Ma Buck eccelleva davvero nel far rispettare l'ordine e nel imporre rispetto.**

De Buck valóban jeleskedett a rendfenntartásban és a tisztelet kivívásában.

**Dave e Solleks accettarono il cambiamento senza preoccupazioni o proteste.**

Dave és Solleks aggodalom vagy tiltakozás nélkül elfogadták a változást.

**Si concentravano solo sul lavoro e tiravano forte le redini.**

Csak a munkára és a gyeplő kemény húzására koncentráltak.

**A loro importava poco chi guidasse, purché la slitta continuasse a muoversi.**

Nem törődtek azzal, ki vezet, amíg a szán mozog.

**Billee, quella allegra, avrebbe potuto comandare per quel che volevano.**

Billee, a vidám lány, akár vezethetett volna is, mindegy volt nekik.

**Ciò che contava per loro era la pace e l'ordine tra i ranghi.**

Ami számított nekik, az a sorokban uralkodó béke és rend volt.


**Il resto della squadra era diventato indisciplinato durante il declino di Spitz.**

A csapat többi tagja Spitz hanyatlása alatt rakoncátlanná vált.

**Rimasero sciocati quando Buck li riportò immediatamente all'ordine.**

Megdöbbentek, amikor Buck azonnal rendet teremtett bennük.

**Pike era sempre stato pigro e aveva sempre tergiversato dietro a Buck.**

Pike mindig is lusta volt, és csak húzta a lábát Buck után.

**Ma ora è stato severamente disciplinato dalla nuova leadership.**

De most az új vezetés keményen megfegyelmezte.

**E imparò rapidamente a dare il suo contributo alla squadra.**

És gyorsan megtanulta, hogyan érvényesítse a súlyát a csapatban.

**Alla fine della giornata, Pike lavorò più duramente che mai.**
A nap végére Pike keményebben dolgozott, mint valaha.
**Quella notte all'accampamento, Joe, il cane scontroso, fu finalmente domato.**
Azon az estén a táborban Joe-t, a savanyú kutyát végre sikerült lecsillapítani.
**Spitz non era riuscito a disciplinarlo, ma Buck non aveva fallito.**
Spitz nem tudta megfegyelmezni, de Buck nem vallott kudarcot.
**Sfruttando il suo peso maggiore, Buck sopraffece Joe in pochi secondi.**
Nagyobb súlyát felhasználva Buck másodpercek alatt legyűrte Joe-t.
**Morse e picchiò Joe finché questi non si mise a piagnucolare e smise di opporre resistenza.**
Addig harapdálta és ütötte Joe-t, amíg az felnyögött és felhagyott az ellenállással.
**Da quel momento in poi l'intera squadra migliorò.**
Az egész csapat attól a pillanattól kezdve fejlődött.
**I cani ritrovarono la loro antica unità e disciplina.**
A kutyák visszanyerték régi egységüket és fegyelmüket.
**A Rink Rapids si sono uniti al gruppo due nuovi husky autoctoni, Teek e Koona.**
Rink Rapidsnél két új őshonos husky, Teek és Koona csatlakozott.
**La rapidità con cui Buck li addestramento stupì perfino François.**
Buck gyors kiképzése még François-t is megdöbbentette.
**"Non è mai esistito un cane come quel Buck!" esclamò stupito.**
„Soha nem volt még ilyen kutya, mint ez a Buck!" – kiáltotta ámulva.
**"No, mai! Vale mille dollari, per Dio!"**
„Nem, soha! Istenemre mondom, ezer dollárt ér!"
**"Eh? Che ne dici, Perrault?" chiese con orgoglio.**
– Hm? Mit szólsz ehhez, Perrault? – kérdezte büszkén.

**Perrault annuì in segno di assenso e controllò i suoi appunti.**
Perrault egyetértően bólintott, és átnézte a jegyzeteit.
**Siamo già in anticipo sui tempi e guadagniamo sempre di più ogni giorno.**
Már most megelőzzük a tervezettet, és napról napra többet nyerünk.
**Il sentiero era compatto e liscio, senza neve fresca.**
Az ösvény keményre döngölt és sima volt, friss hó nem esett.
**Il freddo era costante, con temperature che si aggiravano sempre sui cinquanta gradi sotto zero.**
Állandó volt a hideg, végig ötven fok körül alakult.
**Per scaldarsi e guadagnare tempo, gli uomini si alternavano a cavallo e a correre.**
A férfiak felváltva lovagoltak és futottak, hogy melegen tartsák magukat és időt nyerjenek.
**I cani correvano veloci, fermandosi di rado, spingendosi sempre in avanti.**
A kutyák gyorsan futottak, kevés megállást követően, mindig előre nyomulva.
**Il fiume Thirty Mile era per la maggior parte ghiacciato e facile da attraversare.**
A Harminc Mérföld folyó nagy része be volt fagyva, és könnyen átkelhetett rajta.
**In un giorno realizzarono ciò che per arrivare aveva impiegato dieci giorni.**
Egy nap alatt mentek ki, míg visszafelé tíz napig tartott.
**Percorsero circa 96 chilometri dal lago Le Barge a White Horse.**
Hatvan mérföldes száguldást tettek meg a Le Barge-tótól White Horse-ig.
**Si muovevano a velocità incredibile attraverso i laghi Marsh, Tagish e Bennett.**
Hihetetlenül gyorsan haladtak a Marsh, Tagish és Bennett tavakon át.
**L'uomo che correva veniva trainato dietro la slitta con una corda.**
A futó férfi kötélen vontatta a szánkót.

L'ultima notte della seconda settimana giunsero a destinazione.

A második hét utolsó estéjén megérkeztek úti céljukhoz.

Insieme avevano raggiunto la cima del White Pass.

Együtt érték el a White Pass csúcsát.

Scesero fino al livello del mare, con le luci dello Skaguay sotto di loro.

A tenger szintjére ereszkedtek, alattuk Skaguay fényei világítottak.

Era stata una corsa da record attraverso chilometri di fredda natura selvaggia.

Rekorddöntő futás volt a hideg vadon mérföldjein át.

Per quattordici giorni di fila percorsero in media circa quaranta miglia.

Tizennégy napon keresztül átlagosan negyven mérföldet tettek meg.

A Skaguay, Perrault e François trasportavano merci attraverso la città.

Skaguay-ban Perrault és François rakományt szállítottak a városon keresztül.

Furono applauditi e ricevettero numerose bevande dalla folla ammirata.

A csodáló tömeg éljenezte őket, és sok italt kínált nekik.

I cacciatori di cani e gli operai si sono riuniti attorno alla famosa squadra cinofila.

Kutyavadászok és munkások gyűltek össze a híres kutyás csapat körül.

Poi i fuorilegge del West giunsero in città e subirono una violenta sconfitta.

Ezután nyugati törvényen kívüliek érkeztek a városba, és erőszakos vereséget szenvedtek.

La gente si dimenticò presto della squadra e si concentrò sul nuovo dramma.

Az emberek hamarosan elfelejtették a csapatot, és új drámákra koncentráltak.

Poi arrivarono i nuovi ordini che cambiarono tutto in un colpo.

Aztán jöttek az új parancsok, amelyek egyszerre mindent megváltoztattak.

**François chiamò Buck e lo abbracciò con orgoglio e lacrime.**

François magához hívta Buckot, és könnyes büszkeséggel ölelte át.

**Quel momento fu l'ultima volta che Buck vide di nuovo François.**

Ez volt az utolsó alkalom, hogy Buck újra látta François-t.

**Come molti altri uomini prima di lui, sia François che Perrault se n'erano andati.**

Sok más férfihoz hasonlóan François és Perrault is eltűntek.

**Un meticcio scozzese si prese cura di Buck e dei suoi compagni di squadra con i cani da slitta.**

Egy skót félvér vette át Buck és szánhúzó kutyáinak irányítását.

**Con una dozzina di altre mute di cani, ritornarono lungo il sentiero fino a Dawson.**

Egy tucat másik kutyafogattal együtt visszatértek a Dawsonba vezető ösvényen.

**Non si trattava più di una corsa veloce, ma solo di un duro lavoro con un carico pesante ogni giorno.**

Most már nem volt gyors futás – csak nehéz kínlódás, nehéz teherrel minden nap.

**Si trattava del treno postale che portava notizie ai cercatori d'oro vicino al Polo.**

Ez volt a postavonat, amely hírt vitt az Északi-sark közelében lévő aranyvadászoknak.

**Buck non amava il lavoro, ma lo sopportò bene, essendo orgoglioso del suo impegno.**

Buck nem szerette a munkát, de jól viselte, büszke volt az erőfeszítésére.

**Come Dave e Solleks, Buck dimostrava dedizione in ogni compito quotidiano.**

Dave-hez és Sollekshez hasonlóan Buck is odaadással végezte minden napi feladatát.

**Si è assicurato che tutti i suoi compagni di squadra dessero il massimo.**

Gondoskodott róla, hogy csapattársai mindannyian a rájuk bízott feladatokat végezzék.

**La vita sui sentieri divenne noiosa e si ripeteva con la precisione di una macchina.**

Az ösvényes élet unalmassá vált, gépi pontossággal ismétlődött.

**Ogni giorno era uguale, una mattina si fondeva con quella successiva.**

Minden nap ugyanolyannak tűnt, az egyik reggel beleolvadt a másikba.

**Alla stessa ora, i cuochi si alzarono per accendere il fuoco e preparare il cibo.**

Ugyanebben az órában a szakácsok is felkeltek, hogy tüzet rakjanak és ételt készítsenek.

**Dopo colazione alcuni lasciarono l'accampamento mentre altri attaccarono i cani.**

Reggeli után néhányan elhagyták a tábort, míg mások befogták a kutyákat.

**Raggiunsero il sentiero prima che il pallido segnale dell'alba sfiorasse il cielo.**

Még mielőtt a hajnal halvány figyelmeztetése elérte volna az eget, elindultak az ösvényen.

**Di notte si fermavano per accamparsi, e a ogni uomo veniva assegnato un compito.**

Éjszaka megálltak tábort verni, minden embernek meghatározott feladata volt.

**Alcuni montarono le tende, altri tagliarono la legna da ardere e raccolsero rami di pino.**

Néhányan sátrakat vertek, mások tűzifát vágtak és fenyőágakat gyűjtöttek.

**Acqua o ghiaccio venivano portati ai cuochi per la cena serale.**

Vizet vagy jeget vittek vissza a szakácsoknak vacsorára.

**I cani vennero nutriti e per loro quello fu il momento migliore della giornata.**

A kutyákat megetették, és ez volt a nap legszebb része számukra.

**Dopo aver mangiato il pesce, i cani si rilassarono e oziarono vicino al fuoco.**

Miután elfogyasztották a halat, a kutyák pihentek és heverésztek a tűz közelében.

**Nel convoglio c'erano un centinaio di altri cani con cui socializzare.**

Száz másik kutya is volt a konvojban, akikkel el lehetett beszélgetni.

**Molti di quei cani erano feroci e pronti a combattere senza preavviso.**

Sok ilyen kutya vad volt és gyorsan verekedni kezdett figyelmeztetés nélkül.

**Ma dopo tre vittorie, Buck riuscì a domare anche i combattenti più feroci.**

De három győzelem után Buck még a legádázabb harcosokat is legyőzte.

**Ora, quando Buck ringhiò e mostrò i denti, loro si fecero da parte.**

Amikor Buck morgott és kivillantotta a fogát, félreálltak.

**Forse la cosa più bella di tutte era che a Buck piaceva sdraiarsi vicino al fuoco tremolante.**

Talán a legjobban Buck imádott a pislákoló tábortűz közelében feküdni.

**Si accovacciò, con le zampe posteriori ripiegate e quelle anteriori distese in avanti.**

Leguggolt, hátsó lábait behúzva, első lábait előre nyújtva.

**Teneva la testa sollevata e sbatteva dolcemente le palpebre verso le fiamme ardenti.**

Felemelt fejjel halkan pislogott az izzó lángok felé.

**A volte ricordava la grande casa del giudice Miller a Santa Clara.**

Néha eszébe jutott Miller bíró nagy háza Santa Clarában.

**Pensò alla piscina di cemento, a Ysabel e al carlino di nome Toots.**

A cementmedencére gondolt, Ysabelre és a Toots nevű mopszra.

Ma più spesso si ricordava del bastone dell'uomo con il maglione rosso.

De gyakrabban a piros pulóveres férfi klubjára gondolt.

Ricordava la morte di Curly e la sua feroce battaglia con Spitz.

Emlékezett Göndör halálára és a Spitzcel vívott ádáz csatájára.

Ricordava anche il buon cibo che aveva mangiato o che ancora sognava.

Eszébe jutottak azok a finom ételek is, amiket evett, vagy amikről még mindig álmodozott.

Buck non aveva nostalgia di casa: la valle calda era lontana e irreale.

Buck nem honvágyas volt – a meleg völgy távoli és valószerűtlen volt.

I ricordi della California non avevano più alcun fascino su di lui.

Kalifornia emlékei már nem igazán ragadták meg.

Più forti della memoria erano gli istinti radicati nella sua stirpe.

Az emlékeinél erősebbek voltak a vérvonalában mélyen rejlő ösztönök.

Le abitudini un tempo perdute erano tornate, ravvivate dal sentiero e dalla natura selvaggia.

Az elveszett szokások visszatértek, az ösvény és a vadon újjáélesztette őket.

Mentre Buck osservava la luce del fuoco, a volte questa diventava qualcos'altro.

Miközben Buck a tűzfényt nézte, az néha valami mássá vált.

Vide alla luce del fuoco un altro fuoco, più vecchio e più profondo di quello attuale.

A tűzfényben egy másik tüzet látott, régebbit és mélyebbet a jelenleginél.

Accanto all'altro fuoco era accovacciato un uomo che non somigliava per niente al cuoco meticcio.

A másik tűz mellett egy férfi kuporgott, aki nem hasonlított a félvér szakácshoz.

**Questa figura aveva gambe corte, braccia lunghe e muscoli duri e contratti.**

Ennek az alaknak rövid lábai, hosszú karjai és kemény, csomós izmai voltak.

**I suoi capelli erano lunghi e arruffati, e gli scendevano all'indietro a partire dagli occhi.**

Hosszú és gubancos haja volt, a szemétől hátralógó.

**Emetteva strani suoni e fissava l'oscurità con paura.**

Furcsa hangokat adott ki, és félelemmel bámult a sötétségbe.

**Teneva bassa una mazza di pietra, stretta saldamente nella sua mano lunga e ruvida.**

Hosszú, durva kezében szorosan szorongatott egy kőbotot, ami alacsonyan tartotta.

**L'uomo indossava ben poco: solo una pelle carbonizzata che gli pendeva lungo la schiena.**

A férfi keveset viselt; csak egy elszenesedett bőr lógott a hátán.

**Il suo corpo era ricoperto da una folta peluria sulle braccia, sul petto e sulle cosce.**

Testét vastag szőrzet borította, amely a karján, a mellkasán és a combján húzódott.

**Alcune parti del pelo erano aggrovigliate e formavano chiazze di pelo ruvido.**

A haj egyes részei durva szőrfoltokká kuszadtak össze.

**Non stava dritto, ma era piegato in avanti dai fianchi alle ginocchia.**

Nem állt egyenesen, hanem csípőtől térdig előrehajolt.

**I suoi passi erano elastici e felini, come se fosse sempre pronto a scattare.**

Léptei ruganyosak és macskaszerűek voltak, mintha mindig készen állna az ugrásra.

**C'era una forte allerta, come se vivesse nella paura costante.**

Éles éberség áradt belőle, mintha állandó félelemben élne.

**Quest'uomo anziano sembrava aspettarsi il pericolo, indipendentemente dal fatto che questo venisse visto o meno.**

Ez az ősi ember látszólag számított a veszélyre, akár látta a veszélyt, akár nem.

A volte l'uomo peloso dormiva accanto al fuoco, con la testa tra le gambe.

A szőrös férfi időnként a tűz mellett aludt, fejét a lábai közé dugva.

Teneva i gomiti sulle ginocchia e le mani giunte sopra la testa.

Könyöke a térdén nyugodott, kezei a feje fölött összekulcsolva.

Come un cane, usava le sue braccia pelose per proteggersi dalla pioggia che cadeva.

Mint egy kutya, szőrös karjaival lerázta magáról a hulló esőt.

Oltre la luce del fuoco, Buck vide due carboni ardenti che ardevano nell'oscurità.

A tűzfényen túl Buck kettős parazsat látott izzani a sötétben.

Sempre a due a due, erano gli occhi delle bestie da preda.

Mindig kettesével, lesben álló ragadozók szemei voltak.

Sentì corpi che si infrangevano tra i cespugli e rumori provenienti dalla notte.

Testek csapódását hallotta a bozótosban, és hangokat az éjszakában.

Sdraiato sulla riva dello Yukon, sbattendo le palpebre, Buck sognò accanto al fuoco.

A Yukon partján fekve, pislogva, Buck a tűz mellett álmodozott.

Le immagini e i suoni di quel mondo selvaggio gli fecero rizzare i capelli.

A vad világ látványától és hangjaitól égnek állt a haja.

La pelliccia gli si drizzò lungo la schiena, sulle spalle e sul collo.

A szőr felállt a hátán, a vállán és fel a nyakán.

Gemeva piano o emetteva un ringhio basso dal profondo del petto.

Halkan nyüszített, vagy egy mély morgást hallatott a mellkasában.

Allora il cuoco meticcio urlò: "Ehi, Buck, svegliati!"

Ekkor a félvér szakács felkiáltott: „Hé, te Buck, ébredj fel!"

**Il mondo dei sogni svanì e la vera vita tornò agli occhi di Buck.**

Az álomvilág eltűnt, és a való élet visszatért Buck szemébe.

**Si sarebbe alzato, si sarebbe stiracchiato e avrebbe sbadigliato, come se si fosse svegliato da un pisolino.**

Fel fog kelni, nyújtózkodni és ásítani, mintha szunyókálásból ébredt volna.

**Il viaggio era duro, con la slitta postale che li trascinava dietro.**

Az út nehéz volt, a postaszán húzta őket.

**Carichi pesanti e lavoro duro sfinivano i cani ogni lunga giornata.**

A nehéz terhek és a kemény munka minden hosszú napon kifárasztotta a kutyákat.

**Arrivarono a Dawson magro, stanco e con bisogno di più di una settimana di riposo.**

Lesoványodva, fáradtan érkeztek meg Dawsonba, és több mint egyheti pihenésre volt szükségük.

**Ma solo due giorni dopo ripartirono per lo Yukon.**

De mindössze két nappal később ismét elindultak lefelé a Yukonon.

**Erano carichi di altre lettere dirette al mondo esterno.**

Még több, külvilágnak szánt levéllel voltak megrakodva.

**I cani erano esausti e gli uomini si lamentavano in continuazione.**

A kutyák kimerültek voltak, a férfiak pedig állandóan panaszkodtak.

**Ogni giorno cadeva la neve, ammorbidendo il sentiero e rallentando le slitte.**

Minden nap esett a hó, megpuhítva az ösvényt és lelassítva a szánokat.

**Ciò rendeva la trazione più dura e aumentava la resistenza delle guide.**

Ez nehezebb húzást és nagyobb ellenállást eredményezett a futókon.

**Nonostante ciò, i piloti si sono dimostrati leali e hanno avuto cura delle loro squadre.**

Ennek ellenére a sofőrök korrektek voltak és törődtek a csapataikkal.

**Ogni notte, i cani venivano nutriti prima che gli uomini mangiassero.**

Minden este megetették a kutyákat, mielőtt a férfiak enhettek volna.

**Nessun uomo dormiva prima di controllare le zampe del proprio cane.**

Senki sem aludt el anélkül, hogy meg ne nézte volna a saját kutyája lábát.

**Tuttavia, i cani diventavano sempre più deboli man mano che i chilometri consumavano i loro corpi.**

A kutyák mégis egyre gyengébbek lettek, ahogy a kilométerek megviselték a testüket.

**Avevano viaggiato per milleottocento miglia durante l'inverno.**

Ezernyolcszáz kilométert utaztak a tél folyamán.

**Percorrevano ogni miglio di quella distanza brutale trainando le slitte.**

Szánkókkal tették meg ezt a brutális távolságot minden mérföldön.

**Anche i cani da slitta più resistenti provano tensione dopo tanti chilometri.**

Még a legkeményebb szánhúzókutyák is megerőltetőnek érzik magukat ennyi kilométer után.

**Buck tenne duro, fece sì che la sua squadra lavorasse e mantenne la disciplina.**

Buck kitartott, folyamatosan dolgozott a csapatán, és fegyelmet tartott.

**Ma Buck era stanco, proprio come gli altri durante il lungo viaggio.**

De Buck fáradt volt, akárcsak a többiek a hosszú úton.

**Billee piagnucolava e piangeva nel sonno ogni notte, senza sosta.**

Billee minden éjjel szünet nélkül nyöszörgött és sírt álmában.

**Joe diventò ancora più amareggiato e Solleks rimase freddo e distante.**

Joe még keserűbb lett, Solleks pedig hideg és távolságtartó maradt.

**Ma è stato Dave a soffrire di più di tutta la squadra.**

De az egész csapat közül Dave szenvedett a legjobban.

**Qualcosa dentro di lui era andato storto, anche se nessuno sapeva cosa.**

Valami elromlott benne, bár senki sem tudta, hogy mi.

**Divenne più lunatico e aggredì gli altri con rabbia crescente.**

Egyre szeszélyesebb lett, és egyre növekvő dühvel nyafogott másoknak.

**Ogni notte andava dritto al suo nido, in attesa di essere nutrito.**

Minden este egyenesen a fészkébe ment, és várta az etetést.

**Una volta a terra, Dave non si alzò più fino al mattino.**

Miután Dave lefeküdt, reggelig nem kelt fel.

**Sulle redini, gli improvvisi strattoni o sussulti lo facevano gridare di dolore.**

A gyeplőn a hirtelen rántások vagy ijedtségek fájdalmas felkiáltást váltottak ki belőle.

**L'autista ha cercato di capirne la causa, ma non ha trovato ferite.**

A sofőrje kereste a baleset okát, de sérülést nem talált nála.

**Tutti gli autisti cominciarono a osservare Dave e a discutere del suo caso.**

Minden sofőr Dave-et kezdte figyelni, és megvitatták az esetét.

**Parlarono durante i pasti e durante l'ultima sigaretta della giornata.**

Étkezéskor és a nap utolsó cigarettája alatt beszélgettek.

**Una notte tennero una riunione e portarono Dave al fuoco.**

Egyik este gyűlést tartottak, és Dave-et odavitték a tűzhöz.

**Gli premevano e palpavano il corpo e lui gridava spesso.**

Nyomkodták és tapogatták a testét, és gyakran felkiáltott.

**Era evidente che qualcosa non andava, anche se non sembrava esserci nessuna frattura.**

Nyilvánvalóan valami baj volt, bár úgy tűnt, hogy egyetlen csontja sem tört el.

**Quando arrivarono al Cassiar Bar, Dave stava cadendo.**

Mire elérték a Cassiar Bárt, Dave már zuhant.

Il meticcio scozzese impose uno stop e rimosse Dave dalla squadra.

A skót félvér megálljt parancsolt, és eltávolította Dave-et a csapatból.

Fissò Solleks al posto di Dave, il più vicino possibile alla parte anteriore della slitta.

Solleks-et Dave helyére rögzítette, a szán elejéhez legközelebb.

Voleva lasciare che Dave riposasse e corresse libero dietro la slitta in movimento.

Hagyni akarta Dave-et pihenni, és szabadon szaladgálni a mozgó szánkó mögött.

Ma nonostante la malattia, Dave odiava che gli venisse tolto il lavoro che aveva ricoperto.

De még betegen is utálta Dave, ha elvették az eddigi munkájától.

Ringhiò e piagnucolò quando gli strapparono le redini dal corpo.

Morgott és nyüszített, ahogy a gyeplőt kihúzták a testéből.

Quando vide Solleks al suo posto, pianse disperato.

Amikor meglátta Solleks-et a helyén, megtört szívű fájdalommal sírt.

L'orgoglio per il lavoro sui sentieri era profondo in Dave, anche quando la morte si avvicinava.

A túraútvonalon végzett munka büszkesége mélyen élt Dave-ben, még a halál közeledtével is.

Mentre la slitta si muoveva, Dave arrancava nella neve soffice vicino al sentiero.

Ahogy a szán mozgott, Dave vergődött a puha hóban az ösvény közelében.

Attaccò Solleks, mordendolo e spingendolo giù dal lato della slitta.

Megtámadta Solleks-et, megharapta és a szán oldaláról lökte.

Dave cercò di saltare nell'imbracatura e di riprendersi il suo posto di lavoro.

Dave megpróbált beugrani a hámba, és visszaszerezni a munkaterületét.

**Lui guaiva, si lamentava e piangeva, diviso tra il dolore e l'orgoglio del parto.**

Felsikoltott, nyafogott és sírt, a fájdalom és a vajúdás utáni büszkeség között őrlődve.

**Il meticcio usò la frusta per cercare di allontanare Dave dalla squadra.**

A félvér az ostorát használta, hogy megpróbálja elűzni Dave-et a csapattól.

**Ma Dave ignorò la frustata e l'uomo non riuscì a colpirlo più forte.**

De Dave nem törődött az ostorcsapással, és a férfi nem tudta erősebben megütni.

**Dave rifiutò il sentiero più facile dietro la slitta, dove la neve era compatta.**

Dave nem volt hajlandó a könnyebb utat választani a szánkó mögött, ahol vastag hó volt.

**Invece, si ritrovò a lottare nella neve profonda, ai lati del sentiero, in preda alla miseria.**

Ehelyett a mély hóban küzdött az ösvény mellett, nyomorultul.

**Alla fine Dave crollò, giacendo sulla neve e urlando di dolore.**

Végül Dave összeesett, a hóban feküdt és fájdalmasan üvöltött.

**Lanciò un grido mentre la lunga fila di slitte gli passava accanto una dopo l'altra.**

Felkiáltott, ahogy a szánkók hosszú sora egyesével elhaladt mellette.

**Tuttavia, con le poche forze che gli rimanevano, si alzò e barcollò dietro di loro.**

Mégis, maradék erejével felállt, és botladozva utánuk eredt.

**Quando il treno si fermò di nuovo, lo raggiunse e trovò la sua vecchia slitta.**

Amikor a vonat ismét megállt, utolérte, és megtalálta a régi szánkóját.

**Superò con difficoltà le altre squadre e tornò a posizionarsi accanto a Solleks.**

Elvánszorgott a többi csapat mellett, és ismét Solleks mellé állt.

**Mentre l'autista si fermava per accendere la pipa, Dave colse l'ultima occasione.**

Miközben a sofőr megállt, hogy meggyújtsa a pipáját, Dave megragadta az utolsó esélyt.

**Quando l'autista tornò e urlò, la squadra non avanzò.**

Amikor a sofőr visszatért és kiabált, a csapat nem mozdult előre.

**I cani avevano girato la testa, confusi dall'improvviso arresto.**

A kutyák elfordították a fejüket, zavartan a hirtelen megállást követően.

**Anche il conducente era scioccato: la slitta non si era mossa di un centimetro in avanti.**

A sofőr is megdöbbent – a szán egy tapodtat sem mozdult előre.

**Chiamò gli altri perché venissero a vedere cosa era successo.**

Odakiáltott a többieknek, hogy jöjjenek és nézzék meg, mi történt.

**Dave aveva masticato le redini di Solleks, spezzandole entrambe.**

Dave átrágta Solleks gyeplőjét, mindkettőt széttépve.

**Ora era di nuovo in piedi davanti alla slitta, nella sua giusta posizione.**

Most a szán előtt állt, vissza a jogos helyére.

**Dave alzò lo sguardo verso l'autista, implorandolo silenziosamente di restare al passo.**

Dave felnézett a sofőrre, és magában könyörgött, hogy maradhasson a sínek között.

**L'autista era perplesso e non sapeva cosa fare per il cane in difficoltà.**

A sofőr zavarban volt, nem tudta, mitévő legyen a vergődő kutyával.

**Gli altri uomini parlavano di cani morti perché li avevano portati fuori.**

A többi férfi kutyákról beszélt, amelyek elpusztultak, miközben kivitték őket.

**Raccontavano di cani vecchi o feriti il cui cuore si era spezzato quando erano stati abbandonati.**

Öreg vagy sérült kutyákról meséltek, akiknek a szíve összetört, amikor magukra hagyták őket.

**Concordarono che era un atto di misericordia lasciare che Dave morisse mentre era ancora imbrigliato.**

Egyetértettek, hogy irgalomból hagyták Dave-et meghalni, miközben még a hámjában volt.

**Fu rimesso in sicurezza sulla slitta e Dave tirò con orgoglio.**

Vissza volt kötözve a szánkóhoz, és Dave büszkén húzta.

**Anche se a volte gridava, lavorava come se il dolore potesse essere ignorato.**

Bár időnként felkiáltott, úgy dolgozott, mintha a fájdalmat figyelmen kívül lehetne hagyni.

**Più di una volta cadde e fu trascinato prima di rialzarsi.**

Többször is elesett, és valaki vonszolta, mielőtt újra felkelt.

**A un certo punto la slitta gli rotolò addosso e da quel momento in poi zoppicò.**

Egyszer átgurult rajta a szánkó, és attól a pillanattól kezdve sántikált.

**Nonostante ciò, lavorò finché non raggiunse l'accampamento e poi si sdraiò accanto al fuoco.**

Mégis dolgozott, amíg el nem érte a tábort, majd lefeküdt a tűz mellé.

**Al mattino Dave era troppo debole per muoversi o anche solo per stare in piedi.**

Reggelre Dave túl gyenge volt ahhoz, hogy utazzon, vagy akár csak felegyenesedjen.

**Al momento di allacciare l'imbracatura, cercò di raggiungere il suo autista con sforzi tremanti.**

Amikor be kellett kapcsolnia, remegő erőfeszítéssel próbálta elérni a sofőrjét.

**Si sforzò di rialzarsi, barcollò e crollò sul terreno innevato.**

Feltápászkodott, megtántorodott, és a havas földre rogyott.

**Utilizzando le zampe anteriori, trascinò il suo corpo verso la zona dell'imbracatura.**

Mellső lábait használva vonszolta a testét a hámozási terület felé.

**Si fece avanti, centimetro dopo centimetro, verso i cani da lavoro.**

Apró lépésekkel, centiméterről centiméterre haladt előre a munkáskutyák felé.

**Le forze gli cedettero, ma continuò a muoversi nel suo ultimo disperato tentativo.**

Ereje elhagyta, de utolsó kétségbeesett mozdulatával továbbment.

**I suoi compagni di squadra lo videro ansimare nella neve, ancora desideroso di unirsi a loro.**

Csapattársai látták, ahogy a hóban kapkodva kapkodja a levegőt, és még mindig vágyik rá, hogy csatlakozhasson hozzájuk.

**Lo sentirono urlare di dolore mentre si lasciavano alle spalle l'accampamento.**

Hallották a bánatos üvöltését, miközben elhagyták a tábort.

**Mentre la squadra svaniva tra gli alberi, il grido di Dave risuonava dietro di loro.**

Ahogy a csapat eltűnt a fák között, Dave kiáltása visszhangzott mögöttük.

**Il treno delle slitte si fermò brevemente dopo aver attraversato un tratto di fiume ricco di boschi.**

A szánkóvonat rövid időre megállt, miután átkelt egy folyóparti erdősávon.

**Il meticcio scozzese tornò lentamente verso l'accampamento alle sue spalle.**

A skót félvér lassan visszasétált a mögötte lévő tábor felé.

**Gli uomini smisero di parlare quando lo videro scendere dal treno delle slitte.**

A férfiak elhallgattak, amikor meglátták, hogy leszáll a szánkós vonatról.

**Poi un singolo colpo di pistola risuonò chiaro e netto attraverso il sentiero.**

Aztán egyetlen lövés dördült tisztán és élesen át az ösvényen.
**L'uomo tornò rapidamente e prese il suo posto senza dire una parola.**
A férfi gyorsan visszatért, és szó nélkül elfoglalta a helyét.
**Le fruste schioccavano, i campanelli tintinnavano e le slitte avanzavano sulla neve.**
Ostorok csattantak, csengők csilingeltek, és a szánkók gurultak tovább a hóban.
**Ma Buck sapeva cosa era successo, come tutti gli altri cani.**
De Buck tudta, mi történt – és minden más kutya is.

## La fatica delle redini e del sentiero
## A gyeplő és az ösvény fáradalmai

**Trenta giorni dopo aver lasciato Dawson, la Salt Water Mail raggiunse Skaguay.**
Harminc nappal Dawson elhagyása után a Salt Water Mail megérkezett Skaguayba.
**Buck e i suoi compagni di squadra presero il comando e arrivarono in condizioni pietose.**
Buck és csapattársai átvették a vezetést, szánalmas állapotban érkezve.
**Buck era sceso da 140 a 150 chili.**
Buck száznegyvenről száztizenöt kilóra fogyott.
**Gli altri cani, sebbene più piccoli, avevano perso ancora più peso corporeo.**
A többi kutya, bár kisebb volt, még többet fogyott.
**Pike, che una volta zoppicava fingendo, ora trascinava dietro di sé una gamba veramente ferita.**
Pike, aki egykor csak álsántikált, most egy valóban sérült lábat vonszolt maga után.
**Solleks zoppicava gravemente e Dub aveva una scapola slogata.**
Solleks csúnyán sántított, Dubnak pedig megrándult a lapockája.
**Tutti i cani del team avevano i piedi doloranti a causa delle settimane trascorse sul sentiero ghiacciato.**
A csapat minden kutyájának sajgott a lába a hetekig tartó fagyos ösvényen való tartózkodástól.
**Non avevano più slancio nei loro passi, solo un movimento lento e trascinato.**
Lépteikben már nem volt ruganyosság, csak lassú, vonszoló mozgás.
**I loro piedi colpivano il sentiero con forza e ogni passo aggiungeva ulteriore sforzo al loro corpo.**
Lábaik keményen nyomultak az ösvényen, minden egyes lépés egyre nagyobb terhelést jelentett a testüknek.

**Non erano malati, erano solo stremati oltre ogni possibile guarigione naturale.**

Nem voltak betegek, csak annyira kimerültek, hogy természetes úton semmivé fáradtak.

**Non si trattava della stanchezza di una giornata faticosa, curata con una notte di riposo.**

Ez nem egy nehéz nap fáradtsága volt, amit egy éjszakai pihenéssel gyógyíthattam.

**Era una stanchezza accumulata lentamente attraverso mesi di sforzi estenuanti.**

A kimerültség lassan, hónapokig tartó, kimerítő erőfeszítések során gyűlt össze.

**Non era rimasta alcuna riserva di forze: avevano esaurito ogni energia a loro disposizione.**

Nem maradt tartalék erő – minden tartalékukat elhasználták.

**Ogni muscolo, fibra e cellula del loro corpo era consumato e usurato.**

Testük minden egyes izma, rostja és sejtje elhasználódott és elhasználódott.

**E c'era un motivo: avevano percorso duemilacinquecento miglia.**

És volt is rá ok – kétezerötszáz mérföldet tettek meg.

**Si erano riposati solo cinque giorni durante le ultime milleottocento miglia.**

Az elmúlt tizennyolcszáz mérföld alatt mindössze öt napot pihentek.

**Quando giunsero a Skaguay, sembrava che riuscissero a malapena a stare in piedi.**

Amikor Skaguay-ba értek, alig tudtak lábra állni.

**Facevano fatica a tenere le redini strette e a restare davanti alla slitta.**

Küzdeniük kellett, hogy feszesen tartsák a gyeplőt, és a szán előtt maradjanak.

**Nei pendii in discesa riuscivano solo a evitare di essere investiti.**

A lejtőkön csak az gázolást sikerült elkerülniük.

"Continuate a marciare, poveri piedi doloranti", disse l'autista mentre zoppicavano.

– Rajta, szegény, fájós lábacskáim! – mondta a sofőr, miközben sántikáltak.

"Questo è l'ultimo tratto, poi ci prenderemo tutti un lungo riposo, di sicuro."

„Ez az utolsó szakasz, aztán biztosan mindannyian kapunk egy hosszú pihenőt."

"Un riposo davvero lungo", promise, guardandoli barcollare in avanti.

„Egy igazán hosszú pihenés" – ígérte, miközben nézte, ahogy tántorgó léptekkel előrehaladnak.

Gli autisti si aspettavano una lunga e necessaria pausa.

A sofőrök arra számítottak, hogy most egy hosszú, szükséges szünetet tartanak.

Avevano percorso milleduecento miglia con solo due giorni di riposo.

Ezerkétszáz mérföldet tettek meg mindössze kétnapi pihenővel.

Per correttezza e ragione, ritenevano di essersi guadagnati un po' di tempo per rilassarsi.

Joggal és észszerűen úgy érezték, hogy kiérdemeltek egy kis időt a pihenésre.

Ma troppi erano giunti nel Klondike e troppo pochi erano rimasti a casa.

De túl sokan jöttek a Klondike-ba, és túl kevesen maradtak otthon.

Le lettere delle famiglie continuavano ad arrivare, creando pile di posta in ritardo.

Özönlöttek a családoktól érkező levelek, ami halmokban hozta létre a késedelmes postai küldeményeket.

Arrivarono gli ordini ufficiali: i nuovi cani della Hudson Bay avrebbero preso il sopravvento.

Megérkeztek a hivatalos parancsok – új Hudson-öbölbeli kutyák vették át a hatalmat.

I cani esausti, ormai considerati inutili, dovevano essere eliminati.

A kimerült, most már értéktelennek nevezett kutyákat meg kellett semmisíteni.

**Poiché i soldi erano più importanti dei cani, venivano venduti a basso prezzo.**

Mivel a pénz fontosabb volt a kutyáknál, olcsón akarták eladni őket.

**Passarono altri tre giorni prima che i cani si accorgessero di quanto fossero deboli.**

Még három nap telt el, mire a kutyák igazán érezni kezdték, mennyire gyengék.

**La quarta mattina, due uomini provenienti dagli Stati Uniti acquistarono l'intera squadra.**

A negyedik reggelen két férfi az Államokból megvette az egész csapatot.

**La vendita comprendeva tutti i cani e le loro imbracature usate.**

Az eladás magában foglalta az összes kutyát, plusz a kopott hámjukat.

**Mentre concludevano l'affare, gli uomini si chiamavano tra loro "Hal" e "Charles".**

A férfiak „Hal"-nak és „Charles"-nak szólították egymást, miközben befejezték az üzletet.

**Charles era un uomo di mezza età, pallido, con labbra molli e folti baffi.**

Károly középkorú, sápadt, petyhüdt ajkakkal és vad bajusszal rendelkezett.

**Hal era un giovane, forse diciannove anni, che indossava una cintura imbottita di cartucce.**

Hal egy fiatalember volt, talán tizenkilenc, és töltényekkel tömött övet viselt.

**Nella cintura erano contenuti un grosso revolver e un coltello da caccia, entrambi inutilizzati.**

Az övön egy nagy revolver és egy vadászkés lapult, mindkettő használatlan.

**Dimostrava quanto fosse inesperto e inadatto alla vita nel Nord.**

Ez megmutatta, mennyire tapasztalatlan és alkalmatlan az északi életre.

**Nessuno dei due uomini viveva in natura; la loro presenza sfidava ogni ragionevolezza.**

Egyikük sem tartozott a vadonba; jelenlétük minden ésszerűséget felülmúlt.

**Buck osservava lo scambio di denaro tra l'acquirente e l'agente.**

Buck figyelte, ahogy a vevő és az ügynök között pénz cserélődik.

**Sapeva che i conducenti dei treni postali stavano abbandonando la sua vita come tutti gli altri.**

Tudta, hogy a postavonat-vezetők ugyanúgy elhagyják az életét, mint bárki más.

**Seguirono Perrault e François, ormai scomparsi.**

Perrault-t és François-t követték, akiket mostanra már sehol sem lehetett megjegyezni.

**Buck e la squadra vennero condotti al disordinato accampamento dei loro nuovi proprietari.**

Buckot és a csapatot új tulajdonosaik hanyag táborába vezették.

**La tenda cedeva, i piatti erano sporchi e tutto era in disordine.**

A sátor megereszkedett, a tányérok piszkosak voltak, és minden rendetlenül hevert.

**Anche Buck notò una donna lì: Mercedes, moglie di Charles e sorella di Hal.**

Buck egy nőt is észrevett ott – Mercedest, Charles feleségét és Hal húgát.

**Formavano una famiglia completa, anche se erano tutt'altro che adatti al sentiero.**

Teljes családot alkottak, bár korántsem voltak alkalmasak az ösvényre.

**Buck osservava nervosamente mentre il trio iniziava a impacchettare le provviste.**

Buck idegesen figyelte, ahogy a trió elkezdte pakolgatni a holmikat.

**Lavoravano duro ma senza ordine, solo confusione e sforzi sprecati.**
Keményen dolgoztak, de rend nélkül – csak felhajtás és hiábavaló erőfeszítés.

**La tenda era arrotolata fino a formare una sagoma ingombrante, decisamente troppo grande per la slitta.**
A sátrat ormótlanra tekerték fel, túl nagyra a szánkónak.

**I piatti sporchi venivano imballati senza essere stati né lavati né asciugati.**
A piszkos edényeket anélkül pakolták be, hogy egyáltalán megtisztították volna vagy megszárították volna őket.

**Mercedes svolazzava in giro, parlando, correggendo e intromettendosi in continuazione.**
Mercedes állandóan beszélt, javítgatott és beleavatkozott a dolgokba.

**Quando le misero un sacco davanti, lei insistette perché lo mettesse dietro.**
Amikor egy zsákot előre tettek, ragaszkodott hozzá, hogy hátulra kerüljön.

**Mise il sacco in fondo e un attimo dopo ne ebbe bisogno.**
Bepakolta a zsákot az aljára, és a következő pillanatban szüksége is volt rá.

**Quindi la slitta venne disimballata di nuovo per raggiungere quella specifica borsa.**
Így hát a szánt újra kicsomagolták, hogy elérjék azt az egy bizonyos zsákot.

**Lì vicino, tre uomini stavano fuori da una tenda e osservavano la scena che si svolgeva.**
A közelben három férfi állt egy sátor előtt, és figyelte a kibontakozó jelenetet.

**Sorrisero, ammiccarono e sogghignarono di fronte all'evidente confusione dei nuovi arrivati.**
Mosolyogtak, kacsintottak és vigyorogtak az újonnan érkezők nyilvánvaló zavarodottságán.

**"Hai già un carico parecchio pesante", disse uno degli uomini.**
– Már így is elég nehéz a teher – mondta az egyik férfi.

"Non credo che dovresti portare quella tenda, ma la scelta è tua."

„Szerintem nem kellene cipelned azt a sátrat, de ez a te döntésed."

"Impensabile!" esclamò Mercedes, alzando le mani in segno di disperazione.

– Álmodni sem mertem róla! – kiáltotta Mercedes, kétségbeesetten széttárva a kezét.

"Come potrei viaggiare senza una tenda sotto cui dormire?"

„Hogyan tudnék utazni sátor nélkül, ami alatt megbújhatnék?"

«È primavera, non vedrai più il freddo», rispose l'uomo.

„Tavasz van, nem fogsz többé hideget látni" – felelte a férfi.

Ma lei scosse la testa e loro continuarono ad accumulare oggetti sulla slitta.

De a nő megrázta a fejét, és tovább pakolták a tárgyakat a szánkóba.

Il carico era pericolosamente alto mentre aggiungevano gli ultimi oggetti.

A rakomány veszélyesen magasra tornyosult, miközben az utolsó dolgokat is hozzáadták.

"Pensi che la slitta andrà avanti?" chiese uno degli uomini con aria scettica.

„Gondolod, hogy elmegy a szán?" – kérdezte az egyik férfi szkeptikus pillantással.

"E perché non dovrebbe?" ribatté Charles con netto fastidio.

– Miért ne? – csattant fel Charles éles bosszúsággal.

"Oh, va bene", disse rapidamente l'uomo, evitando di offendersi.

– Ó, rendben van – mondta gyorsan a férfi, és elhárította a sértődést.

"Mi chiedevo solo: mi sembrava un po' troppo pesante nella parte superiore."

„Csak azon tűnődtem – nekem egy kicsit túl nehéznek tűnt a teteje."

Charles si voltò e legò il carico meglio che poté.

Károly elfordult, és amennyire csak tudta, lekötözte a terhet.

Ma le legature erano allentate e l'imballaggio nel complesso era fatto male.

De a kötözés laza volt, és a csomagolás összességében rosszul volt elvégezve.

"Certo, i cani tireranno così tutto il giorno", disse sarcasticamente un altro uomo.

– Persze, a kutyák egész nap húzni fogják – mondta egy másik férfi gúnyosan.

«Certamente», rispose Hal freddamente, afferrando il lungo timone della slitta.

– Természetesen – felelte Hal hidegen, és megragadta a szán hosszú gearboxát.

Tenendo una mano sul palo, faceva roteare la frusta nell'altra.

Az egyik kezével a rúdon, a másikban az ostort lengette.

"Andiamo!" urlò. "Muovetevi!", incitando i cani a partire.

„Gyerünk!" – kiáltotta. „Gyerünk!" – sürgette a kutyákat, hogy induljanak.

I cani si appoggiarono all'imbracatura e si sforzarono per qualche istante.

A kutyák beledőltek a hámba, és néhány pillanatig erőlködtek.

Poi si fermarono, incapaci di spostare di un centimetro la slitta sovraccarica.

Aztán megálltak, képtelenek voltak egy tapodtat sem mozdítani a túlterhelt szánt.

"Quei fannulloni!" urlò Hal, alzando la frusta per colpirli.

„A lusta bestiák!" – kiáltotta Hal, és felemelte az ostort, hogy lecsapjon rájuk.

Ma Mercedes si precipitò dentro e strappò la frusta dalle mani di Hal.

De Mercedes odarohant, és kikapta Hal kezéből az ostort.

«Oh, Hal, non osare far loro del male», gridò allarmata.

– Ó, Hal, ne merészeld bántani őket! – kiáltotta riadtan.

"Promettimi che sarai gentile con loro, altrimenti non farò un altro passo."

„Ígérd meg, hogy kedves leszel hozzájuk, különben egy tapodtat sem megyek tovább."

"Non sai niente di cani", scattò Hal contro la sorella.

– Semmit sem tudsz a kutyákról! – csattant fel Hal a húgára.

"Sono pigri e l'unico modo per smuoverli è frustarli."

„Lusták, és az egyetlen módja annak, hogy megmozdítsuk őket, az az, ha megkorbácsoljuk őket."

"Chiedi a chiunque, chiedi a uno di quegli uomini laggiù se dubiti di me."

„Kérdezz meg bárkit – kérdezz meg egyet azoktól az emberektől ott, ha kételkedsz bennem."

Mercedes guardò gli astanti con occhi imploranti e pieni di lacrime.

Mercedes könyörgő, könnyes szemekkel nézett a bámészkodókra.

Il suo viso rivelava quanto odiasse la vista di qualsiasi dolore.

Az arcán látszott, mennyire gyűlöli a fájdalom látványát.

"Sono deboli, tutto qui", ha detto un uomo. "Sono sfiniti."

„Gyengék, ennyi az egész" – mondta az egyik férfi. „Elfáradtak."

"Hanno bisogno di riposare: hanno lavorato troppo a lungo senza una pausa."

„Pihenésre van szükségük – túl sokáig dolgoztatták őket szünet nélkül."

«Che il resto sia maledetto», borbottò Hal arricciando il labbro.

– A többiek átkozottak legyenek! – motyogta Hal felkunkorodott ajakkal.

Mercedes sussultò, visibilmente addolorata per le parole volgari pronunciate da lui.

Mercedes felnyögött, láthatóan fájt neki a durva szó tőle.

Ciononostante, lei rimase leale e difese immediatamente il fratello.

Ennek ellenére hűséges maradt, és azonnal megvédte a testvérét.

"Non badare a quell'uomo", disse ad Hal. "Sono i nostri cani."

– Ne törődj azzal az emberrel – mondta Halnak. – Ők a mi kutyáink.

**"Li guidi come meglio credi: fai ciò che ritieni giusto."**

„Úgy vezeted őket, ahogy jónak látod – tedd, amit helyesnek látsz."

**Hal sollevò la frusta e colpì di nuovo i cani senza pietà.**

Hal felemelte az ostort, és könyörtelenül ismét megütötte a kutyákat.

**Si lanciarono in avanti, con i corpi bassi e i piedi che affondavano nella neve.**

Előrevetődtek, testük laposan, lábuk a hóba nyomódott.

**Tutta la loro forza era concentrata nel traino, ma la slitta non si muoveva.**

Minden erejüket a húzásra fordították, de a szánkó nem mozdult.

**La slitta rimase bloccata, come un'ancora congelata nella neve compatta.**

A szánkó ott ragadt, mint egy belefagyott horgony a döngölt hóba.

**Dopo un secondo tentativo, i cani si fermarono di nuovo, ansimando forte.**

Egy második erőfeszítés után a kutyák ismét megálltak, lihegve.

**Hal sollevò di nuovo la frusta, proprio mentre Mercedes interferiva di nuovo.**

Hal ismét felemelte az ostort, éppen akkor, amikor Mercedes ismét közbeavatkozott.

**Si lasciò cadere in ginocchio davanti a Buck e gli abbracciò il collo.**

Térdre rogyott Buck előtt, és átölelte a nyakát.

**Le lacrime le riempivano gli occhi mentre implorava il cane esausto.**

Könnyek szöktek a szemébe, miközben könyörgött a kimerült kutyának.

**"Poveri cari", disse, "perché non tirate più forte?"**

– Szegény drágáim – mondta –, miért nem húzzátok csak erősebben?

"Se tiri, non verrai frustato così."

„Ha húzol, akkor nem fognak így megkorbácsolni."

**A Buck non piaceva Mercedes, ma ormai era troppo stanco per resisterle.**

Buck nem szerette Mercedest, de most már túl fáradt volt ahhoz, hogy ellenálljon neki.

**Lui accettò le sue lacrime come se fossero solo un'altra parte di quella giornata miserabile.**

A könnyeit csupán a nyomorúságos nap egy újabb részének fogadta.

**Uno degli uomini che osservavano, dopo aver represso la rabbia, finalmente parlò.**

Az egyik figyelő férfi végre megszólalt, miután visszafojtotta a haragját.

**"Non mi interessa cosa succede a voi, ma quei cani sono importanti."**

„Nem érdekel, mi történik veletek, de azok a kutyák számítanak."

**"Se vuoi aiutare, stacca quella slitta: è ghiacciata e innevata."**

„Ha segíteni akarsz, tedd tönkre azt a szánt – hóhoz fagyott."

**"Spingi con forza il palo della luce, a destra e a sinistra, e rompi il sigillo di ghiaccio."**

„Nyomd meg erősen a gerendarudat jobbra-balra, és törd át a jégzárat."

**Fu fatto un terzo tentativo, questa volta seguendo il suggerimento dell'uomo.**

Harmadszorra is próbálkoztak, ezúttal a férfi javaslatára.

**Hal fece oscillare la slitta da una parte all'altra, facendo staccare i pattini.**

Hal jobbra-balra ringatta a szánt, kioldva a talpakat.

**La slitta, benché sovraccarica e scomoda, alla fine sobbalzò in avanti.**

A szánkó, bár túlterhelt és esetlen volt, végül előrelendült.

**Buck e gli altri tirarono selvaggiamente, spinti da una tempesta di frustate.**

Buck és a többiek vadul húztak, az ostorcsapások vihara hajtotta őket.

Un centinaio di metri più avanti, il sentiero curvava e scendeva in pendenza verso la strada.

Száz méterrel előttük az ösvény kanyargott és lejtős lett az utcába.

Ci sarebbe voluto un guidatore esperto per tenere la slitta in posizione verticale.

Egy ügyes hajtóra lett volna szükség ahhoz, hogy a szánt egyenesen tartsa.

Hal non era abile e la slitta si ribaltò mentre svoltava.

Hal nem volt ügyes, és a szánkó felborult, amikor a kanyarban lengett.

Le cinghie allentate cedettero e metà del carico si rovesciò sulla neve.

A laza kötözőelemek elszabadultak, és a rakomány fele a hóra ömlött.

I cani non si fermarono; la slitta più leggera continuò a procedere su un fianco.

A kutyák nem álltak meg; a könnyebb szán oldalára dőlve repült tovább.

I cani, furiosi per i maltrattamenti e per il peso del carico, corsero più veloci.

A bántalmazás és a nehéz teher miatt dühösen a kutyák gyorsabban futottak.

Buck, infuriato, si lanciò a correre, seguito dalla squadra.

Buck dühösen futásnak eredt, a csapat pedig a nyomában volt.

Hal urlò "Whoa! Whoa!" ma la squadra non gli prestò attenzione.

Hal felkiáltott: „Hűha! Hűha!", de a csapat ügyet sem vetett rá.

Inciampò, cadde e fu trascinato a terra dall'imbracatura.

Megbotlott, elesett, és a hámja magával rántotta a földön.

La slitta rovesciata lo travolse mentre i cani continuavano a correre avanti.

A felborult szán átütközött rajta, miközben a kutyák előreszaladtak.

Il resto delle provviste è sparso lungo la trafficata strada di Skaguay.

A többi készlet szétszórva hevert Skaguay forgalmas utcáján.

**Le persone di buon cuore si precipitarono a fermare i cani e a raccogliere l'attrezzatura.**

Jószívű emberek siettek megállítani a kutyákat és összeszedni a felszerelést.

**Diedero anche consigli schietti e pratici ai nuovi viaggiatori.**

Emellett őszinte és gyakorlatias tanácsokat adtak az új utazóknak.

**"Se vuoi raggiungere Dawson, prendi metà del carico e raddoppia i cani."**

„Ha el akarsz jutni Dawsonba, vidd a rakomány felét és a kutyák dupláját."

**Hal, Charles e Mercedes ascoltarono, anche se non con entusiasmo.**

Hal, Charles és Mercedes hallgatták, bár nem lelkesedéssel.

**Montarono la tenda e cominciarono a sistemare le loro provviste.**

Felverték a sátrat, és elkezdték átválogatni a holmijukat.

**Ne uscirono dei cibi in scatola, che fecero ridere a crepapelle gli astanti.**

Konzervek kerültek elő, amin a bámészkodók hangosan felnevettek.

**"Roba in scatola sul sentiero? Morirai di fame prima che si sciolga", disse uno.**

„Konzerv az ösvényen? Éhen halsz, mielőtt elolvadna" – mondta az egyik.

**"Coperte d'albergo? Meglio buttarle via tutte."**

„Szállodai takarók? Jobban jársz, ha mindet kidobod."

**"Togli anche la tenda e qui nessuno laverà più i piatti."**

„Hagyd el a sátrat is, és itt senki sem mosogat."

**"Pensi di viaggiare su un treno Pullman con dei servitori a bordo?"**

„Azt hiszed, egy Pullman vonaton utazol, amiben szolgák vannak?"

**Il processo ebbe inizio: ogni oggetto inutile venne gettato da parte.**

A folyamat elkezdődött – minden haszontalan tárgyat félredobtak.

**Mercedes pianse quando le sue borse furono svuotate sul terreno innevato.**

Mercedes sírt, amikor a táskáit a havas földre ürítették.

**Singhiozzava per ogni oggetto buttato via, uno per uno, senza sosta.**

Minden egyes kidobott tárgyon zokogott, egyesével, szünet nélkül.

**Giurò di non fare un altro passo, nemmeno per dieci Charles.**

Megfogadta, hogy egy lépést sem tesz többet – még tíz Charlesért sem.

**Pregò ogni persona vicina di lasciarle conservare le sue cose preziose.**

Könyörgött mindenkinek, aki a közelben állt, hogy hadd tartsa meg a drága holmijait.

**Alla fine si asciugò gli occhi e cominciò a gettare via anche i vestiti più importanti.**

Végül megtörölte a szemét, és még a létfontosságú ruháit is elkezdte dobálni.

**Una volta terminato il suo, cominciò a svuotare le scorte degli uomini.**

Miután végzett a sajátjával, elkezdte kiüríteni a férfiak készleteit.

**Come un turbine, fece a pezzi gli effetti personali di Charles e Hal.**

Mint egy forgószél, úgy rohant át Charles és Hal holmijain.

**Sebbene il carico fosse dimezzato, era comunque molto più pesante del necessario.**

Bár a rakományt a felére csökkentették, még mindig sokkal nehezebb volt a kelleténél.

**Quella notte, Charles e Hal uscirono e comprarono sei nuovi cani.**

Azon az estén Charles és Hal elmentek, és hat új kutyát vettek.

**Questi nuovi cani si unirono ai sei originali, più Teek e Koona.**

Ezek az új kutyák csatlakoztak az eredeti hathoz, plusz Teekhez és Koonához.

**Insieme formarono una squadra di quattordici cani attaccati alla slitta.**

Együtt alkottak egy tizennégy kutyából álló csapatot, amelyet a szánhoz kötöttek.

**Ma i nuovi cani erano inadatti e poco addestrati per il lavoro con la slitta.**

De az új kutyák alkalmatlanok és rosszul képzettek voltak a szánhúzásra.

**Tre dei cani erano cani da caccia a pelo corto, mentre uno era un Terranova.**

A kutyák közül három rövid szőrű vizsla, egy pedig újfundlandi volt.

**Gli ultimi due cani erano meticci senza alcuna razza o scopo ben definito.**

Az utolsó két kutya olyan korcs volt, amelyeknek semmilyen egyértelmű fajtája vagy céljuk nem volt.

**Non capivano il percorso e non lo imparavano in fretta.**

Nem értették az ösvényt, és nem is tanulták meg gyorsan.

**Buck e i suoi compagni li osservavano con disprezzo e profonda irritazione.**

Buck és társai megvetéssel és mély ingerültséggel figyelték őket.

**Sebbene Buck insegnasse loro cosa non fare, non poteva insegnare loro il dovere.**

Bár Buck megtanította nekik, mit ne tegyenek, a kötelességtudatra nem taníthatta meg őket.

**Non amavano la vita sui sentieri né la trazione delle redini e delle slitte.**

Nem szerették az élet nyomában járni, vagy a gyeplő és a szánkó vontatását.

**Soltanto i bastardi cercarono di adattarsi, e anche a loro mancava lo spirito combattivo.**

Csak a korcsok próbáltak alkalmazkodni, és még tőlük is hiányzott a harci szellem.

**Gli altri cani erano confusi, indeboliti e distrutti dalla loro nuova vita.**

A többi kutya összezavarodott, legyengült és megtört volt az új életétől.

**Con i nuovi cani all'oscuro e i vecchi esausti, la speranza era flebile.**

Mivel az új kutyák fogalmatlanok, a régiek pedig kimerültek, a remény szerény volt.

**La squadra di Buck aveva percorso duemilacinquecento miglia di sentiero accidentato.**

Buck csapata kétezer-ötszáz mérföldnyi rögös ösvényt tett meg.

**Ciononostante, i due uomini erano allegri e orgogliosi della loro grande squadra di cani.**

A két férfi mégis vidám volt, és büszke a nagy kutyacsapatára.

**Pensavano di viaggiare con stile, con quattordici cani al seguito.**

Azt hitték, stílusosan utaznak, tizennégy kutyával befogva.

**Avevano visto delle slitte partire per Dawson e altre arrivarne.**

Látták, hogy a szánkók elindulnak Dawsonba, és mások megérkeznek onnan.

**Ma non ne avevano mai vista una trainata da ben quattordici cani.**

De még soha nem láttak olyat, amit tizennégy kutya húzott volna.

**C'era un motivo per cui squadre del genere erano rare nelle terre selvagge dell'Artico.**

Volt ok arra, hogy az ilyen csapatok ritkák voltak az arktiszi vadonban.

**Nessuna slitta poteva trasportare cibo sufficiente a sfamare quattordici cani per l'intero viaggio.**

Egyetlen szán sem tudott annyi élelmet szállítani, hogy tizennégy kutyát is megetethessen az útra.

**Ma Charles e Hal non lo sapevano: avevano fatto i calcoli.**

De Charles és Hal ezt nem tudták – ők már kiszámolták.

**Hanno pianificato la razione di cibo: una certa quantità per cane, per un certo numero di giorni, fatta.**

Ceruzával kiszámolták az ételt: ennyi kutyánként, ennyi napra, ennyi időre.

**Mercedes guardò i numeri e annuì come se avessero senso.**

Mercedes a számokra nézett, és bólintott, mintha érthető lenne a dolog.

**Tutto le sembrava molto semplice, almeno sulla carta.**

Minden nagyon egyszerűnek tűnt számára, legalábbis papíron.

**La mattina seguente, Buck guidò lentamente la squadra lungo la strada innevata.**

Másnap reggel Buck lassan felvezette a csapatot a havas utcán.

**Non c'era né energia né spirito in lui e nei cani dietro di lui.**

Sem benne, sem a mögötte lévő kutyákban nem volt energia vagy szellem.

**Erano stanchi morti fin dall'inizio: non avevano più riserve.**

Már a legelejétől fogva halálosan fáradtak voltak – nem maradt semmi tartalék.

**Buck aveva già fatto quattro viaggi tra Salt Water e Dawson.**

Buck már négy utat tett meg Salt Water és Dawson között.

**Ora, di fronte alla stessa pista, non provava altro che amarezza.**

Most, hogy újra ugyanazzal az ösvénnyel kellett szembenéznie, semmi mást nem érzett, csak keserűséget.

**Il suo cuore non c'era, e nemmeno quello degli altri cani.**

A szíve nem volt benne, ahogy a többi kutya szíve sem.

**I nuovi cani erano timidi e gli husky non si fidavano per niente.**

Az új kutyák félénkek voltak, a huskyk pedig teljesen megbízhatatlanok.

**Buck capì che non poteva fare affidamento su quei due uomini o sulla loro sorella.**

Buck érezte, hogy nem számíthat erre a két férfira vagy a húgukra.

Non sapevano nulla e non mostravano alcun segno di apprendimento lungo il percorso.
Semmit sem tudtak, és az ösvényen sem mutattak tanulási jeleit.
**Erano disorganizzati e privi di qualsiasi senso di disciplina.**
Rendetlenek voltak és hiányzott belőlük a fegyelem.
**Ogni volta impiegavano metà della notte per allestire un accampamento malmesso.**
Minden alkalommal fél éjszaka kellett hozzá, hogy rendetlenül tábort verjenek.
**E metà della mattina successiva la trascorsero di nuovo armeggiando con la slitta.**
És a következő délelőtt felét megint a szánnal babrálva töltötték.
**Spesso a mezzogiorno si fermavano solo per sistemare il carico irregolare.**
Délre gyakran már csak azért is megálltak, hogy kijavítsák az egyenetlen terhelést.
**In alcuni giorni percorsero meno di dieci miglia in totale.**
Voltak napok, amikor összesen kevesebb mint tíz mérföldet tettek meg.
**Altri giorni non riuscivano proprio ad abbandonare l'accampamento.**
Más napokon egyáltalán nem sikerült elhagyniuk a tábort.
**Non sono mai riusciti a coprire la distanza alimentare prevista.**
Soha nem kerültek a tervezett élelemszerzési távolság megtételének közelébe.
**Come previsto, il cibo per i cani finì molto presto.**
Ahogy az várható volt, nagyon gyorsan elfogyott az élelem a kutyáknak.
**Nei primi tempi hanno peggiorato ulteriormente la situazione con l'eccesso di cibo.**
A helyzetet tovább rontották azzal, hogy az első napokban túletették őket.
**Ciò rendeva la carestia sempre più vicina, con ogni razione disattenta.**

Ez minden egyes gondatlan adaggal közelebb hozta az éhezést.

**I nuovi cani non avevano ancora imparato a sopravvivere con molto poco.**

Az új kutyák nem tanulták meg, hogyan éljenek túl nagyon kevésből.

**Mangiarono avidamente, con un appetito troppo grande per il sentiero.**

Éhesen ettek, túl nagy étvágyuk volt az ösvényhez.

**Vedendo i cani indebolirsi, Hal pensò che il cibo non fosse sufficiente.**

Látva a kutyák legyengülését, Hal úgy gondolta, hogy az étel nem elég.

**Raddoppiò le razioni, peggiorando ulteriormente l'errore.**

Megduplázta az adagokat, amivel még súlyosbította a hibát.

**Mercedes aggravò il problema con le sue lacrime e le sue suppliche sommesse.**

Mercedes könnyeivel és halk könyörgésével tetézte a problémát.

**Quando non riuscì a convincere Hal, diede da mangiare ai cani di nascosto.**

Amikor nem tudta meggyőzni Halt, titokban megetette a kutyákat.

**Rubò il pesce dai sacchi e glielo diede alle spalle.**

Lopott a halaszsákokból, és a férfi háta mögött odaadta nekik.

**Ma ciò di cui i cani avevano veramente bisogno non era altro cibo: era riposo.**

De a kutyáknak igazán nem több ételre volt szükségük, hanem pihenésre.

**Nonostante la loro scarsa velocità, la pesante slitta continuava a procedere.**

Gyengén haladtak, de a nehéz szán még mindig vonszolta magát.

**Quel peso da solo esauriva ogni giorno le loro forze rimanenti.**

Már csak ez a súly is kiszívta a maradék erejüket minden egyes nap.

Poi arrivò la fase della sottoalimentazione, quando le scorte scarseggiavano.

Aztán jött az alultápláltság szakasza, mivel a készletek fogytán voltak.

Una mattina Hal si accorse che metà del cibo per cani era già finito.

Hal egy reggel rájött, hogy a kutyatáp fele már elfogyott.

Avevano percorso solo un quarto della distanza totale del sentiero.

A teljes ösvény távolságának csak egynegyedét tették meg.

Non si poteva più comprare cibo, a qualunque prezzo.

Több élelmet nem lehetett venni, bármilyen árat is ajánlottak érte.

Ridusse le porzioni dei cani al di sotto della razione giornaliera standard.

A kutyák adagjait a szokásos napi adag alá csökkentette.

Allo stesso tempo, chiese di viaggiare più a lungo per compensare la perdita.

Ugyanakkor hosszabb utazást követelt a veszteség pótlására.

Mercedes e Charles appoggiarono questo piano, ma fallirono nella sua realizzazione.

Mercedes és Charles támogatták ezt a tervet, de a végrehajtás kudarcot vallott.

La loro pesante slitta e la mancanza di abilità rendevano il progresso quasi impossibile.

Nehéz szánjuk és a képességek hiánya szinte lehetetlenné tette az előrehaladást.

Era facile dare meno cibo, ma impossibile forzare uno sforzo maggiore.

Könnyű volt kevesebb ételt adni, de lehetetlen volt több erőfeszítésre kényszeríteni.

Non potevano partire prima, né viaggiare per ore extra.

Nem kezdhettek korán, és nem utazhattak túlórákat sem.

Non sapevano come gestire i cani, e nemmeno loro stessi, a dire il vero.

Nem tudták, hogyan kell dolgozni a kutyákkal, sőt, még magukat sem.

Il primo cane a morire fu Dub, lo sfortunato ma laborioso ladro.

Az első kutya, amelyik meghalt, Dub volt, a balszerencsés, de szorgalmas tolvaj.

Sebbene spesso punito, Dub aveva fatto la sua parte senza lamentarsi.

Bár gyakran megbüntették, Dub panasz nélkül helytállt.

La sua spalla ferita peggiorò se non ricevette cure adeguate e non ebbe bisogno di riposo.

Sérült válla ellátás és pihenés nélkül egyre rosszabb lett.

Alla fine, Hal usò la pistola per porre fine alle sofferenze di Dub.

Végül Hal a revolverrel vetett véget Dub szenvedéseinek.

Un detto comune afferma che i cani normali muoiono se vengono nutriti con razioni di husky.

Egy közmondás szerint a normális kutyák husky takarmányon pusztulnak el.

I sei nuovi compagni di Buck avevano ricevuto solo metà della quota di cibo riservata all'husky.

Buck hat új társa csak a husky adagjának a felét kapta.

Il Terranova morì per primo, seguito dai tre cani da caccia a pelo corto.

Először az újfundlandi pusztult el, majd a három rövidszőrű vizsla.

I due bastardi resistettero più a lungo ma alla fine morirono come gli altri.

A két korcs kutya tovább kitartott, de végül a többiekhez hasonlóan elpusztult.

Ormai tutti i comfort e la gentilezza del Southland erano scomparsi.

Ekkorra már a Délvidék minden kényelme és szelídsége eltűnt.

Le tre persone avevano perso le ultime tracce della loro educazione civile.

A három ember magáról lerázta magáról civilizált neveltetésének utolsó nyomait is.

**Spogliato di glamour e romanticismo, il viaggio nell'Artico è diventato brutalmente reale.**

A csillogástól és romantikától megfosztva a sarkvidéki utazás brutálisan valósággá vált.

**Era una realtà troppo dura per il loro senso di virilità e femminilità.**

Ez a valóság túl kemény volt a férfiasságukról és nőiességükről alkotott képükhöz képest.

**Mercedes non piangeva più per i cani, ma piangeva solo per se stessa.**

Mercedes már nem a kutyákat siratta, hanem csak önmagát.

**Trascorreva il tempo piangendo e litigando con Hal e Charles.**

Az idejét sírással és Hal-lal és Charles-szal való veszekedéssel töltötte.

**Litigare era l'unica cosa per cui non si stancavano mai.**

A veszekedés volt az egyetlen dolog, amihez sosem voltak túl fáradtak.

**La loro irritabilità derivava dalla miseria, cresceva con essa e la superava.**

Ingerlékenységük a nyomorúságból fakadt, vele együtt nőtt, és meghaladta azt.

**La pazienza del cammino, nota a coloro che faticano e soffrono con generosità, non è mai arrivata.**

Az ösvény türelme, melyet azok ismernek, akik kedvesen fáradoznak és szenvednek, soha nem jött el.

**Quella pazienza che rende dolce la parola nonostante il dolore, era a loro sconosciuta.**

Az a türelem, amely a fájdalom közepette is édessé teszi a beszédet, ismeretlen volt előttük.

**Non avevano alcun briciolo di pazienza, nessuna forza derivante dalla sofferenza con grazia.**

Semmi türelem nem volt bennük, semmi erő nem merített a kegyelemmel teli szenvedésből.

**Erano irrigiditi dal dolore: dolori nei muscoli, nelle ossa e nel cuore.**

Fájdalomtól merevek voltak – sajgott az izmaik, a csontjaik és a szívük.

**Per questo motivo, divennero taglienti nella lingua e pronti a pronunciare parole dure.**

Emiatt éles nyelvűek és gyorsak lettek a kemény szavakkal.

**Ogni giorno iniziava e finiva con voci arrabbiate e lamentele amare.**

Minden nap dühös hangokkal és keserű panaszokkal kezdődött és végződött.

**Charles e Hal litigavano ogni volta che Mercedes ne dava loro l'occasione.**

Charles és Hal mindig vitatkoztak, amikor Mercedes lehetőséget adott nekik.

**Ogni uomo credeva di aver fatto più del dovuto.**

Minden férfi úgy gondolta, hogy többet végzett, mint amennyit méltányos részük rá hárult.

**Nessuno dei due ha mai perso l'occasione di dirlo, ancora e ancora.**

Egyikük sem szalasztotta el a lehetőséget, hogy újra meg újra elmondja.

**A volte Mercedes si schierava con Charles, a volte con Hal.**

Mercedes néha Charles, néha Hal oldalára állt.

**Ciò portò a una grande e infinita lite tra i tre.**

Ez egy nagy és véget nem érő veszekedéshez vezetett a három között.

**La disputa su chi dovesse tagliare la legna da ardere divenne incontrollabile.**

A vita arról, hogy kinek kellene tűzifát aprítania, elfajult.

**Ben presto vennero nominati padri, madri, cugini e parenti defunti.**

Hamarosan apákat, anyákat, unokatestvéreket és halott rokonokat neveztek meg.

**Le opinioni di Hal sull'arte o sulle opere teatrali di suo zio divennero parte della lotta.**

Hal művészetről vagy nagybátyja darabjairól alkotott nézetei a harc részévé váltak.

Anche le convinzioni politiche di Carlo entrarono nel dibattito.

Károly politikai nézetei is vitába keveredtek.

Per Mercedes, perfino i pettegolezzi della sorella del marito sembravano rilevanti.

Mercedes számára még a férje húgának pletykái is relevánsnak tűntek.

Espresse la sua opinione su questo e su molti dei difetti della famiglia di Charles.

Véleményt nyilvánított erről és Charles családjának számos hibájáról.

Mentre discutevano, il fuoco rimase spento e l'accampamento mezzo allestito.

Miközben vitatkoztak, a tűz nem gyújtott, és a tábor félig készen állt.

Nel frattempo i cani erano rimasti infreddoliti e senza cibo.

Eközben a kutyák fáztak és ennivaló nélkül maradtak.

Mercedes nutriva un risentimento che considerava profondamente personale.

Mercedesnek volt egy sérelme, amit mélyen személyesnek tartott.

Si sentiva maltrattata in quanto donna e le venivano negati i suoi gentili privilegi.

Úgy érezte, hogy nőként rosszul bánnak vele, megfosztják tőle a nemes kiváltságait.

Era carina e gentile, e per tutta la vita era stata abituata alla cavalleria.

Csinos és gyengéd volt, és egész életében lovagias volt.

Ma suo marito e suo fratello ora la trattavano con impazienza.

De a férje és a bátyja most türelmetlenül bántak vele.

Aveva l'abitudine di comportarsi in modo impotente e loro cominciarono a lamentarsi.

Szokása az volt, hogy tehetetlenül viselkedett, és a gyerekek panaszkodni kezdtek.

Offesa da ciò, rese loro la vita ancora più difficile.

Ezen megsértődve még jobban megnehezítette az életüket.

Ignorò i cani e insistette per guidare lei stessa la slitta.

Nem törődött a kutyákkal, és ragaszkodott hozzá, hogy ő maga üljön a szánon.

Sebbene sembrasse esile, pesava centoventi libbre (circa quaranta chili).

Bár könnyű volt a külseje, százhúsz fontot nyomott.

Quel peso aggiuntivo era troppo per i cani affamati e deboli.

Ez a plusz teher túl sok volt az éhező, gyenge kutyáknak.

Nonostante ciò, continuò a cavalcare per giorni, finché i cani non crollarono nelle redini.

Mégis napokig lovagolt, mígnem a kutyák összeestek a gyeplőben.

La slitta si fermò e Charles e Hal la implorarono di proseguire a piedi.

A szán megállt, Charles és Hal pedig könyörögtek neki, hogy menjen tovább.

Loro la implorarono e la scongiurarono, ma lei pianse e li definì crudeli.

Könyörögtek és könyörögtek, de ő sírt és kegyetlennek nevezte őket.

In un'occasione, la tirarono giù dalla slitta con pura forza e rabbia.

Egyszer puszta erővel és dühvel lerántották a szánról.

Dopo quello che accadde quella volta non ci riprovarono più.

A történtek után soha többé nem próbálkoztak.

Si accasciò come una bambina viziata e si sedette nella neve.

Elernyedt, mint egy elkényeztetett gyerek, és leült a hóba.

Continuarono a muoversi, ma lei si rifiutò di alzarsi o di seguirli.

Továbbmentek, de a lány nem volt hajlandó felkelni vagy követni őket.

Dopo tre miglia si fermarono, tornarono indietro e la riportarono indietro.

Három mérföld után megálltak, visszatértek, és visszavitték.

La ricaricarono sulla slitta, usando ancora una volta la forza bruta.

Újra felrakták a szánra, ismét nyers erőt bevetve.

**Nella loro profonda miseria, erano insensibili alla sofferenza dei cani.**

Mély nyomorúságukban érzéketlenek voltak a kutyák szenvedésével szemben.

**Hal credeva che fosse necessario indurirsi e impose questa convinzione agli altri.**

Hal úgy hitte, hogy az embernek meg kell keményednie, és ezt a hitet másokra is ráerőltette.

**Inizialmente ha cercato di predicare la sua filosofia a sua sorella**

Először a nővérének próbálta hirdetni a filozófiáját.

**e poi, senza successo, predicò al cognato.**

majd sikertelenül prédikált a sógorának.

**Ebbe più successo con i cani, ma solo perché li ferì.**

A kutyákkal több sikert ért el, de csak azért, mert fájdalmat okozott nekik.

**Da Five Fingers, il cibo per cani è rimasto completamente vuoto.**

A Five Fingersnél a kutyatáp teljesen kifogyott.

**Una vecchia squaw sdentata vendette qualche chilo di pelle di cavallo congelata**

Egy fogatlan öreg squaw eladott néhány font fagyasztott lóbőrt

**Hal scambiò la sua pistola con la pelle di cavallo secca.**

Hal elcserélte revolverét a szárított lóbőrre.

**La carne proveniva dai cavalli affamati di allevatori di bovini, morti mesi prima.**

A hús hónapokkal korábban éhen halt marhatenyésztők lovaitól származott.

**Congelata, la pelle era come ferro zincato: dura e immangiabile.**

A megfagyott bőr olyan volt, mint a horganyzott vas; kemény és ehetetlen.

**Per riuscire a mangiarla, i cani dovevano masticare la pelle senza sosta.**

A kutyáknak vég nélkül kellett rágniuk a bőrt, hogy megegyék.

**Ma le corde coriacee e i peli corti non erano certo un nutrimento.**

De a bőrszerű húrok és a rövid haj aligha voltak táplálóak.

**La maggior parte della pelle era irritante e non era cibo in senso stretto.**

A bőr nagy része irritáló volt, és nem igazi étel.

**E nonostante tutto, Buck barcollava davanti a tutti, come in un incubo.**

És mindezek alatt Buck elöl tántorgott, mint egy rémálomban.

**Quando poteva, tirava; quando non poteva, restava lì finché non veniva sollevato dalla frusta o dal bastone.**

Amikor tudta, húzta; amikor nem, addig feküdt, amíg az ostor vagy a bot fel nem emelte.

**Il suo pelo fine e lucido aveva perso tutta la rigidità e la lucentezza di un tempo.**

Finom, fényes bundája elvesztette minden merevségét és fényét, ami valaha volt.

**I suoi capelli erano flosci, spettinati e pieni di sangue rappreso a causa dei colpi.**

Haja ernyedten, kócosan lógott, és az ütésektől megszáradt vértől alvadt.

**I suoi muscoli si ridussero a midolli e i cuscinetti di carne erano tutti consumati.**

Izmai zsinórrá zsugorodtak, és a húspárnái mind elkoptak.

**Ogni costola, ogni osso erano chiaramente visibili attraverso le pieghe della pelle rugosa.**

Minden borda, minden csont tisztán látszott a ráncos bőr redői között.

**Fu straziante, ma il cuore di Buck non riuscì a spezzarsi.**

Szívszorító volt, de Buck szíve nem tudott megtörni.

**L'uomo con il maglione rosso lo aveva testato e dimostrato molto tempo prima.**

A piros pulóveres férfi ezt már régen bebizonyította és kipróbálta.

Così come accadde a Buck, accadde anche a tutti i suoi compagni di squadra rimasti.

Ahogy Buckkal történt, úgy volt ez az összes megmaradt csapattársával is.

Ce n'erano sette in totale, ognuno uno scheletro ambulante di miseria.

Összesen heten voltak, mindegyik a nyomorúság élő csontváza.

Erano diventati insensibili alle fruste e sentivano solo un dolore distante.

Elzsibbadtak az ostorcsapásoktól, csak távoli fájdalmat éreztek.

Anche la vista e i suoni li raggiungevano debolmente, come attraverso una fitta nebbia.

Még a látvány és a hang is halványan ért el hozzájuk, mintha sűrű ködön keresztül.

Non erano mezzi vivi: erano ossa con deboli scintille al loro interno.

Nem voltak félig élők – csontok voltak, bennük halvány szikrák csillogtak.

Una volta fermati, crollarono come cadaveri, con le scintille quasi del tutto spente.

Amikor megálltak, holttestekként rogytak össze, szikráik szinte kialudtak.

E quando la frusta o il bastone colpivano di nuovo, le scintille sfarfallavano debolmente.

És amikor az ostor vagy a bot újra lecsapott, a szikrák gyengén lobogtak.

Poi si alzarono, barcollarono in avanti e trascinarono le loro membra in avanti.

Aztán felálltak, előretántorodtak, és a végtagjaikat vonszolva maguk után indultak.

Un giorno il gentile Billee cadde e non riuscì più a rialzarsi.

Egy nap a kedves Billee elesett, és már egyáltalán nem tudott felkelni.

Hal aveva scambiato la sua pistola con quella di Billee, così decise di ucciderla con un'ascia.

Hal elcserélte a revolverét, ezért inkább egy fejszével ölte meg Billee-t.

**Lo colpì alla testa, poi gli tagliò il corpo e lo trascinò via.**

Fejbe ütötte, majd levágta a testét és elhurcolta.

**Buck se ne accorse, e così fecero anche gli altri: sapevano che la morte era vicina.**

Buck látta ezt, és a többiek is; tudták, hogy a halál közeleg.

**Il giorno dopo Koona se ne andò, lasciando solo cinque cani nel gruppo affamato.**

Másnap Koona elment, és csak öt kutyát hagyott maga után az éhező csapatban.

**Joe, non più cattivo, era ormai troppo fuori di sé per rendersi conto di nulla.**

Joe, aki már nem volt gonosz, túl messzire ment ahhoz, hogy bármiről is tudomást vegyen.

**Pike, ormai non fingeva più di essere ferito, era appena cosciente.**

Pike, már nem színlelte a sérülését, alig volt eszméleténél.

**Solleks, ancora fedele, si rammaricava di non avere più la forza di dare.**

A hűséges Solleks gyászolta, hogy nincs ereje adni.

**Teek fu battuto più di tutti perché era più fresco, ma stava calando rapidamente.**

Teeket azért verték meg leginkább, mert frissebb volt, de gyorsan fogyott.

**E Buck, ancora in testa, non mantenne più l'ordine né lo fece rispettare.**

És Buck, aki továbbra is az élen járt, már nem tartotta fenn a rendet, és nem is érvényesítette azt.

**Mezzo accecato dalla debolezza, Buck seguì la pista solo a tentoni.**

Buck félig vakon, gyengeségtől tátva, egyedül az érzésekre hagyatkozva követte a nyomokat.

**Era una bellissima primavera, ma nessuno di loro se ne accorse.**

Gyönyörű tavaszi idő volt, de egyikük sem vette észre.

**Ogni giorno il sole sorgeva prima e tramontava più tardi.**

Minden nap korábban kelt és később nyugodott a nap, mint
azelőtt.
**Alle tre del mattino era già spuntata l'alba; il crepuscolo
durò fino alle nove.**
Hajnali háromra megvirradt; az alkonyat kilencig tartott.
**Le lunghe giornate erano illuminate dal sole primaverile.**
A hosszú napokat a tavaszi napsütés teljes ragyogása töltötte
be.
**Il silenzio spettrale dell'inverno si era trasformato in un
caldo mormorio.**
A tél kísérteties csendje meleg morajlássá változott.
**Tutta la terra si stava svegliando, animata dalla gioia degli
esseri viventi.**
Az egész föld ébredezett, az élő dolgok örömétől elevenedett.
**Il suono proveniva da ciò che era rimasto morto e immobile
per tutto l'inverno.**
A hang onnan jött, ami halottan és mozdulatlanul feküdt
egész télen át.
**Ora quelle cose si mossero di nuovo, scrollandosi di dosso il
lungo sonno del gelo.**
Most azok a dolgok újra megmozdultak, lerázva magukról a
hosszú, fagyos álmot.
**La linfa saliva attraverso i tronchi scuri dei pini in attesa.**
Nedv szállt fel a várakozó fenyőfák sötét törzsei közül.
**Salici e pioppi tremuli fanno sbocciare giovani gemme
luminose su ogni ramoscello.**
A fűzfák és a nyárfák minden ágon fényes fiatal rügyeket
hoznak.
**Arbusti e viti si tingono di un verde fresco mentre il bosco si
anima.**
A cserjék és indák friss zöldelltek, ahogy az erdő életre kelt.
**Di notte i grilli cantavano e di giorno gli insetti strisciavano
nella luce del sole.**
Éjszaka tücskök ciripeltek, nappali fényben bogarak
mászkáltak.
**Le pernici gridavano e i picchi picchiavano in profondità tra
gli alberi.**

Foglyok dübörögtek, és harkályok kopogtak a fák mélyén.
**Gli scoiattoli chiacchieravano, gli uccelli cantavano e le oche starnazzavano per richiamare l'attenzione dei cani.**
Mókusok csicseregtek, madarak énekeltek, és libák kürtöltek a kutyák felett.
**Gli uccelli selvatici arrivavano a cunei affilati, volando in alto da sud.**
A vadmadarak éles ékekben repültek dél felől.
**Da ogni pendio giungeva la musica di ruscelli nascosti e impetuosi.**
Minden domboldalról rejtett, sebesen csobogó patakok zenéje hallatszott.
**Tutto si scongelava e si spezzava, si piegava e ricominciava a muoversi.**
Minden felengedett, eltört, meggörbült, majd újra mozgásba lendült.
**Lo Yukon si sforzò di spezzare le fredde catene del ghiaccio ghiacciato.**
A Yukon erőlködve próbálta megtörni a megfagyott jég hidegláncait.
**Il ghiaccio si scioglieva sotto, mentre il sole lo scioglieva dall'alto.**
A jég alul elolvadt, míg felülről a nap olvasztotta.
**Si aprirono dei buchi, si allargarono delle crepe e dei pezzi caddero nel fiume.**
Szellőzőlyukak nyíltak meg, repedések terjedtek, és darabok hullottak a folyóba.
**In mezzo a tutta questa vita sfrenata e sfrenata, i viaggiatori barcollavano.**
E pezsgő és lángoló élet közepette az utazók tántorogtak.
**Due uomini, una donna e un branco di husky camminavano come morti.**
Két férfi, egy nő és egy husky falka úgy sétálgatott, mint a halottak.
**I cani cadevano, Mercedes piangeva, ma continuava a guidare la slitta.**

A kutyák hullottak, Mercedes sírt, de azért még mindig szánkózott.

**Hal imprecò debolmente e Charles sbatté le palpebre con gli occhi lacrimanti.**

Hal erőtlenül káromkodott, Charles pedig könnyező szemekkel pislogott.

**Si imbatterono nell'accampamento di John Thornton, nei pressi della foce del White River.**

Belebotlottak John Thornton táborába White River torkolatánál.

**Quando si fermarono, i cani caddero a terra, come se fossero stati tutti colpiti a morte.**

Amikor megálltak, a kutyák hanyatt estek, mintha mind meghaltak volna.

**Mercedes si asciugò le lacrime e guardò John Thornton.**

Mercedes letörölte a könnyeit, és John Thorntonra nézett.

**Charles si sedette su un tronco, lentamente e rigidamente, dolorante per il sentiero.**

Károly egy rönkön ült, lassan és mereven, sajgott az ösvénytől.

**Hal parlava mentre Thornton intagliava l'estremità del manico di un'ascia.**

Hal beszélt helyette, miközben Thornton egy fejsze nyelének végét faragta.

**Tagliò il legno di betulla e rispose con frasi brevi e decise.**

Nyírfát faragva rövid, határozott válaszokat adott.

**Quando gli veniva chiesto, dava un consiglio, certo che non sarebbe stato seguito.**

Amikor megkérdezték, tanácsot adott, biztos volt benne, hogy azt nem fogják betartani.

**Hal spiegò: "Ci avevano detto che il ghiaccio lungo la pista si stava staccando".**

Hal elmagyarázta: „Azt mondták nekünk, hogy a jég elkezd olvadni az ösvényen."

**"Ci avevano detto che dovevamo restare fermi, ma siamo arrivati a White River."**

„Azt mondták, maradjunk otthon – de eljutottunk White Riverbe."

Concluse con un tono beffardo, come per cantare vittoria nelle difficoltà.

Gúnyos hangon fejezte be, mintha a nehézségek közepette aratott győzelmet.

"E ti hanno detto la verità", rispose John Thornton a bassa voce ad Hal.

– És igazat mondtak neked – felelte John Thornton halkan Halnak.

"Il ghiaccio potrebbe cedere da un momento all'altro: è pronto a staccarsi."

„A jég bármikor megadhatja magát – készen áll a leválásra."

"Solo la fortuna cieca e gli sciocchi avrebbero potuto arrivare vivi fin qui."

„Csak a vakszerencse és a bolondok juthattak el idáig élve."

"Te lo dico senza mezzi termini: non rischierei la vita per tutto l'oro dell'Alaska."

„Őszintén megmondom, hogy Alaszka összes aranyáért sem kockáztatnám az életemet."

"Immagino che tu non sia uno stupido", rispose Hal.

– Gondolom, azért, mert nem vagy bolond – felelte Hal.

"Comunque, andiamo avanti con Dawson." Srotolò la frusta.

– Mindegy, megyünk tovább Dawsonba. – Kibontotta az ostorát.

"Sali, Buck! Ehi! Alzati! Forza!" urlò con voce roca.

„Menj fel, Buck! Szia! Kelj fel! Rajta!" – kiáltotta rekedten.

Thornton continuò a intagliare, sapendo che gli sciocchi non volevano sentire ragioni.

Thornton tovább faragta a dolgokat, tudván, hogy a bolondok nem hallják meg az észt.

Fermare uno stupido era inutile, e due o tre stupidi non cambiavano nulla.

Egy bolondot megállítani hiábavaló volt – és két-három bolond semmit sem változtatott.

Ma la squadra non si mosse al suono del comando di Hal.

De a csapat nem mozdult Hal parancsára.

Ormai solo i colpi potevano farli sollevare e avanzare.

Mostanra már csak ütésekkel tudták őket felkelni és előrehúzni.

**La frusta schioccava ripetutamente sui cani indeboliti.**

Az ostor újra meg újra csattant a legyengült kutyákon.

**John Thornton strinse forte le labbra e osservò in silenzio.**

John Thornton összeszorította a száját, és csendben figyelt.

**Solleks fu il primo a rialzarsi sotto la frusta.**

Solleks volt az első, aki talpra állt a korbácsütés alatt.

**Poi Teek lo seguì, tremando. Joe urlò mentre barcollava.**

Teek remegve követte. Joe felkiáltott, ahogy felbotlott.

**Pike cercò di alzarsi, fallì due volte, poi alla fine si rialzò barcollando.**

Pike megpróbált felállni, kétszer is kudarcot vallott, majd végül bizonytalanul állt.

**Ma Buck rimase lì dov'era caduto, senza muoversi affatto.**

De Buck ott feküdt, ahol elesett, és ezalatt egy pillanatig sem mozdult.

**La frusta lo colpì più volte, ma lui non emise alcun suono.**

Az ostor újra meg újra lecsapott rá, de nem adott ki hangot.

**Lui non sussultò né oppose resistenza, rimase semplicemente immobile e in silenzio.**

Nem hátrált meg, nem ellenkezett, egyszerűen mozdulatlan és csendben maradt.

**Thornton si mosse più di una volta, come per dire qualcosa, ma non lo fece.**

Thornton többször is megmozdult, mintha beszélni akarna, de nem tette.

**I suoi occhi si inumidirono, ma la frusta continuava a schioccare contro Buck.**

Könnyek szöktek a szemébe, és az ostor még mindig csapkodott Buckra.

**Alla fine Thornton cominciò a camminare lentamente, incerto sul da farsi.**

Thornton végül lassan járkálni kezdett, bizonytalanul, hogy mitévő legyen.

**Era la prima volta che Buck falliva e Hal si infuriò.**

Ez volt az első alkalom. hogy Buck kudarcot vallott, és Hal dühbe gurult.

**Gettò via la frusta e prese al suo posto il pesante manganello.**

Lehajította az ostort, és helyette a nehéz botot vette fel.

**La mazza di legno colpì con violenza, ma Buck non si alzò per muoversi.**

A fabunkó keményen lecsapódott, de Buck még mindig nem kelt fel, hogy megmozduljon.

**Come i suoi compagni di squadra, era troppo debole, ma non solo.**

Csapattársaihoz hasonlóan ő is túl gyenge volt – de ennél több.

**Buck aveva deciso di non muoversi, qualunque cosa accadesse.**

Buck úgy döntött, hogy nem mozdul, bármi is történjék ezután.

**Sentì qualcosa di oscuro e sicuro incombere proprio davanti a sé.**

Érezte, hogy valami sötét és biztos dolog lebeg közvetlenül előtte.

**Quel terrore lo aveva colto non appena aveva raggiunto la riva del fiume.**

A félelem azonnal elfogta, amint a folyópartra ért.

**Quella sensazione non lo aveva abbandonato da quando aveva sentito il ghiaccio assottigliarsi sotto le zampe.**

Az érzés nem múlt el belőle, mióta vékony jeget érzett a mancsai alatt.

**Qualcosa di terribile lo stava aspettando: lo sentiva proprio lungo il sentiero.**

Valami szörnyűség várt rá – érezte már az ösvényen.

**Non avrebbe camminato verso quella cosa terribile davanti a lui**

Nem fog az előtte álló szörnyűség felé sétálni

**Non avrebbe obbedito a nessun ordine che lo avrebbe condotto a quella cosa.**

Nem fog engedelmeskedni semmilyen parancsnak, ami odavitte.

**Ormai il dolore dei colpi non lo sfiorava più: era troppo stanco.**

Az ütések fájdalma már alig érintette – túl messze volt.

**La scintilla della vita tremolava lentamente, affievolita da ogni colpo crudele.**

Az élet szikrája halványan pislákolt, minden kegyetlen csapás alatt elhalványyult.

**Gli arti gli sembravano distanti; tutto il corpo sembrava appartenere a un altro.**

Végtagjai távolinak tűntek; az egész teste mintha valaki másé lett volna.

**Sentì uno strano torpore mentre il dolore scompariva completamente.**

Furcsa zsibbadást érzett, ahogy a fájdalom teljesen elmúlt.

**Da lontano, sentiva che lo stavano picchiando, ma non se ne rendeva conto.**

Már messziről érezte, hogy verik, de alig tudta.

**Poteva udire debolmente i tonfi, ma ormai non gli facevano più male.**

Halványan hallotta a puffanásokat, de már nem fájtak igazán.

**I colpi andarono a segno, ma il suo corpo non sembrava più il suo.**

Az ütések becsapódtak, de a teste már nem tűnt a sajátjának.

**Poi, all'improvviso, senza alcun preavviso, John Thornton lanciò un grido selvaggio.**

Aztán hirtelen, minden előzetes figyelmeztetés nélkül, John Thornton vad kiáltást hallatott.

**Era inarticolato, più il grido di una bestia che di un uomo.**

Artikulálatlan volt, inkább egy állat, mint egy ember kiáltása.

**Si lanciò sull'uomo con la mazza e fece cadere Hal all'indietro.**

Ráugrott a bottal szorongatott férfira, és hátralökte Halt.

**Hal volò come se fosse stato colpito da un albero, atterrando pesantemente al suolo.**

Hal úgy repült, mintha egy fa csapódott volna belé, és keményen a földre zuhant.

**Mercedes urlò a gran voce in preda al panico e si portò le mani al viso.**

Mercedes pánikba esve hangosan felsikoltott, és az arcához kapott.

**Charles si limitò a guardare, si asciugò gli occhi e rimase seduto.**

Károly csak nézte, megtörölte a szemét, és ülve maradt.

**Il suo corpo era troppo irrigidito dal dolore per alzarsi o contribuire alla lotta.**

A teste túl merev volt a fájdalomtól ahhoz, hogy felálljon vagy segítsen a harcban.

**Thornton era in piedi davanti a Buck, tremante di rabbia, incapace di parlare.**

Thornton Buck felett állt, dühösen remegett, és képtelen volt megszólalni.

**Tremava di rabbia e lottò per trovare la voce.**

Dühösen remegett, és küzdött, hogy megtalálja a hangját a dühöngésen keresztül.

**"Se colpisci ancora quel cane, ti uccido", disse infine.**

– Ha még egyszer megütöd azt a kutyát, megöllek – mondta végül.

**Hal si asciugò il sangue dalla bocca e tornò avanti.**

Hal letörölte a vért a szájáról, és ismét előrelépett.

**"È il mio cane", borbottò. "Togliti di mezzo o ti sistemo io."**

– A kutyám az – motyogta. – Menj az útból, különben elintézem!

**"Vado da Dawson e tu non mi fermerai", ha aggiunto.**

„Dawsonba megyek, és te nem fogsz megállítani" – tette hozzá.

**Thornton si fermò tra Buck e il giovane arrabbiato.**

Thornton szilárdan állt Buck és a dühös fiatalember között.

**Non aveva alcuna intenzione di farsi da parte o di lasciar passare Hal.**

Esze ágában sem volt félreállni, vagy Halt elengedni.

Hal tirò fuori il suo coltello da caccia, lungo e pericoloso nella sua mano.

Hal előhúzta a kezében hosszú és veszélyes vadászkését.

Mercedes urlò, poi pianse, poi rise in preda a un'isteria selvaggia.

Mercedes sikított, majd sírt, végül vad hisztérikus nevetésben tört ki.

Thornton colpì la mano di Hal con il manico dell'ascia, con forza e rapidità.

Thornton fejszéje nyelével erősen és gyorsan Hal kezére csapott.

Il coltello si liberò dalla presa di Hal e volò a terra.

A kés kiesett Hal markából, és a földre repült.

Hal cercò di raccogliere il coltello, ma Thornton gli batté di nuovo le nocche.

Hal megpróbálta felvenni a kést, de Thornton ismét rácsapott az ujjperceire.

Poi Thornton si chinò, afferrò il coltello e lo tenne fermo.

Aztán Thornton lehajolt, megragadta a kést, és a kezében tartotta.

Con due rapidi colpi del manico dell'ascia, tagliò le redini di Buck.

Két gyors csapással elvágta Buck gyeplőjét a fejsze nyelével.

Hal non aveva più voglia di combattere e si allontanò dal cane.

Halnak már nem volt harci kedve, és hátralépett a kutya elől.

Inoltre, ora Mercedes aveva bisogno di entrambe le braccia per restare in piedi.

Különben is, Mercedesnek most már mindkét karjára szüksége volt, hogy egyenesen maradjon.

Buck era troppo vicino alla morte per poter nuovamente tirare la slitta.

Buck túl közel volt a halálhoz ahhoz, hogy újra hasznos legyen szánhúzásra.

Pochi minuti dopo, ripartirono, dirigendosi verso il fiume.

Néhány perccel később kifutottak, és lefelé indultak a folyón.

**Buck sollevò debolmente la testa e li guardò lasciare la banca.**

Buck gyengén felemelte a fejét, és nézte, ahogy elhagyják a bankot.

**Pike guidava la squadra, con Solleks dietro al volante.**

Pike vezette a csapatot, Solleks pedig hátul a keréken.

**Joe e Teek camminavano in mezzo, zoppicando entrambi per la stanchezza.**

Joe és Teek közöttük sétáltak, mindketten kimerülten sántikáltak.

**Mercedes si sedette sulla slitta e Hal afferrò la lunga pertica.**

Mercedes a szánkón ült, Hal pedig a hosszú gearbotet szorongatta.

**Charles barcollava dietro di lui, con passi goffi e incerti.**

Károly botladozva hátulról lépett, léptei esetlenek és bizonytalanok voltak.

**Thornton si inginocchiò accanto a Buck e tastò delicatamente per vedere se aveva ossa rotte.**

Thornton letérdelt Buck mellé, és gyengéden kitapogatta, hogy nincs-e eltört csontja.

**Le sue mani erano ruvide, ma si muovevano con gentilezza e cura.**

A kezei érdesek voltak, de kedvesen és gondosan mozogtak.

**Il corpo di Buck era pieno di lividi, ma non presentava lesioni permanenti.**

Buck teste zúzódásokkal volt tele, de maradandó sérülés nem látszott rajta.

**Ciò che restava era una fame terribile e una debolezza quasi totale.**

Ami maradt, az a szörnyű éhség és a szinte teljes gyengeség volt.

**Quando la situazione fu più chiara, la slitta era già andata molto a valle.**

Mire ez kitisztult, a szán már messzire lejjebb ment a folyón.

**L'uomo e il cane osservavano la slitta avanzare lentamente sul ghiaccio che si rompeva.**

Férfi és kutya nézték, ahogy a szán lassan kúszik a repedező jégen.

**Poi videro la slitta sprofondare in una cavità.**

Aztán látták, hogy a szánkó belesüllyed egy mélyedésbe.

**La pertica volò in alto, ma Hal vi si aggrappò ancora invano.**

A gearbota felrepült, Hal pedig hiába kapaszkodott bele.

**L'urlo di Mercedes li raggiunse attraverso la fredda distanza.**

Mercedes sikolyát a hideg messzeségen át hallhatták.

**Charles si voltò e fece un passo indietro, ma era troppo tardi.**

Károly megfordult és hátralépett – de már túl késő volt.

**Un'intera calotta di ghiaccio cedette e tutti precipitarono.**

Egy egész jégtakaró leomlott, és mindannyian átestek rajta.

**Cani, slitte e persone scomparvero nelle acque nere sottostanti.**

Kutyák, szánkók és emberek tűntek el a lenti fekete vízben.

**Nel punto in cui erano passati era rimasto solo un largo buco nel ghiaccio.**

Csak egy széles lyuk maradt a jégben ott, ahol elhaladtak.

**Il fondo del sentiero era crollato, proprio come aveva previsto Thornton.**

Az ösvény alja leszakadt – pontosan ahogy Thornton figyelmeztette.

**Thornton e Buck si guardarono l'un l'altro, in silenzio per un momento.**

Thornton és Buck egymásra néztek, egy pillanatig hallgattak.

**"Povero diavolo", disse Thornton dolcemente, e Buck gli leccò la mano.**

– Szegény ördög! – mondta Thornton halkan, mire Buck megnyalta a kezét.

## Per amore di un uomo
Egy férfi szerelmére


John Thornton si congelò i piedi per il freddo del dicembre precedente.

John Thorntonnak megfagyott a lába az előző decemberi hidegben.

I suoi compagni lo fecero sentire a suo agio e lo lasciarono guarire da solo.

Partnerei kényelembe helyezték, és magára hagyták a felépülést.

Risalirono il fiume per raccogliere una zattera di tronchi da sega per Dawson.

Felmentek a folyón, hogy fűrészrönköt gyűjtsenek Dawsonnak.

Zoppicava ancora leggermente quando salvò Buck dalla morte.

Még enyhén sántított, amikor megmentette Buckot a haláltól.

Ma con il persistere del caldo, anche quella zoppia è scomparsa.

De a meleg idő folytatódásával még ez a sántítás is eltűnt.

Sdraiato sulla riva del fiume durante le lunghe giornate primaverili, Buck si riposò.

Buck a hosszú tavaszi napokon a folyóparton fekve pihent.

Osservava l'acqua che scorreva e ascoltava gli uccelli e gli insetti.

Nézte a folyó vizet, és hallgatta a madarakat és rovarokat.

Lentamente Buck riacquistò le forze sotto il sole e il cielo.

Buck lassan visszanyerte erejét a nap és az ég alatt.

Dopo aver viaggiato tremila miglia, riposarsi è stato meraviglioso.

Csodálatosan éreztem magam pihenve háromezer mérföldes utazás után.

Buck diventò pigro man mano che le sue ferite guarivano e il suo corpo si riempiva.

Buck ellustult, ahogy a sebei begyógyultak és a teste kiteljesedett.

**I suoi muscoli si rassodarono e la carne tornò a ricoprire le sue ossa.**

Izmai megfeszültek, és hús borította vissza csontjait.

**Stavano tutti riposando: Buck, Thornton, Skeet e Nig.**

Mindannyian pihentek – Buck, Thornton, Skeet és Nig.

**Aspettarono la zattera che li avrebbe portati a Dawson.**

Várták a tutajt, amivel levitték őket Dawsonba.

**Skeet era un piccolo setter irlandese che fece amicizia con Buck.**

Skeet egy kis ír szetter volt, aki összebarátkozott Buckkal.

**Buck era troppo debole e malato per resisterle al loro primo incontro.**

Buck túl gyenge és beteg volt ahhoz, hogy ellenálljon neki az első találkozásukkor.

**Skeet aveva la caratteristica di guaritore che alcuni cani possiedono per natura.**

Skeetnek megvolt az a gyógyító tulajdonsága, ami egyes kutyákban természetes módon megvan.

**Come una gatta, leccò e pulì le ferite aperte di Buck.**

Mint egy anyamacska, nyalogatta és tisztogatta Buck sebeit.

**Ogni mattina, dopo colazione, ripeteva il suo attento lavoro.**

Reggeli után minden reggel megismételte gondos munkáját.

**Buck finì per aspettarsi il suo aiuto tanto quanto quello di Thornton.**

Buck ugyanúgy számított a segítségére, mint Thorntonéra.

**Anche Nig era amichevole, ma meno aperto e meno affettuoso.**

Nig is barátságos volt, de kevésbé nyitott és kevésbé szeretetteljes.

**Nig era un grosso cane nero, in parte segugio e in parte levriero.**

Nig egy nagy fekete kutya volt, részben véreb, részben szarvaseb.

**Aveva occhi sorridenti e un'infinita bontà d'animo.**

Nevető szemek és végtelen jó természet lakozott a lelkében.

**Con sorpresa di Buck, nessuno dei due cani mostrò gelosia nei suoi confronti.**

Buck meglepetésére egyik kutya sem mutatott féltékenységet iránta.

**Sia Skeet che Nig condividevano la gentilezza di John Thornton.**

Skeet és Nig is osztoztak John Thornton kedvességében.

**Man mano che Buck diventava più forte, lo attiravano in stupidi giochi da cani.**

Ahogy Buck egyre erősebb lett, bolondos kutyajátékokba csábították.

**Anche Thornton giocava spesso con loro, incapace di resistere alla loro gioia.**

Thornton is gyakran játszott velük, képtelen volt ellenállni az örömüknek.

**In questo modo giocoso, Buck passò dalla malattia a una nuova vita.**

Ezzel a játékos módon Buck a betegségből egy új életbe lépett.

**L'amore, quello vero, ardente e passionale, era finalmente suo.**

A szerelem – az igaz, lángoló és szenvedélyes szerelem – végre az övé volt.

**Non aveva mai conosciuto questo tipo di amore nella tenuta di Miller.**

Soha nem ismert ilyen szeretetet Miller birtokán.

**Con i figli del giudice aveva condiviso lavoro e avventure.**

A Bíró fiaival közös munkát és kalandot élt át.

**Nei nipoti notò un orgoglio rigido e vanitoso.**

Az unokáknál merev és kérkedő büszkeséget látott.

**Con lo stesso giudice Miller aveva un rapporto di rispettosa amicizia.**

Magával Miller bíróval tiszteletteljes barátságot ápolt.

**Ma l'amore che era fuoco, follia e adorazione era ciò che accadeva con Thornton.**

De a szerelem, ami tűz, őrület és imádat volt, Thorntonnal érkezett.

**Quest'uomo aveva salvato la vita di Buck, e questo di per sé significava molto.**

Ez az ember megmentette Buck életét, és már önmagában ez is sokat jelentett.

**Ma più di questo, John Thornton era il tipo ideale di maestro.**

De mi több, John Thornton volt az ideális fajta mester.

**Altri uomini si prendevano cura dei cani per dovere o per necessità lavorative.**

Más férfiak kötelességből vagy üzleti szükségszerűségből gondoskodtak kutyákról.

**John Thornton si prendeva cura dei suoi cani come se fossero figli.**

John Thornton úgy gondoskodott a kutyáiról, mintha a gyermekei lennének.

**Si prendeva cura di loro perché li amava e semplicemente non poteva farne a meno.**

Törődött velük, mert szerette őket, és egyszerűen nem tehetett mást.

**John Thornton vide molto più lontano di quanto la maggior parte degli uomini riuscisse mai a vedere.**

John Thornton még messzebbre látott, mint a legtöbb férfi valaha is képes volt látni.

**Non dimenticava mai di salutarli gentilmente o di pronunciare una parola di incoraggiamento.**

Soha nem felejtette el kedvesen üdvözölni őket, vagy egy bátorító szót szólni.

**Amava sedersi con i cani per fare lunghe chiacchierate, o "gassy", come diceva lui.**

Imádott leülni a kutyákkal hosszas beszélgetésekre, vagy ahogy ő mondta, „gázoskodni".

**Gli piaceva afferrare bruscamente la testa di Buck tra le sue mani forti.**

Szerette durván megragadni Buck fejét erős kezei között.

**Poi appoggiò la testa contro quella di Buck e lo scosse delicatamente.**

Aztán a fejét Buckéhoz hajtotta, és gyengéden megrázta.

**Nel frattempo, chiamava Buck con nomi volgari che per lui significavano affetto.**

Mindeközben durva szavakkal illette Buckot, amik a szerelmet jelentették számára.

**Per Buck, quell'abbraccio rude e quelle parole portarono una gioia profonda.**

Buck számára az a durva ölelés és azok a szavak mély örömet okoztak.

**A ogni movimento il suo cuore sembrava sussultare di felicità.**

A szíve minden mozdulatnál felszabadultan remegett a boldogságtól.

**Quando poi balzò in piedi, la sua bocca sembrava ridere.**

Amikor utána felugrott, úgy nézett ki a szája, mintha nevetett volna.

**I suoi occhi brillavano intensamente e la sua gola tremava per una gioia inespressa.**

Szeme ragyogott, torka pedig remegett a kimondatlan örömtől.

**Il suo sorriso rimase immobile in quello stato di emozione e affetto ardente.**

Mosolya mozdulatlanná dermedt az érzelmek és a ragyogó szeretet közepette.

**Allora Thornton esclamò pensieroso: "Dio! Riesce quasi a parlare!"**

Thornton ekkor elgondolkodva felkiáltott: „Istenem! Majdnem tud beszélni!"

**Buck aveva uno strano modo di esprimere l'amore che quasi gli causava dolore.**

Bucknak furcsa, szinte fájdalmat okozó módja volt a szeretet kifejezésére.

**Spesso stringeva forte la mano di Thornton tra i denti.**

Gyakran nagyon erősen szorította Thornton kezét a fogai közé.

**Il morso avrebbe lasciato segni profondi che sarebbero rimasti per qualche tempo.**

A harapás mély nyomokat hagyott, amelyek egy ideig megmaradtak.

**Buck credeva che quei giuramenti fossero amore, e Thornton la pensava allo stesso modo.**

Buck hitte, hogy ezek az eskük a szerelem jelei, és Thornton is tudta ezt.

**Il più delle volte, l'amore di Buck si manifestava in un'adorazione silenziosa, quasi silenziosa.**

Buck szerelme leggyakrabban csendes, szinte néma imádatban nyilvánult meg.

**Sebbene fosse emozionato quando veniva toccato o gli si parlava, non cercava attenzione.**

Bár izgatott volt, ha megérintették vagy beszéltek hozzá, nem kereste a figyelmet.

**Skeet spinse il naso sotto la mano di Thornton finché lui non la accarezzò.**

Skeet addig bökte az orrát Thornton keze alá, amíg az meg nem simogatta.

**Nig si avvicinò silenziosamente e appoggiò la sua grande testa sulle ginocchia di Thornton.**

Nig csendesen odalépett, és nagy fejét Thornton térdére hajtotta.

**Buck, al contrario, si accontentava di amare da una rispettosa distanza.**

Buck ezzel szemben megelégedett azzal, hogy tiszteletteljes távolságból szeressen.

**Rimase sdraiato per ore ai piedi di Thornton, vigile e attento.**

Órákon át feküdt Thornton lábánál, éber és feszült figyelő tekintettel.

**Buck studiò ogni dettaglio del volto del suo padrone, perfino il più piccolo movimento.**

Buck gazdája arcának minden részletét, a legkisebb mozdulatát is alaposan szemügyre vette.

**Oppure sdraiati più lontano, studiando in silenzio la sagoma dell'uomo.**

Vagy távolabb feküdt, csendben tanulmányozva a férfi alakját.

**Buck osservava ogni piccolo movimento, ogni cambiamento di postura o di gesto.**

Buck minden apró mozdulatot, minden testtartás- vagy gesztusváltást figyelt.

**Questo legame era così potente che spesso catturava lo sguardo di Thornton.**

Olyan erős volt ez a kapcsolat, hogy gyakran magára vonta Thornton tekintetét.

**Incontrò lo sguardo di Buck senza dire parole, e il suo amore traspariva chiaramente.**

Szótlanul nézett Buck szemébe, a szerelem tisztán ragyogott benne.

**Per molto tempo dopo essere stato salvato, Buck non perse mai di vista Thornton.**

Miután megmentették, Buck sokáig nem tévesztette szem elől Thorntont.

**Ogni volta che Thornton usciva dalla tenda, Buck lo seguiva da vicino all'esterno.**

Valahányszor Thornton elhagyta a sátrat, Buck szorosan követte kifelé.

**Tutti i severi padroni delle Terre del Nord avevano fatto sì che Buck non riuscisse più a fidarsi.**

Észak minden kemény ura miatt Buck félt bízni bennük.

**Temeva che nessun uomo potesse restare suo padrone se non per un breve periodo.**

Attól félt, hogy senki sem maradhat az ura egy rövid időnél tovább.

**Temeva che John Thornton sarebbe scomparso come Perrault e François.**

Attól félt, hogy John Thornton úgy fog eltűnni, mint Perrault és François.

**Anche di notte, la paura di perderlo tormentava il sonno agitato di Buck.**

Még éjszaka is kísértette Buck nyugtalan álmát az elvesztésétől való félelem.

**Quando Buck si svegliò, si trascinò fuori al freddo e andò nella tenda.**

Amikor Buck felébredt, kimászott a hidegbe, és elment a sátorhoz.

**Ascoltò attentamente il leggero suono del suo respiro interiore.**

Figyelmesen hallgatózott, hallja-e belülről a halk légzést.

**Nonostante il profondo amore di Buck per John Thornton, la natura selvaggia sopravvisse.**

Buck John Thornton iránti mély szeretete ellenére a vadon életben maradt.

**Quell'istinto primitivo, risvegliatosi nel Nord, non scomparve.**

Az északon felébredt primitív ösztön nem tűnt el.

**L'amore portava devozione, lealtà e il caldo legame attorno al fuoco.**

A szerelem odaadást, hűséget és a tűz melletti meleg köteléket hozott magával.

**Ma Buck mantenne anche i suoi istinti selvaggi, acuti e sempre all'erta.**

De Buck megőrizte vad ösztöneit is, melyek élesek és örökké éberek voltak.

**Non era solo un animale domestico addomesticato proveniente dalle dolci terre della civiltà.**

Nem csupán egy megszelídített háziállat volt a civilizáció puha földjeiről.

**Buck era un essere selvaggio che si era seduto accanto al fuoco di Thornton.**

Buck vad teremtmény volt, aki Thornton tüzéhez jött leülni.

**Sembrava un cane del Southland, ma in lui albergava la natura selvaggia.**

Úgy nézett ki, mint egy délvidéki kutya, de vadság lakozott benne.

**Il suo amore per Thornton era troppo grande per permettersi un furto da parte di quell'uomo.**

Túl nagy volt a szerelme Thornton iránt ahhoz, hogy megengedje magának a lopást.

**Ma in qualsiasi altro campo ruberebbe con audacia e senza esitazione.**

De bármely más táborban bátran és szünet nélkül lopott volna.

**Era così abile nel rubare che nessuno riusciva a catturarlo o accusarlo.**

Olyan ravasz volt a lopásban, hogy senki sem tudta elkapni vagy megvádolni.

**Il suo viso e il suo corpo erano coperti di cicatrici dovute a molti combattimenti passati.**

Arcát és testét számos korábbi harc hegei borították.

**Buck continuava a combattere con ferocia, ma ora lo faceva con maggiore astuzia.**

Buck továbbra is hevesen küzdött, de most már ravaszabb módon.

**Skeet e Nig erano troppo docili per combattere, ed erano di Thornton.**

Skeet és Nig túl gyengédek voltak ahhoz, hogy harcoljanak, és ők Thorntonéi voltak.

**Ma qualsiasi cane estraneo, non importa quanto forte o coraggioso, cedeva.**

De minden idegen kutya, bármilyen erős vagy bátor is, megadta magát.

**Altrimenti, il cane si ritrovò a combattere contro Buck, lottando per la propria vita.**

Különben a kutya Buckkal küzdött; az életéért küzdött.

**Buck non ebbe pietà quando decise di combattere contro un altro cane.**

Buck nem volt irgalmas, miután úgy döntött, hogy egy másik kutyával harcol.

**Aveva imparato bene la legge del bastone e della zanna nel Nord.**

Jól elsajátította az északi fánk és agyar szabályát.

**Non ha mai rinunciato a un vantaggio e non si è mai tirato indietro dalla battaglia.**

Soha nem adott fel előnyt, és soha nem hátrált meg a csatában.

**Aveva studiato Spitz e i cani più feroci della polizia e della posta.**

Tanulmányozta a spitzeket és a legvadabb posta- és rendőrkutyákat.

Sapeva chiaramente che non esisteva via di mezzo in un combattimento selvaggio.

Világosan tudta, hogy a vad harcban nincs középút.

Doveva governare o essere governato; mostrare misericordia significava mostrare debolezza.

Uralkodnia kellett, vagy őt uralták; az irgalom kimutatása gyengeséget jelentett.

La pietà era sconosciuta nel mondo crudo e brutale della sopravvivenza.

A kegyelem ismeretlen volt a túlélés nyers és brutális világában.

Mostrare pietà era visto come un atto di paura, e la paura conduceva rapidamente alla morte.

Az irgalmasság kimutatása félelemnek számított, a félelem pedig gyorsan halálhoz vezetett.

La vecchia legge era semplice: uccidere o essere uccisi, mangiare o essere mangiati.

A régi törvény egyszerű volt: ölj vagy megölnek, egyél vagy megesznek.

Quella legge proveniva dalle profondità del tempo e Buck la seguì alla lettera.

Ez a törvény az idők mélyéről származik, és Buck teljes mértékben követte.

Buck era più vecchio dei suoi anni e del numero dei suoi respiri.

Buck idősebb volt a koránál és a lélegzetvételek számánál.

Collegava in modo chiaro il passato remoto con il momento presente.

Világosan összekapcsolta a régmúlt időket a jelennel.

I ritmi profondi dei secoli si muovevano attraverso di lui come le maree.

A korok mély ritmusai úgy kavarogtak benne, mint az árapály.

Il tempo pulsava nel suo sangue con la stessa sicurezza con cui le stagioni muovevano la terra.

Az idő olyan biztosan lüktetett a vérében, mint ahogy az évszakok mozgatták a földet.

Sedeva accanto al fuoco di Thornton, con il petto forte e le zanne bianche.

Thornton tüzénél ült, erős mellkassal és fehér agyarral.

La sua lunga pelliccia ondeggiava, ma dietro di lui lo osservavano gli spiriti dei cani selvatici.

Hosszú bundája lengedezett, de mögötte vadkutyák szellemei figyelték.

Lupi mezzi e lupi veri si agitavano nel suo cuore e nei suoi sensi.

Fél farkasok és teli farkasok kavarogtak a szívében és az érzékeiben.

Assaggiarono la sua carne e bevvero la stessa acqua che bevve lui.

Megkóstolták a húsát. és ugyanabból a vízből ittak, mint ő.

Annusarono il vento insieme a lui e ascoltarono la foresta.

Mellette szimatolták a szelet, és hallgatták az erdőt.

Sussurravano il significato dei suoni selvaggi nell'oscurità.

A vad hangok jelentését suttogták a sötétben.

Modellavano il suo umore e guidavano ciascuna delle sue reazioni silenziose.

Formálták a hangulatait és irányították minden csendes reakcióját.

Giacevano accanto a lui mentre dormiva e diventavano parte dei suoi sogni profondi.

Vele feküdtek, miközben aludt, és mély álmainak részévé váltak.

Sognavano con lui, oltre lui, e costituivano il suo stesso spirito.

Vele álmodtak, rajta túl, és alkották meg a lelkét.

Gli spiriti della natura selvaggia chiamavano con tanta forza che Buck si sentì attratto.

A vadon szellemei olyan erősen szóltak, hogy Buck úgy érezte, vonszolják.

Ogni giorno che passava, l'umanità e le sue rivendicazioni si indebolivano nel cuore di Buck.

Az emberiség és annak igényei napról napra gyengültek Buck szívében.

**Nel profondo della foresta si stava per udire un richiamo strano ed emozionante.**

Mélyen az erdőben egy furcsa és izgalmas hívás fog felhangzani.

**Ogni volta che sentiva la chiamata, Buck provava un impulso a cui non riusciva a resistere.**

Valahányszor meghallotta a hívást, Buck egy ellenállhatatlan késztetést érzett.

**Avrebbe voltato le spalle al fuoco e ai sentieri battuti dagli uomini.**

Elfordult a tűztől és a kitaposott emberi ösvényektől.

**Stava per addentrarsi nella foresta, avanzando senza sapere il perché.**

Be akart vetődni az erdőbe, előrement anélkül, hogy tudta volna, miért.

**Non mise in discussione questa attrazione, perché la chiamata era profonda e potente.**

Nem kérdőjelezte meg ezt a vonzást, mert a hívás mély és erőteljes volt.

**Spesso raggiungeva l'ombra verde e la terra morbida e intatta**

Gyakran elérte a zöld árnyékot és a puha, érintetlen földet

**Ma poi il forte amore per John Thornton lo riportò al fuoco.**

De aztán a John Thornton iránti erős szerelem visszarántotta a tűzhöz.

**Soltanto John Thornton riuscì davvero a tenere stretto il cuore selvaggio di Buck.**

Csak John Thornton tartotta igazán a markában Buck vad szívét.

**Per Buck il resto dell'umanità non aveva alcun valore o significato duraturo.**

Az emberiség többi részének nem volt maradandó értéke vagy jelentése Buck számára.

**Gli sconosciuti potrebbero lodarlo o accarezzargli la pelliccia con mani amichevoli.**

Az idegenek dicsérhetik, vagy barátságosan simogathatják a bundáját.

**Buck rimase impassibile e se ne andò per eccesso di affetto.**

Buck mozdulatlan maradt, és elsétált a túl sok szeretettől.

**Hans e Pete arrivarono con la zattera che era stata attesa a lungo**

Hans és Pete megérkeztek a régóta várt tutajjal

**Buck li ignorò finché non venne a sapere che erano vicini a Thornton.**

Buck nem törődött velük, amíg meg nem tudta, hogy Thornton közelében vannak.

**Da allora in poi li tollerò, ma non dimostrò mai loro tutto il suo calore.**

Ezután tolerálta őket, de soha nem mutatott teljes melegséget irántuk.

**Accettava da loro cibo o gentilezza come se volesse fare loro un favore.**

Úgy fogadott el tőlük ételt vagy kedvességet, mintha szívességet tenne nekik.

**Erano come Thornton: semplici, onesti e lucidi nei pensieri.**

Olyanok voltak, mint Thornton – egyszerűek, őszinték és világosan gondolkodtak. ·

**Tutti insieme viaggiarono verso la segheria di Dawson e il grande vortice**

Mindannyian együtt utaztak Dawson fűrészmalmához és a nagy örvényhez

**Nel corso del loro viaggio impararono a comprendere profondamente la natura di Buck.**

Útjuk során mélyen megértették Buck természetét.

**Non cercarono di avvicinarsi come avevano fatto Skeet e Nig.**

Nem próbáltak meg közeledni egymáshoz, ahogy Skeet és Nig tették.

**Ma l'amore di Buck per John Thornton non fece che aumentare con il tempo.**

De Buck John Thornton iránti szeretete az idő múlásával csak mélyült.

**Solo Thornton poteva mettere uno zaino sulla schiena di Buck durante l'estate.**

Csak Thornton tudott hátizsákot tenni Buck hátára nyáron.
**Buck era disposto a eseguire senza riserve qualsiasi ordine impartito da Thornton.**
Amit Thornton parancsolt, Buck hajlandó volt maradéktalanul teljesíteni.
**Un giorno, dopo aver lasciato Dawson per le sorgenti del Tanana,**
Egy nap, miután elhagyták Dawsont a Tanana forrásvidéke felé,
**il gruppo era seduto su una rupe che scendeva per un metro fino a raggiungere la nuda roccia.**
A csoport egy sziklán ült, amely egy méterrel a csupasz alapkőzetig ért.
**John Thornton si sedette vicino al bordo e Buck si riposò accanto a lui.**
John Thornton a szélén ült, Buck pedig mellette pihent.
**Thornton ebbe un'idea improvvisa e richiamò l'attenzione degli uomini.**
Thorntonnak hirtelen ötlete támadt, és felhívta a férfiak figyelmét.
**Indicò l'altro lato del baratro e diede a Buck un unico comando.**
Átmutatott a szakadékon, és egyetlen parancsot adott Bucknak.
**"Salta, Buck!" disse, allungando il braccio oltre il precipizio.**
„Ugorj, Buck!" – mondta, és kinyújtotta a karját a szakadék fölé.
**Un attimo dopo dovette afferrare Buck, che stava saltando per obbedire.**
Egy pillanat múlva el kellett kapnia Buckot, aki ugrott, hogy engedelmeskedjen.
**Hans e Pete si precipitarono in avanti e tirarono entrambi indietro per metterli in salvo.**
Hans és Pete előrerohantak, és mindkettőjüket biztonságba húzták.
**Dopo che tutto fu finito e che ebbero ripreso fiato, Pete prese la parola.**

Miután minden véget ért, és kapkodták a levegőt, Pete megszólalt.

«È un amore straordinario», disse, scosso dalla feroce devozione del cane.

– Kísérteties ez a szerelem – mondta, megrendítve a kutya heves odaadásától.

Thornton scosse la testa e rispose con calma e serietà.

Thornton megrázta a fejét, és nyugodt komolysággal válaszolt.

«No, l'amore è splendido», disse, «ma anche terribile».

– Nem, a szerelem csodálatos – mondta –, de szörnyű is.

"A volte, devo ammetterlo, questo tipo di amore mi fa paura."

„Be kell vallanom, hogy néha félelemmel tölt el az ilyen szerelem."

Pete annuì e disse: "Mi dispiacerebbe tanto essere l'uomo che ti tocca".

Pete bólintott, és azt mondta: „Nem szeretnék én lenni az az ember, aki hozzád ér."

Mentre parlava, guardava Buck con aria seria e piena di rispetto.

Miközben beszélt, komolyan és tiszteletteljesen nézett Buckra.

"Py Jingo!" esclamò Hans in fretta. "Neanch'io, no signore."

– Py Jingo! – mondta Hans gyorsan. – Én sem, uram.

Prima che finisse l'anno, i timori di Pete si avverarono a Circle City.

Még az év vége előtt Pete félelmei beigazolódtak Circle Cityben.

Un uomo crudele di nome Black Burton attaccò una rissa nel bar.

Egy Black Burton nevű kegyetlen férfi verekedést szított a bárban.

Era arrabbiato e cattivo, e si scagliava contro un novellino.

Dühös és rosszindulatú volt, és egy új zsenge lábúnak rontott.

John Thornton intervenne, calmo e bonario come sempre.

John Thornton lépett közbe, nyugodtan és jóindulatúan, mint mindig.

**Buck giaceva in un angolo, con la testa bassa, e osservava Thornton attentamente.**
Buck egy sarokban feküdt, lehajtott fejjel, és Thorntont figyelte.

**Burton colpì all'improvviso e il suo pugno fece girare Thornton.**
Burton hirtelen lecsapott, az ütése megpörgette Thorntont.

**Solo la ringhiera della sbarra gli impedì di cadere violentemente a terra.**
Csak a korlát korlátja akadályozta meg, hogy a földre zuhanjon.

**Gli osservatori hanno sentito un suono che non era un abbaio o un guaito**
A megfigyelők egy hangot hallottak, ami nem ugatás vagy vonyítás volt

**Buck emise un profondo ruggito mentre si lanciava verso l'uomo.**
Mély ordítás hallatszott Buckból, miközben a férfi felé indult.

**Burton alzò il braccio e per poco non si salvò la vita.**
Burton felemelte a karját, és alig mentette meg az életét.

**Buck si schiantò contro di lui, facendolo cadere a terra.**
Buck nekiütközött, és a férfi a földre zuhant.

**Buck gli diede un morso profondo al braccio, poi si lanciò alla gola.**
Buck mélyen beleharapott a férfi karjába, majd a torkára vetette magát.

**Burton riuscì a parare solo in parte e il suo collo fu squarciato.**
Burton csak részben tudott blokkolni, és a nyaka szétszakadt.

**Gli uomini si precipitarono dentro, brandendo i manganelli e allontanarono Buck dall'uomo sanguinante.**
Férfiak rohantak be, felemelt buzogányokkal, és leterítették Buckot a vérző férfiról.

**Un chirurgo ha lavorato rapidamente per impedire che il sangue fuoriuscisse.**
Egy sebész gyorsan dolgozott, hogy elállítsa a vérzést.

Buck camminava avanti e indietro ringhiando, tentando di
attaccare ancora e ancora.
Buck fel-alá járkált és morgott, újra meg újra támadni
próbálva.
Soltanto i bastoni oscillanti gli impedirono di raggiungere
Burton.
Csak a lendítő botok tartották vissza attól, hogy elérje Burtont.
Proprio lì, sul posto, venne convocata una riunione dei
minatori.
Bányászgyűlést hívtak össze és tartottak meg ott helyben.
Concordarono sul fatto che Buck era stato provocato e
votarono per liberarlo.
Egyetértettek abban, hogy Buckot provokálták, és
megszavazták szabadon bocsátását.
Ma il nome feroce di Buck risuonava ormai in ogni
accampamento dell'Alaska.
De Buck vad neve mostanra Alaszka minden táborában
visszhangzott.
Più tardi, quello stesso autunno, Buck salvò Thornton di
nuovo in un modo nuovo.
Később, azon az őszön, Buck új módon mentette meg
Thorntont.
I tre uomini stavano guidando una lunga barca lungo delle
rapide impetuose.
A három férfi egy hosszú csónakot irányított lefelé a
zuhatagokon.
Thornton manovrava la barca, gridando indicazioni per
raggiungere la riva.
Thornton a csónakot kormányozta, és a partvonal felé kiabált.
Hans e Pete correvano sulla terraferma, tenendo una corda
da un albero all'altro.
Hans és Pete a szárazföldön futottak, egy kötelet tartva fától
fáig.
Buck procedeva a passo d'uomo sulla riva, tenendo sempre
d'occhio il suo padrone.
Buck lépést tartott a parton, mindig a gazdáját figyelve.

**In un punto pericoloso, delle rocce sporgevano dall'acqua veloce.**

Egyik kellemetlen helyen sziklák álltak ki a sebes víz alól.

**Hans lasciò andare la cima e Thornton tirò la barca verso la larghezza.**

Hans elengedte a kötelet, Thornton pedig szélesre kormányozta a csónakot.

**Hans corse a percorrerla di nuovo, superando le pericolose rocce.**

Hans rohanva próbálta utolérni a csónakot a veszélyes sziklák között.

**La barca superò la sporgenza ma trovò una corrente più forte.**

A hajó átjutott a sziklaperemen, de az áramlat egy erősebb szakaszába ütközött.

**Hans afferrò la cima troppo velocemente e fece perdere l'equilibrio alla barca.**

Hans túl gyorsan megragadta a kötelet, és kibillentette az egyensúlyából a csónakot.

**La barca si capovolse e sbatté contro la riva, con la parte inferiore rivolta verso l'alto.**

A csónak felborult, és alulról felfelé a partnak csapódott.

**Thornton venne scaraventato fuori e trascinato nella parte più selvaggia dell'acqua.**

Thorntont kidobták, és a víz legvadabb részébe sodorták.

**Nessun nuotatore sarebbe sopravvissuto in quelle acque pericolose e pericolose.**

Egyetlen úszó sem élhette volna túl azokban a halálos, száguldó vizekben.

**Buck si lanciò all'istante e inseguì il suo padrone lungo il fiume.**

Buck azonnal közbelépett, és üldözőbe vette gazdáját a folyó mentén.

**Dopo trecento metri finalmente raggiunse Thornton.**

Háromszáz yard után végre elérte Thorntont.

**Thornton afferrò la coda di Buck, e Buck si diresse verso la riva.**

Thornton megragadta Buck farkát, és Buck a part felé fordult.

**Nuotò con tutte le sue forze, lottando contro la forte resistenza dell'acqua.**

Teljes erőből úszott, küzdve a víz vad sodrásával.

**Si spostarono verso valle più velocemente di quanto riuscissero a raggiungere la riva.**

Gyorsabban haladtak lefelé a folyón, mint ahogy elérték a partot.

**Più avanti, il fiume ruggiva più forte, precipitando in rapide mortali.**

Előttük a folyó hangosabban zúgott, ahogy halálos zuhatagokba zuhant.

**Le rocce fendevano l'acqua come i denti di un enorme pettine.**

A sziklák úgy hasítottak a vízbe, mint egy hatalmas fésű fogai.

**La forza di attrazione dell'acqua nei pressi del dislivello era selvaggia e ineluttabile.**

A csepp közelében lévő víz vonzása vad és elkerülhetetlen volt.

**Thornton sapeva che non sarebbero mai riusciti a raggiungere la riva in tempo.**

Thornton tudta, hogy soha nem érhetnek partra időben.

**Raschiò una roccia, ne sbatté una seconda,**

Átsúrolt egy sziklát, áttört egy másikon,

**Poi si schiantò contro una terza roccia, afferrandola con entrambe le mani.**

Aztán egy harmadik sziklának csapódott, és mindkét kezével megragadta.

**Lasciò andare Buck e urlò sopra il ruggito: "Vai, Buck! Vai!"**

Elengedte Buckot, és túlkiabálta a bömbölést: „Rajt, Buck! Rajt!"

**Buck non riuscì a restare a galla e fu trascinato dalla corrente.**

Buck nem tudott a felszínen maradni, és az áramlat elsodorta.

**Lottò con tutte le sue forze, cercando di girarsi, ma non fece alcun progresso.**

Keményen küzdött, küszködött a megfordulással, de sehogy sem jutott előre.

**Poi sentì Thornton ripetere il comando sopra il fragore del fiume.**

Aztán hallotta, ahogy Thornton megismétli a parancsot a folyó morajlása felett.

**Buck si impennò fuori dall'acqua e sollevò la testa come per dare un'ultima occhiata.**

Buck kiágaskodott a vízből, és felemelte a fejét, mintha utoljára pillantana rá.

**poi si voltò e obbedì, nuotando verso la riva con risolutezza.**

majd megfordult, engedelmeskedett és elszántan a part felé úszott.

**Pete e Hans lo tirarono a riva all'ultimo momento possibile.**

Pete és Hans az utolsó lehetséges pillanatban húzták partra.

**Sapevano che Thornton avrebbe potuto aggrapparsi alla roccia solo per pochi minuti.**

Tudták, hogy Thornton már csak percekig kapaszkodhat a sziklába.

**Corsero su per la riva fino a un punto molto più in alto rispetto al punto in cui lui era appeso.**

Felrohantak a parton egy helyre, messze afelett, ahol felakasztották.

**Legarono con cura la cima della barca al collo e alle spalle di Buck.**

Gondosan Buck nyakához és vállához kötötték a csónak zsinórját.

**La corda era stretta ma abbastanza larga da permettere di respirare e muoversi.**

A kötél feszes volt, de elég laza a légzéshez és a mozgáshoz.

**Poi lo gettarono di nuovo nel fiume impetuoso e mortale.**

Aztán ismét beledobták a sebesen hömpölygő, halálos folyóba.

**Buck nuotò coraggiosamente ma non riuscì a prendere l'angolazione giusta per affrontare la forza della corrente.**

Buck merészen úszott, de elhibázta a megfelelő szöget az áramlat erejével szemben.

**Si accorse troppo tardi che stava per superare Thornton.**

Túl későn vette észre, hogy el fog sodródni Thornton mellett.

**Hans tirò forte la corda, come se Buck fosse una barca che si capovolge.**

Hans megrántotta a kötelet, mintha Buck egy felboruló csónak lenne.

**La corrente lo trascinò sott'acqua e lui scomparve sotto la superficie.**

Az áramlat magával rántotta, és eltűnt a felszín alatt.

**Il suo corpo colpì la riva prima che Hans e Pete lo tirassero fuori.**

Teste a partnak csapódott, mielőtt Hans és Pete kihúzták volna.

**Era mezzo annegato e gli tolsero l'acqua dal corpo.**

Félig megfulladt, és kiöntötték belőle a vizet.

**Buck si alzò, barcollò e crollò di nuovo a terra.**

Buck felállt, megtántorodott, majd ismét a földre rogyott.

**Poi udirono la voce di Thornton portata debolmente dal vento.**

Aztán meghallották Thornton hangját, melyet halkan vitt a szél.

**Sebbene le parole non fossero chiare, sapevano che era vicino alla morte.**

Bár a szavak nem voltak világosak, tudták, hogy a halál szélén áll.

**Il suono della voce di Thornton colpì Buck come una scossa elettrica.**

Thornton hangja úgy érte Buckot, mint egy elektromos lökés.

**Saltò in piedi e corse su per la riva, tornando al punto di partenza.**

Felugrott és felrohant a parton, visszatérve az indítóálláshoz.

**Legarono di nuovo la corda a Buck, e di nuovo lui entrò nel fiume.**

Újra Buckhoz kötötték a kötelet, és ő ismét belépett a patakba.

**Questa volta nuotò direttamente e con decisione nell'acqua impetuosa.**

Ezúttal egyenesen és határozottan úszott a sebesen áramló vízbe.

Hans lasciò scorrere la corda con regolarità, mentre Pete impediva che si aggrovigliasse.

Hans egyenletesen engedte ki a kötelet, miközben Pete ügyelt arra, hogy ne gubancolódjon össze.

Buck nuotò con forza finché non si trovò allineato appena sopra Thornton.

Buck keményen úszott, amíg közvetlenül Thornton felett nem egy vonalban nem volt.

Poi si voltò e si lanciò verso di lui come un treno a tutta velocità.

Aztán megfordult, és úgy száguldott lefelé, mint egy teljes sebességgel száguldó vonat.

Thornton lo vide arrivare, si preparò e gli abbracciò il collo.

Thornton meglátta közeledni, felkészült, és átkarolta a nyakát.

Hans legò saldamente la corda attorno a un albero mentre entrambi venivano tirati sott'acqua.

Hans erősen körbekötötte a kötelet egy fán, miközben mindkettőjüket aláhúzták.

Caddero sott'acqua, schiantandosi contro rocce e detriti del fiume.

Víz alatt zuhantak, szikláknak és folyami törmeléknek csapódva.

Un attimo prima Buck era in cima e un attimo dopo Thornton si alzava ansimando.

Az egyik pillanatban Buck még felült, a következőben Thornton zihálva emelkedett fel.

Malconci e soffocati, si diressero verso la riva e si misero in salvo.

Összeverődve és fuldokolva a part felé vették az irányt, biztonságba menekülve.

Thornton riprese conoscenza mentre era sdraiato su un tronco alla deriva.

Thornton egy sodródási rönkön fekve tért magához.

Hans e Pete lavorarono duramente per riportarlo a respirare e a vivere.

Hans és Pete keményen dolgoztatták, hogy visszaadja a lélegzetét és az életerejét.

Il suo primo pensiero fu per Buck, che giaceva immobile e inerte.

Első gondolata Buck volt, aki mozdulatlanul és ernyedten feküdt.

Nig ululò sul corpo di Buck e Skeet gli leccò delicatamente il viso.

Nig Buck teste fölött üvöltött, Skeet pedig gyengéden megnyalta az arcát.

Thornton, dolorante e contuso, esaminò Buck con mano attenta.

Thornton, sebesülten és zúzódásokkal, óvatos kézzel vizsgálgatta Buckot.

Ha trovato tre costole rotte, ma il cane non presentava ferite mortali.

Három eltört bordát talált, de a kutyán nem voltak halálos sérülések.

"Questo è tutto", disse Thornton. "Ci accamperemo qui". E così fecero.

– Ez eldöntötte a dolgot – mondta Thornton. – Itt táborozunk. És így is tettek.

Rimasero lì finché le costole di Buck non guarirono e lui poté di nuovo camminare.

Addig maradtak, amíg Buck bordái be nem gyógyultak, és újra járni tudott.


Quell'inverno Buck compì un'impresa che accrebbe ulteriormente la sua fama.

Azon a télen Buck egy olyan hőstettre tett szert, amely tovább növelte hírnevét.

Fu un gesto meno eroico del salvataggio di Thornton, ma altrettanto impressionante.

Kevésbé volt hősies, mint Thornton megmentése, de ugyanolyan lenyűgöző.

A Dawson, i soci avevano bisogno di provviste per un viaggio lontano.

Dawsonban a partnereknek ellátmányra volt szükségük egy hosszú útra.

Volevano viaggiare verso est, in terre selvagge e
incontaminate.
Keletre akartak utazni, érintetlen vadonba.
Quel viaggio fu possibile grazie all'impresa compiuta da
Buck nell'Eldorado Saloon.
Buck Eldorado Saloonban tett üzlete tette lehetővé ezt az utat.
Tutto cominciò con degli uomini che si vantavano dei loro
cani bevendo qualcosa.
Azzal kezdődött, hogy a férfiak iszogatás közben a kutyáikkal
hencegtek.
La fama di Buck lo rese bersaglio di sfide e dubbi.
Buck hírneve kihívások és kétségek célpontjává tette.
Thornton, fiero e calmo, rimase fermo nel difendere il nome
di Buck.
Thornton büszkén és nyugodtan, határozottan kiállt Buck
nevének védelmében.
Un uomo ha affermato che il suo cane riusciva a trainare
facilmente duecentocinquanta chili.
Egy férfi azt mondta, hogy a kutyája könnyedén elhúzhat
ötszáz fontot.
Un altro disse seicento, e un terzo si vantò di settecento.
Egy másik hatszázat mondott, egy harmadik pedig hétszázzal
dicsekedett.
"Pfft!" disse John Thornton, "Buck può trainare una slitta da
mille libbre."
– Pfúj! – mondta John Thornton. – Buck el tud húzni egy ezer
kilós szánt is.
Matthewson, un Bonanza King, si sporse in avanti e lo sfidò.
Matthewson, egy Bonanza King, előrehajolt és kihívást
jelentett neki.
"Pensi che possa spostare tutto quel peso?"
„Szerinted ekkora súlyt tud mozgatni?"
"E pensi che riesca a sollevare il peso per cento metri?"
„És azt hiszed, hogy képes elhúzni a súlyt száz méteren
keresztül?"
Thornton rispose freddamente: "Sì. Buck è abbastanza cane
da farlo."

Thornton hűvösen válaszolt: „Igen. Buck elég kutya ahhoz, hogy megcsinálja."

"Metterà in moto mille libbre e la tirerà per cento metri."

„Ezer fontot mozgat meg, és száz métert is elhúz."

**Matthewson sorrise lentamente e si assicurò che tutti gli uomini udissero le sue parole.**

Matthewson lassan elmosolyodott, és megbizonyosodott róla, hogy mindenki hallja a szavait.

**"Ho mille dollari che dicono che non può. Eccoli."**

„Van egy ezer dollárom, ami azt jelenti, hogy nem teheti meg. Itt van."

**Sbatté sul bancone un sacco di polvere d'oro grande quanto una salsiccia.**

Egy kolbásznyi nagyságú aranyporos zsákot vágott a bárpultra.

**Nessuno disse una parola. Il silenzio si fece pesante e teso intorno a loro.**

Senki sem szólt egy szót sem. A csend egyre súlyosabbá és feszültté vált körülöttük.

**Il bluff di Thornton, se mai lo fu, era stato preso sul serio.**

Thornton blöffjét – ha egyáltalán blöffnek számított – komolyan vették.

**Sentì il calore salirgli al viso mentre il sangue gli affluiva alle guance.**

Érezte, hogy forróság száll az arcába, ahogy a vér az arcába ömlik.

**In quel momento la sua lingua aveva preceduto la ragione.**

A nyelve abban a pillanatban megelőzte az eszét.

**Non sapeva davvero se Buck sarebbe riuscito a spostare mille libbre.**

Tényleg nem tudta, hogy Buck képes-e ezer kilót megmozgatni.

**Mezza tonnellata! Solo la sua mole gli faceva sentire il cuore pesante.**

Fél tonna! Már a mérete is nehézzé tette a szívét.

**Aveva fiducia nella forza di Buck e lo riteneva capace.**

Bízott Buck erejében, és képesnek tartotta rá.

Ma non aveva mai affrontato una sfida di questo tipo, non in questo modo.

De még soha nem nézett szembe ilyen kihívással, nem ehhez hasonlóval.

Una dozzina di uomini lo osservavano in silenzio, in attesa di vedere cosa avrebbe fatto.

Egy tucat férfi figyelte csendben, várva, mit fog tenni.

Lui non aveva i soldi, e nemmeno Hans e Pete.

Nem volt rá pénze – Hansnak és Pete-nek sem.

"Ho una slitta fuori", disse Matthewson in modo freddo e diretto.

– Van kint egy szánkóm – mondta Matthewson hidegen és határozottan.

"È carico di venti sacchi, da cinquanta libbre ciascuno, tutti di farina.

„Húsz zsákkal van megrakva, mindegyik ötven font, mind liszt."

Quindi non lasciare che la scomparsa della slitta diventi la tua scusa", ha aggiunto.

Szóval ne egy eltűnt szánkó legyen most a kifogásod" – tette hozzá.

Thornton rimase in silenzio. Non sapeva che parole dire.

Thornton némán állt. Nem tudta, mit mondjon.

Guardò i volti intorno a sé senza vederli chiaramente.

Körülnézett az arcokon anélkül, hogy tisztán látta volna őket.

Sembrava un uomo immerso nei suoi pensieri, che cercava di ripartire.

Úgy nézett ki, mint aki gondolataiba merülve próbál újrakezdeni.

Poi incontrò Jim O'Brien, un amico dei tempi dei Mastodon.

Aztán meglátta Jim O'Brient, a Mastodon-kori barátját.

Quel volto familiare gli diede un coraggio che non sapeva di avere.

Az ismerős arc olyan bátorságot adott neki, amiről nem is tudott.

Si voltò e chiese a bassa voce: "Puoi prestarmi mille dollari?"

Megfordult, és halkan megkérdezte: „Tudnál kölcsönadni nekem ezrest?"

"Certo", disse O'Brien, lasciando cadere un pesante sacco vicino all'oro.

– Persze – mondta O'Brien, és máris elejtett egy nehéz zsákot az arany mellett.

"Ma sinceramente, John, non credo che la bestia possa fare questo."

„De őszintén szólva, John, nem hiszem, hogy a szörnyeteg képes lenne erre."

Tutti quelli presenti all'Eldorado Saloon si precipitarono fuori per assistere all'evento.

Az Eldorado Szalonban mindenki kiszaladt, hogy lássa az eseményt.

Lasciarono tavoli e bevande e perfino le partite furono sospese.

Elhagyták az asztalokat és az italokat, sőt, még a játékokat is szüneteltették.

Croupier e giocatori accorsero per assistere alla conclusione di questa audace scommessa.

Osztók és szerencsejátékosok gyűltek össze, hogy tanúi legyenek a merész fogadás végének.

Centinaia di persone si radunarono attorno alla slitta sulla strada ghiacciata.

Több százan gyűltek össze a szánkó körül a jeges, nyílt utcán.

La slitta di Matthewson era carica di un carico completo di sacchi di farina.

Matthewson szánja tele volt liszteszsákokkal.

La slitta era rimasta ferma per ore a temperature sotto lo zero.

A szán órák óta állt mínuszokban.

I pattini della slitta erano congelati e incollati alla neve compatta.

A szánkó talpai szorosan odafagytak a letaposott hóhoz.

Gli uomini scommettevano due a uno che Buck non sarebbe riuscito a spostare la slitta.

A férfiak kétszeres oddsot tettek arra, hogy Buck nem tudja megmozdítani a szánt.

**Scoppiò una disputa su cosa significasse realmente "break out".**

Vita alakult ki arról, hogy mit is jelent valójában a „kitörés".

**O'Brien ha affermato che Thornton dovrebbe allentare la base ghiacciata della slitta.**

O'Brien azt mondta Thorntonnak, hogy lazítsa meg a szánkó befagyott talpát.

**Buck potrebbe quindi "rompere" una partenza solida e immobile.**

Buck ezután „kitörhetett" egy szilárd, mozdulatlan kezdetből.

**Matthewson sosteneva che anche il cane doveva liberare i corridori.**

Matthewson azzal érvelt, hogy a kutyának a futókat is ki kell szabadítania.

**Gli uomini che avevano sentito la scommessa concordavano con Matthewson.**

A férfiak, akik hallották a fogadást, egyetértettek Matthewson nézetével.

**Con questa sentenza, le probabilità contro Buck salirono a tre a uno.**

Ezzel a döntéssel az esélyek három az egyhez ugrottak Buck ellen.

**Nessuno si fece avanti per accettare le crescenti quote di tre a uno.**

Senki sem lépett elő, hogy elfogadja a növekvő háromszoros esélyt.

**Nessuno credeva che Buck potesse compiere la grande impresa.**

Egyetlen ember sem hitte, hogy Buck képes lenne erre a nagy tettre.

**Thornton era stato spinto a scommettere, pieno di dubbi.**

Thorntont sietve, kétségek gyötörték, sürgették a fogadást.

**Ora guardava la slitta e la muta di dieci cani accanto ad essa.**

Most a szánt és a mellette lévő tízkutyás fogatot nézte.

Vedere la realtà del compito lo faceva sembrare ancora più impossibile.

A feladat valóságának láttán az még lehetetlenebbnek tűnt.

In quel momento Matthewson era pieno di orgoglio e sicurezza.

Matthewson abban a pillanatban tele volt büszkeséggel és magabiztossággal.

"Tre a uno!" urlò. "Ne scommetto altri mille, Thornton!

– Három az egyhez! – kiáltotta. – Fogadok még ezerbe, Thornton!

"Cosa dici?" aggiunse, abbastanza forte da farsi sentire da tutti.

– Mit mondasz? – tette hozzá elég hangosan ahhoz, hogy mindenki hallja.

Il volto di Thornton esprimeva i suoi dubbi, ma il suo spirito era sollevato.

Thornton arcán látszottak a kétségek, de a lelkesedés már javult.

Quello spirito combattivo ignorava le avversità e non temeva nulla.

Ez a harci szellem figyelmen kívül hagyta az esélyeket, és semmitől sem félt.

Chiamò Hans e Pete perché portassero tutti i loro soldi al tavolo.

Felhívta Hanst és Pete-et, hogy hozzák össze az összes pénzüket.

Non gli era rimasto molto altro: solo duecento dollari in tutto.

Kevés pénzük maradt – összesen csak kétszáz dollár.

Questa piccola somma costituiva la loro intera fortuna nei momenti difficili.

Ez a kis összeg jelentette a teljes vagyonukat a nehéz időkben.

Ciononostante puntarono tutta la loro fortuna contro la scommessa di Matthewson.

Mégis, az összes vagyonukat Matthewson fogadására tették fel.

**La muta composta da dieci cani venne sganciata e allontanata dalla slitta.**

A tíz kutyából álló csapatot leválasztották a szánról, és elhúztak a szánkótól.

**Buck venne messo alle redini, indossando la sua consueta imbracatura.**

Buckot a gyeplőbe helyezték, és a hátán viselte a megszokott hámját.

**Aveva colto l'energia della folla e ne aveva percepito la tensione.**

Érezte a tömeg energiáját és a feszültséget.

**In qualche modo sapeva che doveva fare qualcosa per John Thornton.**

Valahogy tudta, hogy tennie kell valamit John Thorntonért.

**La gente mormorava ammirata di fronte alla figura fiera del cane.**

Az emberek csodálattal mormogtak a kutya büszke alakjára.

**Era magro e forte, senza un solo grammo di carne in più.**

Sovány és erős volt, egyetlen grammnyi felesleges hús nélkül.

**Il suo peso di centocinquanta chili era sinonimo di potenza e resistenza.**

Százötven fontnyi teljes súlya csupa erő és kitartás volt.

**Il mantello di Buck brillava come la seta, denso di salute e forza.**

Buck bundája selyemként csillogott, egészségtől és erőtől átitatva.

**La pelliccia sul collo e sulle spalle sembrava sollevarsi e drizzarsi.**

A nyakán és a vállán a szőr mintha felpúposodott volna és felborzolódott volna.

**La sua criniera si muoveva leggermente, ogni capello era animato dalla sua grande energia.**

Sörénye kissé megmozdult, minden egyes szőrszála életre kelt hatalmas energiájától.

**Il suo petto ampio e le sue gambe forti si sposavano bene con la sua corporatura pesante e robusta.**

Széles mellkasa és erős lábai tökéletesen illettek nehézkes, szívós testalkatához.

**I muscoli si tesero sotto il cappotto, tesi e sodi come ferro legato.**

Izmai hullámoztak a kabátja alatt, feszesek és szilárdak, mint a megkötött vas.

**Gli uomini lo toccavano e giuravano che era fatto come una macchina d'acciaio.**

A férfiak megérintették, és megesküdtek, hogy úgy van felépítve, mint egy acélszerkezet.

**Le probabilità contro il grande cane sono scese leggermente a due a uno.**

Az esélyek kissé csökkentek, kettő az egyhez a nagy kutya ellen.

**Un uomo dei banchi di Skookum si fece avanti balbettando.**

Egy férfi a Skookum padokról dadogva előretolta magát.

**"Bene, signore! Offro ottocento per lui... prima della prova, signore!"**

„Rendben van, uram! Nyolcszázat ajánlok érte… a próba előtt, uram!"

**"Ottocento, così com'è adesso!" insistette l'uomo.**

„Nyolcszáz, ahogy most áll!" – erősködött a férfi.

**Thornton fece un passo avanti, sorrise e scosse la testa con calma.**

Thornton előrelépett, elmosolyodott, és nyugodtan megrázta a fejét.

**Matthewson intervenne rapidamente con tono ammonitore e aggrottando la fronte.**

Matthewson gyorsan közbelépett figyelmeztető hangon és összevont szemöldökkel.

**"Devi allontanarti da lui", disse. "Dagli spazio."**

„El kell távolodnod tőle" – mondta. „Adj neki teret."

**La folla tacque; solo i giocatori continuavano a offrire due a uno.**

A tömeg elcsendesedett; csak a szerencsejátékosok ajánlottak még mindig kettőt az egyhez.

**Tutti ammiravano la corporatura di Buck, ma il carico sembrava troppo pesante.**

Mindenki csodálta Buck testalkatát, de a rakomány túl nagynak tűnt.

**Venti sacchi di farina, ciascuno del peso di cinquanta libbre, sembravano decisamente troppi.**

Húsz zsák liszt – egyenként ötven font súlyú – túl soknak tűnt.

**Nessuno era disposto ad aprire la borsa e a rischiare i propri soldi.**

Senki sem volt hajlandó kinyitni az erszényét és kockáztatni a pénzét.

**Thornton si inginocchiò accanto a Buck e gli prese la testa tra entrambe le mani.**

Thornton letérdelt Buck mellé, és két kezébe fogta a fejét.

**Premette la guancia contro quella di Buck e gli parlò all'orecchio.**

Arcát Buck arcához nyomta, és a fülébe suttogott.

**Non c'erano più né scossoni giocosi né insulti affettuosi sussurrati.**

Most nem volt játékos rázogatás vagy suttogott szerelmes sértések.

**Mormorò solo dolcemente: "Quanto mi ami, Buck."**

Csak halkan mormolta: „Amennyire szeretsz, Buck."

**Buck emise un gemito sommesso, trattenendo a stento la sua impazienza.**

Buck halkan nyüszített, alig fékezte a lelkesedését.

**Gli astanti osservavano con curiosità la tensione che aleggiava nell'aria.**

A nézők kíváncsian figyelték, ahogy a feszültség betöltötte a levegőt.

**Quel momento sembrava quasi irreale, qualcosa che trascendeva la ragione.**

A pillanat szinte valószerűtlennek tűnt, mint valami értelmetlen dolog.

**Quando Thornton si alzò, Buck gli prese delicatamente la mano tra le fauci.**

Amikor Thornton felállt, Buck gyengéden megfogta a kezét.

Premette con i denti, poi lasciò andare lentamente e delicatamente.

Fogaival lenyomta, majd lassan és gyengéden elengedte.

Fu una risposta silenziosa d'amore, non detta, ma compresa.

A szeretet néma válasza volt, nem kimondva, hanem megértve.

Thornton si allontanò di molto dal cane e diede il segnale.

Thornton jó messzire hátrébb lépett a kutyától, és megadta a jelet.

"Ora, Buck", disse, e Buck rispose con calma concentrata.

– Na, Buck – mondta, mire Buck nyugodtan válaszolt.

Buck tese le corde, poi le allentò di qualche centimetro.

Buck meghúzta a szíjakat, majd néhány centivel meglazította őket.

Questo era il metodo che aveva imparato; il suo modo per rompere la slitta.

Ezt a módszert tanulta meg; így törte össze a szánt.

"Caspita!" urlò Thornton, con voce acuta nel silenzio pesante.

– Hűha! – kiáltotta Thornton éles hangon a nehéz csendben.

Buck si girò verso destra e si lanciò con tutto il suo peso.

Buck jobbra fordult, és teljes súlyával előrelendült.

Il gioco svanì e tutta la massa di Buck colpì le timonerie strette.

A lazaság eltűnt, és Buck teljes súlyával a feszes sínre csapódott.

La slitta tremò e i pattini produssero un suono secco e scoppiettante.

A szán remegett, a talpak pedig ropogós, ropogó hangot adtak ki.

"Haw!" ordinò Thornton, cambiando di nuovo direzione a Buck.

– Haw! – parancsolta Thornton, ismét Buck irányát váltva.

Buck ripeté la mossa, questa volta tirando bruscamente verso sinistra.

Buck megismételte a mozdulatot, ezúttal élesen balra húzódott.

**La slitta scricchiolava più forte, i pattini schioccavano e si spostavano.**

A szán hangosabban recsegett, a talpak recsegtek és mozdultak.

**Il pesante carico scivolò leggermente di lato sulla neve ghiacciata.**

A nehéz teher kissé oldalra csúszott a fagyott havon.

**La slitta si era liberata dalla presa del sentiero ghiacciato!**

A szánkó kiszabadult a jeges ösvény szorításából!

**Gli uomini trattennero il respiro, inconsapevoli di non stare nemmeno respirando.**

A férfiak visszatartották a lélegzetüket, nem is sejtették, hogy nem lélegznek.

**"Ora, TIRA!" gridò Thornton nel silenzio glaciale.**

„Most HÚZZATOK!" – kiáltotta Thornton a dermedt csendben.

**Il comando di Thornton risuonò netto, come lo schiocco di una frusta.**

Thornton parancsa élesen harsant, mint egy ostor csattanása.

**Buck si lanciò in avanti con un affondo violento e violento.**

Buck egy vad és rázkódással előrevetette magát.

**Tutto il suo corpo si irrigidì e si contrasse sotto l'enorme sforzo.**

Az egész teste megfeszült és összerándult a hatalmas nyomástól.

**I muscoli si muovevano sotto la pelliccia come serpenti che prendevano vita.**

Izmai úgy hullámoztak a bundája alatt, mint életre kelő kígyók.

**Il suo grande petto era basso e la testa era protesa in avanti verso la slitta.**

Hatalmas mellkasa alacsonyan volt, feje előrenyújtva a szánkó felé.

**Le sue zampe si muovevano come fulmini e gli artigli fendevano il terreno ghiacciato.**

Mancsai villámként mozogtak, karmaikkal hasították a fagyott földet.

I solchi erano profondi mentre lottava per ogni centimetro di trazione.

Mély barázdákat vágott a talaj, miközben minden négyzetcentiméternyi tapadásért küzdött.

La slitta ondeggiò, tremò e cominciò a muoversi lentamente e in modo inquieto.

A szánkó ringatózott, remegett, és lassú, nyugtalan mozgásba kezdett.

Un piede scivolò e un uomo tra la folla gemette ad alta voce.

Megcsúszott az egyik lába, és egy férfi a tömegben hangosan felnyögött.

Poi la slitta si lanciò in avanti con un movimento brusco e a scatti.

Aztán a szánkó rángatózó, durva mozdulattal előrelendült.

Non si fermò più: mezzo pollice...un pollice...cinque pollici in più.

Nem állt meg újra – fél hüvelyk... egy hüvelyk... még öt hüvelyk.

Gli scossoni si fecero più lievi man mano che la slitta cominciava ad acquistare velocità.

A rándulások egyre kisebbek lettek, ahogy a szánkó sebességet kezdett gyűjteni.

Presto Buck cominciò a tirare con una potenza fluida e uniforme.

Buck hamarosan sima, egyenletes, guruló erővel húzott.

Gli uomini sussultarono e finalmente si ricordarono di respirare di nuovo.

A férfiak felnyögtek, és végre eszébe jutott újra levegőt venni.

Non si erano accorti che il loro respiro si era fermato per lo stupore.

Nem vették észre, hogy a lélegzetük elállt a félelemtől.

Thornton gli corse dietro, gridando comandi brevi e allegri.

Thornton mögöttük futott, rövid, vidám parancsokat kiabálva.

Davanti a noi c'era una catasta di legna da ardere che segnava la distanza.

Előttük egy tűzifahalom jelezte a távolságot.

**Mentre Buck si avvicinava al mucchio, gli applausi diventavano sempre più forti.**

Ahogy Buck közeledett a halomhoz, az éljenzés egyre hangosabb lett.

**Gli applausi crebbero fino a diventare un boato quando Buck superò il traguardo.**

Az éljenzés üvöltéssé erősödött, ahogy Buck elhaladt a végpont mellett.

**Gli uomini saltarono e gridarono, perfino Matthewson sorrise.**

A férfiak ugráltak és kiabáltak, még Matthewson is elvigyorodott.

**I cappelli volavano in aria e i guanti venivano lanciati senza pensarci o mirare.**

Kalapok repültek a levegőbe, kesztyűk dobálóztak gondolkodás és céltalanul.

**Gli uomini si afferrarono e si strinsero la mano senza sapere chi.**

A férfiak megragadták egymást, és kezet fogtak egymással, anélkül, hogy tudták volna, kivel.

**Tutta la folla era in delirio, in un tripudio di gioia e di entusiasmo.**

Az egész tömeg vad, örömteli ünneplésben zümmögött.

**Thornton cadde in ginocchio accanto a Buck con le mani tremanti.**

Thornton remegő kézzel rogyott térdre Buck mellett.

**Premette la testa contro quella di Buck e lo scosse delicatamente avanti e indietro.**

Fejét Buck fejéhez nyomta, és gyengéden előre-hátra rázta.

**Chi si avvicinava lo sentiva maledire il cane con amore silenzioso.**

Akik közeledtek, hallották, ahogy csendes szeretettel átkozza a kutyát.

**Imprecò a lungo contro Buck, con dolcezza, calore, emozione.**

Hosszan káromkodott Buckkal – halkan, melegen, érzelmesen.

"Bene, signore! Bene, signore!" esclamò di corsa il re della panchina di Skookum.

– Jó, uram! Jó, uram! – kiáltotta sietve a Skookum pad királya.

"Le darò mille, anzi milleduecento, per quel cane, signore!"

„Ezret... nem, ezerkétszázat... adok azért a kutyáért, uram!"

Thornton si alzò lentamente in piedi, con gli occhi brillanti di emozione.

Thornton lassan feltápászkodott, szeme csillogott az érzelmektől.

Le lacrime gli rigavano le guance senza alcuna vergogna.

Könnyek patakokban folytak az arcán, minden szégyenkezés nélkül.

"Signore", disse al re della panchina di Skookum, con fermezza e fermezza

– Uram – mondta a Skookum pad királyának szilárdan és határozottan.

"No, signore. Può andare all'inferno, signore. Questa è la mia risposta definitiva."

„Nem, uram. Mehet a pokolba, uram. Ez a végső válaszom."

Buck afferrò delicatamente la mano di Thornton tra le sue forti mascelle.

Buck erős állkapcsával gyengéden megragadta Thornton kezét.

Thornton lo scosse scherzosamente; il loro legame era più profondo che mai.

Thornton játékosan megrázta, a köztük lévő kötelék továbbra is mély volt.

La folla, commossa dal momento, fece un passo indietro in silenzio.

A pillanatnyi meghatottságtól meghatott tömeg csendben hátrált.

Da quel momento in poi nessuno osò più interrompere un affetto così sacro.

Attól kezdve senki sem merte félbeszakítani ezt a szent szeretetet.

## Il suono della chiamata
A hívás hangja

**Buck aveva guadagnato milleseicento dollari in cinque minuti.**
Buck öt perc alatt tizenhatszáz dollárt keresett.
**Il denaro permise a John Thornton di saldare alcuni dei suoi debiti.**
A pénz lehetővé tette John Thornton számára, hogy kifizesse adósságainak egy részét.
**Con il resto del denaro si diresse verso est insieme ai suoi soci.**
A maradék pénzzel keletre indult a társaival.
**Cercarono una leggendaria miniera perduta, antica quanto il paese stesso.**
Egy legendás elveszett bányát kerestek, amely olyan régi, mint maga az ország.
**Molti uomini avevano cercato la miniera, ma pochi l'avevano trovata.**
Sokan keresték a bányát, de kevesen találták meg.
**Molti uomini erano scomparsi durante la pericolosa ricerca.**
A veszélyes küldetés során jó néhány ember tűnt el.
**Questa miniera perduta era avvolta nel mistero e nella vecchia tragedia.**
Ez az elveszett bánya rejtélybe és régi tragédiába burkolózott.
**Nessuno sapeva chi fosse stato il primo uomo a scoprire la miniera.**
Senki sem tudta, ki volt az első ember, aki megtalálta a bányát.
**Le storie più antiche non menzionano nessuno per nome.**
A legrégebbi történetek senkit sem említenek név szerint.
**Lì c'era sempre stata una vecchia capanna fatiscente.**
Mindig is állt ott egy régi, romos kunyhó.
**I moribondi avevano giurato che vicino a quella vecchia capanna ci fosse una miniera.**
A haldoklók megesküdtek, hogy egy bánya van a régi kunyhó mellett.

**Hanno dimostrato le loro storie con un oro che non ha eguali altrove.**

Olyan arannyal bizonyították történetüket, amilyet sehol máshol nem találtak.

**Nessuna anima viva aveva mai saccheggiato il tesoro da quel luogo.**

Élő lélek sem zsákmányolta még soha a kincset arról a helyről.

**I morti erano morti e i morti non raccontano storie.**

A halottak halottak voltak, és a halottak nem mesélnek.

**Così Thornton e i suoi amici si diressero verso Est.**

Thornton és barátai tehát kelet felé vették az irányt.

**Si unirono a noi Pete e Hans, portando con sé Buck e sei cani robusti.**

Pete és Hans csatlakoztak, magukkal hozva Buckot és hat erős kutyát.

**Si avviarono lungo un sentiero sconosciuto dove altri avevano fallito.**

Ismeretlen ösvényen indultak el, ahol mások kudarcot vallottak.

**Percorsero in slitta settanta miglia lungo il fiume Yukon ghiacciato.**

Hetven mérföldet szánkóztak felfelé a befagyott Yukon folyón.

**Girarono a sinistra e seguirono il sentiero verso lo Stewart.**

Balra fordultak, és követték az ösvényt a Stewart-folyóba.

**Superarono il Mayo e il McQuestion e proseguirono oltre.**

Elhagyták a Mayo és a McQuestion folyót, és egyre messzebbre nyomultak.

**Lo Stewart si restringeva fino a diventare un ruscello, infilandosi tra cime frastagliate.**

A Stewart folyóvá zsugorodott, csipkézett csúcsok között kanyarogva.

**Queste vette aguzze rappresentavano la spina dorsale del continente.**

Ezek az éles csúcsok jelölték a kontinens gerincét.

**John Thornton pretendeva poco dagli uomini e dalla terra selvaggia.**

John Thornton keveset követelt az emberektől vagy a vad
földtől.

**Non temeva nulla della natura e affrontava la natura
selvaggia con disinvoltura.**

Semmitől sem félt a természetben, és könnyedén szembenézett
a vadonnal.

**Con solo del sale e un fucile poteva viaggiare dove voleva.**

Csak sóval és egy puskával utazhatott, ahová csak akart.

**Come gli indigeni, durante il viaggio cacciava per procurarsi
il cibo.**

A bennszülöttekhez hasonlóan ő is vadászott élelemre,
miközben utazott.

**Se non prendeva nulla, continuava ad andare avanti,
confidando nella fortuna che lo attendeva.**

Ha nem fogott semmit, folytatta útját, bízva a szerencsében.

**Durante questo lungo viaggio, la carne era l'alimento
principale di cui si nutrivano.**

Ezen a hosszú úton a hús volt a fő táplálékuk.

**La slitta trasportava attrezzi e munizioni, ma non c'era un
orario preciso.**

A szán szerszámokat és lőszert tartalmazott, de nem volt
szigorú menetrend.

**Buck amava questo vagabondare, la caccia e la pesca senza
fine.**

Buck imádta ezt a vándorlást; a végtelen vadászatot és
horgászatot.

**Per settimane viaggiarono senza sosta, giorno dopo giorno.**

Heteken át utaztak nap mint nap.

**Altre volte si accampavano e restavano fermi per settimane.**

Máskor tábort vertek, és hetekig mozdulatlanul maradtak.

**I cani riposarono mentre gli uomini scavavano nel terreno
ghiacciato.**

A kutyák pihentek, miközben a férfiak a fagyott földben ástak.

**Scaldavano le padelle sul fuoco e cercavano l'oro nascosto.**

Tűz felett melegítették a serpenyőket, és rejtett aranyat
kerestek.

C'erano giorni in cui pativano la fame, altri in cui
banchettavano.

Voltak napok, amikor éheztek, és voltak napok, amikor
lakomákat rendeztek.

Il loro pasto dipendeva dalla selvaggina e dalla fortuna della
caccia.

Étkezésük a vadtól és a vadászat szerencséjétől függött.

Con l'arrivo dell'estate, uomini e cani caricavano carichi
sulle spalle.

Amikor eljött a nyár, a férfiak és a kutyák rakományt pakoltak
a hátukra.

Fecero rafting sui laghi azzurri nascosti nelle foreste di
montagna.

Hegyi erdőkben megbúvó kék tavakon eveztek át.

Navigavano su imbarcazioni sottili su fiumi che nessun
uomo aveva mai mappato.

Karcsú csónakokkal vitorláztak olyan folyókon, amelyeket
ember még soha nem térképezett fel.

Quelle barche venivano costruite con gli alberi che avevano
segato in natura.

Azokat a hajókat a vadonban kivágott fákból építették.


Passarono i mesi e loro viaggiarono attraverso terre selvagge
e sconosciute.

Teltek a hónapok, ők pedig vad, ismeretlen vidékeken
bolyongtak.

Non c'erano uomini lì, ma vecchie tracce lasciavano
intendere che alcuni di loro fossero presenti.

Nem voltak ott férfiak, de a régi nyomok arra utaltak, hogy
voltak ott férfiak.

Se la Capanna Perduta fosse esistita davvero, allora altre
persone in passato erano passate da lì.

Ha az Elveszett Kunyhó valóságos volt, akkor mások is jártak
már erre.

Attraversavano passi alti durante le bufere di neve, anche
d'estate.

Magas hágókon keltek át hóviharokban, még nyáron is.

**Rabbrividivano sotto il sole di mezzanotte sui pendii brulli delle montagne.**
Vacogtak az éjféli nap alatt a kopár hegyoldalakon.
**Tra il limite degli alberi e i campi di neve, salivano lentamente.**
A fasor és a hómezők között lassan kapaszkodtak felfelé.
**Nelle valli calde, scacciavano nuvole di moscerini e mosche.**
Meleg völgyekben szúnyog- és legyfelhőket csapkodtak.
**Raccolsero bacche dolci vicino ai ghiacciai nel pieno della fioritura estiva.**
Teljes nyári virágzásban édes bogyókat szedtek a gleccserek közelében.
**I fiori che trovarono erano belli quanto quelli del Southland.**
A virágok, amiket találtak, ugyanolyan szépek voltak, mint a Délvidéken.
**Quell'autunno giunsero in una regione solitaria piena di laghi silenziosi.**
Azon az őszön egy magányos vidékre értek, tele csendes tavakkal.
**La terra era triste e vuota, un tempo brulicava di uccelli e animali.**
A föld szomorú és üres volt, valaha madaraktól és állatoktól élt.
**Ora non c'era più vita, solo il vento e il ghiaccio che si formava nelle pozze.**
Most már nem volt élet, csak a szél és a tócsákban képződő jég.
**Le onde lambivano le rive deserte con un suono dolce e lugubre.**
A hullámok halk, gyászos hanggal csapkodták az üres partokat.


**Arrivò un altro inverno e loro seguirono di nuovo deboli e vecchi sentieri.**
Újabb tél jött, és ismét halvány, régi ösvényeket követtek.
**Erano le tracce di uomini che avevano cercato molto prima di loro.**

Ezek azoknak a férfiaknak a nyomai voltak, akik már jóval előttük kerestek.

**Una volta trovarono un sentiero che si inoltrava nel profondo della foresta oscura.**

Egyszer csak találtak egy ösvényt, ami mélyen a sötét erdőbe vezetett.

**Era un vecchio sentiero e sentivano che la baita perduta era vicina.**

Régi ösvény volt, és úgy érezték, hogy az elveszett kunyhó a közelben van.

**Ma il sentiero non portava da nessuna parte e si perdeva nel fitto del bosco.**

De az ösvény sehová sem vezetett, és beleveszett a sűrű erdőbe.

**Nessuno sapeva chi avesse tracciato il sentiero e perché lo avesse fatto.**

Ki tette meg az ösvényt, és miért, senki sem tudta.

**Più tardi trovarono i resti di una capanna nascosta tra gli alberi.**

Később megtalálták a fák között megbúvó kunyhó roncsait.

**Coperte marce erano sparse dove un tempo qualcuno aveva dormito.**

Rohadó takarók hevertek szanaszét ott, ahol valaha valaki aludt.

**John Thornton trovò sepolto all'interno un fucile a pietra focaia a canna lunga.**

John Thornton egy hosszú csövű kovás puskát talált elásva a belsejében.

**Sapeva fin dai primi tempi che si trattava di un cannone della Hudson Bay.**

Tudta, hogy ez egy Hudson Bay-i fegyver, még a kereskedés korai napjaiból.

**A quei tempi, tali armi venivano barattate con pile di pelli di castoro.**

Azokban az időkben az ilyen fegyvereket hódbőrkötegekért adták el.

**Questo era tutto: non rimaneva alcuna traccia dell'uomo che aveva costruito la loggia.**

Ennyi volt az egész – semmi nyoma sem maradt annak az embernek, aki a kunyhót építette.

**Arrivò di nuovo la primavera e non trovarono traccia della Capanna Perduta.**

Újra eljött a tavasz, és az Elveszett Kunyhónak semmi jelét nem találták.

**Invece trovarono un'ampia valle con un ruscello poco profondo.**

Ehelyett egy széles völgyet találtak sekély patakkal.

**L'oro si stendeva sul fondo della pentola come burro giallo e liscio.**

Az arany sima, sárga vajként feküdt a serpenyők alján.

**Si fermarono lì e non cercarono oltre la cabina.**

Megálltak ott, és nem keresték tovább a kunyhót.

**Ogni giorno lavoravano e ne trovavano migliaia di pezzi in polvere d'oro.**

Minden nap dolgoztak, és ezreket találtak aranyporban.

**Confezionarono l'oro in sacchi di pelle di alce, da cinquanta libbre ciascuno.**

Ötven font súlyú jávorszarvasbőr zsákokba csomagolták az aranyat.

**I sacchi erano accatastati come legna da ardere fuori dal loro piccolo rifugio.**

A zsákok tűzifaként hevertek egymásra halmozva a kis kunyhójuk előtt.

**Lavoravano come giganti e i giorni trascorrevano veloci come sogni.**

Óriásokként dolgoztak, a napok pedig gyorsan teltek, mint az álom.

**Accumularono tesori mentre gli infiniti giorni trascorrevano rapidamente.**

Kincset halmoztak fel, ahogy a végtelen napok gyorsan teltek.

**I cani avevano ben poco da fare, se non trasportare la carne di tanto in tanto.**

A kutyáknak nem sok dolguk akadt, azon kívül, hogy néha-néha húst cipeltek.

**Thornton cacciò e uccise la selvaggina, mentre Buck si sdraiò accanto al fuoco.**

Thornton vadászott és ejtette a vadat, Buck pedig a tűz mellett feküdt.

**Trascorse lunghe ore in silenzio, perso nei pensieri e nei ricordi.**

Hosszú órákat töltött csendben, elveszve a gondolataiban és az emlékeiben.

**L'immagine dell'uomo peloso tornava sempre più spesso alla mente di Buck.**

A szőrös férfi képe egyre gyakrabban jelent meg Buck elméjében.

**Ora che il lavoro scarseggiava, Buck sognava mentre sbatteva le palpebre verso il fuoco.**

Most, hogy kevés volt a munka, Buck a tűzbe pislogva álmodozott.

**In quei sogni, Buck vagava con l'uomo in un altro mondo.**

Ezekben az álmokban Buck a férfival bolyongott egy másik világban.

**La paura sembrava il sentimento più forte in quel mondo lontano.**

A félelem tűnt a legerősebb érzésnek abban a távoli világban.

**Buck vide l'uomo peloso dormire con la testa bassa.**

Buck látta, hogy a szőrös férfi lehajtott fejjel alszik.

**Aveva le mani giunte e il suo sonno era agitato e interrotto.**

Kezei összekulcsolva voltak, álma nyugtalan és megszakadt volt.

**Si svegliava di soprassalto e fissava il buio con timore.**

Riadtan ébredt, és félelemmel bámult a sötétbe.

**Poi aggiungeva altra legna al fuoco per mantenere viva la fiamma.**

Aztán még fát tett a tűzre, hogy a láng élénk maradjon.

**A volte camminavano lungo una spiaggia in riva a un mare grigio e infinito.**

Néha a szürke, végtelen tenger partján sétáltak.

**L'uomo peloso raccolse i frutti di mare e li mangiò mentre camminava.**

A szőrös férfi kagylókat szedett és evett belőlük menet közben.

**I suoi occhi cercavano sempre pericoli nascosti nell'ombra.**

Szeme mindig a homályban rejlő veszélyeket kereste.

**Le sue gambe erano sempre pronte a scattare al primo segno di minaccia.**

A lábai mindig készen álltak, hogy az első fenyegetésre sprintelni tudjanak.

**Avanzavano furtivamente nella foresta, silenziosi e cauti, uno accanto all'altro.**

Némán és óvatosan, egymás mellett lopakodtak át az erdőn.

**Buck lo seguì alle calcagna, ed entrambi rimasero all'erta.**

Buck a nyomában követte, és mindketten éberek maradtak.

**Le loro orecchie si muovevano e si contraevano, i loro nasi fiutavano l'aria.**

Fülük rángatózott és mozgott, orruk a levegőt szimatolta.

**L'uomo riusciva a sentire e ad annusare la foresta in modo altrettanto acuto quanto Buck.**

A férfi ugyanolyan élesen hallotta és szagolta az erdőt, mint Buck.

**L'uomo peloso si lanciò tra gli alberi a velocità improvvisa.**

A szőrös férfi hirtelen sebességgel átlendült a fák között.

**Saltava da un ramo all'altro senza mai perdere la presa.**

Ágról ágra ugrált, soha nem tévedett el a szorításából.

**Si muoveva con la stessa rapidità con cui si muoveva sopra e sopra il terreno.**

Ugyanolyan gyorsan mozgott a föld felett, mint rajta.

**Buck ricordava le lunghe notti passate sotto gli alberi a fare la guardia.**

Buck emlékezett a fák alatt töltött hosszú éjszakákra, miközben virrasztott.

**L'uomo dormiva appollaiato sui rami, aggrappandosi forte.**

A férfi az ágakon aludt, szorosan kapaszkodva.

**Questa visione dell'uomo peloso era strettamente legata al richiamo profondo.**

A szőrös férfiról alkotott vízió szorosan kötődött a mély híváshoz.

Il richiamo risuonava ancora nella foresta con una forza inquietante.

A hívás még mindig kísérteties erővel hallatszott az erdőn keresztül.

La chiamata riempì Buck di desiderio e di un inquieto senso di gioia.

A hívás vágyakozással és nyugtalan örömmel töltötte el Buckot.

Sentì strani impulsi e stimoli a cui non riusciva a dare un nome.

Furcsa késztetéseket és izgalmakat érzett, amiket nem tudott megnevezni.

A volte seguiva la chiamata inoltrandosi nel silenzio dei boschi.

Néha követte a hívást a csendes erdő mélyére.

Cercava il richiamo, abbaiando piano o bruscamente mentre camminava.

Kereste a hívást, menet közben halkan vagy élesen ugatott.

Annusò il muschio e il terreno nero dove cresceva l'erba.

Megszagolgatta a mohát és a fekete földet, ahol a fű nőtt.

Sbuffò di piacere sentendo i ricchi odori della terra profonda.

Gyönyörrel felhorkant a mély föld gazdag illatától.

Rimase accovacciato per ore dietro i tronchi ricoperti di funghi.

Órákig kuporgott gombával borított fatörzsek mögött.

Rimase immobile, ascoltando con gli occhi sgranati ogni minimo rumore.

Mozdulatlanul állt, tágra nyílt szemekkel figyelve minden apró neszre.

Forse sperava di sorprendere la cosa che aveva emesso la chiamata.

Talán abban reménykedett, hogy meglepi azt, ami a hívást kezdeményezte.

**Non sapeva perché si comportava in quel modo: lo faceva e basta.**

Nem tudta, miért viselkedett így – egyszerűen csak tudta.

**Questi impulsi provenivano dal profondo, al di là del pensiero o della ragione.**

A késztetések mélyről fakadtak, a gondolaton és az észszerűségen túlról.

**Buck fu colto da impulsi irresistibili, senza preavviso o motivo.**

Ellenállhatatlan késztetések vették hatalmába Buckot minden előzetes figyelmeztetés és ok nélkül.

**A volte sonnecchiava pigramente nell'accampamento, sotto il caldo di mezzogiorno.**

Időnként lustán szundikált a táborban a déli hőségben.

**All'improvviso sollevò la testa e le sue orecchie si drizzarono in allerta.**

Hirtelen felemelte a fejét, és fülei éberen hegyezték a levegőt.

**Poi balzò in piedi e si lanciò nella natura selvaggia senza fermarsi.**

Aztán felugrott, és megállás nélkül berohant a vadonba.

**Corse per ore attraverso sentieri forestali e spazi aperti.**

Órákon át futott erdei ösvényeken és nyílt tereken.

**Amava seguire i letti asciutti dei torrenti e spiare gli uccelli sugli alberi.**

Szerette a kiszáradt patakmedreket követni és a fákon ülő madarakat kémlelni.

**Poteva restare nascosto tutto il giorno, osservando le pernici che si pavoneggiavano in giro.**

Egész nap rejtőzködhetett volna, és nézhette volna a ficánkoló foglyokat.

**Suonavano i tamburi e marciavano, ignari della presenza immobile di Buck.**

Doboltak és meneteltek, mit sem sejtve Buck jelenlétéről.

**Ma ciò che amava di più era correre al crepuscolo estivo.**

De amit a legjobban szeretett, az a nyári alkonyatkor való futás volt.

La luce fioca e i suoni assonnati della foresta lo riempivano di gioia.

A halvány fény és az álmos erdei hangok örömmel töltötték el.

Leggeva i cartelli della foresta con la stessa chiarezza con cui un uomo legge un libro.

Olyan tisztán olvasta az erdei jeleket, mint ahogy egy ember egy könyvet.

E cercava sempre la strana cosa che lo chiamava.

És mindig kereste azt a különös dolgot, ami hívta.

Quella chiamata non si è mai fermata: lo raggiungeva sia da sveglio che nel sonno.

A hívás soha nem szűnt meg – elérte őt ébren vagy alva.

Una notte si svegliò di soprassalto, con gli occhi acuti e le orecchie tese.

Egyik éjjel riadtan ébredt, éles szemekkel és felemelt fülekkel.

Le sue narici si contrassero mentre la sua criniera si rizzava in onde.

Orrlyukai megrándultak, miközben sörénye hullámokban állt.

Dal profondo della foresta giunse di nuovo quel suono, il vecchio richiamo.

Az erdő mélyéről ismét felhangzott a hang, a régi hívás.

Questa volta il suono risuonò chiaro, un ululato lungo, inquietante e familiare.

Ezúttal a hang tisztán csengett, egy hosszú, kísérteties, ismerős üvöltés.

Era come il verso di un husky, ma dal tono strano e selvaggio.

Olyan volt, mint egy husky kiáltása, de furcsa és vad hangvételű.

Buck riconobbe subito quel suono: lo aveva già sentito molto tempo prima.

Buck azonnal felismerte a hangot – régen már hallotta pontosan ugyanazt a hangot.

Attraversò con un balzo l'accampamento e scomparve rapidamente nel bosco.

Átugrott a táboron, és gyorsan eltűnt az erdőben.

Avvicinandosi al suono, rallentò e si mosse con cautela.
Ahogy közeledett a hanghoz, lelassított és óvatosan mozgott.
Presto raggiunse una radura tra fitti pini.
Hamarosan egy tisztásra ért sűrű fenyőfák között.
Lì, ritto sulle zampe posteriori, sedeva un lupo grigio alto e magro.
Ott, egyenesen a guggoló lábaira ereszkedve, egy magas, sovány, fafarkas ült.
Il naso del lupo puntava verso il cielo, continuando a rieccheggiare il richiamo.
A farkas orra az ég felé meredt, még mindig a kiáltást visszhangozva.
Buck non aveva emesso alcun suono, eppure il lupo si fermò e ascoltò.
Buck nem adott ki hangot, a farkas mégis megállt és hallgatózott.
Percependo qualcosa, il lupo si irrigidì e scrutò l'oscurità.
A farkas megérzett valamit, megfeszült, és a sötétséget kutatta.
Buck si fece avanti furtivamente, con il corpo basso e i piedi ben appoggiati al terreno.
Buck bekúszott a látómezőbe, alacsony testtel, mozdulatlan lábbal a földön.
La sua coda era dritta e il suo corpo era teso e teso.
Farka egyenes volt, teste feszülten gömbölyödött.
Manifestava sia un atteggiamento minaccioso che una sorta di rude amicizia.
Fenyegetést és egyfajta durva barátságot is mutatott.
Era il saluto cauto tipico delle bestie selvatiche.
Ez volt a vadállatok által megszokott óvatos üdvözlés.
Ma il lupo si voltò e fuggì non appena vide Buck.
De a farkas megfordult és elmenekült, amint meglátta Buckot.
Buck si lanciò all'inseguimento, saltando selvaggiamente, desideroso di raggiungerlo.
Buck üldözőbe vette, vadul ugrálva, alig várva, hogy utolérje.
Seguì il lupo in un ruscello secco bloccato da un ingorgo di tronchi.

Követte a farkast egy kiszáradt patakhoz, amelyet egy fatorlódás zárt el.

**Messo alle strette, il lupo si voltò e rimase fermo.**

A sarokba szorított farkas megpördült, és megállt a helyén.

**Il lupo ringhiò e schiocco i denti come un husky intrappolato in una rissa.**

A farkas vicsorgott és csattant, mint egy verekedésben csapdába esett husky.

**I denti del lupo schioccarono rapidamente e il suo corpo si irrigidì per la furia selvaggia.**

A farkas fogai gyorsan kattantak, teste vad dühtől izzott.

**Buck non attaccò, ma girò intorno al lupo con attenta cordialità.**

Buck nem támadott, hanem óvatos barátságossággal kerülte meg a farkast.

**Cercò di bloccargli la fuga con movimenti lenti e innocui.**

Lassú, ártalmatlan mozdulatokkal próbálta megakadályozni a menekülést.

**Il lupo era cauto e spaventato: Buck lo superava di peso tre volte.**

A farkas óvatos és félős volt – Buck háromszor is túlerőben volt nála.

**La testa del lupo arrivava a malapena all'altezza della spalla massiccia di Buck.**

A farkas feje alig ért fel Buck hatalmas válláig.

**Il lupo, attento a individuare un varco, si lanciò e l'inseguimento ricominciò.**

A farkas egy rést keresve elszaladt, és az üldözés újra kezdődött.

**Buck lo mise alle strette più volte e la danza si ripeté.**

Buck többször is sarokba szorította, és a tánc megismétlődött.

**Il lupo era magro e debole, altrimenti Buck non avrebbe potuto catturarlo.**

A farkas sovány és gyenge volt, különben Buck nem kaphatta volna el.

**Ogni volta che Buck si avvicinava, il lupo si girava di scatto e lo affrontava spaventato.**

Valahányszor Buck közelebb ért, a farkas megpördült és félelemmel telve nézett rá.

**Poi, alla prima occasione, si precipitò di nuovo nel bosco.**

Aztán az első adandó alkalommal ismét berontott az erdőbe.

**Ma Buck non si arrese e alla fine il lupo imparò a fidarsi di lui.**

De Buck nem adta fel, és végül a farkas megbízott benne.

**Annusò il naso di Buck e i due diventarono giocosi e attenti.**

Megszagolta Buck orrát, mire a két férfi játékossá és éberté vált.

**Giocavano come animali selvaggi, feroci ma timidi nella loro gioia.**

Úgy játszottak, mint a vadállatok, vadak, mégis félénkek az örömükben.

**Dopo un po' il lupo trotterellò via con calma e decisione.**

Egy idő múlva a farkas nyugodt céltudatosan elügetett.

**Dimostrò chiaramente a Buck che intendeva essere seguito.**

Világosan megmutatta Bucknak, hogy követni akarja.

**Correvano fianco a fianco nel buio della sera.**

Egymás mellett futottak az alkonyati homályban.

**Seguirono il letto del torrente fino alla gola rocciosa.**

A patak medrét követve felértek a sziklás szurdokba.

**Attraversarono un freddo spartiacque nel punto in cui aveva avuto origine il fiume.**

Átkeltek egy hideg szakadékon, ahol a patak elkezdődött.

**Sul pendio più lontano trovarono un'ampia foresta e molti corsi d'acqua.**

A túlsó lejtőn széles erdőre és számos patakra bukkantak.

**Corsero per ore senza fermarsi attraverso quella terra immensa.**

Órákon át rohantak megállás nélkül ezen a hatalmas földön.

**Il sole saliva sempre più alto, l'aria si faceva calda, ma loro continuavano a correre.**

A nap magasabbra emelkedett, a levegő melegedett, de ők tovább futottak.

**Buck era pieno di gioia: sapeva di aver risposto alla sua chiamata.**

Buckot öröm töltötte el – tudta, hogy válaszol a hívására.

**Corse accanto al fratello della foresta, più vicino alla fonte della chiamata.**

Erdőtestvére mellett futott, közelebb a hívás forrásához.

**I vecchi sentimenti ritornano, potenti e difficili da ignorare.**

Régi érzések tértek vissza, erősen és nehezen figyelmen kívül hagyva őket.

**Queste erano le verità nascoste nei ricordi dei suoi sogni.**

Ezek voltak az álmaiban rejlő emlékek mögött rejlő igazságok.

**Tutto questo lo aveva già fatto in un mondo lontano e oscuro.**

Mindezt már megtette korábban egy távoli és árnyékos világban.

**Questa volta lo fece di nuovo, scatenandosi con il cielo aperto sopra di lui.**

Most megint ezt tette, vadul rohant a szabad ég alatt.

**Si fermarono presso un ruscello per bere l'acqua fredda che scorreva.**

Megálltak egy pataknál, hogy igyanak a hideg, folyó vízből.

**Mentre beveva, Buck si ricordò improvvisamente di John Thornton.**

Miközben ivott, Bucknak hirtelen eszébe jutott John Thornton.

**Si sedette in silenzio, lacerato dal sentimento di lealtà e dalla chiamata.**

Csendben ült le, a hűség és az elhívás vonzása tépte szét.

**Il lupo continuò a trottare, ma tornò indietro per incitare Buck ad andare avanti.**

A farkas továbbügetett, de visszatért, hogy ösztökélje Buckot.

**Gli annusò il naso e cercò di convincerlo con gesti gentili.**

Megszagolta az orrát, és halk mozdulatokkal próbálta rávenni.

**Ma Buck si voltò e riprese a tornare indietro per la strada da cui era venuto.**

De Buck megfordult, és elindult visszafelé, amerről jött.

**Il lupo gli corse accanto per molto tempo, guaindo piano.**

A farkas sokáig futott mellette, halkan nyüszítve.

**Poi si sedette, alzò il naso ed emise un lungo ululato.**

Aztán leült, felhúzta az orrát, és hosszan felüvöltött.

**Era un grido lugubre, che si addolcì mentre Buck si allontanava.**

Gyászos kiáltás volt, amely elhalkult, ahogy Buck elsétált.

**Buck ascoltò mentre il suono del grido svaniva lentamente nel silenzio della foresta.**

Buck hallgatta, ahogy a sírás hangja lassan elhalványul az erdő csendjében.

**John Thornton stava cenando quando Buck irruppe nell'accampamento.**

John Thornton éppen vacsorázott, amikor Buck berontott a táborba.

**Buck gli saltò addosso selvaggiamente, leccandolo, mordendolo e facendolo rotolare.**

Buck vadul ráugrott, nyalogatta, harapdálta és fel-le gördítette.

**Lo fece cadere, gli saltò sopra e gli baciò il viso.**

Fellökte, ráugrott, és megcsókolta az arcát.

**Thornton lo definì con affetto "fare il buffone".**

Thornton szeretettel „az általános hülye megjátszásának" nevezte ezt.

**Nel frattempo, imprecava dolcemente contro Buck e lo scuoteva avanti e indietro.**

Közben gyengéden átkozta Buckot, és előre-hátra rázogatta.

**Per due interi giorni e due notti, Buck non lasciò l'accampamento nemmeno una volta.**

Két teljes napon és két éjszakán át Buck egyszer sem hagyta el a tábort.

**Si teneva vicino a Thornton e non lo perdeva mai di vista.**

Thornton közelében maradt, és soha nem tévesztette szem elől.

**Lo seguiva mentre lavorava e lo osservava mentre mangiava.**

Követte őt munka közben, és figyelte evés közben.

**Di notte vedeva Thornton avvolto nelle sue coperte e ogni mattina lo vedeva uscire.**

Éjszaka látta Thorntont a takaróiba bújni, reggelente pedig kiment.

**Ma presto il richiamo della foresta ritornò, più forte che mai.**

De hamarosan visszatért az erdő hívása, hangosabban, mint valaha.

**Buck si sentì di nuovo irrequieto, agitato dal pensiero del lupo selvatico.**

Buck ismét nyugtalanná vált, a vad farkas gondolatai kavargatták.

**Ricordava la terra aperta e le corse fianco a fianco.**

Emlékezett a nyílt terepre és az egymás mellett futásra.

**Ricominciò a vagare nella foresta, solo e vigile.**

Újra elindult az erdőbe, egyedül és éberen.

**Ma il fratello selvaggio non tornò e l'ululato non fu udito.**

De a vad testvér nem tért vissza, és az üvöltés sem hallatszott.

**Buck cominciò a dormire all'aperto, restando lontano anche per giorni interi.**

Buck kint kezdett aludni, napokig is távol maradt.

**Una volta attraversò l'alto spartiacque dove aveva origine il torrente.**

Miután átkelt a magas vízválasztón, ahol a patak elkezdődött.

**Entrò nella terra degli alberi scuri e dei grandi corsi d'acqua.**

Sötét erdők és széles patakok földjére lépett.

**Vagò per una settimana alla ricerca di tracce del fratello selvaggio.**

Egy hétig barangolt, a vad testvér nyomait keresve.

**Uccideva la propria carne e viaggiava a passi lunghi e instancabili.**

Saját maga ölte meg a zsákmányát, és hosszú, fáradhatatlan léptekkel haladt.

**Pescò salmoni in un ampio fiume che arrivava fino al mare.**

Lazacra halászott egy széles folyóban, amely a tengerig ért.

**Lì lottò e uccise un orso nero reso pazzo dagli insetti.**

Ott harcolt és megölt egy bogaraktól megőrjített fekete medvét.

**L'orso stava pescando e corse alla cieca tra gli alberi.**

A medve horgászott, és vakon szaladgált a fák között.

**La battaglia fu feroce e risvegliò il profondo spirito combattivo di Buck.**

A csata ádáz volt, felébresztve Buck mély harci szellemét.

Due giorni dopo, Buck tornò e trovò dei ghiottoni nei pressi della sua preda.

Két nappal később Buck visszatért, és rozsomákokat talált a zsákmányánál.

Una dozzina di loro litigarono furiosamente e rumorosamente per la carne.

Egy tucatnyian veszekedtek hangos dühvel a húson.

Buck caricò e li disperse come foglie al vento.

Buck rohamra kelt, és szétszórta őket, mint a faleveleket a szélben.

Due lupi rimasero indietro: silenziosi, senza vita e immobili per sempre.

Két farkas maradt hátra – csendben, élettelenül és örökre mozdulatlanul.

La sete di sangue divenne più forte che mai.

A vér utáni szomjúság erősebb lett, mint valaha.

Buck era un cacciatore, un assassino, che si nutriva di creature viventi.

Buck vadász volt, gyilkos, élőlényekkel táplálkozott.

Sopravvisse da solo, affidandosi alla sua forza e ai suoi sensi acuti.

Egyedül élte túl, erejére és éles érzékeire támaszkodva.

Prosperava nella natura selvaggia, dove solo i più forti potevano sopravvivere.

A vadonban élt, ahol csak a legkeményebbek élhettek.

Da ciò nacque un grande orgoglio che riempì tutto l'essere di Buck.

Ettől nagy büszkeség támadt, és Buck egész lényét betöltötte.

Il suo orgoglio traspariva da ogni passo, dal fremito di ogni muscolo.

Büszkesége minden lépésében, minden izma hullámzásában megmutatkozott.

Il suo orgoglio era evidente, come si vedeva dal suo comportamento.

Büszkesége olyan nyilvánvaló volt, mint a szavak, ami a viselkedésén látszott.

Persino il suo spesso mantello appariva più maestoso e splendeva di più.

Még vastag bundája is fenségesebbnek tűnt és fényesebben csillogott.

**Buck avrebbe potuto essere scambiato per un lupo grigio gigante.**

Buckot akár egy óriási erdei farkasnak is nézhették volna.

**A parte il marrone sul muso e le macchie sopra gli occhi.**

Kivéve a barna foltokat az orrán és a szeme felett.

**E la striscia bianca di pelo che gli correva lungo il centro del petto.**

És a fehér szőrcsík, ami a mellkasa közepén végigfutott.

**Era addirittura più grande del più grande lupo di quella feroce razza.**

Még a vad fajta legnagyobb farkasánál is nagyobb volt.

**Suo padre, un San Bernardo, gli ha trasmesso la stazza e la corporatura robusta.**

Apja, egy bernáthegyi, nagy és masszív testalkatú lányt adott neki.

**Sua madre, una pastorella, plasmò quella mole conferendole la forma di un lupo.**

Az anyja, egy pásztor, farkas alakúra formálta ezt a testet.

**Aveva il muso lungo di un lupo, anche se più pesante e largo.**

Hosszú, farkasorrú volt, bár nehezebb és szélesebb.

**La sua testa era quella di un lupo, ma di dimensioni enormi e maestose.**

A feje farkasra hasonlított, de hatalmas, fenséges méretekben épült fel.

**L'astuzia di Buck era l'astuzia del lupo e della natura selvaggia.**

Buck ravaszsága a farkasok és a vadon ravaszsága volt.

**La sua intelligenza gli venne sia dal Pastore Tedesco che dal San Bernardo.**

Intelligenciáját mind a németjuhásztól, mind a bernáthegyitől kapta.

**Tutto ciò, unito alla dura esperienza, lo rese una creatura temibile.**

Mindez, a kemény tapasztalatokkal együtt, félelmetes teremtménnyé tette.

**Era formidabile quanto qualsiasi animale che vagasse nelle terre selvagge del nord.**

Olyan félelmetes volt, mint bármelyik vadállat, amely az északi vadonban barangolt.

**Nutrendosi solo di carne, Buck raggiunse l'apice della sua forza.**

Buck, aki kizárólag húson élt, ereje csúcsára ért.

**Trasudava potenza e forza maschile in ogni fibra del suo corpo.**

Minden porcikájában áradt az erő és a férfias erő.

**Quando Thornton gli accarezzò la schiena, i peli brillarono di energia.**

Amikor Thornton megsimogatta a hátát, a szőrszálak energiától szikráztak.

**Ogni capello scricchiolava, carico del tocco di un magnetismo vivente.**

Minden egyes hajszál roppant, az élő mágnesesség érintésével feltöltve.

**Il suo corpo e il suo cervello erano sintonizzati sulla tonalità più fine possibile.**

Teste és agya a lehető legfinomabb hangmagasságra volt hangolva.

**Ogni nervo, ogni fibra e ogni muscolo lavoravano in perfetta armonia.**

Minden ideg, rost és izom tökéletes harmóniában működött.

**A qualsiasi suono o visione che richiedesse un intervento, rispondeva immediatamente.**

Bármilyen beavatkozást igénylő hangra vagy látványra azonnal reagált.

**Se un husky saltava per attaccare, Buck poteva saltare due volte più velocemente.**

Ha egy husky támadásba lendült volna, Buck kétszer olyan gyorsan tudott volna ugrani.

Reagì più rapidamente di quanto gli altri potessero vedere o sentire.

Gyorsabban reagált, mint ahogy mások láthatták vagy hallhatták volna.

Percezione, decisione e azione avvennero tutte in un unico, fluido istante.

Az érzékelés, a döntés és a cselekvés mind egyetlen folyékony pillanatban történt.

In realtà si tratta di atti separati, ma troppo rapidi per essere notati.

Valójában ezek a cselekedetek különállóak voltak, de túl gyorsak ahhoz, hogy észrevegyék.

Gli intervalli tra questi atti erano così brevi che sembravano uno solo.

Olyan rövidek voltak a szünetek e két aktus között, hogy egyetlen egységnek tűntek.

I suoi muscoli e il suo essere erano come molle strettamente avvolte.

Izmai és lénye olyanok voltak, mint a szorosan összefonódó rugók.

Il suo corpo traboccava di vita, selvaggia e gioiosa nella sua potenza.

Teste élettel teli volt, vadul és örömtelien telt erejével.

A volte aveva la sensazione che la forza stesse per esplodere completamente dentro di lui.

Időnként úgy érezte, mintha teljesen ki akarna törni belőle az erő.

"Non c'è mai stato un cane simile", disse Thornton un giorno tranquillo.

– Soha nem volt még ilyen kutya a világon – mondta Thornton egy csendes napon.

I soci osservarono Buck uscire fiero dall'accampamento.

A társak figyelték, ahogy Buck büszkén vonul ki a táborból.

"Quando è stato creato, ha cambiato il modo in cui un cane può essere", ha detto Pete.

„Amikor megalkották, megváltoztatta azt, hogy milyen lehet egy kutya" – mondta Pete.

"Per Dio! Lo penso anch'io", concordò subito Hans.

– Jézusomra! Én is így gondolom – helyeselt gyorsan Hans.

**Lo videro allontanarsi, ma non il cambiamento che avvenne dopo.**

Látták elvonulni, de a utána következő változást nem látták.

**Non appena entrò nel bosco, Buck si trasformò completamente.**

Amint Buck belépett az erdőbe, teljesen átváltozott.

**Non marciava più, ma si muoveva come uno spettro selvaggio tra gli alberi.**

Már nem menetelt, hanem vad szellemként mozgott a fák között.

**Divenne silenzioso, come un gatto, un bagliore che attraversava le ombre.**

Elhallgatott, macskalábú lett, egy fénycsóva suhant át az árnyékokon.

**Usava la copertura con abilità, strisciando sulla pancia come un serpente.**

Ügyesen használta a fedezéket, kígyóként mászott a hasán.

**E come un serpente, sapeva balzare in avanti e colpire in silenzio.**

És mint egy kígyó, előre tudott ugrani és csendben lecsapni.

**Potrebbe rubare una pernice bianca direttamente dal suo nido nascosto.**

Ellophatott egy hófajdot egyenesen a rejtett fészkéből.

**Uccideva i conigli addormentati senza emettere alcun suono.**

Egyetlen hang nélkül ölte meg az alvó nyulakat.

**Riusciva a catturare gli scoiattoli a mezz'aria anche se fuggivano troppo lentamente.**

Elkaphatta a levegőben a lassan menekülő mókusokat.

**Nemmeno i pesci nelle pozze riuscivano a sfuggire ai suoi attacchi improvvisi.**

Még a medencében lévő halak sem menekülhettek hirtelen csapásai elől.

**Nemmeno i furbi castori impegnati a riparare le dighe erano al sicuro da lui.**

Még az okos hódok sem voltak biztonságban tőle, akik gátakat javítottak.

**Uccideva per nutrirsi, non per divertirsi, ma preferiva uccidere le proprie vittime.**

Élelemért ölt, nem szórakozásból – de a saját zsákmányát szerette a legjobban.

**Eppure, un umorismo subdolo permeava alcune delle sue cacce silenziose.**

Mégis, ravasz humor futott át néma vadászatainak némelyikén.

**Si avvicinò furtivamente agli scoiattoli, solo per lasciarli scappare.**

Közel osont a mókusokhoz, csak hogy aztán hagyja őket elmenekülni.

**Stavano per fuggire tra gli alberi, chiacchierando con rabbia e paura.**

Félelmükben és felháborodásukban csacsogva a fák közé menekültek.

**Con l'arrivo dell'autunno, le alci cominciarono ad apparire in numero maggiore.**

Ahogy beköszöntött az ősz, a jávorszarvasok egyre nagyobb számban kezdtek megjelenni.

**Si spostarono lentamente verso le basse valli per affrontare l'inverno.**

Lassan beköltöztek az alacsony völgyekbe, hogy várják a telet.

**Buck aveva già abbattuto un giovane vitello randagio.**

Buck már elejtett egy fiatal, kóbor borjút.

**Ma lui desiderava ardentemente affrontare prede più grandi e pericolose.**

De vágyott arra, hogy nagyobb, veszélyesebb prédával nézzen szembe.

**Un giorno, sul crinale, alla sorgente del torrente, trovò la sua occasione.**

Egy nap a vízválasztórál, a patak forrásánál, meglátta a lehetőséget.

**Una mandria di venti alci era giunta da terre boscose.**

Húsz jávorszarvasból álló csorda kelt át erdős vidékekről.

Tra loro c'era un possente toro, il capo del gruppo.

Köztük volt egy hatalmas bika; a csoport vezetője.

Il toro era alto più di due metri e mezzo e appariva feroce e selvaggio.

A bika több mint két méter magas volt, és vadnak, vadnak látszott.

Lanciò le sue grandi corna, le cui quattordici punte si diramavano verso l'esterno.

Széles agancsait meglóbálta, tizennégy ágból álló ágakat.

Le punte di quelle corna si estendevano per due metri.

Az agancsok végei hét láb szélesre nyúltak.

I suoi piccoli occhi ardevano di rabbia quando vide Buck lì vicino.

Apró szemei dühtől égtek, amikor meglátta Buckot a közelben.

Emise un ruggito furioso, tremando di rabbia e dolore.

Dühösen felordított, remegett a dühtől és a fájdalomtól.

Vicino al suo fianco spuntava la punta di una freccia, appuntita e piumata.

Egy tollas, hegyes nyílvég állt ki az oldala közelében.

Questa ferita contribuì a spiegare il suo umore selvaggio e amareggiato.

Ez a seb segített megmagyarázni vad, keserű hangulatát.

Buck, guidato dall'antico istinto di caccia, fece la sua mossa.

Buck, az ősi vadászösztön által vezérelve, megtette a lépést.

Il suo obiettivo era separare il toro dal resto della mandria.

Célja az volt, hogy elkülönítse a bikát a csorda többi részétől.

Non era un compito facile: richiedeva velocità e una grande astuzia.

Ez nem volt könnyű feladat – gyorsaságra és ravaszságra volt szükség hozzá.

Abbaiava e danzava vicino al toro, appena fuori dalla sua portata.

Ugatott és táncolt a bika közelében, éppen csak lőtávon kívül.

L'alce si lanciò con enormi zoccoli e corna mortali.

A jávorszarvas hatalmas patákkal és halálos agancsokkal rontott előre.

Un colpo avrebbe potuto porre fine alla vita di Buck in un batter d'occhio.

Egyetlen ütés egy szempillantás alatt véget vethetett volna Buck életének.

Incapace di abbandonare la minaccia, il toro si infuriò.

Mivel nem tudta maga mögött hagyni a fenyegetést, a bika dühbe gurult.

Lui caricava con furia, ma Buck riusciva sempre a sfuggirgli.

Dühösen támadott, de Buck mindig elhúzódott.

Buck finse di essere debole, allontanandosi ulteriormente dalla mandria.

Buck gyengeséget színlelt, és ezzel távolabb csalogatta a csordától.

Ma i giovani tori sarebbero tornati alla carica per proteggere il capo.

De a fiatal bikák visszarohantak, hogy megvédjék a vezetőt.

Costrinsero Buck a ritirarsi e il toro a ricongiungersi al gruppo.

Kényszerítették Buckot a visszavonulásra, a bikát pedig arra, hogy csatlakozzon újra a csoporthoz.

C'è una pazienza nella natura selvaggia, profonda e inarrestabile.

Van egyfajta türelem a vadonban, mély és megállíthatatlan.

Un ragno resta immobile nella sua tela per innumerevoli ore.

Egy pók órákon át mozdulatlanul várakozik a hálójában.

Un serpente si avvolge su se stesso senza contrarsi e aspetta il momento giusto.

Egy kígyó rángatózás nélkül tekeredik, és várja, míg eljön az ideje.

Una pantera è in agguato, finché non arriva il momento.

Egy párduc lesben áll, míg el nem jön a pillanat.

Questa è la pazienza dei predatori che cacciano per sopravvivere.

Ez a ragadozók türelme, akik a túlélésért vadásznak.

La stessa pazienza ardeva dentro Buck mentre gli restava accanto.

Ugyanez a türelem égett Buckban is, miközben közel maradt.

**Rimase vicino alla mandria, rallentandone la marcia e incutendo timore.**

A csorda közelében maradt, lelassítva annak menetét és félelmet keltve benne.

**Provocava i giovani tori e molestava le mucche madri.**

Cukkolta a fiatal bikákat és zaklatta az anyateheneket.

**Spinse il toro ferito in una rabbia ancora più profonda e impotente.**

Még mélyebb, tehetetlen dühbe gurította a sebesült bikát.

**Per mezza giornata il combattimento si trascinò senza alcuna tregua.**

Fél napig elhúzódott a harc pihenés nélkül.

**Buck attaccò da ogni angolazione, veloce e feroce come il vento.**

Buck minden szögből támadott, gyorsan és vadul, mint a szél.

**Impedì al toro di riposare o di nascondersi con la mandria.**

Megakadályozta, hogy a bika pihenjen vagy elbújjon a csordájával.

**Buck logorò la volontà dell'alce più velocemente del suo corpo.**

Buck gyorsabban ölte le a jávorszarvas akaratát, mint a testét.

**Il giorno passò e il sole tramontò basso nel cielo a nord-ovest.**

A nap telt el, és a nap alacsonyan ereszkedett le az északnyugati égbolton.

**I giovani tori tornarono più lentamente per aiutare il loro capo.**

A fiatal bikák lassabban tértek vissza, hogy segítsenek vezetőjüknek.

**Erano tornate le notti autunnali e il buio durava ormai sei ore.**

Visszatértek az őszi éjszakák, és a sötétség már hat órán át tartott.

**L'inverno li spingeva verso valli più sicure e calde.**

A tél a biztonságosabb, melegebb völgyekbe taszította őket lefelé.

**Ma non riuscirono comunque a sfuggire al cacciatore che li tratteneva.**

De még így sem tudtak elmenekülni a vadász elől, aki visszatartotta őket.

**Era in gioco solo una vita: non quella del branco, ma quella del loro capo.**

Csak egyetlen élet forgott kockán – nem a csordáé, csak a vezetőjüké.

**Ciò rendeva la minaccia lontana e non una loro preoccupazione urgente.**

Ez távolivá tette a fenyegetést, és nem a sürgető aggodalmukká.

**Col tempo accettarono questo prezzo e lasciarono che Buck prendesse il vecchio toro.**

Idővel elfogadták ezt az árat, és hagyták, hogy Buck elvigye az öreg bikát.

**Mentre calava il crepuscolo, il vecchio toro rimase in piedi con la testa bassa.**

Ahogy leszállt az alkonyat, az öreg bika lehajtott fejjel állt.

**Guardò la mandria che aveva guidato svanire nella luce morente.**

Nézte, ahogy a csorda, amelyet vezetett, eltűnik a halványuló fényben.

**C'erano mucche che aveva conosciuto, vitelli che un tempo aveva generato.**

Voltak tehenek, akiket ismert, borjak, akiknek egykor ő volt az apja.

**C'erano tori più giovani con cui aveva combattuto e che aveva dominato nelle stagioni passate.**

Voltak fiatalabb bikák is, akikkel a múlt szezonokban harcolt és uralkodott.

**Non poteva seguirli, perché davanti a lui era di nuovo accovacciato Buck.**

Nem követhette őket – mert Buck ismét leguggolt előtte.

**Il terrore spietato e zannuto gli bloccava ogni via che potesse percorrere.**

A könyörtelen, agyaras rettegés minden útját elállta.

Il toro pesava più di trecento chili di potenza densa.
A bika több mint háromszáz fontnyi sűrű erőt nyomott.
Aveva vissuto a lungo e lottato duramente in un mondo di difficoltà.
Hosszú életet élt és keményen küzdött egy küzdelmes világban.
Eppure, alla fine, la morte gli venne commessa da una bestia molto più bassa di lui.
Mégis, most, a végén a halál egy messze alatta lévő szörnyetegtől érkezett.
La testa di Buck non arrivò nemmeno alle enormi ginocchia noccate del toro.
Buck feje még a bika hatalmas, bütykös térdéig sem ért fel.
Da quel momento in poi, Buck rimase con il toro notte e giorno.
Attól a pillanattól kezdve Buck éjjel-nappal a bikával maradt.
Non gli dava mai tregua, non gli permetteva mai di brucare o bere.
Soha nem hagyta pihenni, soha nem engedte legelni vagy inni.
Il toro cercò di mangiare giovani germogli di betulla e foglie di salice.
A bika megpróbált fiatal nyírfahajtásokat és fűzfaleveleket enni.
Ma Buck lo scacciò, sempre all'erta e sempre all'attacco.
De Buck elűzte, mivel mindig éber és támadó volt.
Anche nei torrenti che scorrevano, Buck bloccava ogni assetato tentativo.
Még a csordogáló patakoknál is Buck minden szomjas kísérletet hárított.
A volte, in preda alla disperazione, il toro fuggiva a tutta velocità.
Néha kétségbeesésében a bika teljes sebességgel menekült.
Buck lo lasciò correre, avanzando tranquillamente dietro di lui, senza mai allontanarsi troppo.
Buck hagyta futni, nyugodtan lopakodott mögötte, soha nem messze.
Quando l'alce si fermò, Buck si sdraiò, ma rimase pronto.

Amikor a jávorszarvas megállt, Buck lefeküdt, de készenlétben maradt.

**Se il toro provava a mangiare o a bere, Buck colpiva con tutta la sua furia.**

Ha a bika megpróbált enni vagy inni, Buck teljes dühvel csapott le rá.

**La grande testa del toro si abbassava sotto le enormi corna.**

A bika hatalmas feje egyre mélyebbre csuklott hatalmas agancsai alatt.

**Il suo passo rallentò, il trotto divenne pesante, un'andatura barcollante.**

A lépései lelassultak, az ügetés nehézkessé, botladozó járássá vált.

**Spesso restava immobile con le orecchie abbassate e il naso rivolto verso il terreno.**

Gyakran mozdulatlanul állt, lelógó fülekkel és a földhöz szorított orral.

**In quei momenti Buck si prese del tempo per bere e riposare.**

Ezekben a pillanatokban Buck időt szakított az ivásra és a pihenésre.

**Con la lingua fuori e gli occhi fissi, Buck sentì che la terra stava cambiando.**

Kinyújtott nyelvvel, fürkésző tekintettel Buck érezte, hogy a táj változik.

**Sentì qualcosa di nuovo muoversi nella foresta e nel cielo.**

Érezte, hogy valami új mozog az erdőn és az égen keresztül.

**Con il ritorno delle alci tornarono anche altre creature selvatiche.**

Ahogy a jávorszarvasok visszatértek, úgy tették ezt a vadon más állatai is.

**La terra sembrava viva di una presenza invisibile ma fortemente nota.**

A föld élőnek és jelenvalónak érződött, láthatatlanul, mégis erősen ismertté.

**Buck non lo sapeva tramite l'udito, la vista o l'olfatto.**

Buck nem hallás, látás vagy szag alapján tudta ezt.

Un sentimento più profondo gli diceva che nuove forze
erano in movimento.
Egy mélyebb érzés azt súgta neki, hogy új erők vannak
mozgásban.
Una strana vita si agitava nei boschi e lungo i corsi d'acqua.
Különös élet kavarogott az erdőkben és a patakok mentén.
Decise di esplorare questo spirito una volta completata la
caccia.
Elhatározta, hogy felfedezi ezt a szellemet, miután befejezte a
vadászatot.
Il quarto giorno, Buck riuscì finalmente a catturare l'alce.
A negyedik napon Buck végre leterítette a jávorszarvast.
Rimase nei pressi della preda per un giorno e una notte
interi, nutrendosi e riposandosi.
Egy teljes napot és egy éjszakát töltött a zsákmány mellett,
evett és pihent.
Mangiò, poi dormì, poi mangiò ancora, finché non fu forte e
sazio.
Evett, aztán aludt, majd újra evett, míg meg nem erősödött és
jóllakott.
Quando fu pronto, tornò indietro verso l'accampamento e
Thornton.
Amikor készen állt, visszafordult a tábor és Thornton felé.
Con passo costante iniziò il lungo viaggio di ritorno verso
casa.
Egyenletes tempóval indult meg a hosszú hazaútra.
Correva con la sua andatura instancabile, ora dopo ora, senza
mai smarrirsi.
Fáradhatatlanul rohant, óránként, egyszer sem tévedve el.
Attraverso terre sconosciute, si muoveva dritto come l'ago di
una bussola.
Ismeretlen vidékeken haladt, egyenesen, mint az iránytű tűje.
Il suo senso dell'orientamento faceva sembrare deboli, al
confronto, l'uomo e la mappa.
Tájékozódása miatt az ember és a térkép gyengének tűnt
hozzá képest.

Mentre Buck correva, sentiva sempre più forte l'agitazione nella terra selvaggia.

Ahogy Buck futott, egyre erősebben érezte a vad tájon zajló nyüzsgést.

Era un nuovo tipo di vita, diverso da quello dei tranquilli mesi estivi.

Ez egy újfajta élet volt, ellentétben a nyugodt nyári hónapokkal.

Questa sensazione non giungeva più come un messaggio sottile o distante.

Ez az érzés már nem finom vagy távoli üzenetként érkezett.

Ora gli uccelli parlavano di questa vita e gli scoiattoli chiacchieravano.

A madarak most erről az életről beszéltek, a mókusok pedig csacsogtak róla.

Persino la brezza sussurrava avvertimenti tra gli alberi silenziosi.

Még a szellő is figyelmeztetéseket suttogott a néma fák között.

Più volte si fermò ad annusare l'aria fresca del mattino.

Többször is megállt, és beleszippantott a friss reggeli levegőbe.

Lì lesse un messaggio che lo fece fare un balzo in avanti più velocemente.

Egy üzenetet olvasott ott, amitől gyorsabban ugrott előre.

Fu pervaso da un forte senso di pericolo, come se qualcosa fosse andato storto.

Súlyos veszélyérzet töltötte el, mintha valami baj történt volna.

Temeva che la calamità stesse per arrivare, o che fosse già arrivata.

Attól félt, hogy katasztrófa közeleg – vagy már bekövetkezett.

Superò l'ultima cresta ed entrò nella valle sottostante.

Átkelt az utolsó gerincen, és beért az alatta lévő völgybe.

Si muoveva più lentamente, attento e cauto a ogni passo.

Lassabban, minden lépéssel éberebbé és óvatosabbá vált.

Dopo tre miglia trovò una pista fresca che lo fece irrigidire.

Három mérfölddel odébb egy friss ösvényre bukkant, amitől megmerevedett.

**I peli sul collo si rizzarono e si rizzarono in segno di allarme.**
A nyakán a szőr riadtan hullámzott és égnek állt.
**Il sentiero portava dritto all'accampamento dove Thornton aspettava.**
Az ösvény egyenesen a tábor felé vezetett, ahol Thornton várakozott.
**Buck ora si muoveva più velocemente, con passi silenziosi e rapidi.**
Buck most gyorsabban mozgott, léptei egyszerre voltak nesztelenek és gyorsak.
**I suoi nervi si irrigidirono mentre leggeva segnali che altri non avrebbero notato.**
Feszültek az idegei, miközben olyan jeleket olvasott, amelyeket mások nem fognak észrevenni.
**Ogni dettaglio del percorso raccontava una storia, tranne l'ultimo pezzo.**
Az ösvény minden részlete egy történetet mesélt – kivéve az utolsó darabot.
**Il suo naso gli raccontò della vita che aveva trascorso lì.**
Az orra árulkodott az itt eltelt életről.
**L'odore gli fornì un'immagine mutevole mentre lo seguiva da vicino.**
Az illat változó képet festett róla, ahogy szorosan a nyomában követte.
**Ma la foresta stessa era diventata silenziosa, innaturalmente immobile.**
De maga az erdő elcsendesedett; természetellenesen mozdulatlanná vált.
**Gli uccelli erano scomparsi, gli scoiattoli erano nascosti, silenziosi e immobili.**
A madarak eltűntek, a mókusok elrejtőztek, csendben és mozdulatlanul.
**Vide solo uno scoiattolo grigio, sdraiato su un albero morto.**
Csak egyetlen szürke mókust látott, egy kiszáradt fán feküdt.
**Lo scoiattolo si mimetizzava, rigido e immobile come una parte della foresta.**

A mókus beleolvadt a környezetébe, mereven és mozdulatlanul, mint egy erdő része.

**Buck si muoveva come un'ombra, silenzioso e sicuro tra gli alberi.**

Buck árnyékként mozgott, csendben és magabiztosan a fák között.

**Il suo naso si mosse di lato come se fosse stato tirato da una mano invisibile.**

Az orra oldalra rándult, mintha egy láthatatlan kéz húzta volna.

**Si voltò e seguì il nuovo odore nel profondo di un boschetto.**

Megfordult, és követte az új illatot egy bozótos mélyére.

**Lì trovò Nig, steso morto, trafitto da una freccia.**

Ott találta Niget holtan fekve, nyílvesszővel átszúrva.

**La freccia gli attraversò il corpo, lasciando ancora visibili le piume.**

A nyíl áthatolt a testén, a tollai még látszottak.

**Nig si era trascinato fin lì, ma era morto prima di riuscire a raggiungere i soccorsi.**

Nig vonszolta magát oda, de meghalt, mielőtt a segítséghez érkezhetett volna.

**Cento metri più avanti, Buck trovò un altro cane da slitta.**

Száz méterrel odébb Buck egy másik szánhúzó kutyára bukkant.

**Era un cane che Thornton aveva comprato a Dawson City.**

Egy kutya volt, amit Thornton vett még Dawson Cityben.

**Il cane lottava con tutte le sue forze, dimenandosi violentemente sul sentiero.**

A kutya haláltusát vívva, keményen vergődött az ösvényen.

**Buck gli passò accanto senza fermarsi, con gli occhi fissi davanti a sé.**

Buck elhaladt mellette, meg sem állva, maga elé szegezve tekintetét.

**Dalla direzione dell'accampamento proveniva un canto lontano e ritmico.**

A tábor irányából távoli, ritmikus ének hallatszott.

**Le voci si alzavano e si abbassavano con un tono strano, inquietante, cantilenante.**

A hangok furcsa, hátborzongató, éneklő hangon emelkedtek és süllyedtek.

**Buck strisciò in silenzio fino al limite della radura.**

Buck csendben kúszott előre a tisztás széléig.

**Lì vide Hans disteso a faccia in giù, trafitto da numerose frecce.**

Ott látta Hanst arccal lefelé feküdni, sok nyílvesszővel átszúrva.

**Il suo corpo sembrava quello di un porcospino, irto di penne.**

A teste egy tarajos sülre hasonlított, tollas nyilak borították.

**Nello stesso momento, Buck guardò verso la capanna in rovina.**

Ugyanebben a pillanatban Buck a romos kunyhó felé nézett.

**Quella vista gli fece rizzare i capelli sul collo e sulle spalle.**

A látványtól meredeken állt a nyakán és a vállán a szőr.

**Un'ondata di rabbia selvaggia travolse tutto il corpo di Buck.**

Vad dühvihar söpört végig Buck egész testén.

**Ringhiò forte, anche se non ne era consapevole.**

Hangosan morgott, bár nem tudta, hogy így tett.

**Il suono era crudo, pieno di una furia terrificante e selvaggia.**

A hang nyers volt, tele félelmetes, vad dühvel.

**Per l'ultima volta nella sua vita, Buck perse la ragione a causa delle emozioni.**

Buck életében utoljára elvesztette az érzelmei feletti uralmat.

**Fu l'amore per John Thornton a spezzare il suo attento controllo.**

A John Thornton iránti szerelem törte meg gondos önuralmát.

**Gli Yeehats ballavano attorno alla baita in legno di abete rosso distrutta.**

A Yeehat család a romos lucfenyőkunyhó körül táncolt.

**Poi si udì un ruggito e una bestia sconosciuta si lanciò verso di loro.**

Aztán egy üvöltés hallatszott – és egy ismeretlen fenevad rohant feléjük.

**Era Buck: una furia in movimento, una tempesta vivente di vendetta.**

Buck volt az; mozgásban lévő düh; a bosszú eleven vihara.

**Si gettò in mezzo a loro, folle di voglia di uccidere.**

Közéjük vetette magát, őrjöngve a gyilkolás vágyától.

**Si lanciò contro il primo uomo, il capo Yeehat, e colpì nel segno.**

Ráugrott az első emberre, a yeehat főnökre, és célt lőtt.

**La sua gola era squarciata e il sangue schizzava a fiotti.**

A torkát feltépték, és vére patakként ömlött belőle.

**Buck non si fermò, ma con un balzo squarciò la gola dell'uomo successivo.**

Buck nem állt meg, hanem egyetlen ugrással eltépte a következő férfi torkát.

**Era inarrestabile: squarciava, tagliava, non si fermava mai a riposare.**

Megállíthatatlan volt – tépett, vagdalt, és soha nem állt meg pihenni.

**Si lanciò e balzò così velocemente che le loro frecce non riuscirono a toccarlo.**

Olyan gyorsan száguldott és ugrott, hogy a nyilaik nem érték el.

**Gli Yeehats erano in preda al panico e alla confusione.**

A Yeehat családot elfogta a pánik és a zavarodottság.

**Le loro frecce non colpirono Buck e si colpirono tra loro.**

Nyilaik elvétették Buckot, és inkább egymást találták el.

**Un giovane scagliò una lancia contro Buck e colpì un altro uomo.**

Az egyik fiatalember lándzsát dobott Buckra, és eltalált egy másik férfit.

**La lancia gli trapassò il petto e la punta gli trafisse la schiena.**

A lándzsa átfúródott a mellkasán, a hegye pedig a hátát ütötte ki.

**Il terrore travolse gli Yeehats, che si diedero alla ritirata.**

Rettegés söpört végig a Yeehatokon, és teljes visszavonulásba kezdtek.

**Urlarono allo Spirito Maligno e fuggirono nelle ombre della foresta.**

A Gonosz Szellemre kiáltottak, és az erdő árnyékába menekültek.

**Buck era davvero come un demone mentre inseguiva gli Yeehats.**

Buck valóban démonként üldözte a Yeehat családot.

**Li inseguì attraverso la foresta, abbattendoli come cervi.**

Utánuk rohant az erdőn át, és úgy terítette le őket, mint a szarvasokat.

**Divenne un giorno di destino e terrore per gli spaventati Yeehats.**

A sors és a rettegés napja lett ez a megriadt Yeehat-ek számára.

**Si dispersero sul territorio, fuggendo in ogni direzione.**

Szétszóródtak az országban, minden irányban messzire menekülve.

**Passò un'intera settimana prima che gli ultimi sopravvissuti si incontrassero in una valle.**

Egy teljes hét telt el, mire az utolsó túlélők egy völgyben találkoztak.

**Solo allora contarono le perdite e raccontarono quanto accaduto.**

Csak ezután számoltak be a veszteségeikről és beszéltek a történtekről.

**Buck, stanco dell'inseguimento, ritornò all'accampamento in rovina.**

Buck, miután megunta az üldözést, visszatért a romos táborba.

**Trovò Pete, ancora avvolto nelle coperte, ucciso nel primo attacco.**

Pete-et még mindig takarókban találta, az első támadásban holtan.

**I segni dell'ultima lotta di Thornton erano visibili nella terra lì vicino.**

Thornton utolsó küzdelmének nyomai látszottak a közeli földben.

**Buck seguì ogni traccia, annusando ogni segno fino al punto finale.**

Buck minden nyomot követett, minden egyes jelet megszagolt a végső pontig.

**Sul bordo di una profonda pozza trovò il fedele Skeet, immobile.**

Egy mély medence szélén megtalálta a hűséges Skeetet, amint mozdulatlanul fekve fekszik.

**La testa e le zampe anteriori di Skeet erano nell'acqua, immobili nella morte.**

Skeet feje és mellső mancsai a vízben voltak, mozdulatlanul a halálban.

**La piscina era fangosa e contaminata dai liquidi di scarico delle chiuse.**

A medence sáros volt, és a zsilipekből lefolyó víz szennyezte.

**La sua superficie torbida nascondeva ciò che si trovava sotto, ma Buck conosceva la verità.**

Felhős felszíne elrejtette, ami alatta rejlett, de Buck tudta az igazságot.

**Seguì l'odore di Thornton nella piscina, ma non lo portò da nessun'altra parte.**

Thornton szagát követte a medencében – de a szag sehova sem vezetett.

**Non c'era alcun odore che provenisse, solo il silenzio dell'acqua profonda.**

Semmilyen illat nem vezetett ki belőle – csak a mély víz csendje.

**Buck rimase tutto il giorno vicino alla piscina, camminando avanti e indietro per l'accampamento, addolorato.**

Buck egész nap a medence közelében maradt, bánatában fel-alá járkálva a táborban.

**Vagava irrequieto o sedeva immobile, immerso nei suoi pensieri.**

Nyugtalanul bolyongott, vagy mozdulatlanul ült, nehéz gondolatokba merülve.

Conosceva la morte, la fine della vita, la scomparsa di ogni movimento.

Ismerte a halált; az élet végét; minden mozgás eltűnését.

Capì che John Thornton se n'era andato e non sarebbe mai più tornato.

Megértette, hogy John Thornton elment, és soha többé nem tért vissza.

La perdita lasciò in lui un vuoto che pulsava come la fame.

A veszteség űrt hagyott benne, ami lüktetett, mint az éhség.

Ma questa era una fame che il cibo non riusciva a placare, non importava quanto ne mangiasse.

De ez egy olyan éhség volt, amit az étel nem tudott csillapítani, bármennyit is evett.

A volte, mentre guardava i cadaveri di Yeehats, il dolore si attenuava.

Időnként, ahogy a halott Yeehatekre nézett, a fájdalom alábbhagyott.

E poi dentro di lui nacque uno strano orgoglio, feroce e totale.

És akkor furcsa büszkeség támadt benne, vad és teljes.

Aveva ucciso l'uomo, la preda più alta e pericolosa di tutte.

Embert ölt, ami a legnemesebb és legveszélyesebb játék mind közül.

Aveva ucciso in violazione dell'antica legge del bastone e della zanna.

A bunkó és agyar ősi törvényét megszegve ölt.

Buck annusò i loro corpi senza vita, curioso e pensieroso.

Buck kíváncsian és elgondolkodva szaglászott élettelen testükön.

Erano morti così facilmente, molto più facilmente di un husky in combattimento.

Olyan könnyen haltak meg – sokkal könnyebben, mint egy husky egy verekedésben.

Senza le armi non avrebbero avuto vera forza né avrebbero rappresentato una minaccia.

Fegyvereik nélkül nem éreztek igazi erőt vagy fenyegetést.

**Buck non avrebbe più avuto paura di loro, a meno che non fossero stati armati.**

Buck soha többé nem fog félni tőlük, hacsak nem lesznek felfegyverezve.

**Stava attento solo quando portavano clave, lance o frecce.**

Csak akkor óvakodott, ha bunkókat, lándzsákat vagy nyilakat vittek magukkal.

**Calò la notte e la luna piena spuntò alta sopra le cime degli alberi.**

Leszállt az éj, és a telihold magasan a fák teteje fölé emelkedett.

**La pallida luce della luna avvolgeva la terra in un tenue e spettrale chiarore, come se fosse giorno.**

A hold halvány fénye lágy, kísérteties nappalhoz hasonló derengésbe fürdette a földet.

**Mentre la notte avanzava, Buck continuava a piangere presso la pozza silenziosa.**

Ahogy egyre sötétedett, Buck még mindig gyászolta a csendes tó partját.

**Poi si accorse di un diverso movimento nella foresta.**

Aztán valami másfajta morajlásra lett figyelmes az erdőben.

**L'agitazione non proveniva dagli Yeehats, ma da qualcosa di più antico e profondo.**

A morajlás nem a Yeehat családtól származott, hanem valami régebbitől és mélyebbtől.

**Si alzò in piedi, drizzò le orecchie e tastò con attenzione la brezza con il naso.**

Felállt, fülét felemelve orrával óvatosan simogatva a szellőt.

**Da lontano giunse un debole e acuto grido che squarciò il silenzio.**

Messziről egy halk, éles sikoly hallatszott, ami megtörte a csendet.

**Poi un coro di grida simili seguì subito dopo il primo.**

Majd hasonló kiáltások kórusa követte szorosan az elsőt.

**Il suono si avvicinava sempre di più, diventando sempre più forte con il passare dei minuti.**

A hang közelebb ért, és minden egyes eltelt pillanattal
erősödött.

**Buck conosceva quel grido: proveniva da quell'altro mondo
nella sua memoria.**

Buck ismerte ezt a kiáltást – abból a másik világból jött, ami az
emlékeiben élt.

**Si recò al centro dello spazio aperto e ascoltò attentamente.**

A nyílt tér közepére sétált, és figyelmesen hallgatózott.

**L'appello risuonò più forte che mai, più sentito e più potente
che mai.**

A hívás felhangzott, sokhangúan és erőteljesebben, mint
valaha.

**E ora, più che mai, Buck era pronto a rispondere alla sua
chiamata.**

És most, minden eddiginél jobban, Buck készen állt válaszolni
a hívására.

**John Thornton era morto e in lui non era rimasto alcun
legame con l'uomo.**

John Thornton halott volt, és semmiféle kötelék nem maradt
benne az emberhez.

**L'uomo e tutte le pretese umane erano svaniti: era
finalmente libero.**

Az ember és minden emberi igény eltűnt – végre szabad volt.

**Il branco di lupi era a caccia di carne, proprio come un
tempo avevano fatto gli Yeehats.**

A farkasfalka úgy kergette a prédát, mint egykor a Yeehat-ek.

**Avevano seguito le alci mentre scendevano dalle terre
boscose.**

Jávorszarvasokat követtek le az erdős vidékekről.

**Ora, selvaggi e affamati di prede, attraversarono la sua valle.**

Most, vadul és zsákmányra éhesen, átkeltek a völgyébe.

**Giunsero nella radura illuminata dalla luna, scorrendo come
acqua argentata.**

Ezüstös vízként folytak ki a holdfényes tisztásra.

**Buck rimase immobile al centro, in attesa.**

Buck mozdulatlanul állt középen, és várta őket.

La sua presenza calma e imponente lasciò il branco senza parole, tanto da farlo restare per un breve periodo in silenzio.

Nyugodt, nagy jelenléte egy pillanatra elnémította a falkát.

Allora il lupo più audace gli saltò addosso senza esitazione.

Akkor a legbátrabb farkas habozás nélkül egyenesen ráugrott.

Buck colpì rapidamente e spezzò il collo del lupo con un solo colpo.

Buck gyorsan csapott le, és egyetlen csapással eltörte a farkas nyakát.

Rimase di nuovo immobile mentre il lupo morente si contorceva dietro di lui.

Mozdulatlanul állt ismét, miközben a haldokló farkas megpördült mögötte.

Altri tre lupi attaccarono rapidamente, uno dopo l'altro.

Még három farkas támadt gyorsan, egymás után.

Ognuno di loro si ritrasse sanguinante, con la gola o le spalle tagliate.

Mindegyikük vérzőn vonult vissza, felvágott torokkal vagy vállakkal.

Ciò fu sufficiente a scatenare una carica selvaggia da parte dell'intero branco.

Ez elég volt ahhoz, hogy az egész falka vad rohamra keljen.

Si precipitarono tutti insieme, troppo impazienti e troppo ammassati per colpire bene.

Együtt rohantak be, túl lelkesen és zsúfoltan ahhoz, hogy jól csapjanak le.

La velocità e l'abilità di Buck gli permisero di anticipare l'attacco.

Buck sebessége és ügyessége lehetővé tette számára, hogy a támadás előtt maradjon.

Girò sulle zampe posteriori, schioccando i denti e colpendo in tutte le direzioni.

Hátsó lábain pördült, minden irányba csapkodott és csapkodott.

Ai lupi sembrò che la sua difesa non si fosse mai aperta o avesse vacillato.

A farkasok számára úgy tűnt, mintha a védekezése soha nem nyílt volna ki, vagy megingott volna.

**Si voltò e colpì così velocemente che non riuscirono a raggiungerlo alle spalle.**

Megfordult és olyan gyorsan lecsapott, hogy nem tudtak mögé kerülni.

**Ciononostante, il loro numero lo costrinse a cedere terreno e a ritirarsi.**

Mindazonáltal a létszámuk arra kényszerítette, hogy engedjen a helyzeten és visszavonuljon.

**Superò la piscina e scese nel letto roccioso del torrente.**

Elhaladt a medence mellett, és leereszkedett a sziklás patakmederbe.

**Lì si imbatté in un ripido pendio di ghiaia e terra.**

Ott egy meredek kavicsos és földes partra ütközött.

**Si è infilato in un angolo scavato durante i vecchi scavi dei minatori.**

A bányászok régi ásása közben egy sarokvágásba csúszott.

**Ora, protetto su tre lati, Buck si trovava di fronte solo al lupo frontale.**

Buck, akit most három oldalról is védtek, csak az első farkassal nézett szembe.

**Lì rimase in attesa, pronto per la successiva ondata di assalto.**

Ott állt távol, készen a következő támadási hullámra.

**Buck mantenne la posizione con tanta ferocia che i lupi indietreggiarono.**

Buck olyan dühösen tartotta magát, hogy a farkasok visszahúzódtak.

**Dopo mezz'ora erano sfiniti e visibilmente sconfitti.**

Fél óra múlva kimerültek és láthatóan vereséget szenvedtek.

**Le loro lingue pendevano fuori e le loro zanne bianche brillavano alla luce della luna.**

Nyelvük kilógott, fehér agyaraik csillogtak a holdfényben.

**Alcuni lupi si sdraiano, con la testa alzata e le orecchie dritte verso Buck.**

Néhány farkas lefeküdt, felemelt fejjel, hegyezett fülekkel Buck felé.

**Altri rimasero immobili, attenti e osservarono ogni suo movimento.**

Mások mozdulatlanul álltak, éberen figyelték minden mozdulatát.

**Qualcuno si avvicinò alla piscina e bevve l'acqua fredda.**

Néhányan odamentek a medencéhez, és hideg vizet kortyolgattak.

**Poi un lupo grigio, lungo e magro, si fece avanti furtivamente, con passo gentile.**

Aztán egy hosszú, sovány szürke farkas szelíden előrelopózott.

**Buck lo riconobbe: era il fratello selvaggio di prima.**

Buck felismerte – a korábbi vad testvér volt az.

**Il lupo grigio uggiolò dolcemente e Buck rispose con un guaito.**

A szürke farkas halkan nyüszített, Buck pedig egy nyüszítéssel válaszolt.

**Si toccarono il naso, silenziosamente, senza timore o minaccia.**

Csendesen, fenyegetés vagy félelem nélkül megérintették az orrukat.

**Poi venne un lupo più anziano, scarno e segnato dalle numerose battaglie.**

Utána egy idősebb farkas következett, sovány és a sok csata által sebhelyes.

**Buck cominciò a ringhiare, ma si fermò e annusò il naso del vecchio lupo.**

Buck vicsorogni kezdett, de megállt, és megszagolta az öreg farkas orrát.

**Il vecchio si sedette, alzò il naso e ululò alla luna.**

Az öreg leült, felhúzta az orrát, és a holdra üvöltött.

**Il resto del branco si sedette e si unì al lungo ululato.**

A falka többi tagja leült, és csatlakozott a hosszú üvöltéshez.

**E ora la chiamata giunse a Buck, inequivocabile e forte.**

És most Buckhoz érkezett a hívás, félreérthetetlenül és erőteljesen.

**Si sedette, alzò la testa e ululò insieme agli altri.**

Leült, felemelte a fejét, és a többiekkel együtt üvöltött.

**Quando l'ululato cessò, Buck uscì dal suo riparo roccioso.**

Amikor a vonyítás véget ért, Buck kilépett sziklás menedékéből.

**Il branco si strinse attorno a lui, annusando con gentilezza e cautela.**

A falka körülvette, kedvesen és óvatosan szaglászva.

**Allora i capi lanciarono un grido e si precipitarono nella foresta.**

Aztán a vezetők felkiáltottak, és elrohantak az erdőbe.

**Gli altri lupi li seguirono, guaendo in coro, selvaggi e veloci nella notte.**

A többi farkas követte, kórusban ugatva, vadul és gyorsan az éjszakában.

**Buck corse con loro, accanto al suo selvaggio fratello, ululando mentre correva.**

Buck velük futott, vad testvére mellett, futás közben vonyítva.


**Qui la storia di Buck giunge al termine.**

Itt Buck története jól végződik.

**Negli anni a seguire, gli Yeehats notarono degli strani lupi.**

Az elkövetkező években a Yeehat család furcsa farkasokra lett figyelmes.

**Alcuni avevano la testa e il muso marroni e il petto bianco.**

Némelyiknek barna volt a fején és az orrán, fehér a mellkasán.

**Ma ancora di più temevano la presenza di una figura spettrale tra i lupi.**

De még jobban féltek egy szellemalaktól a farkasok között.

**Parlavano a bassa voce del Cane Fantasma, il capo del branco.**

Suttogva beszéltek a Szellemkutyáról, a falkavezérről.

**Questo Ghost Dog era più astuto del più audace cacciatore di Yeehat.**

Ez a Szellemkutya ravaszabb volt, mint a legvakmerőbb
Yeehat vadász.

**Il cane fantasma rubava dagli accampamenti nel cuore
dell'inverno e faceva a pezzi le loro trappole.**

A szellemkutya a tél mélyén táborokból lopkodott, és
széttépte a csapdáikat.

**Il cane fantasma uccise i loro cani e sfuggì alle loro frecce
senza lasciare traccia.**

A szellemkutya megölte a kutyáikat, és nyomtalanul
megszökött a nyilaik elől.

**Perfino i guerrieri più coraggiosi avevano paura di
affrontare questo spirito selvaggio.**

Még a legbátrabb harcosaik is féltek szembenézni ezzel a vad
szellemmel.

**No, la storia diventa ancora più oscura con il passare degli
anni trascorsi nella natura selvaggia.**

Nem, a történet egyre sötétebbé válik, ahogy telnek az évek a
vadonban.

**Alcuni cacciatori scompaiono e non fanno più ritorno ai loro
accampamenti lontani.**

Néhány vadász eltűnik, és soha nem tér vissza távoli táborába.

**Altri vengono trovati con la gola squarciata, uccisi nella
neve.**

Másokat feltépett torokkal, a hóban agyonverve találnak.

**Intorno ai loro corpi ci sono delle impronte più grandi di
quelle che un lupo potrebbe mai lasciare.**

Testük körül nyomok húzódnak – nagyobbak, mint amiket
bármelyik farkas képes lenne hagyni.

**Ogni autunno, gli Yeehats seguono le tracce dell'alce.**

Minden ősszel a Yeehat-ek a jávorszarvasok nyomát követik.

**Ma evitano una valle perché la paura è scolpita nel profondo
del loro cuore.**

De egy völgyet elkerülnek, a félelem mélyen a szívükbe
vésődik.

**Si dice che la valle sia stata scelta dallo Spirito Maligno
come sua dimora.**

Azt mondják, a völgyet a Gonosz Szellem választotta otthonául.

**E quando la storia viene raccontata, alcune donne piangono accanto al fuoco.**

És amikor a történet elhangzik, néhány asszony sír a tűz mellett.

**Ma d'estate, c'è un visitatore che giunge in quella valle sacra e silenziosa.**

De nyáron egy látogató érkezik abba a csendes, szent völgybe.

**Gli Yeehats non lo conoscono e non potrebbero capirlo.**

A Yeehat család nem tud róla, és nem is érthetnék.

**Il lupo è un animale grandioso, ricoperto di gloria, come nessun altro della sua specie.**

A farkas hatalmas, dicsőséges bundában pompázó állat, semmihez sem fogható a fajtájából.

**Lui solo attraversa il bosco verde ed entra nella radura della foresta.**

Egyedül kel át a zöld erdőn, és lép be az erdei tisztásra.

**Lì, la polvere dorata contenuta nei sacchi di pelle d'alce si infiltra nel terreno.**

Ott a jávorszarvasbőr zsákokból aranyló por szivárog a talajba.

**L'erba e le foglie vecchie hanno nascosto il giallo del sole.**

A fű és az öreg levelek eltakarták a sárgát a nap elől.

**Qui il lupo resta in silenzio, pensando e ricordando.**

Itt a farkas csendben áll, gondolkodik és emlékezik.

**Urla una volta sola, a lungo e lugubremente, prima di girarsi e andarsene.**

Egyszer felüvölt – hosszan és gyászosan –, mielőtt megfordul, hogy elmenjen.

**Ma non è sempre solo nella terra del freddo e della neve.**

Mégsem mindig van egyedül a hideg és hó földjén.

**Quando le lunghe notti invernali scendono sulle valli più basse.**

Amikor hosszú téli éjszakák ereszkednek az alsó völgyekre.

**Quando i lupi seguono la selvaggina attraverso il chiaro di luna e il gelo.**

Amikor a farkasok holdfényben és fagyban követik a vadat.

**Poi corre in testa al gruppo, saltando in alto e in modo selvaggio.**

Aztán a falka élén fut, magasra és vadul ugrálva.

**La sua figura svetta sulle altre, la sua gola risuona di canto.**

Alakja a többiek fölé magasodik, torka dalra fakad.

**È il canto del mondo più giovane, la voce del branco.**

Ez a fiatalabb világ dala, a falka hangja.

**Canta mentre corre: forte, libero e per sempre selvaggio.**

Futás közben énekel – erős, szabad és örökké vad.